THE
WHOLE FOODS
ENCYCLOPEDIA

THE
WHOLE FOODS
ENCYCLOPEDIA

A Shopper's Guide

REBECCA WOOD

Foreword by
MICHIO KUSHI

PRENTICE HALL PRESS

NEW YORK   LONDON   TORONTO   SYDNEY   TOKYO

Prentice Hall Press
Gulf+Western Building
One Gulf+Western Plaza
New York, New York   10023

PRENTICE HALL PRESS and colophon are registered trademarks of Simon & Schuster, Inc.

Library of Congress Cataloging-in-Publication Data

Wood, Rebecca.
   The whole foods encyclopedia.

   Bibliography: p.
   1. Food, Natural—Dictionaries.   I. Title.
TX369.W67   1988   641.3'02'0321   87-43152
ISBN 0-13-958554-0

Designed by C. Linda Dingler

Manufactured in the United States of America

10 9 8 7 6 5 4 3 2 1

First Edition

*I lovingly dedicate this book
to my father and mother*

Acknowledgments

Thanks to all you with whom I have broken bread and learned about the different levels of nurturing. Thanks to my children—Roanna, Asa, and Elizabeth Greenwood. Thanks to my sisters—Peggy Markel, Christine Palafox, Arifa Goodman, and Nancy Farrar. Thank you, my teachers—Michio and Aveline Kushi, Herman and Cornelia Aihara, Lino Stanchich, David La Chapelle, Bertha Gotterup, Ron Kurtz, Naboru Muramoto, Jack Worsley, John H. F. Shen, and the Carmelites at Nada.

To my many students over the years: Your interest has deeply fed me, thank you. For your initial support of this book, Mark Retzloff and Hass Hassan, thank you. To all my friends in the natural food industry, and especially to Lenny Jacobs, Susan Carskadon, Mike Potter, Bill Aufricht, Steve Gorad, and Don McKinnley, thank you.

Sincere thanks to Leon and Belle Atkind, Fred Bauder, Taylor and Dorothy Benson, Pat and John Caverly, Kizzen Dennett, Rebecca Dubawsky, Laine Gerritsen, Esther Quintana Grant, Lorraine Higbie, Corrine Holder, Ron Le Mir, Jeffrey Markel, Charlie Papazian, Ann Philleo, Jane Randolph, Michael and Peggy Rossoff, Gregory Sams, Carole Shane, Alma and Arverna Theurer, Chris Webster, and Ratie Balser Young.

Special thanks to my dear friends and fellow natural food professionals who have read the text and made suggestions. Pamela Bertin, Buzz Burrell, Susan Sim, Lino Stanchich, and Barbara Svening: I greatly appreciate your time and expertise. I claim full responsibility for any errors contained herein.

Sincere thanks to Isadora Ann Storey, Linda Bevard, Stephen W. Whitehead, and Prentice Hall Press.

While writing this book, I've drawn great strength from the mountains and high desert valley of my home.

Foreword

As the last and most recent development of the universal spiral of life, human beings have taken within themselves all preceding qualities and stages of evolution, including the various species of animals and plants. Accordingly, human beings are capable of eating and taking within themselves all levels of the animal and plant kingdoms in the form of food. How we balance our food—plant versus animal, whole versus processed, cooked versus raw, seasonal versus unseasonal, locally grown versus imported—and how we use fire, water, temperature, pressure, and seasoning in cooking largely determines our daily health and consciousness.

In order to create optimal conditions for continuing health and happiness, we can observe the following dietary principles:

1. *Eating according to human tradition.* For thousands of years, our ancestors observed a way of eating in harmony with their environment. The majority of the world's population based their diet around whole cereal grains supplemented by beans, seeds, cooked vegetables from land and sea, fruits and nuts, and, if desired, an occasional small amount of animal food, usually fresh fish or seafood. With few exceptions this pattern occurred worldwide, appearing in dietary practices in the east, west, north, and south. In fact, the use of wild or domesticated grains as principal food can be traced back to the origins of human life itself. Animal products, including dairy foods, were used much less frequently than they are now, generally under unusual circumstances such as prolonged cold weather or a mother's inability to produce breast milk.

2. *Varying diet according to climate.* The diet of someone living in Africa or Central America obviously differs from that of someone living in the United States or Europe. In northern climates the selection of slightly stronger food items is required, along with an emphasis on seasoning and other contractive factors in cooking. In tropical climates balance is maintained through the selection of more expansive food items with less salt and lower pressure and cooking time. We violate the ecological order of eating when we begin to include items in our diet that have come from climates that differ from our own. Our natural immunity weakens, and we become more susceptible to disease. Therefore people living in temperate, four-season climates are advised to avoid, whenever possible, bananas, mangoes, coffee, spices, and other products that originate in the tropics. It is possible to maintain our health, however, by importing high-quality food items that have originated in climates similar to those in which we live, such as sea vegetables from temperate regions of the Far East or Europe.

3. *Varying diet with the changing seasons.* Today, most people eat a relatively uniform diet throughout the year. Ice cream and cold soft drinks are often consumed throughout the winter, while meat, chicken, eggs, and other animal products are frequently consumed during the summer. A diet based on yearlong uniformity permits very little adaptability to the changing seasons. Traditionally, our ancestors and grandparents tried to harmonize with seasonal changes by

emphasizing slightly stronger foods and cooking methods during the cold winter months and by serving more relaxing, fresh, and lightly cooked foods during the warmer months. As much as possible, our diet should be based on foods that are naturally available in our area and eaten during the season in which they grow or foods that can be stored without artificial methods of freezing, canning, or chemical preservation.

4. *Varying diet according to personal needs.* Since everyone is unique, no two people can or should eat in exactly the same way. Everyone has different needs based on factors such as age, sex, season and year of birth, previous eating habits, constitution and condition of health, type of activity or work, and others. All of these must be taken into account when we select and prepare our daily food.

In modern times, the traditional human habits of eating based on these principles has rapidly declined. The result has been a wave of biological degeneration, including the spread of cancer, heart disease, diabetes, mental illness, and infertility. Hardly a family remains that has not been touched by one of these illnesses. The breakdown of the family itself, the decline of traditional religious and cultural values, and the spread of crime, social disorder, and war may also be traced to a foundation of improper nourishment leading to weakened physical health and impaired mental and spiritual judgment.

Unless this trend is reversed, our species will decline, and millions of years of evolution will come to an end. To help prevent this catastrophe, my wife and I, along with our associates and students, started advocating macrobiotics—the universal way of health, happiness, and peace—and making low-cost, quality foods available to everyone. More than twenty years ago, we began to promote the terms *natural foods* and *whole foods* to distinguish whole, unprocessed or natural foods that have been processed in a minimal, traditional way, from *health foods.* At that time health foods included various vitamin and mineral supplements, enzymes, extracts, and powders that in some cases helped balance the refining, artificial processing, and chemicalization of modern foods. To secure humanity's continued biological and spiritual evolution, however, it was necessary to return to a traditional way of eating centered on foods in their natural, whole form.

Since then, whole natural foods have caught on around the world, and modern society has begun to move in a healthier direction. Millions of individuals and families have modified their eating habits. Hospitals, schools, restaurants, and other facilities are serving brown rice, millet, and barley; whole-grain bread and sugar-free desserts; lentils, chickpeas, tofu, tempeh, and other beans and bean products; sautéed vegetables and fresh garden salads; and other nutritious foods. The American Heart Association, the American Cancer Society, and other medical and scientific associations have linked diet and degenerative disease for the first time and have issued guidelines for better health and well-being.

However, we have a long way to go, and there is still widespread confusion about just which foods are appropriate to eat. We cannot automatically assume that everything in the natural foods store, health food store, or whole foods supermarket is appropriate for daily health. *The Whole Foods Encyclopedia* is a valuable step toward remedying this situation. From *abalone* to *zucchini* it clarifies and makes order out of the hundreds of foods and dietary items now commonly available.

Included here is a wealth of useful information on food history and folklore, nutritional content, medical use, and proper storage methods. The author describes foods acceptable for better health (grains, beans, seeds, organic produce, and so on) and foods temporarily suitable (organic meats, dairy foods, natural honey, and so on) for making the transition from the standard modern diet to the traditional well-balanced diet that leads to enduring health and harmony.

For nearly twenty years Rebecca Wood has been active in teaching, writing, and promoting natural health and living. In recent years she has devoted herself to popularizing quinoa, a traditional grain of the Americas, and other "heirloom" varieties of crops and seeds. Rebecca is a true bridge between the ancient and future world communities. I salute her dedication and perseverance and sincerely hope that readers of this work will put her knowledge and insight to good use. Together, we can return to a balanced way of eating in harmony with our natural environment, restore our health and that of our families, and contribute to realizing one happy, peaceful world.

MICHIO KUSHI
BROOKLINE, MASSACHUSETTS

Introduction

Horrors at the thought of anyone reading this book from cover to cover! The intellectual categorization of endless food facts, figures, and trivia is at counter-purpose to learning about food. The real study of food requires eating it, savoring it, and being aware of how it makes you feel.

I wrote this book hoping that you, my reader, will use a page here or an entry there. I like to imagine you becoming more curious about the foods you eat and permitting your own intuition, sensory organs, and common sense to lead you to the food choices that are most pleasing to you. I hope this book will serve you with practical information about everyday as well as new foods.

In today's world, few are blessed with abundant food. Many of us who have enough are still hungry. We hunger to experience our inner, or higher, selves. We hunger for meaningful livelihoods, relationships, and life-styles. One valid way of becoming more whole, fully integrated human beings is to nourish ourselves with whole, integral foods. A food that has its own energy intact, that is energized through mindful preparation, and that is eaten with appreciation is more than calories.

The energizing properties of food have always fascinated me. The difference between a garden-fresh carrot and one from the supermarket is vast. Likewise, a fresh-cooked carrot is not the same as one that has been frozen or canned. Their measurable nutrients may be similar; however, even a child knows which tastes best.

I rarely discuss frozen foods in this book. Freezing a food diminishes its energizing potential. If you doubt this, I invite you to eat *only* frozen foods for ten days and then see how you feel. I suspect that my lack of endorsement will not freeze up freezer sales; however, if it helps even a few people rely less on such foods, I will be warmed.

In the same spirit, I do not give directions for microwave use. Try the following experiment: Bake a potato in a standard range and another in a microwave. Now taste each. Which has the most flavor? Which retains its heat the longest (and therefore is more warming and satisfying)? I rest my case.

For foods with the greatest amount of energy, favor seasonal and regional foods grown organically from heirloom seed (rather than hybridized or genetically engineered seed). Also, favor whole foods or lightly refined foods rather than highly refined foods. Once you have these foods in your kitchen, prepare them with a song and serve them with a flourish. May all the children of the world be well nourished.

REBECCA WOOD
CRESTONE, COLORADO

A Note on the Medicinal Properties of Foods

Some medicinal properties of foods are mentioned in this book. These observations are introductory rather than comprehensive. They are not medical advice. Using food to heal specific health problems requires the supervision of a qualified health practitioner. Nevertheless, the more we familiarize ourselves with the energizing properties of foods, the more they can serve us.

The energizing or medicinal properties of a food include, but do not end with, its nutritional properties. Below are brief descriptions of some additional ways to assess a food's "energy." For detailed explanations of why these systems work, see the Recommended Reading List in this book.

If you have a scientific orientation, looking at the energizing properties of foods may require a leap of faith. However, quantum physics, molecular biology, astronomy, and advanced studies of the human brain support the concept of the interrelatedness of all life forms, which supports this expanded view of food. The historical use of food also demonstrates this perspective. Using the energizing properties of foods is fundamental to traditional medicines throughout the world. In the least, discovering how foods make us feel is a worthwhile exploration.

The five methods listed below are metaphorical processes. The universal bent of the primitive mind was to note and personalize the shape, growth, pattern, and habitat of plants. By such observations the potential medicinal property of a given plant was intuited and, through experience, substantiated.

TEMPERATURE

A "cooling" food is one that tends to make you feel cool, such as watermelon and cucumbers. Cooling foods are naturally favored in hot weather. They include most fruits and many vegetables, beverages, and sweets. A high vitamin C content generally indicates a cooling food.

Foods that help generate body warmth are flesh foods, oils, nuts, seeds, grains, and beans. These properties vary from category to category (beef is more warming than beans). They also vary within each category (red flesh is more warming than white flesh). Warming foods build energy and are emphasized in cold weather. An ideal meal is an appropriate blend of both cooling and warming foods balanced for the season, the day, and your individual needs.

FLAVOR

According to Oriental medical systems, foods are divided into five flavors or tastes: bitter, sweet, pungent (or spicy), salty, and sour. Each of these flavors is associated with specific body organs and may be used medicinally to energize those organs. According to this model, bitter nourishes the heart and small intestine; sweet nourishes the spleen, pancreas, and stomach; pungent nourishes the lungs and large intestine; salt nourishes the kidneys and bladder; and sour nourishes the liver and gallbladder. A balanced diet includes all five flavors; however, to benefit a specific organ some flavors may be emphasized or de-emphasized.

EXPANSIVE-CONTRACTIVE

Salt on a scratch closes or contracts the scratch. Sugar opens it more. Soybeans made into tofu and cooked with sugar become an expansive food; soybeans made into salty miso are a contractive food. We think of someone who eats a lot of sugar or too much fruit or who uses drugs as being "spaced out," or expansive. Someone who eats a lot of meat or eggs is more apt to be contracted and called "uptight." It is a quality of health to be emotionally and physically balanced rather than to live at either extreme.

MOVEMENT

Some foods tend to disperse energy, some tend to collect it, while others move it either up or down or to a specific organ. In the spring when green plants are sprouting, we feel our energy spring up and move out. For someone whose energy is too heavy or rooted, eating early spring greens and stalk vegetables— such as asparagus—helps provide a touch of "spring fever." A good gardener knows the peculiarities of each plant variety and tends them accordingly. Observe how a particular plant grows and intuit what subtle energizing properties it affords you.

LAW OF SIGNATURE

The law of signature is used in all traditional healing systems. It simply means that if a food looks like a particular organ (or body part), then it may have medicinal properties for that organ. Some foods resemble certain organs. Beans that are the color and shape of kidneys are medicinal to the kidneys. Ginseng, which looks like a human body, has remarkable healing potential for the whole body.

SYMBOLS USED IN THIS BOOK

To facilitate finding quick answers to specific questions, symbols are used throughout this manual. For example, anyone who wants to know how to choose a ripe fig, rather than read the whole fig entry, should look for the symbol denoting "pointers for selection" for the answer. Here are the symbols used throughout the manual:

¤ Cooking	☆ Preferred Choice	◗ Pointers for Selection	✗ Not Preferred
▷ Storage Advised	◆ Medicinal Properties	+ Nutritional Value	

THE
WHOLE FOODS
ENCYCLOPEDIA

Abalone   The abalone, a sweet-fleshed mollusk, is a gastronomic treat. It has a single, ear-shaped shell lined with diaphanous mother-of-pearl. More than seventy-five varieties are found in warm coastal waters and are gathered at low tide or collected by divers. If you find abalone you will need a crowbar to pry it off the rock and then a mallet to pound its flesh to make it tender enough to be palatable. Once pounded, the abalone looks like a large, unappetizing sea scallop. Its flavor, however, delights the senses as much as its beautiful shell pleases the eye.

Due to the limited availability of California abalone, it is illegal to sell it outside of the state or to gather any under seven inches in size. Mexican, Chinese, and Japanese abalone are available frozen, dried, and canned. The canned product, which needs no further cooking, may be added directly to salads.

Abalone is a good source of protein and is low in fat. As a kitchen remedy it is used in treating coughs and is considered an aphrodisiac by some.

See **Shellfish** for selection, storage, use, and nutritional and medicinal highlights.

Acidophilus   *Lactobacillus acidophilus,* referred to as acidophilus, is a bacteria strain often added to yogurt. Foods with a living (not pasteurized) culture of acidophilus afford remarkable nutritional and medicinal properties.

Acidophilus increases B vitamins and enzymes in addition to producing natural antibiotics. Acidophilus reduces cholesterol and inhibits the growth of toxin-producing microorganisms. Research suggests it has beneficial effects for *Candida albicans* (thrush), vaginitis, skin problems, and some forms of cancer.[1]

In a dairy product such as yogurt, acidophilus renders the milk more digestible. More than half the world's population is lactose-intolerant. Many people lose their ability to digest lactose in early childhood, and then milk consumption causes digestive problems or allergic reactions. Acidophilus consumption enables some of these individuals to assimilate dairy products without discomfort.

Acidophilus is available as a supplement in dairy or soy formulas. Acidophilus milk is made by inoculating sterilized low-fat milk with an *L. acidophilus* culture. For maximum benefit a product must contain significant numbers of live organisms. The National Nutritional Foods Association is initiating industry standards for acidophilus products. Analysis will emphasize viable cell count and organism identification.

*   *   *

The Good, the Bad, and the Acidophilus

Many health care practitioners prescribe acidophilus, or fermented foods, to those taking antibiotics. There are "good" intestinal bacteria that assist assimilation, and there are "bad" bacteria associated with infection. Antibiotics indiscriminately destroy *all* bacteria. Some research indicates that acidophilus helps reestablish a healthy population of intestinal bacteria.

*   *   *

Acorn Squash   Also known as *Table Queen.* As its name suggests, this winter squash is shaped like an acorn but, unlike an acorn, it is deeply ribbed. Its skin is bright orange or dark green. Compared to a buttercup or butternut squash, the acorn's flesh is more yellow and fibrous, less sweet and moist.

Acorn squash may be baked, boiled, or steamed. Cut it into desired shapes and cook and *then* peel it. For beautiful flower shapes, slice it into thin horizontal rounds. Acorn squash takes well to sweet or savory glazes and stuffings.

As with other winter squash, the acorn is an excellent source of potassium, beta carotene, and the provitamin A. It is considered a warming food, with medicinal properties for the stomach and spleen.

See **Squash, Winter** for information on selection, storage, use, and medicinal and nutritional highlights.

A

*   *   *

High-Fiber Snack

Squash seeds are a superior source of fiber and zinc. They are so chewy that some find them bothersome to eat, but others find the succulent kernels well worth the exercise.

1 cup acorn squash seeds (other winter squash or pumpkin may be substituted; thin-hulled seeds are favored)
2 teaspoons soy sauce
2 teaspoons mirin (optional)

Separate squash seeds from pulp. Rinse and drain. Place seeds in a hot wok or thin steel pan and toast, stirring continually. Once they start popping, reduce heat to medium and continue to stir until they are golden. Pour into a bowl. Stir in seasonings. Return to wok and toast until the flavorings are absorbed. Use seeds as a tasty out-of-hand treat or garnish.

*   *   *

Aduki   Also known as *Adzuki* and *Azuki.* The "king of beans," according to the Japanese, is the aduki. Cultivated for centuries in Asia, it is now also grown commercially in the United States. Adukis imported from Japan are lightly polished to a bright sheen and are the most costly. Domestic and Chinese adukis are not polished and, as a result, have a just-noticeable gritty texture.

The aduki is easier to assimilate than other legumes. It is a good source of carbohydrate, phosphorus, potassium, iron, and calcium and contains some A and B vitamins. The amino acid content of the aduki makes it an excellent protein complement to grain.

In Oriental medicine the aduki has excellent healing potential for the kidneys. As a kitchen remedy it is enhanced when cooked with glutenous sweet rice (see **Rice**), or when just the liquid from cooked adukis is consumed twenty minutes before each meal.

See **Beans** for information on selection, storage, use, and medicinal and nutritional highlights.

Agar   Also known as *Agar-Agar* and *Kanten.* "Vegetable Jell-O" is another term for the marine algae known as agarophytes but more commonly called agar. It is easy to use and contains absolutely no calories! Agar, which you may remember from your school days, is the growth medium used in petri dishes. Throughout the world it is used as a gelling agent in such products as jam, jelly, yogurt, and candy and other confections.

The healthful agar gel not only enhances the flavors of other foods but also acts as a mild laxative and lends bulk. Agar soothes the entire digestive tract, which makes it an excellent food for invalids and infants. It bonds with toxic and radioactive pollutants and helps to expel them from the body.[2] Agar is rich in iodine, calcium, iron, phosphorus, and vitamins A, B complex, C, D, and K.

Agar is available in a variety of forms including flaked, powdered, granular, and bars. The bars are called **Kanten** and comprise numerous agar varieties. Flaked, powdered, or granulated agar is usually made from one variety of seaweed imported from South America.

Agar does not gel when combined with acetic acid (found in wine and distilled vinegars) or with oxalic acid (found in chocolate, rhubarb, and spinach). Agar yields more gelatin per gram weight than does gelatin extracted from animal sources. It is stable at temperatures up to 98 degrees and will not "water out."

See **Kanten**, which includes an agar recipe; see also **Sea Vegetables** for additional information.

*   *   *

*Gelatin Is **Not** Just Cows' Hooves*

Contrary to popular belief, gelatin is not made from only cattle hooves and horns. Commercial gelatin is also extracted from the cartilage, ligaments, tendons, bones, and hides of cattle, horses, and pigs. Agar is a more natural and healthful gelatin substitute.

*   *   *

Agar-Agar   See **Agar**.

Alaria   A domestic sea vegetable harvested in Maine, alaria is biologically almost identical to Japanese wakame. Alaria has a wilder taste and requires longer cooking. See **Sea Vegetables** and **Wakame**.

Albi   See **Taro**.

Alfalfa Seed   See **Seeds**.

Alfalfa Sprouts   See **Sprouts**.

Algae   See **Sea Vegetables**.

Almond   The oldest and most widely cultivated of nuts, the almond is closely related to the peach and apricot. Almonds grow in most temperate fruit-growing regions and are native to northern Africa and western Asia. California supplies most of our domestic almonds.

Two types of almonds are grown: sweet and bitter. The sweet is the only one used as a nut, and its oil has both culinary and cosmetic uses. The bitter is made into almond extract and is also used in cosmetics. Of the sweet varieties, Nonpareil is the most popular, and it is sold both shelled and in shell. During recent years many new varieties have been bred to make commercial production and harvest easier.

On a shelled almond, the thin brown skin should be intact and unscratched; it provides some protection from rancidity. Therefore, for freshness, purchase whole almonds (rather than almond pieces or slices) and then slice or chop just prior to use.

Almonds contain about 18 percent protein, several B vitamins, calcium, iron, potassium, and phosphorus. Like most nuts, they are high in unsaturated fats. Possible cancer inhibiters, cyanogenic glucosides, occur in almonds. As a home remedy, almonds are used as a muscle relaxer and for the relief of a dry cough (but not a productive cough).

See **Nuts** for information on selection, storage, use, and nutritional and medicinal properties of almonds.

*   *   *

How to Test for Rancid Almonds

Slice an almond kernel in half and examine its texture. A solid white nutmeat denotes freshness. A honeycomb-textured kernel, or yellow color, indicates rancidity. Discard *any* rancid food.

*   *   *

Almond Butter   Peanut butter has been the undisputed favorite American nut butter. However, the price of almond butter has plummeted in recent years, and this wonderfully sweet and delicious spread may become the favorite. Almond butter affords the same richness and versatility as peanut butter and, many people find, is more digestible.

Refrigeration of nut butters, including almond, is suggested. Once the container is opened, use the contents within three months.

See **Nut and Seed Butters** for information on selection, storage, and use and for nutritional and medicinal highlights.

Almond Milk   Almonds make a delicately sweet and satisfying dairy-free and soy-free milk. Substitute this nut-milk for milk in soups, casseroles, desserts, and beverages.

Almond milk is not available commercially but is easily made at home. Simply blend blanched almonds with water or apple juice and a pinch of sea salt to make a smooth beverage. Use immediately.

* * *

Kathy Hoshijo's Almond Fool

⅔ cup raw almonds (or other nut)
1 cup water
1 tablespoon honey
½ teaspoon vanilla
⅛ teaspoon cinnamon (optional)
Chilled, puréed fruit in season

Soak almonds in water for 24 hours or at least overnight. Then put the soaked almonds and ⅔ cup soaking water in blender with honey, vanilla, and cinnamon. Blend till smooth and fluffy. Pour into a bowl and chill in refrigerator.

To make a "fool," purée enough fruit in a blender or processor to equal about half the amount of fluffy almond mixture. (Sweeten fruit with honey if desired.) Chill puree in a separate bowl. At serving time, divide the almond mixture into serving bowls and top with fruit puree. Fold the fruit puree into the almond mixture to make a swirled effect. Makes 4 servings.[3]

* * *

Almond Oil   Any good-quality oil has an aroma and flavor similar to the food from which it is made. I have yet to find an almond oil that passes this test, and thus I cannot recommend it. Almond oil is costly and is reputed to have several cosmetic and therapeutic uses.

See **Oil** for information on selection, storage, use, and medicinal and nutritional highlights.

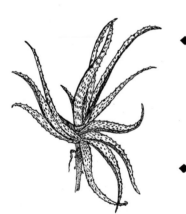

Aloe Vera   The juice from the succulent tropical plant Aloe vera has been used for centuries to treat such ailments as burns, wounds, and digestive problems. There are nearly two hundred species of aloe. The Aloe vera species (which means "true aloe" in Latin) is considered to be the most therapeutic.

The gelatinous inner leaf of this plant is an effective home remedy for minor burns. Judging from the many kitchens that boast a potted Aloe vera it is indeed considered healing. And it's good for more than just burns. Scientists have found that the aloe plant acts as an antibiotic, astringent, coagulating agent, pain inhibitor, and growth stimulator. It appears to contain a "wound hormone" that accelerates the rate of healing of injured surfaces. The enzymatic activity of aloe reportedly reduces or eliminates scars. Nonabrasive and soothing to the intestinal tract, Aloe vera is widely used as a bowel regulator.[4]

The juice of aloe is preserved and sold in various concentrations that can be termed drink, extract, gel, or juice. As of yet, no labeling standards have been established regarding aloe content.

Amaranth   Amaranth was a major crop of the Aztecs. The conquering Spaniard, Hernán Cortés, forbade amaranth cultivation and the religious rituals that included mixing human blood with amaranth meal and forming it into cakelike replicas of Aztec gods.[5]

Its Greek form, *amaranton,* means "deathless" or "unfading." Zuni legends relate that it was one of the plants brought up from the underworld at the time of the Zunis' emergence, and it was a staple until the Corn Maiden gave them corn.

The seed is appreciated for its remarkable vitality. The energizing qualities of amaranth are far more potent than those of our common grains that have been highly cultivated for centuries. It thrives in adverse conditions. The amaranth family includes more than sixty different species on five of seven continents. Several wild amaranths are still found in North America.

The seeds of the amaranth are very small, as small as poppy seeds. Their color ranges from purple-black to buff-yellow. Up to five hundred seeds may appear on one seed head, and any one plant has multiple seed heads. Unlike a true cereal grain, amaranth leaves, either wild or cultivated, are a nutritious green vegetable.

The United Nations Food and Agriculture Organization (FAO) has been fostering the resurrection of amaranth since 1967, and it is just now gaining acceptance. Some cookies, graham crackers, breakfast cereals, and other packaged foods containing a small percentage of amaranth flour are promoted as amaranth products. Watch for its increasing use.

This spunky-tasting grain is higher in protein (16 percent) than cereal grains and is exceptionally rich in the key amino acid lysine. Amaranth is higher in calcium and phosphorus than any other grain except millet, is a good source of fiber, and is low in calories.

For selection, storage, use, and nutritional and medicinal highlights, see **Grain**.

*   *   *

Nobody Cooks Plain Amaranth Twice

Amaranth has a gooey, slimy, gelatinous consistency that most find unpalatable. To *enjoy* amaranth, don't cook it plain. Rather, add up to 15 percent amaranth to another whole grain such as buckwheat, millet, or rice. In low proportions its pleasant flavor enhances other grains and does not detract from their texture.

*   *   *

Amaranth Flour   Amaranth flour has a distinctive yet pleasing flavor and blends well with other flours in numerous dishes. Nonglutenous amaranth flour is appreciated by people with grain or gluten sensitivities. Generally a small portion is used in leavened products. Flat breads may use a higher percentage of amaranth flour.

See **Flour** for information on selection, storage, and use.

Amasake   A balmy and refreshingly sweet beverage, amasake (am-a-ZOCK-ee), which means "sweet sake" in Japanese, is made by introducing koji enzymes into cooked sweet rice and incubating it. The enzymes convert the complex carbohydrates into simple sugars. (Malting barley for beer is a similar process.)

Domestic amasake is sold as either a plain or flavored beverage. Imported amasake is thick and rich like rice pudding. Amasake is eaten as is and is used in baking or as a base for beverages and nondairy ice cream. Blended with fruit it makes delicious smoothies.

Because amasake is a fermented food, it is readily digestible itself and it also aids digestion. It is thus an excellent food for infants, the elderly, and invalids. Amasake acts as a leavener in baked goods and may be used as a substitute for other sweetening agents.

Many natural food stores sell amasake or amasake beverages. Most sell koji, which is packaged with directions for making homemade amasake. To make amasake, mix koji with any freshly cooked, unsalted grain and incubate at 130 degrees for about twelve hours. The koji mold produces enzymes that break down proteins, starches, and fats into more readily digestible amino acids, simple sugars, and fatty acids.

See **Fermented Food** and **Koji** for additional information.

*   *   *

On the Run

The complex carbohydrates in amasake are converted to a readily assimilable high-energy food ideal for endurance athletes.

*   *   *

Amino Acids   The second most plentiful substance in our bodies (after water), amino acids are the essential components of protein. They are commonly thought of as the "building blocks of protein." This is simplistic. Our enzymes, hormones, neurotransmitters, and fat metabolism as well as our protein depend on amino acids. Twenty-two amino acids are known to be necessary for human health. Fourteen of these are synthesized by the human body and are therefore classified as nonessential. Eight amino acids not produced by the human body are termed essential.

The eight essential amino acids are tryptophan, lysine, methionine, phenylalanine, threonine, valine, leucine, and isoleucine. Two additional amino acids, needed to support fast growth, are considered essential for children: They are histidine and arginine.

Medical research has been uncovering the relationship of amino acids to health maintenance. For example, lysine appears to be effective for certain viral conditions, such as herpes. Phenylalanine may be effective in helping the body combat depression and suppress appetite.

Supplements are available as individual amino acids and in formulas. See **Protein.**

Anabaena   This blue-green freshwater microalgae is a superior source of protein and vitamins. Anabaena is one of several vegetable planktons that are increasingly becoming popular as nutritional supplements. A similar food is spirulina. See **Green Foods** for additional information.

Anaheim Chile   See **Chile Peppers**.

Anasazi Bean   *Anasazi* comes from a Navaho word that means "ancient ones." The anasazi bean was popularized in the Southwest, and though generally beans are not headline material, this one comes close. Some people in the food industry say the anasazi is a hot item because of its full flavor and its ability to hold its shape when cooked. Others say it is because the anasazi is an energetically superior food. Cynics observe that the romance associated with American Indian food—and especially an "ancient" American Indian food—explains why the anasazi fetches a high price.

The mottled maroon-and-white anasazi bean is similar to a pinto bean in size and shape but contains 35 percent more sodium.[6] When cooked it is sweet and has a slightly mealy texture. It may be freely substituted for pinto and bolita beans.

See **Beans** for information on selection, storage, and use and for cooking chart and nutritional and medicinal highlights.

*   *   *

Bean Bunk

There is a popular myth that ancient seed cached in Indian cliff dwellings or Egyptian tombs is viable and will sprout and grow. Despite their great emotional appeal, such stories are scientifically untenable. After thirty years of storage a seed's food supply is exhausted, its vital structure denatured, and its enzymes broken down.[7]

*   *   *

Ancho Chile   See **Chile Peppers**.

Anchovy A warm-water fish and member of the herring family, the anchovy deteriorates quickly and therefore is rarely available fresh. Immediately after the catch, anchovies are pickled, canned in oil, salted in brine, or smoked. Although the anchovy may attain a length of eight inches, the size most commonly sold rarely exceeds three inches.

Anchovies are a good source of protein, vitamins, and minerals. A medium anchovy is low in calories (about twenty-four) but high in sodium content (ninety-nine mg.).

See **Fish** for additional information.

Annatto This is a salmon-red-colored seed from a South American evergreen tree, which are used as a natural coloring for foods such as butter, margarine, cheese, and confections.

Apple

> Apple pies and apple fritters,
> Apple cores to feed the critters,
> Tasty apple cider in a glass.
> Apples baked and boiled and frizzled,
> Taffy apples hot and sizzled,
> And there's always good old apple sass.
>
> —WALT DISNEY'S *JOHNNY APPLESEED*

Remember the taste of apples when you were a kid? Remember all the different varieties, and how each excelled in its own way? Today six varieties comprise 75 percent of commercial production with Delicious (both red and yellow) accounting for 25 percent of production. Food writer Waverly Root observed that the flavor of the Delicious "has been reduced to the lowest common denominator, which has been discovered to be productive of the largest number of sales (neutral taste offends no one), and its yellow variety has become even worse."[8] Expand your culinary horizons and seek out different apple varieties, be they old or new. Be prepared to do some hunting in the countryside or persistent requesting of your greengrocer.

Apples are the most popular temperate-zone fruit and grow in almost every state. Washington produces more than one-quarter of the U.S. apple crop. The parent of all apples is the wild crab apple, *Malus sylvestris,* which is occasionally used in preserves but otherwise is scarcely edible.

The fact that apples store well and are versatile helps account for their popularity. If the apple is not organically grown, peel and discard the skin; although rich in vitamins and minerals, it may cause indigestion due to pesticide residues.

When well chewed, apples are quickly digested. Their medicinal uses include the following: grated raw to reduce fevers in children; steamed with honey to ease dry coughs; juiced as a laxative; and cooked with agar to eliminate mucus from the lungs. Apples are an excellent low-calorie source of pectin, fiber, and nutrients.

Apples taste best when stored at 35 degrees in a cool pantry or cellar. If cool storage is not available, refrigerate them. Peak season for apples is from September to March. Apples may be classified according to use:

Eating apples, enjoyed raw for their crisp, juicy, firm texture, include Cortland, Red and Golden Delicious, Granny Smith, Jonathan, McIntosh, Newton Pippin, Stayman, and Winesap.

Cooking apples—such as Cortland, Golden Delicious, Granny Smith, McIntosh, Newton Pippin, and Rome Beauty—are excellent for pies, baking, and applesauce and are generally tart, juicy, and firm-fleshed. While Jonathan apples do well in a pie, they are less suited for baking.

All-purpose apples include Golden Delicious, McIntosh, Jonathan, and Winesap.

★ ★ ★

Adam's Apple

Some say that a chunk of forbidden fruit stuck in Adam's throat and created a protuberance. Others view the Adam's apple as a projection of thyroid cartilage.

★ ★ ★

Today's Apple a Day Will Not Keep the Doctor Away

The growth hormone daminozide applied to 38 percent of the nation's fresh apples is a carcinogen. In 1985 the Environmental Protection Agency (EPA) announced that it would ban daminozide but then gave it an extension through 1988, when long-term animal studies would be completed.

This sobering story contains a hopeful note. Consumer concern over daminozide has triggered several states, supermarket chains, and manufacturers to boycott daminozide-treated apples.[9] Does your retailer deal in tainted products? Make your preference known! Grapes, peanuts, peaches, cherries, and tomatoes may be treated as well.

★ ★ ★

Apple Cider   Although the names *cider* and *juice* are commonly interchanged, there is a profound difference. Real apple cider is pressed from fresh apples and is not pasteurized. It is less sweet but more flavorful than apple juice. It must be refrigerated and used within ten days.

Cider and "hard" cider were popular in America from before the Revolution up until Prohibition. The repeal of Prohibition brought the resurgence of brewing and distilling but not of cider pressing. The trend toward natural foods is responsible for reintroducing this delicious beverage.

Available in the fall and early winter from local sources, cider can be found at roadside fruit stands and natural food stores.

Apple cider is cleansing to the liver and gallbladder.

Apple juice is a pasteurized beverage. See also **Juice, Fruit**.

★ ★ ★

Homemade Hard Cider

It is easy and fun to make alcoholic cider. Fill a jug with fresh pressed apple cider. Stretch a balloon over the jug's mouth to serve as a fermentation lock. Set it out at room temperature and the wild yeasts that were on the apples will multiply. In two to ten days the cider will become effervescent from carbon dioxide, and mildly alcoholic (1 to 2 percent). To control fermentation and increase the alcohol content to 6 to 8 percent, introduce wine yeast at the outset.

★ ★ ★

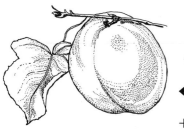

Apricot   For those who have dallied near apricot trees bearing dead-ripe fruit, it makes perfect sense that nectar was the drink of the Greek and Roman Gods. Though my Oxford English Dictionary does not associate the apricot with nectar, it is an association that I never doubted.

For an apricot to have a good flavor it must be fully ripe when picked, and then it keeps no more than three to four days. This explains why only 8 percent of the total commercial crop is sold fresh. Look for apricots during June and July that are soft to the touch and golden all over.

This peach and almond relative is said to have medicinal properties for the heart, according to Oriental medicine. Its vibrant gold color correctly marks it as a superior source of vitamin A and carotene. Dried apricots are a good source of iron.

California produces 90 percent of the domestic apricot crop, with Washington, Colorado, Idaho, and Utah supplying the rest.

Arame The sea vegetable arame is a kelp that is closely related to wakame and kombu, but in the package or cooked it looks like black and stringy hijiki. It has a mild, sweet taste that most Westerners enjoy from the start.

In addition to the numerous medicinal properties of sea vegetables in general, arame is noted for treatment of the spleen, pancreas, female disorders, and high blood pressure. It is an excellent source of protein. This ocean weed contains starch, sugar, unsaturated fat, vitamins A and B complex and all the minerals, with significant amounts of iodine, calcium, and iron.

Arame blades, which grow in wide leaves up to a foot in length, are sliced into long, stringlike strands, cooked for seven hours, then sun dried and packaged. Japan is the only country that is a significant producer of arame.

Arame is delicious sautéed alone, or combined with land vegetables and eaten as a side dish, or used to fill turnovers and strudels.

See **Sea Vegetables** for information on selection, storage, and use and for nutritional and medicinal highlights. See also **Hijiki, Kombu,** and **Wakame** for additional information.

⋆   ⋆   ⋆

Unsuitable for Soup!

Can you imagine trying to spoon black strands of chewy seaweed out of a soup? A soup is at its best when its ingredients are melt-in-your-mouth soft and easily maneuvered with a spoon. Arame doesn't qualify.

⋆   ⋆   ⋆

Arrowroot The root of the tropical arrowroot plant yields a fine-grained starch that makes a thickener that is superior to highly refined cornstarch. Arrowroot flour should be substituted, measure for measure, for cornstarch. Arrowroot is easily digestible.

Most of our arrowroot comes from the West Indian island of St. Vincent. The root is ground, sun dried, and then powdered. Dissolve it in cold water prior to use.

⋆   ⋆   ⋆

Baby's Bottom

Arrowroot flour is the powder of choice for diaper rash. It is absorbent, soothing, natural, and nontoxic. The talc and chemical fragrances of commercial baby powders can be abrasive to an infant's lungs.

⋆   ⋆   ⋆

Artichoke Draw the tender pulpy artichoke leaf base through your front teeth, consuming the plant leaf by leaf, and your reward is the luscious heart. Eating an artichoke is not like eating a piece of toast, and therein lies its charm.

This iodine-rich thistle originated in the Arabian-Mediterranean area, was popular in Rome, and is a close relative of the cardoon. Recent research on its medicinal properties indicates that the artichoke may neutralize the effect of certain toxic substances and benefit the gastrointestinal tract, blood-clotting time, and heart activity.[10]

Nearly all our domestic supply of artichokes is of the globe variety, which is grown south of San Francisco in the "artichoke capital of the world," Castroville. Globes are available in many sizes, from baby to jumbo. There are many European artichoke varieties that are colored and shaped differently from the globe—several may be eaten in their entirety when young.

The peak season for artichokes is in the spring. Premier artichokes are winter-kissed by frost, and their outer leaves are colored bronze to brown. Choose artichokes that are heavy for their size, compact and firm in the winter and spring, somewhat flared and conical in the summer and fall. Look for heavy, compact scales of a healthy green color. Old artichokes are lighter in weight and have tannish leaves that have pulled away from each other.

◁ Sprinkle fresh artichokes with a little water, seal them in a plastic bag, and refrigerate. Artichokes will keep up to a week. This vegetable has moderate

+ amounts of vitamins and minerals. It is low in protein and fat, moderate in carbohydrate. See **Sunflower Oil, Seed.**

Arugula Also known as *Rocket.* This Mediterranean-region vegetable grows wild and so plentifully that it was not cultivated until just recently. Arugula (ah-ROO-guh-lah) has an appealing but sharp flavor that is both earthy and mustardlike. It is favored in salads when the serrated leaves are no more than

⊐ three inches long. When the plant is older it can be used as a potherb, as for parsley.

◀ Avoid overgrown, yellowing, or wilted leaves and leaves from a plant that has flowered. Arugula is available most of the year but is at its best in the summer. Refrigerate in plastic for up to two to three days.

◆ As a home remedy, arugula stimulates the lungs and liver and tends to bring energy up and outward. Like other dark leafy greens of the cabbage family,

+ arugula is a good source of calcium and is recommended as a preventive food by the American Cancer Society.

See **Cabbage Family** for additional information.

Asparagus One intuitively knows that the asparagus is a primitive plant. Its broad point poking up through the ground looks alien compared to other garden denizens. Cultivated asparagus has been a luxury vegetable from ancient times. Wild, it is free for the harvesting along roadsides and in meadows in the early spring. As with other foraged foods, it is not fair to compare a wild food to a cultivated variety.

Botanically, asparagus is unusual in that there are distinct male and female plants and also in that it grows so rapidly. One spear may grow as much as ten inches in a day. Only the young green shoots or spears are eaten. If allowed to mature, a beautiful fern develops. The popular hanging plant, the asparagus fern, is a species of asparagus.

◀ Buy bright green, fresh-looking spears with compact tips. Use asparagus as soon as possible after purchase or harvest. Angular or flat stalks indicate woodiness and should be avoided. For uniform cooking, select those of uniform thickness.

◁ Store asparagus loosely covered in the refrigerator. To maintain freshness, wrap a moist paper towel around the stem ends, or stand upright in two inches of cold water. To remove the fibrous stalk end, hold the stalk by each end and bend it until it snaps in two. Use the stalk ends for soup stock, or peel to remove

⊐ the fibrous skin and use in salad or as finger food, or cook as you would the upper stalk.

+ Asparagus contains good amounts of vitamins A, B complex, C, and E as well as potassium and zinc. It contains a substance called rutin, which helps prevent

◆ small blood vessels from rupturing. This explains its traditional use for heart palpitations. Asparagus is also used as a diuretic. (Given its shape, it is inevitable that asparagus has been considered an aphrodisiac.)

Asparagus Bean See **Yard-Long Bean.**

✻ **Aspartame** The brand names for aspartame, a synthetic sweetener made by the drug company G. D. Searle & Co., are NutraSweet and Equal. Calorically, aspartame is equal to white sugar; as a sweetener it is two hundred times more intense.[11] Common sense indicates that any substance that is two hundred times more intense than sugar is two hundred times worse than sugar. Most health authorities suggest avoiding any chemical that, like aspartame, is linked to brain tumors, seizures, and birth defects.

NutraSweet is a combination of two amino acids: aspartic acid and phenylalanine. These amino acids occur naturally in some foods, but in this sweetener they are synthesized from petroleum. Aspartame has had the heaviest advertising campaign ever given to an ingredient, and many people are convinced that it is a "natural" sweetener. This is grossly misleading.

As of April 1, 1987, the Department of Health and Human Services had reviewed 3,192 consumer complaints about "adverse reactions associated with aspartame ingestion." Yet the Food and Drug Administration (FDA) continues to sanction the use of aspartame.[12] This sweetener is only used in cold foods (it loses its sweetness when heated). It is found in soft drinks, breakfast cereals, orange juice, and yogurt. See **Sweeteners**.

Atemoya   Cross a cherimoya and a sugar apple and the creamy result is an atemoya. This tough-skinned, grayish hybrid fruit is, by size and appearance, reminiscent of an artichoke. An atemoya's creamy, lush, ivory-colored flesh tastes like mango-flavored custard. If not well ripened, its flavor is starchy.

This West Indian delicacy is available in the fall. Select unblemished, thin-skinned atemoyas that are somewhat tender. Allow to ripen at room temperature until they are soft, then consume immediately or refrigerate for a few days. Do *not* refrigerate until the fruit is ripened. Upon ripening it may split at the stem end.

Atemoyas are used in fruit salads or riced and served as a fruit sauce. They are also eaten out of their rind, a spoonful at a time.

Aubergine   See **Eggplant**.

Avocado   Although technically a fruit and chemically more like a nut, avocados are commonly considered a vegetable. They contain up to 22 percent fat, most of which is monosaturated. This accounts for their creamy, sensual texture but also suggests limited use by those wishing to reduce their consumption of saturated fats.

The name *avocado* originates from an Aztec word that means "testicle tree," possibly because the rounded fruits grow in pairs. Many varieties of this native American plant are grown, but two types, grown only in California, account for 80 percent of the commercial crop. They are Hass (a dark, rough-skinned, high-oil, summer fruit) and Fuerte (a medium-green, leathery-skinned, fall and winter fruit). Florida supplies the remaining avocados, which contain less oil, are usually larger, and have bright green skins.

Avocados are a good source of protein and contain vitamin E and are good for gaining weight and for helping hyperactive people slow down. A versatile food, they can be used raw in a variety of dishes, dips (especially guacamole), and desserts.

Select avocados that are fairly heavy for their size and free of irregularities. When the fruit yields to gentle finger pressure, it is ripe. Store at room temperature until ripened, then refrigerate until use.

Azuki Bean   See **Aduki**.

B

Baking Powder   Most commercially available baking powders contain aluminum compounds that are deleterious to health as well as flavor (they impart a bitter aftertaste). There are further objections to baking powder because of its sodium content. Homemade baking powder takes seconds to make, performs as well as the commercial variety, and leaves no bitter aftertaste.

Baking powders have been in use for more than one hundred years as a yeast substitute. They are a mixture of various simple chemical substances. When baking powder is mixed into a batter, carbon dioxide gas is released from sodium or potassium bicarbonate by the action of an acid or an acid salt. In order to inhibit a premature reaction, the individual particles are often coated with a thin layer of starch.

* * *

Aluminum-Free Baking Powder

¼ cup baking soda*
½ cup cream of tartar
½ cup arrowroot flour

Mix together. Substitute equal parts for commercial baking powder. Store in an airtight container to prevent lumping.

*To make low-sodium baking powder, substitute potassium bicarbonate (available from pharmacists) for the baking soda.

* * *

Banana   Bananas as we know them are a hybrid with sterile, seedless fruits. They grow on a giant herb that is probably the largest plant without a woody stem. A bunch of bananas is technically called a "hand," and each fruit is a "finger." This fruit has a remarkably high yield per acre. One thousand square feet of land produce up to four thousand pounds of bananas. Thirty-three pounds of wheat or ninety-nine pounds of potatoes require the same space.

Bananas have a high sugar content (about 17 to 19 percent) and are richer in minerals than any other soft fruit except strawberries. They have twice the vitamin C of apples and a high caloric value, but they are low in carbohydrate and protein. Underripe bananas are difficult to digest, but ripened ones are easily digested and are soothing to the intestines, especially for children.

The United States consumes about 60 percent of the world's banana crop. Most are the blunt-ended Cavendish variety and are consumed raw. There is a small production of dried bananas and banana flour. There are several high-starch varieties, used for cooking, which are called plantains. See **Plantains.**

Commercial bananas are picked green and then treated with ethylene gas to speed their ripening. Bananas that are green have not been gassed. Allow them to ripen at home at room temperature (placing them in a closed paper bag speeds the process). When the skin is yellow and speckled with brown, the banana is ready for consumption, or it may be refrigerated for several days until use. Refrigeration will turn the skin a dark brown but will not affect the flavor.

Banana Squash   In shape and skin color, this winter squash is reminiscent of a banana. It grows up to two feet in length and about six inches in diameter. Its bright orange flesh is sweet.

Banana squash is often available cut into smaller pieces. As soon as any vegetable is cut, however, it loses flavor and nutrients. Thus, unless serving a multitude, you may prefer preparing smaller squash that can be utilized in one meal.

See **Squash, Winter** for information on selection, storage, and use and for nutritional and medicinal highlights.

Bancha Tea   Bancha (bon-CHA) is to the macrobiotic diet what milk is to the standard American diet. Macrobiotics often use it as a digestive aid. "Three tea" is the literal translation of *bancha* because it is composed of twigs and leaves from the tea plant that are at least three years old before harvesting. Harvest is in the fall when the caffeine content is at its lowest level; thus it is considered a low grade of tea by commercial standards.

Bancha has one-fifth the caffeine of green tea and contains minute quantities of calcium and magnesium. Before it is imported to this country the processors roast it in cast-iron cauldrons to lessen its bitterness and to decrease its tannin. Unlike other teas, bancha may be simmered.

Kukicha tea is similar to bancha, but is composed only of twigs. See **Kukicha** and **Tea** for additional information.

Barley   Possibly the oldest cultivated cereal, barley was used as money by the Sumerians around 4000 B.C. Today most people think of it in connection with soup—it makes a tasty, hearty soup base—but the bulk of barley is drunk in a malted form, otherwise known as beer.

Whole barley is a dark grain and is larger and plumper than all others except corn. Its tough hull and bran adhere so tightly to the grain's starchy core that milling leaves only a small white "pearl" of barley. Whole barley, which is sometimes available in natural food stores, has only its outer hull removed. Its vitamin and mineral content is intact, and it is significantly higher in protein, potassium, calcium, and iron than is pearl barley.

This grain cooks into a chewy, sustaining dish. Try it plain, combined with another grain, combined with beans, or cooked with extra water to make a breakfast porridge.

Barley is soothing to the digestive tract and to the liver. In Britain a thin gruel called barley water is a traditional food for convalescents.

See **Grain** for information on selection, storage, and use and for nutritional highlights of barley.

Hato mugi barley is a prized grain of Southeast Asia. See **Job's Tears**.

Hulled barley has the outer husk removed, is rarely available, and requires strenuous chewing in order to digest it.

Pearled, or pearl, barley has had its bran polished off and has lost all of its fiber and one-half of its protein, fat, and minerals. Pearled barley is the most commonly available barley. Oftentimes the pearled barley found in natural food stores has undergone fewer pearlings than that found in a supermarket, as is indicated by its larger size.

Semihulled barley has been lightly pearled (its tough hull scoured off). It is more flavorful and nutritious than pearl barley and easier to masticate than whole barley. The demand for semihulled barley is not large, and it is available only sporadically.

*   *   *

Tsampa

The diet of many rural Tibetans approaches a monodiet based on barley. Roasted barley flour, called *tsampa,* is mixed with black tea and yak butter and eaten as a gruel or dough ball.

*   *   *

Barley Flour   Barley flour is starchy, soft, and has a sweet, earthy taste. It yields a cakelike crumb and curiously—because the grain as well as the flour is white—when baked, it imparts a grayish color.

Barley is low in gluten. Although no more than 15 percent barley flour is generally added to bread, it imparts a softer and denser texture. In cookies and cakes it gives a light crumb. Barley pancakes are sensational (see recipe in **Flour** entry). Toasting the flour prior to use gives a rich flavor.

See **Flour** for information on selection, storage, and use.

*   *   *

Barely Addicted to Barley

"Although, owing to its greyish crumb, barley bread may not look immediately appetizing, those who acquire a taste for it are likely to become addicts. I am one. An addiction which is not always easily satisfied." So writes Elizabeth David in the classic British text on bread, *English Bread and Yeast Cookery.* [1]

*   *   *

+   **Barley Grass**   The chlorophyll-rich grass of young barley has some use as a health food supplement. It is consumed freshly juiced or dried and powdered. See **Wheat Grass Juice** and **Green Foods**.

☆   **Barley Malt Powder**   *Barley malt* technically refers to malt sugar, which is a buff-colored, crystalline powder. It is made by evaporating the water out of barley malt syrup. Malt sugar has been primarily used for brewing; however, it is becoming increasingly available in quality stores as a superior sugar replacement that is less sweet, but adds a better texture and pleasing nutty flavor to baked goods.

◁   Malt sugar absorbs moisture very easily and then becomes hard as a rock. To prevent this, store sugar in a closed glass jar, which gives it a lengthy shelf life. Use in place of sugar or other natural sweeteners.

See **Sweeteners** for information on use and for nutritional and medicinal highlights.

*   *   *

Easy Sugar Substitute

Most high-quality natural sweeteners are liquid, thus when they are used to upgrade a recipe, the other liquid ingredients must be reduced. This can be tricky. Malt sugar is easy to substitute for sugar, and unlike natural liquid sweeteners, it gives the same tender crumb that sugar does. Substitute measure for measure. The result is a lighter sweetness with a pleasing malt flavor.

*   *   *

Barley Malt Syrup   Sprout whole barley, roast it, and then extract it to a liquid form, and you've got barley malt syrup. Combine the syrup with hops, ferment with yeast, and the result is beer. Hop-flavored barley malt was sold "strictly as a sweetener" during Prohibition. Add bitter-tasting hopped barley to a batch of cookies, and the result would be inedible!

Liquid barley malt is available in two forms: barley extract and barley-corn malt. The extract is 100 percent barley malt and usually tastes as strong as blackstrap molasses. Imported 100 percent malts have a rich but less intense flavor, which gives them wider culinary applications. They are more costly than domestic malts.

A pleasantly flavored and versatile blend of barley and corn is a more popular malt. The higher the percentage of corn, the less expensive the product and the milder the flavor. Corn cannot be malted by itself, but when corn grits are combined with malt, the barley enzymes reduce the cornstarch to maltose. Some manufacturers mix commercial corn syrup with malt syrup to form an inferior product.

+   Barley malt is mostly carbohydrate, and though it contains small quantities of vitamins and minerals, the amount is negligible. Barley malt is the least expensive of the quality natural sweeteners. Compared to honey, barley malt syrup is less sweet.

◁   Store barley malt syrup in a glass or plastic container in a cool, dark cupboard. If stored a long time (longer than twelve months) or in a warm place, the malt may ferment. A sign of fermentation is bubbles percolating up through the malt or foam on top. Should this occur, refrigerate and use quickly, or discard if it has an unpleasant aroma.

See **Sweeteners** for additional information.

Basil   Basil, also known in French as *l'herbe royale* ("the royal herb"), is a relative of mint, native to India, and widely grown in the Mediterranean. It is especially savored as an Italian pesto ingredient and has a great affinity for tomato, fish, and egg dishes.

See **Herbs and Spices** for information on selection, storage, and use and for nutritional and medicinal highlights.

Bass   Bass is a collective name for various spiny-finned salt- and freshwater fish whose flesh resembles that of perch and whose shape and color are similar to that of salmon. Although rather bony, the flesh is firm and lean and has a delicate and delicious flavor. Prepare like salmon, but avoid overly rich sauces that compete with its delicate flavor.

See **Fish** for information on selection, storage, and use and for nutritional and medicinal highlights.

Bay Leaf   Bay laurel, as the Greeks and Romans believed, is the only plant never struck by lightning. It is also the plant they used for wreaths to crown the victorious. An early example of preventive medicine?

One of our most common herbs, the bay leaf comes from an evergreen shrub native to the Mediterranean area, called the bay laurel. It retains much of its strength as a dried herb. Bay leaves perk up a variety of dishes, especially soups and stews. They are often used in bouquets garnis.

See **Herbs and Spices** for related information on bay leaves.

*   *   *

Keeping Grain Infestation at Bay

To prevent insect infestation of stored cereal grain, place several bay leaves in the grain container. The aroma of the bay leaves seems to inhibit the hatching of undesirable guests. Storage at low temperatures also helps.

*   *   *

Beans   Beans, peas, peanuts, and lentils are all fruits contained within the pods of leguminous plants. Legumes are one of the earliest cultivated crops and are grown just about everywhere. Throughout history, beans have been a daily staple, but in highly civilized cultures they have been largely displaced by animal foods. As more and more Americans become concerned with health and fitness, beans are regaining their popularity.

Annemarie Colbin, in her remarkable book, *Food and Healing*, comments, "Because of their protein content, beans are body-building, warming foods. They provide us with the protein needed for body repair without saddling us with the cholesterol, fat, and toxic nitrogen by-products of meats. . . . As a protein food, beans are weighty and keep us tied to the material world."[2]

Some varieties of legumes, like green beans and peas, are eaten fresh in the shell or as seeds. Once they are mature and dried, only the seed is used. Dried beans are highly impervious to infestation and have an excellent shelf life.

Select dry legumes that contain few or no broken, chipped, or split seeds. Uniformity of shape and color is not desirable, for it indicates a hybrid, which is less vital than an heirloom variety. Before adding water, pick over beans and remove any small pebbles, debris, and broken beans. A damaged bean has no vitality.

Nutritionally, most legumes range from 17 to 25 percent protein, which is roughly double that of cereals, and higher than that of eggs and most meats.

Soybeans rate exceptionally high with 38 percent protein. Most beans are low in fat and are good sources of calcium, iron, vitamin B_1, and niacin.

◆ According to Oriental medicine, beans strengthen the kidneys, especially aduki beans and those similar in color and shape to the kidneys. White beans tend to be more healing to the liver. Beans are considered warming foods; however, soybeans and soy products are cooling.

The glucose in beans is released more slowly into the bloodstream than is the glucose of other foods. This makes beans a valuable food for people suffering

◆ from diabetes and hypoglycemia, since this slow release helps stabilize blood-sugar levels. Several tablespoons of beans with a meal are ample.

Beans are the most difficult food of the vegetable realm to digest, except for nuts and vegetable oils. Here is how to enhance their digestibility and thus to

⛾ decrease intestinal flatulence:

- Soak beans for several hours before cooking. To reduce soaking time, bring beans to a boil, remove from heat, and then allow to soak. Discard soaking water if you tend toward flatulence. If not, cook the beans in their soaking water as it contains minerals and vitamins leached from the beans. Soybeans are the exception—their soaking water should always be discarded.
- Cook a 2-inch strip of kombu sea vegetable with each cup of dry beans. Kombu tenderizes the beans and makes them more digestible, flavorful, and mineral-rich.
- Bring uncovered beans to a hard boil for twenty to thirty minutes, then cover and simmer (or pressure-cook) until completely soft. Next add ¼ teaspoon salt per cup of dry beans and cook for 10 minutes more. If flatulence persists, increase salt to ½ teaspoon. Salt helps make beans more digestible.
- Eat moderate portions of beans, or combine beans with vegetables to create lighter, and therefore more digestible, dishes.
- If you follow the above and find that beans are still hard to digest, then possibly your intestinal flora need replenishing (see **Fermented Foods**).

See **Aduki, Anasazi Bean, Black-eyed Pea, Black Turtle Bean, Bolita, Chickpea, Fava Bean, Great Northern Bean, Kidney Bean, Lentil, Lima Bean, Mung Bean, Pinto,** and **Soybean**.

Oats, peas, beans and barley grow,
Oats, peas, beans and barley grow.
Do you or I or anyone know
How oats, peas, beans and barley grow?

—TRADITIONAL FOLKSONG

*   *   *

The Bean-Soaking-Water Debate

Some advise to discard bean soaking water because it contains phytates, which reputedly bind up calcium and other minerals. There is no indication that phytic acid causes a substantial loss of minerals. If one were to eat vast amounts of foods containing phytate, to the exclusion of all other foods, then using the soaking water could theoretically pose a problem.

*   *   *

Bean Cooking Chart

Soak beans first. For optimum digestibility soak *all* beans and legumes prior to cooking.
⛾ Lentils, split peas, and dried peas get by with the least soaking (one hour) whereas chickpeas and soybeans prefer the most (up to ten hours).

BOILED BEANS

1 Cup Dried Beans	Water	Cooking Time	Yield
Aduki	3½ cups	45 minutes	3 cups
Anasazi	3 cups	2½ hours	2 cups
Black-eyed peas	3 cups	1 hour	2¼ cups
Black Turtle	3 cups	1½ hours	2 cups
Bolita	3 cups	2½ hours	2 cups
Chickpeas	4 cups	3 hours	3 cups
Great Northern	3½ cups	2 hours	2 cups
Kidney	3 cups	2 hours	2 cups
Lentils	3 cups	45 minutes	2 cups
Lima	2½ cups	1½ hours	1½ cups
Mung—best sprouted			
Navy	3 cups	1½ hours	2 cups
Pinto	3 cups	2½ hours	2 cups
Soybeans	4 cups	3–4 hours	2 cups
Split peas	4 cups	2½ hours	2¼ cups

PRESSURE-COOKED BEANS

1 Cup Dried Beans	Water	Cooking Time	Yield
Aduki	3 cups	30 minutes	3 cups
Anasazi	2½ cups	1 hour	2 cups
Black-eyed Peas	2½ cups	45 minutes	2¼ cups
Black turtle	2½ cups	45 minutes	2 cups
Bolita	2½ cups	1 hour	2 cups
Chickpeas	3 cups	1¼ hours	3 cups
Great Northern	3 cups	1 hour	2 cups
Kidney	2½ cups	1 hour	2 cups
Lentils	2½ cups	30 minutes	2 cups
Lima	2 cups	1 hour	1½ cups
Mung—best sprouted			
Navy	2½ cups	50 minutes	2 cups
Pinto	2½ cups	1 hour	2 cups
Soybeans	3½ cups	2–2½ hours	2 cups
Split peas	2 cups	25 minutes	2¼ cups

Caution: Some advise not to pressure-cook beans because the beans' outer skins may plug the steam escape valve. This is especially true of soybeans. Others pressure-cook all beans. They allow ample space in the pot, and listen to the pressure regulator to make sure that it hasn't become clogged.

* * *

Bean Sprouts See **Sprouts**.

Beef Per capita beef consumption has dropped as Americans become more health conscious. Overconsumption of flesh food, and especially of red flesh food, is implicated in numerous degenerative health problems.

The quality of the beef consumed also is receiving attention. Concern is increasing about the health consequences of eating meat that has been treated with growth stimulants, antibiotics, and hormones and fed with chemically grown feed. Fatty meats are one of the biggest dietary sources of pesticide residues. According to the Government Operations Committee, twenty thousand individual substances are given to animals by farmers and veterinarians, and more than 90 percent of these drugs have not been tested by the Food and Drug Administration (FDA).[4]

* * *

Unadulterated Beef

In 1983 cattleman Mel Coleman of Saguache, Colorado, started producing natural beef to serve the health-conscious market. Now other ranchers are following suit. Their beef costs up to twice as much as commercial, yet they are currently selling all they can produce. The U.S. Department of Agriculture (USDA) permits such suppliers to print the following on their labels:

- No antibiotics, hormones, or growth promotants are ever administered to the animals.
- No artificial or synthetic ingredients are added to this product.
- The USDA does not permit preservatives in this product.
- This product is only minimally processed.

*   *   *

To be assured of quality meat, purchase *only* meat that is produced specifically for the natural-food market. Unfortunately, the USDA allows any meat that has had nothing added to it *after* butchering to be labeled "natural." Thus, almost all fresh meat on the market today qualifies as USDA natural.

*   *   *

"Fresh" Meat Held Together with Seaweed

Since September of 1986 the USDA has allowed restructured meat products to be sold as fresh. Restructuring is the process of taking flaked, sectioned, or chunked meat and binding it to resemble intact cuts of meat. Sodium alginate (a seaweed), calcium carbonate, lactic acid, and calcium lactate are used as the binders.

*   *   *

The USDA has approved of a "light" label for beef in which the fat content has been reduced by 25 percent. Animals are currently bred and fed to decrease their saturated fats as well as their overall fat content.

Beef is an excellent source of protein and contains all the essential amino acids. It is rich in iron and is an excellent source of the B vitamins—niacin, thiamin, riboflavin, B_6, and B_{12}. It is also high in zinc, phosphorus, and magnesium. It contains some potassium, copper, chromium, sodium, aluminum, molybdenum, and selenium.

Good beef is tender, juicy, and flavorful. It is judged by the maturity of the carcass, marbling (flecks of fat within the lean), and the color, firmness, and texture of the lean. Color is an indicator of quality. Beef is bright red, and the fat on grain-fed beef is creamy white.

Range cattle that are not grain fed before slaughter are termed grass-fed beef. Their fat covering has a dark or yellow cast, resulting from the carotene (vitamin A) in the grass.

When natural fresh meat is available, it is the best choice. Select those pieces with the least fat, and remove excess fat before cooking. If only frozen organic meat is available, select that which has been properly wrapped and frozen and is free of white or brownish areas that would indicate freezer burn. Freezer burn is the drying out of the meat's surface tissues. It is not harmful, but the dehydrated area will be tough and tasteless when cooked. Keep meat frozen until ready to use. To prevent spoilage, allow it to defrost in the refrigerator, rather than on the counter.

Meat must be refrigerated quickly and properly after purchase or it begins to lose flavor and to spoil. Ground meat and variety meats (organ meats) should be used within twenty-four hours. Fresh meats, to be at their best, should be used within two to three days. Larger pieces, such as roasts, keep for up to five days because less of their surface area is exposed to air. Store all varieties of meat in the coldest part of the refrigerator. The temperature should be as low as possible, but not freezing.

If fresh meat is to be used within the first two days of purchase, it may be refrigerated in its original wrapper. If it is to be kept for a longer period, loosen the ends of the wrapper. This allows air partially to dry the surface of the meat and thus retard the growth of bacteria.

Meat that is vacuum packaged or vacuum sealed has had most of the air eliminated from the package. This increases the length of time it can be kept and reduces shrinkage caused by moisture loss.

You can determine whether uncooked meat is spoiled if the color changes from a bright red for beef and pink for veal to a dull gray. An off-odor develops and possibly a slippery surface. Spoiled meat should be discarded.

The cuts of meat are related to the bone structure and location on the carcass and carry similar names for beef, veal, and lamb. Cuts from the middle section along the backbone are generally more tender than those from the shoulders, legs, breasts, and flanks. Porterhouse, T-bone, and sirloin are more tender, and therefore more costly, cuts. Cuts from the forequarter tend to have more fat than those from the hindquarter. The amount of fat is also related to the age of the animal and the kind and length of feeding. Young, grass-fed animals have less fat than mature, grain-fed beef. If the beef is well-trimmed of fat before eating, there is relatively little difference in nutritive value among the various grades of beef.

The seven groups of retail cuts are identified by the bone. They are shoulder-arm cuts, from the arm bone; shoulder-blade cuts, from cross-sections of the blade bone near the neck, center cuts, and near the rib; rib cuts, from the backbone and rib bones; short loin cuts, from the backbone and T-bone; hip, or sirloin cuts (cross-sections of hip bone), including the pin bone near the short loin, the flat bone, center cuts, and wedge bone near the round; and breast or brisket cuts, from the breast and rib bones.

* * *

Where's the Corn in Corned Beef?

Corn formerly meant a small particle or seed. When beef was cured it was sprinkled with corns of coarse salt. The corning of beef soon led to the term *corned beef.*

* * *

Beefsteak Leaf   Also known as *Shiso* or *Chiso.* A herb popular in Japanese cookery is the the purple-red shiso. It gives umeboshi its characteristic pink color, which is similar to a medium-rare steak and thus explains its English name.

Beefsteak leaf is found in macrobiotic staples and condiments. It is exceptionally high in iron and calcium and builds blood hemoglobin.[5]

Bee Pollen   Pollen, the sticky male seed of flowers, is gathered and stored on the hind legs of worker bees. Beekeepers harvest it by placing a wire mesh pollen trap over the hive entrance. As the bees struggle to get through the mesh, pollen gets brushed off their legs and drops into a pollen-retaining drawer.

Many researchers claim that bee pollen is *the* superior supplement because it is natural and it contains every substance needed to maintain life. Bee pollen has up to 35 percent protein, of which approximately half is free-form amino acids. It is high in vitamins A, C, D, E, and B complex, and it contains minerals, enzymes, carbohydrates, and other micronutrients.

Bee pollen is said to help in the prevention of colds, cancer, asthma, and allergies; to increase sexual potency and desire; to control and reduce weight; to alleviate rheumatism and arthritis; and to enhance athletic endurance.[3]

Bee pollen is available in capsule, tablet, granule, extract, and fresh form. Fresh pollen is the most potent and requires refrigeration. Do not purchase pollen dried at temperatures exceeding 130 degrees. Pollen is appearing as a primary or secondary ingredient in a number of health-food products, such as energy bars. It is also said to help increase female hormones in both sexes.

All pollen experts caution first-time users to sample only a few granules initially to test for allergic reactions. Most experts recommend taking one teaspoon per day (the equivalent of three grams, or six 500-mg tablets or capsules).

The best pollen comes from the high desert regions of the United States because the pollen water content there is low, and thus the product requires minimal drying. The ideal moisture content makes the pollen feel somewhat soft when pressed between your fingers. If it is hard and unyielding from too low a water content, it is dead. Excessive water causes the pollen to turn moldy and to lose nutrients. See also **Propolis**.

Beet A member of the ubiquitous goosefoot family, beets are related to chard, spinach, sugar beets, and quinoa. Like chard, beet greens are high in oxalic acid; and like sugar beets, beet roots are high in natural sugar. The original beet still grows wild in Mediterranean countries as well as Asia Minor and the Near East.

Beets are best known as a blood tonic. They have notable amounts of calcium, iron, magnesium, and phosphorus; they also contain vitamins A, B complex, and C.

Although some beets are yellow (and some new varieties are white) most are identified by their bright-red-to-dark-purplish skin and flesh that turn the cooking water (as well as one's stools) red. Beets are often pickled, boiled for use in salads, baked, or added to soups. A popular Russian soup, borscht, uses beets as a principle ingredient.

Select firm beets that are uniform in color. A brown top indicates toughness. See **Goosefoot Family**.

Beet Greens The tender young leaves of beets are tart and make a good salad green. They also may be sautéed, steamed, or prepared as collard greens. See **Goosefoot Family**.

Belgian Endive The pale yellow Belgian endive, shaped like a fat cigar, is a sweet gourmet delicacy air-freighted from Belgium. It is the blanched greens of a chicory root. Once cut, each is wrapped in paper to protect it from the light. Belgian endive is an exquisite salad green. When braised, it is frequently served with game. See **Chicory** and **Curly Endive**.

Bell Pepper See **Sweet Pepper**.

Berries The fruits that most seem to engender cheerfulness are the berries. Their nature inherently delights. Hundreds of wild fruits are called berries, but true berries are small, simple fruits like grapes, tomatoes, and gooseberries. About ten of these are commonly domesticated and are much larger in size than their wild relatives.

Berries are costly. They are an energy-intensive crop to produce and the most fragile of fruits. For optimum flavor they must be picked ripe and consumed within a day or two. Berries are packed in small containers because they are so fragile. Look for ripe, plump berries with no moldy, green, or withered fruits.

These tiny fruits provide vitamins A and C and small amounts of B complex as well as some minerals. Cooking, freezing, or drying berries greatly reduces their vitamin C content. Berries are cooling foods and are used in a variety of desserts, preserves, and beverages.

See **Blackberry, Blueberry, Boysenberry, Cranberry, Currant, Gooseberry, Loganberry, Raspberry,** and **Strawberry**.

Bibb Lettuce See **Butterhead Lettuce**.

Bitter Melon Also known as *Chinese Bitter Melon*. The warty-skinned bitter melon is not a melon but rather a summer squash shaped like an Anaheim pepper. Its lumpy, ridged skin is the color of pale jade. Its flesh is the same tone, only lighter, and it contains brown seeds. The bitter melon is a popular ingredient in Indian and Asian cookery and for most Americans is a novelty food. It goes well in stir-fries, soups, or baked vegetable dishes.

As its name implies, the bitter melon is indeed bitter, and (immature fruits excepted) should be soaked in salted water or parboiled prior to use. Foods with a bitter flavor, like this squash, are salutary to the heart.[6] Nutritionally it is comparable to summer squash.

Select fruits with shiny, even-colored skins and store them in the refrigerator. They are available from the summer into winter.

See **Squash, Summer** for information on selection, storage, and use, and for medicinal and nutritional highlights.

Blackberry Also known as *Brambles*. Plump, sweet blackberries are similar to raspberries but are larger, juicier, and have a grainier texture and a more assertive flavor. Their core does not separate from the fruit.

Blackberries grow wild in temperate regions of the Northern Hemisphere. They deteriorate faster than most fruits and should be used the day they are gathered or purchased. When ripe, the berry is a shiny purple-black, soft, and lush.

This luxury crop is available in late summer. It provides vitamins A and C and some B complex and minerals. The blackberry is a cooling food.

See **Berries** for information on selection, storage, use, and nutritional and medicinal properties.

*   *   *

How Many Fruits in a Cluster?

Each tiny bump on a blackberry or raspberry is actually a minuscule fruit, technically a drupelet. Blackberries and raspberries are not true berries but rather clusters of little drupelets. Popping a single blackberry or raspberry into your mouth is literally eating more than eighty single fruits at a time.

*   *   *

Black-eyed Pea Also known as *Cowpea* and *China Bean*. The classic New Year's Day menu in many Southern homes includes black-eyed peas and collards—not a bad way to start off the year. This legume originated in Africa, where it may still be found growing wild. It is cream-colored with a distinctive black spot. "Soft," or quick-cooking beans, black-eyed peas may also be eaten fresh in the pod.

See **Beans** for information on selection, storage, use, and medicinal and nutritional properties.

Black Forest Mushroom See **Shiitake**.

Black Salsify See **Scorzonera**.

Black Soybean See **Soybean**.

Black Turtle Bean Also known as *Black Bean*. This Mexican native is a member of the kidney bean family and may be interchanged with pinto beans in any recipe. The black turtle is sweet but hardy and is delicious in soups or refried (*refritos negros*).

At first glance black turtles and black soybeans may look like the same bean. However, the soy is shiny and rounded, whereas the turtle has a dull appearance and is slightly square-shaped.

See **Beans** for information on selection, storage, and use and for medicinal and nutritional highlights.

Blood Orange See **Orange**.

Blueberry Not too juicy and not too sweet, it is no wonder that the delectable blueberry has become the second most popular berry after the strawberry. Because of its superior shipping properties, the blueberry is apt to become more, rather than less, apparent. It also dries well and is used in numerous prepared foods.

This native American plant is related to huckleberries, cranberries, and azaleas. The wild blueberry is still found in many parts of the country and is smaller and more tart than the commercial variety.

Blueberries are "boxed" with a cellophane covering, and it is hard to check their quality. Stains on the carton exterior or bottom indicate mashed and moldy berries. To know for sure, slip off the wrapper and look. Avoid withered or green fruits; favor fresh, plump berries with a powdery bloom. Blueberries keep far better than other berries, but they should be used within a week of picking. This lush berry is at its peak in midsummer.

Of the fresh, temperate region fruits, the blueberry is the highest in iron. It is a cooling food and is said to be salutary to the kidneys.

See **Berries** for information on selection, storage, and use and for nutritional and medicinal highlights.

Blue Corn See **Corn, Blue**.

Bluefish A member of the sea-bass family, the bluefish is named for the blue tint of its sweet, oily, rich flesh. In shape and size it resembles the mackerel. Found throughout the world, its peak seasons are spring and fall.

Bluefish do not keep well and are considered by macrobiotics as less health-promoting than white- or red-fleshed fish. The bluefish is an excellent protein source, is low in fat, and has appreciable calcium and phosphorus.

See **Fish** for additional information.

Bok Choy Also known as *Chinese Chard, Pak Choy,* and *Tai Sai.* This sweet, crisp-textured and mild-tasting vegetable has broad white or greenish-white stalks with loose, dark green leaves. One advantage that bok choy shares with many members of the leafy green cabbage family members is an excellent shelf life. Select fresh, crisp, firm heads. Refrigerate in a plastic bag. Stir-fry, serve raw in salads, or add to soups.

Bok choy is an excellent source of vitamins A and C. According to Oriental medicine, stalk vegetables, including bok choy, bring energy up and are expansive and cooling foods.

See **Chinese Cabbage** and **Cabbage Family** for information on selection, storage, and use and for nutritional and medicinal highlights

Bolete Mushroom Also known as *Cèpe* and *Porcino.* The bolete has a texture reminiscent of filet mignon but is even more sensuous. This mushroom is famed throughout the world for its piny, earthy, pungent, and memorable flavor. Widespread in birch and aspen forests of the United States it is occasionally available in the spring, but most often in late summer and early fall. Bolete are not grown commercially but independent collectors sell them in some markets. Occasionally, fresh bolete are imported at an exorbitant price from France and Italy. They are more readily available dried.

The spore-bearing part of bolete is spongelike, and some people discard this part because they object to its texture when cooked. I savor it in its inimitable entirety. You may wish to allow longer cooking time for the more fibrous stem, or cut it into smaller pieces so that it will cook at the same rate as the cap. Bolete mushrooms range in color from whitish to dark red and may be substituted in any recipe calling for cooked mushrooms. Do not serve raw.

This mushroom is highly perishable. Purchase bolete that are firm, bruise-free, and show no sign of insect infestation in the stem-end. They deteriorate rapidly, and so plan to use them soon after purchase. Prepare in a simple way such as lightly sautéed in olive oil with or without garlic and parsley.

Bolete are low in calories and a good vitamin D source. Medicinally they are a cooling food, stimulate the appetite, and are best eaten in moderation.

See **Mushroom Family** for information on selection, storage, use, and nutritional and medicinal properties.

* * *

$10.00 an Ounce

Imported, dried bolete sell for over $10.00 an ounce. Pounds of fresh bolete are free for the taking in many forested areas. True, you have to be at the right place at the right time, and you must have a reputable mushroom identification book (there are poisonous bolete varieties). Be forewarned: Once you have feasted on fresh-foraged bolete, you may become addicted.

* * *

Bolita   Also known as *Pink Bean.* A handful of bolita beans looks as diverse as pebbles in a creek. The color of bolitas is predominately pink but ranges from buff to yellow. They are obviously a pinto relative but highly irregular in size and shape. Such lack of cosmetic uniformity denotes an heirloom seed with great adaptability. Favor heirloom seeds whenever available as they afford greater vitality and flavor than our more common, hybridized commercial bean varieties.

This sweet and rich tasting bean is higher in calcium and sodium than most other beans.[7] Bolitas may be used in any pinto or kidney bean recipe.

See **Beans** for information on selection, storage, use and for medicinal and nutritional highlights.

* * *

The Bean That Escaped Hybridization

In the United States, the bolita is known to specialty food store shoppers and to southwestern Hispanics and Amerindians. Its low commercial profile has enabled it to escape hybridization, making it a first-choice bean.

* * *

Boniato   See **Sweet Potato**.

Bonito Flakes   Bonito is a dried fish product integral to Japanese and macrobiotic cooking. This fish is a member of the mackerel family and is steamed, sun dried, smoked, and then fermented. It is most commonly available in flakes that are a standard ingredient in the soup base dashi. Bonito flakes impart a mild fish flavor.

Borage   Herbalists esteem borage for its ability to drive away sorrow, increase joyfulness, and strengthen the heart. This bland, cooling herb, with a flavor reminiscent of cucumbers, is a valuable remedy for reducing high fever and for chronic catarrh. Because borage contains gamma-linolenic acid, interest in it is apt to increase.

The leaf (when young and chopped fine) and vivid blue flowers are excellent salad ingredients. Borage is also used as a culinary herb.
   See **Herbs and Spices**.

Boston Lettuce   See **Butterhead Lettuce**.

Boysenberry   In 1923, Rudolph Boysen crossed a blackberry and a raspberry and created a namesake. Boysenberries are red and more acid than blackberries.

Grown primarily for canning, boysenberries are similar to yet another blackberry and raspberry hybrid, the loganberry.

See **Berries** for information on selection, storage, use, and nutritional and medicinal properties.

Bran See **Wheat Bran**.

Brassicas See **Cabbage Family**.

Brazil Nut Brazils are the one commercial nut that is foraged. Brazil nut trees are not cultivated and have thus far resisted attempts at cultivation in Florida. They grow wild in the Amazon Valley.

At 66.9 percent fat, the Brazil is high in oil and therefore becomes rancid quickly. If purchasing shelled Brazil nuts, select those whose brown skin is intact and that look plump and fresh; avoid those that are yellowed, dark, or bruised. Brazils in the shell should feel heavy when shaken. Reddish brown shelled Brazils are dyed for cosmetic purposes.

See **Nuts** for information on selection, storage, use, and medicinal and nutritional properties.

* * *

Occupational Hazard

Brazil nuts are collected from the ground, rather than being plucked from their 150-foot-tall trees. The coconutlike pods contain up to twenty-four nuts, which fit together like orange segments. These heavy pods break off and crash to the ground with such force that sometimes the outer shell breaks open and the nuts may actually be driven into the soil. Harvesters prudently wear protective headgear.

* * *

Broad Bean See **Fava Bean**.

Broccoli Broccoli is suspect because it is so widely consumed. The greater a product's commercial value, the more likely it has been intensely hybridized. This is the case with broccoli, which has been designed to grow fast, harvest easily, and ship well. It has been accomplished at the sacrifice of flavor and vitality, however. Organically grown broccoli tastes clearly superior to most commercial broccoli.

This popular cabbage-family member does rank high in nutrients, with twice as much vitamin C as an orange, almost as much calcium as whole milk, and appreciable amounts of iron and B vitamins. The broccoli head is actually the plant's flower. If the stalks are fibrous they may be peeled before eating.

Select broccoli that has a fresh smell, bright and compact green florets, and firm stalks. Avoid any with a rank smell, yellow florets, and woody or hollowed stalks, as these are overmature.

See **Cabbage Family** for information on selection, storage, and use and for medicinal and nutritional highlights.

* * *

The Broccoli Connection

New York City area residents spend over $85 million each year for California broccoli. Commercial quantities of broccoli could easily be grown closer to New York, for a significant increase in freshness and flavor.

Favor local produce whenever available. This strengthens the local economy and reduces the use of fossil fuels for long-distance transport.

* * *

Broccoli Rabe Also known as *Cima di Rapa, Choy Sum, Rapini,* and *Turnip Tops.* One would never call broccoli rabe mild. It is aggressively pungent and bitter.

A nonheading variety of broccoli, it adds zest to bland dishes and can even hold its own with savory ones. Stalk, leaf, and flower are used.

Rabe is at its best when the leaves are fresh and free from discoloration and when the buds are still tight or just starting to open. Prepare it as you would broccoli; however, it requires less cooking. Available in the fall, winter, and early spring, most is grown in California. Use within two days of purchase.

Broccoli rabe is high in vitamins A and C and the minerals potassium and calcium. It is considered beneficial to the heart, lungs, and intestines.

See **Cabbage Family** for information on selection, storage, and use and for nutritional and medicinal highlights.

Brown Rice   See **Rice**.

Brown Sugar   You can easily make your own brown sugar: Just take some white sugar and add a bit of molasses or "caramel coloring" (burnt white sugar). This is precisely how brown sugar is made. Brown sugar made with molasses does contain more nutrients than white sugar, but the amount is insignificant.

See **Sugar** and **Sweeteners**.

Brussels Sprouts   Of all garden vegetables, Brussels sprouts look the strangest. From twenty to eighty auxiliary buds (or baby cabbages) grow close together along a tall, single stalk with cabbagelike leaves at the top. Brussels sprouts supposedly originated in Brussels, Belgium, and thus their name. The Germans more aptly call them Rosenkohl, "rose cabbage."

Brussels sprouts are an excellent cold-weather vegetable—their flavor improves with a frost—and so they are a favored fall and winter food. Select firm and compact Brussels sprouts; puffiness indicates a bland flavor. Avoid overmature Brussels sprouts with yellow or spreading leaves. When fresh the flavor is robust and nutlike; when old it is disagreeable and bitter.

Brussels sprouts are an excellent source of vitamin C and phosphorus and a good source of vitamin A and calcium. Energetically, they are contractive.

See **Cabbage Family** for information on selection, storage, and use and for nutritional and medicinal properties.

* * *

Brussels Sprouts and Mistletoe

In a traditional British Christmas dinner Brussels sprouts are a given. Not a bad custom considering that these beauties are then at their peak and, when cooked properly, appropriate fare for the grandest of feasts.

* * *

Buckwheat   The similarity of buckwheat's shape and color to the rust-colored, three-sided beechnut accounts for its name. The words *beech* and *book* derive from the same Anglo-Saxon root *buk,* probably because beech bark was written upon to make books. Thus the term *buckwheat* identifies the food as a "wheat" that looks like a beechnut.

Buckwheat is often grouped with cereal grains because of its similar culinary use and nutritional value. However, this fruit is a rhubarb relative. Buckwheat originated, and is still a staple, in Siberia and Manchuria.

Buckwheat has a strong, robust flavor. It helps increase body heat and is ideal cold-weather fare. Buckwheat-eating populations, which tend to live in damp and cold climates, include the Finns, Austrians, northern Chinese, Russians, Japanese, Italians, and French. Buckwheat is also popular in Jewish cooking. Soba, a buckwheat pasta, is popular in Japanese cuisine.

A good blood-building food, buckwheat neutralizes toxic acidic wastes. It is a contracting food and may prevent cells from cleansing themselves. Therefore it is not recommended for anyone with skin allergies or cancer (leukemia ex-

cepted). Buckwheat is considered a medicinal food for the kidneys, especially in cold climates.

The most outstanding nutritional characteristic of buckwheat is its high lysine content (6.1 percent), which is greater than any of the cereal grains. Buckwheat has up to 100 percent more calcium than other grains, is rich in vitamin E, and contains almost the entire range of B-complex vitamins.

See **Pasta** for buckwheat noodles. See **Grain** for information on selection, storage, and use and for information on its medicinal and nutritional properties.

★　★　★

Buckwheat is a Warming Food

When someone comes in out of a blizzard, frost-nipped and chilled to the bone, don't serve him or her a cooling slice of melon. Take the chill out with a steaming bowl of hearty buckwheat.

★　★　★

Buckwheat groats (*groat* refers to any hulled grain) are available either unroasted, or roasted. Roasted groats, called Kasha, are chestnut colored and have a hearty flavor. White, or unroasted, groats are mild flavored. For maximum vitality, buy unroasted groats and roast them before cooking. To roast groats, simply place them in a wok or thin pan over a flame and stir continually until the groats brown.

Whole buckwheat, with its black hull intact, is suitable only for sprouting.

Grits are cereals cracked into pieces to shorten their cooking time. Because whole buckwheat cooks in only ten minutes, the time saved cooking grits is insignificant. Furthermore, a buckwheat grit, like any broken grain, lacks vitality and loses freshness as the exposed oils oxidize.

Buckwheat Flour　Add 30 percent or more buckwheat flour to bread, and your loaf will have the density of a brick and the moistness of a pudding. For a dark, soft-textured baked product with a hearty flavor, add 10 percent buckwheat flour and use a high-gluten wheat flour.

Buckwheat flour is unsurpassed in pancakes, waffles, and crepes. The French term for buckwheat is *sarrasin,* and the twelve-inch, paper-thin Breton crepe, the *galette de sarrasin,* is commonly sold by Parisian street vendors.

Buckwheat flour is available light or dark. The dark flour, ground from unhulled groats, is gray in color, with black specks, and has more fiber and flavor than does the light.

See **Flour** for information on selection, storage, and use and for medicinal and nutritional highlights.

★　★　★

Galettes de Sarrasin (Buckwheat Crepes)

1　cup buckwheat flour (light or dark)
2　tablespoons whole wheat flour
3　cups water
¼　teaspoon sea salt
1　egg, beaten

Combine the dry ingredients. Blend the wet ingredients and stir, 1 cup at a time, into the dry. Mix until the batter is smooth. Allow it to rest for 45 minutes. Pour the batter into a pitcher. Heat a crepe pan (skillet with a ¼-inch lip), and brush it lightly with oil. Hold the pan in one hand and the pitcher in the other. Pour a small amount of batter onto the pan while rotating it so that a thin layer of batter covers the surface. Return the pan to a medium fire. Cook for 2 to 3 minutes or until the top dries, as with pancakes. Turn and cook an additional minute or just until it is lightly browned.

Roll the crepes around a variety of fillings, from curried shrimp to vegetables to apple butter. Enjoy them for breakfast, lunch, or dinner. They are excellent in packed lunches and on picnics. Makes twelve 9-inch crepes.

★　　★　　★

Buffalo　In 1899, there were fewer than 100 buffalo (technically bison) in North America. Today there are more than 75,000, raised for commercial use. Buffalo meat, a gourmet food, has the distinction of also being healthful. Buffalo has 70 percent less fat, 30 percent more protein, 50 percent less cholesterol, and 50 percent fewer calories than beef. Buffalo is also lower in calories, cholesterol, and fat than pork or chicken; and it is higher in protein than pork or chicken.[8]

Buffalo appears identical to beef except for a deeper, rich red coloring. It is tender (unless overcooked) and does not have a gamy flavor. Buffalo meat is not marbled like beef so it has less fat insulation and it absorbs heat more readily. Cook buffalo slower and at a lower temperature than beef. If broiling, move your rack an extra notch away from the flame. Otherwise substitute buffalo meat for beef in any recipe.

Store or freeze as for beef. Buffalo is USDA inspected. To determine quality, selection, and storage guidelines see **Beef.**

Bulgur　Wheat that has been steamed and then dried and cracked is called bulgur. This process yields a quicker-cooking, lighter-textured, and nuttier-flavored dish than does cracked wheat or whole wheat. Bulgur, a popular Mideast staple, has also become a staple in the new American whole-foods cuisine. It is tasty with any meal, by itself, cooked with vegetables, or as a salad base (as in tabbouleh).

Dark bulgur is made from hard red wheat. White bulgar is made from soft white wheat and has a more delicate flavor. See **Grain** and **Wheat** for information on selection, storage, use and for medicinal and nutritional highlights.

★　　★　　★

For the Discerning—Homemade Bulgur

Just as fresh pasta cannot be compared to dry pasta, so fresh bulgur is a totally different taste experience from purchased bulgur. It is surprisingly easy to make.

2 cups whole wheat berries
4 cups water

Soak wheat berries in water overnight. Bring to a boil and boil for one hour or until the wheat is slightly tender. Drain and reserve cooking liquid for soup stock. Spread wheat on a cookie sheet and sun-dry, or oven-dry at 250 degrees for 45 to 60 minutes. Stir wheat berries occasionally. When wheat is completely dry, grind coarsely in a grain mill, food processor, or blender. Store in a glass container until used.

★　　★　　★

Burdock　Also known as *Gobo.* Imagine the rich, heady aroma of freshly dug earth—that's the aroma of burdock. Add sweetness, and you've got its flavor, which is also similar to artichoke hearts or salsify. Burdock skin is brown; its somewhat fibrous flesh is white. Popularized by the Japanese, who call it gobo, the burdock taproot grows up to two feet in length yet remains as slender as a carrot.

Ignore any recipe instructions that call for scrubbing off its dark skin. Simply wash to remove any sand, but leave the skin intact. Sliver or cut it into chunks, and cook burdock as you would a carrot, but allow longer cooking. Burdock is not used raw. Add it to stews, soups, sautéed or baked vegetables, bean or grain dishes, and sea-vegetable combinations.

Burdock is unbelievably difficult to dig; it penetrates deeply into the soil and clings tenaciously there. The law of signature indicates that such strength is imparted to our "roots," or kidneys. It is also esteemed for its blood-purifying qualities and for strengthening the sexual organs.

Throughout many parts of the world, including the United States, burdock thrives as a common weed. Identify it by its large, elephant-ear-like leaves and its burrs, which cling to socks and sweaters. It is available in Oriental markets and natural-food stores throughout the year. Select plump, firm roots. Limp roots are acceptable if they are not dehydrated. Wrap in damp paper towels and refrigerate. Use within a week. If they dry, soak in water prior to use.

Burdock has more protein, calcium, and phosphorus than carrots and is an excellent source of potassium. It is a Sunflower family member.

★　　★　　★

Burdock Burrs Are Clingers

Don't curse the burrs that tenaciously cling to socks and sweaters after an autumn stroll through open fields. Grab a shovel and dig for their delicious roots. One ingenious person looked closely to see why burdock burrs are such clingers, went to the drawing board, and invented Velcro.

★　　★　　★

Butter The pendulum swings, and butter, which was denigrated because it contains saturated fat, is regaining its healthful image. This is indeed good news for all of us who love sensual foods, for there is nothing that quite takes the place of butter.

Here's why the fat of butter is valued. Clarified butter contains a significant 30 percent polyunsaturated fat (sesame oil contains 44 percent).[9] Unlike other vegetable oils (sesame and virgin olive excepted) butter oil is obtained by low heat, and it does not become rancid.

Famed scientist and medical researcher Dr. Roger Williams has determined that "butterfat, itself, appears to protect *against* arteriosclerosis." He conclusively disproves what "has come to be almost an orthodox position that if one wishes to protect oneself against heart disease, one should avoid eating saturated (animal) fats. While this idea may not be entirely in error, it is misleading in its emphasis. The evidence shows that high fat consumption, when accompanied by plenty of the essential nutrients which all cells need, does *not* cause arteriosclerosis or heart disease."[10]

Butter is vastly superior to margarine. The most healthful butter is made from raw cream; however, some states prohibit the sale of raw butter. Favor sweet (unsalted) butter over salted. Sweet butter has a more delicate flavor and a shorter life; thus, the manufacturer must use fresher cream to make it. Federal standards do not permit preservatives or additives except approved food colorings (annatto and beta-carotene).

Butter is a rich source of vitamin A and also contains vitamin D. For peak flavor, opened butter should be refrigerated in a covered dish. See also **Dairy** and **Fat**.

Clarified butter is the butterfat that remains when milk solids and water are removed from butter. It contains 30 percent polyunsaturated fat, is prepared at low temperatures, and does not go rancid. Slowly heat unsalted butter until it melts. Skim off the foam and discard. Strain the oil through a fine sieve, being careful to omit the sediment residue at the bottom of the pan. Ghee, the most commonly used fat in India's cuisine, is a similar product to clarified butter.

Low-cholesterol butter. There are several processes that remove cholesterol from butter. One, called supercritical fluid extraction, uses carbon dioxide under controlled temperature and pressure to reduce 95 percent of the cholesterol in butter. Another uses enzymes to change the cholesterol to a form that cannot be utilized or absorbed by the body. Common sense indicates favoring natural butter over highly processed butter.

Whipped butter is butter that has had its volume increased through whipping air or inert gas into it. This process results in a product that is easier to spread.

Buttercup Squash   The buttercup has a dark green skin "crowned" with a blue-green "turban" at its blossom end. The bright orange flesh ranks just under that of the kabucha as the sweetest squash. The word *creamy* describes its texture. In shape, buttercups are similar to but generally smaller and sweeter than the orange- and red-skinned turban squash. They average around three pounds.

Cut into chunks and bake, steam, or purée as you would other squash. Select hard-shelled squash with stems intact that are free of soft spots or pitting. Like other winter squash, the buttercup stores from harvest through March in a cold room. Do not refrigerate.

See **Kabucha** and **Squash, Winter** for information on selection, storage, use, and medicinal and nutritional properties.

Butterhead Lettuce   Also known as *Boston* or *Bibb Lettuce*. The butterhead has tender leaves bunched almost like rose petals. As its name suggests, butterhead is delicate and tasty.

For information on selection, storage, use, and medicinal and nutritional properties, see **Lettuce.**

Buttermilk   Real buttermilk is hard to find. It is a natural by-product of butter churned from raw, unpasteurized cream. Buttermilk is available in some natural-food stores where permitted by state law. Buttermilk is thicker than regular milk, lower in fat, and has a tangy, distinctive taste comparable to that of yogurt.

See **Dairy** for medicinal and nutritional information.

Buttermilk, Cultured   Cultured buttermilk is pasteurized skim milk that has been inoculated with a lactic acid culture and then incubated. It may contain stabilizers and is frequently made from old milk that has gone out of date and has been reclaimed from retail stores. See **Buttermilk.**

Butternut Squash   Butternut squash is reminiscent of a peanut in shape and color (thus its name), although it is actually more bell shaped. Its flesh is most similar to that of the buttercup squash.

Because its skin is thinner and lighter in color than those of other winter squash, butternut may be cooked and puréed with its skin intact. This saves preparation time and increases nutritional value.

For information on selection, storage, and use and for nutritional and medicinal highlights see **Squash, Winter.**

*   *   *

Delicious Squash Pie

Can a pie have only four ingredients, be quick to make, and be satisfying and delicious? Yes! Serve this pie as a side dish for brunch, lunch, or dinner rather than as a dessert.

    1   medium-size butternut* squash (6 cups cut into one-inch cubes)
    ¼   teaspoon sea salt
    ¼   cup maple syrup
    1   baked pie crust
    5   almonds, roasted and slivered

Wash the squash and cut it into chunks. Place squash and salt in a steamer and steam until tender (about 10 minutes). Purée the squash in a food mill or blender. Blend in the maple syrup. Pour into a baked pie shell. Garnish with almond slices. Serve.

*Other bright orange, dense-fleshed squash such as buttercup or kabucha may be used. Remove their green skin prior to puréeing. Pumpkin is not suited for this recipe.

★　　★　　★

Cabbage The cabbage, one of the oldest cultivated vegetables, is eaten in almost every country and has had more bad press than any other vegetable. Its modest price made it a staple in low-income cooking, and if overcooked it has an odor some find highly offensive. Today cabbage is fast becoming an uptown vegetable. Its alleged ability to protect against cancer has everyone talking about—and cooking—cabbage and other cabbage-family varieties.

Avoid purchasing cabbages with wilted leaves or cracked heads. Favor those whose coarse outer leaves are in place, as this indicates freshness. Uncut, a cabbage keeps for two weeks or more refrigerated in a plastic bag. If you are not using the whole cabbage, remove its outer leaves as you need them rather than slicing into the head. When cut it suffers nutrient and flavor loss.

The greener a cabbage, the more chlorophyll it contains. High in vitamins A, C, and K, cabbage is also a good source for many minerals. As a home remedy cabbage is considered salutary for the stomach.

Green cabbage forms a tight head that may be round or pointed in shape. In warmer climates, their heads are less compact.

Red (or purple) cabbage takes longer to mature than green varieties and thus frequently has tougher leaves.

Savoy cabbage has loose, crinkly leaves and is the most tender and sweet of the cabbages.

For information on selection, storage, and use and for medicinal and nutritional highlights, see **Cabbage Family**.

*   *   *

Bubble and Squeak

A decidedly British expression and dish, *bubble and squeak* is sautéed cabbage cooked with boiled potatoes. Dice the potatoes that have "bubbled" (boiled), place in a skillet containing warm oil with sliced cabbage, and listen for the "squeak." Cook until warmed through and serve.

*   *   *

Cabbage Family Also known as *Brassicas* and *Crucifers*. Historically and nutritionally, the cabbage, or brassica, family is probably the most important vegetable family. It is an extremely diverse clan—who would imagine that a kohlrabi is related to a daikon? However, when any of the brassicas go to seed, their common ancestry is apparent in the similarity of their flowers, inflorescences, fruits, and leaves. Their flowers are composed of four petals in a cross formation, which gives the family its Latin name, *crucifer*.

When purchasing leafy cabbage-family members, look for those that are crisp and firm and without insect damage or discoloration. Some members, like cabbage and Chinese cabbage, keep well refrigerated, whereas others are best used within a day or two of purchase. Wrap the more delicate greens in damp towels, place inside a plastic bag, and refrigerate.

Purchase cabbage-family roots that are uniformly colored and plump and hard rather than withered and dry. Oversize roots are frequently pithy and flavorless. Remove their tops prior to refrigeration to increase their life span.

Most dark leafy crucifers are exceptional sources of calcium, vitamins A and C, and beta-carotenes. Their unique nutrients called indoles "may enhance the detoxification of active carcinogens."[1] Collards, mustard greens, broccoli rabe, and kale are the most esteemed of the dark leafy greens. (Broccoli is a flower rather than a leafy green.)

Try to include dark leafy cabbage-family vegetables in your diet frequently. They're delicious boiled, steamed, sautéed, baked, and in soups, and some lend themselves to salads.

See also **Arugula, Broccoli, Broccoli Rabe, Bok Choy, Brussels Sprouts, Cabbage, Cauliflower, Chinese Cabbage, Collard Greens, Daikon, Horserad-**

ish, **Kale, Kohlrabi, Mustard Greens, Radish, Romanesque Broccoli, Ruta-baga, Turnip,** and **Watercress.**

★   ★   ★

Cancer Prevention

The American Cancer Society, the National Academy of Sciences, and the National Cancer Institute endorse cabbage-family vegetable consumption. These vegetables appear to protect against colonic, rectal, stomach, and respiratory cancers.

★   ★   ★

Cabbage Perfume

What causes the characteristic cabbage aroma? Long cooking releases enzymes in cabbage and other cabbagelike vegetables that emit hydrogen sulfide—the odor of rotten eggs. To avoid an assertive cabbage smell, lightly sauté, steam, or briefly boil. "The amount of hydrogen sulfide produced in boiled cabbage doubles in the fifth through the seventh minute of cooking."[2]

★   ★   ★

Cactus Pad   See **Nopale**.

Cactus Pear   See **Prickly Pear**.

Canola   Also known as *Rapeseed*. An all-purpose vegetable oil popular in India and Europe is pressed from the seed of the rape plant and called rapeseed oil. With a name like that, it has never caught on in the United States. Currently it is being developed under its Canadian name, *canola*, both as a snack seed and for oil production.

The seed is about the size of millet but round and ranges in color from sienna to brown-black. It has a nutty flavor similar to that of a sesame seed but with a surprising sweetness and tang.

Canola is a cabbage-family member closely related to the rutabaga. Imported organic, 100 percent expeller-pressed rapeseed oil has limited availability in quality food markets. It is light tasting and excellent on salads.

Cantaloupe   See **Melon Family**.

Cape Gooseberry   See **Ground Cherry**.

Carageen   See **Irish Moss**.

Carambola   See **Star Fruit**.

Cardoon   An artichoke look-alike, the cardoon is just becoming popular in the United States. This Mediterranean vegetable grows to heights of four feet and has gray-green leaves; the outer leaves are trimmed away before the plant reaches market. The blanched inner stalks are eaten like asparagus or celery in salads, soups, and stews. The root may also be used as a cooked vegetable. Unlike the artichoke, its flower is not consumed. Its dried flowers are used to curdle milk for making fresh cheese.[3]

Cardoon is most available in the winter and early spring. Because it is blanched, it is an energy-intensive crop, and thus an expensive one.

Look for fresh, crisp heads no larger than one foot long. Avoid heads with wilt or rust. As with all fresh greens, refrigerate and use as soon after purchase as possible.

Carob   Saint John the Baptist lived in the wilderness on locusts and wild honey. Locusts refers not to insects but the leguminous pods of the locust tree, which we call carob. This explains the alternate name for carob—Saint John's Bread.

Roasted and ground, carob pods yield carob powder. The longer it is roasted, the more its taste approximates that of chocolate. I use the term *approximates* loosely. Many people enjoy the carob flavor for what it is, namely carob. To expect a real chocolate flavor from carob is asking too much of any legume.

Carob is nearly 50 percent sugar (including sucrose), has 8 percent protein, and contains significantly less fat and calories than chocolate. Unlike chocolate, carob is free of caffeine and oxalic acids, and it is naturally sweet (chocolate is bitter unless sweetened with sugar). Carob, an excellent source of calcium, contains more than three times more calcium than milk! It also has vitamins A and B and other minerals.

Carob contains tannin (as does cocoa), and because tannic acid reduces the absorption of protein through the intestinal wall, it may depress the growth rate of young animals. It is therefore recommended that carob be used in moderation, especially in children's diets.

Carob pods are imported from the Mediterranean area and ground and roasted in the United States. Carob powder needs no refrigeration. Carob powder is used as a healthful chocolate and cocoa substitute in baking. However, prepared carob candies, carob chips, and blocks of carob are *not* to be confused with carob powder. Carob in a "chocolate" candy form is an inferior choice to chocolate. An additional chocolate substitute is **Dahlia.**

★   ★   ★

Carob Candies—Healthier Than What?

Carob "chocolatelike" candies contain fractionated palm kernel or coconut oil. Under no circumstances are these oils considered healthful, and *especially* not when fractionated. (See **Oil.**) Many carob candies also contain brown sugar, fructose, or other questionable sweeteners.

★   ★   ★

Carp Although disparaged by some (because it is a scavenger), the carp is considered a delicacy by others and is used in many ethnic dishes. Carp originated in Asia but now are found throughout the world. This soft-finned fish lives to a great age and ranges in size from six inches to more than six feet.

The carp, which prefers slow-moving water, often burrows into the muddy bottoms of rivers and ponds; thus it sometimes has a muddy flavor that several washings will eliminate. The spleen must be carefully removed before cooking. Some carp are covered with scales, and others have few. These may or may not be left on, depending on the recipe.

The best season for eating carp is from November to April. It may be cooked in beer or wine, baked, stuffed, poached, or braised. Gefilte fish, eaten on Jewish Sabbaths and holidays, is sometimes made with carp. A Japanese soup, koi-koku, is made of whole carp (bones and all) and eaten by postpartum women as an especially strengthening dish.

Carp is high in protein and vitamin A. It is low in fat and calories and is a fair source of calcium and some B vitamins.

See **Fish** for information on selection, storage, and use and for medicinal and nutritional highlights.

Carrot What is the longest period of time you have gone without carrots? From soups to salads, from juice to cakes, carrots figure so prominently in our daily fare that it is hard to imagine life without them. This Afghan native has become one of the most valuable root crops grown for human consumption. Carrots are derived from the wild carrot, called Queen Anne's Lace, and are related to celery, parsnips, caraway, cumin, and dill.

Select whole, unbroken carrots that look vibrant. Avoid those that are oversize, pale, or that have withered root tips. Refrigerate in plastic for up to a week.

The ancient Greek word for carrot, *philon,* comes from the Greek word for *love,* as this root was considered an aphrodisiac. The law of signature substantiates this use, as does the fact that root vegetables, especially penetrating root vegetables rather than round ones, are more energizing to our lower organs. Long cooking enhances a carrot's contractive, energizing properties; whereas raw carrots or carrot juice is more expansive.

Carrots are a rich source of vitamin A and carotenoids and sugar, as indicated by their sweetness. They also contain B vitamins, phosphorus, iodine, and calcium. Because these nutrients are concentrated in and near their skin, use them whole.

There are several hundred varieties of carrots. The most popular in the United States is the Mediterranean type, which is fairly long, cylindrical, and orange. Round carrots and baby carrots are now appearing on the market to meet the demand for new and exotic produce.

When fresh and young the nutrient-rich carrot greens may be finely chopped and sautéed or added to soups. Remove and discard their more fibrous stem. Dried or fresh, carrot tops may be used like parsley. See **Carrot Family**.

Carrot Family   The umbellifer family is named for its clustered flowers, which resemble an upside-down umbrella. The most commonly used of all the umbellifers is the carrot.

The aromatic umbellifer seeds include caraway, coriander, cumin, dill, and fennel.

The umbellifers grown for their leaves include chervil, dill, lovage, parsley, samphire, and sweet cicely.

Umbellifers cultivated for their leaf stems include celery, angelica, and fennel.

The umbellifer root crops include carrot, celeriac, chervil root, parsnip, and parsley root.

Carrot Juice   See **Juice, Vegetable**.

Casaba   See **Melon Family**.

Cashew   This sweet-tasting, kidney-shaped nut grows in a curious manner. It hangs from a pear-shaped, orange cashew fruit called an apple. The cashew apple is eaten fresh or made into preserves or liqueur. The cashew, a tropical evergreen, is native to Brazil and a relative of poison ivy.

Cashews are lower in fat than other nuts (except chestnuts), and most of their fat is unsaturated. They contain 20 percent protein and high amounts of magnesium, phosphorus, and potassium.

Between the cashew's inner and outer shell is a toxic oil, cardol, which—if touched—burns the skin. Cardol is released from the uncracked nuts by roasting them at 350 degrees. They are then cracked and roasted once again to remove an inner shell. These cashews are marketed as "raw."

Because they are not shelled domestically, cashews are frequently stale. Fresh cashews are crisp, solid, and white. Even though whole cashews are more expensive, they are definitely fresher and a better purchase than cashew pieces. Raw cashews are hard to digest; roasting enhances their flavor and digestibility.

About 90 percent of our domestic supply of cashews comes from India. The remainder comes from South America. Annual production is from both wild and cultivated cashew trees. See **Nuts**.

Catfish   Catfish is the second most harvested fish in the United States. But if you live north of the Mason-Dixon line, its availability is limited. There are more than thirty species of catfish. Channel catfish are grown by 98 percent of today's aquaculture farmers and are usually marketed at about one and a half pounds each.

Short on eye appeal but long on flavor, the catfish is ugly! It is scaleless and has long barbs around its mouth. However, appearance doesn't seem to affect catfish sales, which were a $300-million business in 1985. Catfish farming, a "new idea" in the late 1960s, has obviously caught on.[4]

The catfish of Huck Finn fame is the blue, which can weigh up to 150 pounds. Some people prefer the wild varieties, which, they claim, have the best flavor. Others favor the mildness of farmed catfish, which have a consistent flavor and texture because they are raised in clean water and fed a controlled diet.

Catfish flesh is lean, white, and flaky; has a delicate texture and flavor; and is available year round.

See **Fish, Freshwater** for additional information.

Cauliflower   Cauliflower, cultivated for its undeveloped white flower buds, is in peak supply in the fall. Select one with a firm, compact head, clean and creamy white color. Size is no indication of quality. If it is wearing a collar of outer leaves, these should be fresh. Cauliflower with brown spots or spreading florets is past its prime.

Similar in use and flower to broccoli, the cauliflower contains significantly lower proportions of vitamins and minerals (and, obviously, chlorophyll) than does broccoli. It is said to be good brain food. Refrigerate it stem end up to prevent moisture from collecting on the cauliflower top, which would speed deterioration.

See **Cabbage Family** for information on selection, storage, use, and nutritional and medicinal properties.

Cayenne   See **Chile Peppers**.

Celeriac   Also known as *Celery Root* and *Knob Celery*. Celeriac is closely related to celery and tastes a lot like a pungent celery heart. Not a true root but rather a swollen stem base, celeriac looks like an irregular, brown turnip with many small roots extending from its base.

You rarely see a celeriac with its stems intact. If you grow this vegetable or find one with its greens, use them sparingly—they are bitter—to flavor soups and stews. The greens are said to have medicinal properties for the heart.

Favor small roots over the large, as the latter tend to be pithy. Press the stalk end of the knob with your thumb and only select those that are firm. Cut off any stems and refrigerate both. The root will keep up to a week. Peel and discard the skin just prior to use. Celeriac is primarily available in the fall and winter.

Julienne or grate and marinate with a vinaigrette for a zesty salad. Or use the knob as you would turnip. It blends beautifully with other foods, yet still retains its own flavor. If overcooked, it may become mushy.

See **Carrot Family** for additional information.

Celery   Celery and its close relative parsley were called by the same name in classical times. They were primarily used as medicine for constipation, as diuretics, to break up gallstones, to soothe nerves, and to heal wounds. In the seventeenth century, the bitterness was bred out of celery, and it has since enjoyed increasing popularity.

This vegetable has one of the highest sodium contents. It is valued today for treating arthritis and diseases involving chemical imbalances. It is said to help bring energy up and is good if one is feeling constipated or heavy. Celery is a favorite reducing food.

Unfortunately, celery—along with mushrooms and iceberg lettuce—is one of the most chemically altered food crops. It is blanched of its green color to make it less bitter. Blanching is most often achieved by applying ethylene gas. Virtually all supermarket celery is blanched. Stalks that are a vivid, deep green have not been blanched. For optimum nutrition, chlorophyll, and strengthening properties, favor organic, unblanched celery. It tastes much stronger but is delicious in cooked dishes.

Avoid celery with yellow leaves or wilted or cracked stalks, and choose firm celery with no signs of damage. Refrigerate in a plastic bag. For longer storage keep the stalks intact until use.

See **Carrot Family** for additional information.

Celtuce   Also known as *Stem Lettuce.* A vegetable that looks and tastes like both celery and lettuce is called, logically enough, celtuce. The young leaves are edible raw but are preferred as a cooked green. The stem, like celery in taste and texture, is the choicest part of celtuce. Use the stem raw or cooked as you would celery.

Celtuce is a relative newcomer to domestic markets. This sunflower-family member is available throughout the year except during the heat of summer.

Cèpe   See **Bolete Mushroom**.

Cereal, Cooked Breakfast   Cereal grains are often processed in order to create a quick-cooking hot breakfast. Grain, or a combination of grains, is coarsely ground, flaked, or sprouted. Sprouted grain combinations are naturally sweeter because the sprouting process converts starch into maltose. Favor whole cereals rather than refined and enriched grain products. See **Grain**.

Cereal, Ready-to-Eat   Ready-to-eat cereals suit our fast-paced mornings. While appreciating the convenience, let us not delude ourselves about quality. Grains that are flaked, puffed, toasted, or shredded are nutritionally and energetically inferior to whole grains.

The heat treatment used for puffing cereals damages the quality of the cereal protein. It causes a significant destruction of the essential amino acid lysine and most of the B vitamins. The milling often removes those portions of the grain, bran, and germ that are the richest source of vitamins, minerals, and fiber.

Commercial ready-to-eat cereals can incorporate overprocessed grain, sugar, artificial colors and flavors, chemical preservatives, vitamins, and minerals. The package containing the cereal may itself contain the preservatives BHA and BHT, so that the manufacturer can claim "no preservatives added."

Quality cereals use whole grains and have no preservatives. These cereals use natural sweeteners such as barley malt or honey. Almost all natural cereals are salt free, or they contain sea salt. See **Grain**.

* * *

Fragmented Foods

Profit is made in the food industry by partitioning foods—taking them, breaking them into pieces, and selling the pieces more profitably than the whole. For example, one of the highest-priced foods, per weight, is breakfast cereals. Ten ounces of corn, flaked and packaged attractively, costs around two dollars. That same two dollars could purchase ten pounds of whole corn.

* * *

Cereal Grains   See **Grain**.

Chanterelle   The uncommonly superb chanterelle mushroom is egg-yellow in color and shaped like a curving trumpet. It has a faint aroma reminiscent of apricots and its delicate taste is delicious. Wild fresh chanterelles appear in markets in late summer. Year round they are available dried and canned.

Select fresh chanterelles that are not withered or bruised. Use immediately. Subtly flavored dishes are enhanced by chanterelles. However, gourmets rarely combine these delicacies with any other food. For maximum enjoyment, lightly sauté this fungus in olive oil and add a dash of salt or tamari.

See **Mushroom Family** for information on selection, storage, and use and for nutritional and medicinal highlights.

Chard   Also known as *Swiss Chard.* Chard is a zesty beetlike vegetable that was developed for its large leaf stalk. Two varieties of chard are available in the United States, and they are distinguished by the color of their leaf rib. The green variety is white ribbed, and the red variety is red ribbed.

Like other members of the goosefoot family, chard contains oxalic acid but does not taste strongly acidic.

Look for clear white or red ribs that show no discoloration and have crisp, curly leaves. Chard is available throughout the year. The young leaves may go into a salad. The older leaves may be prepared in the same way as spinach or Chinese cabbage.

See **Goosefoot Family** for information on selection, storage, and use and for nutritional and medicinal highlights.

* * *

Christmas Cheer

Chop red-ribbed chard and lightly steam it with a dash of umeboshi vinegar or a pinch of sea salt. The perky red ribs along with the vivid green leaves almost evoke yuletide spirit.

* * *

Chayote   Also known as *Vegetable Pear.* The squashlike fruit of the chayote (chi-O-te) plant is becoming commonly available in domestic markets. In Central America and the Caribbean the whole plant (roots, young leaves, fruits, and shoots) is eaten and is an important food source.

A fresh chayote has a delicate flavor and texture that is rather like a blend of cucumber and apple. When old it is decidedly flavorless. Substitute chayotes in any recipe calling for summer squash; however, discard its skin and large, inedible seed.

The chayote is round to pear shaped. The female fruit is smooth skinned and lumpy with slight ridges. It is fleshier and is preferred over the male fruit, which is covered with warty spines. Look for a chayote with a solid appearance and with an unblemished skin from dark green to ivory white in color. Store at 50 to 55 degrees; the refrigerator is too cold. See also **Squash, Summer.**

Cheese   Cheese dresses up and increases the palatability and nutritional value of almost every food but watermelon. U.S. cheese consumption has consistently increased during the past twenty years, as have the types available (two thousand different cheeses are used throughout the world).

Many people are substituting cheese for meat as their primary protein source. Others are reducing their cheese consumption because cheeses are a highly concentrated form of milk and therefore contain higher concentrations of the toxins present in milk. Also, cheese is very high in fat (30 percent by weight) unless it is a skim-milk cheese. New nutritional data, however, suggest that whole-milk products are actually more healthful than skim-milk products.[5]

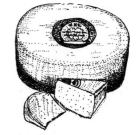

Cheese made from whole, unpasteurized milk is decidedly superior, in terms of nutrition and flavor, to that made from pasteurized milk. Making cheese from fresh, raw milk is an art. It's a living food and requires careful tending during its maturation period, as well as an experienced touch and nose to determine exactly when it has come of age. Once cut, its maturation ceases. Europeans disdain cheese made from pasteurized milk as dead food.

Unfortunately, due to U.S. importation laws, all foreign cheese must be made of pasteurized milk. Furthermore, these same laws require that imported cheeses contain salt or other preservatives and a determined percentage of butterfat. Domestic cheeses made of raw milk are permitted in all states.

Cheese is made by inoculating heated milk with a coagulant. Most European cheeses are still traditionally made with a rennet or pepsin coagulant. These coagulants are enzymes extracted from the stomachs of suckling calves, sheep, or pigs. Domestic cheese coagulants utilize cost-effective enzyme starters. These coagulants are cultures based on nettles, thistleheads, safflower seeds, or grains. If pasteurized milk is used, then calcium chloride is also added.

The variety of cheese produced depends upon the following factors:

- Milk used (cow, sheep, goat, and so on)
- Raw or pasteurized
- Coagulant used
- Amount of salt (if any)
- Other ingredients such as herbs, spices, and chemicals
- Method used for preparing and forming the curd
- Length of time cheese ages
- Temperature and humidity at which cheese ripens

All cheeses may be further classified into one of two categories: either ripened or unripened.

An unripened, or fresh, cheese has a high moisture content, is highly perishable, and is made to be consumed soon after manufacture. Examples are cottage cheese, cream cheese, farmer cheese, and ricotta. There are also firm, unripened cheeses like mozzarella, gjetost, and mysost.

Cheeses allowed to age under conditions favorable to the growth of certain bacteria and molds are termed "ripened." The five types of ripened cheeses, and examples of each, are:

- Soft-ripened—Brie, Camembert, feta, and Limburger.
- Semisoft-ripened—Muenster, Monterey Jack, brick, and Port du Salut.
- Firm-ripened—the Cheddars, Cheshire, Swiss, Colby, Derby, Jarlsberg, Edam, Gouda, provolone and Tilsit.
- Hard-ripened—Provolone, Parmesan, Romano, and Asiago.
- Blue-vein mold-ripened—blue, Gorgonzola, Roquefort, and Stilton.

★ ★ ★

Surprise Ingredients in Natural Cheese!

The word *natural* is used to distinguish cheese made directly of milk from pasteurized process cheese. Natural cheese may contain artificial dyes and chemical additives. Request chemical-free cheese, which is available from quality markets.

★ ★ ★

Pasteurized process cheese, which is a high-tech "plastic" food, should be avoided by consumers who enjoy fine foods. Its advantage is consistent flavor and texture, and it melts and spreads easily. To obtain these properties, emulsifiers, chemicals, acids, stabilizers, and artificial flavors and colors are added to ground or shredded natural cheese. This concoction is then extruded through dies at high temperatures.

Process cheeses include pasteurized process cheese, blended cheese, pasteurized process cheese food, cold-pack cheese, and pasteurized process cheese spread. Cheese-flavored snacks, dips, and crackers primarily use process cheeses.

Imitation Soy Cheese is a comparable sham to processed cheese. This soy-based counterfeit is nutritionally inferior to regular cheese. It contains artificial flavors and colors and usually has a gum or starch to hold it together. Sometimes it has a small amount of the cheese it is mimicking, refined vegetable oil, and some skim or nonfat milk. Most contain two milk-derived chemicals, casein and calcium caseinate.[6]

Cherimoya   Also known as *Custard Apple.* The rough, armadillolike shell of the cherimoya (cheree-MOY-a) looks uninviting. But do not be put off by appearances. Inside the yellow-green skin is a lush, silky smooth, sweet white flesh that has a slightly musky and decidedly tropical taste.

Cherimoya is an Incan word, and the fruit is native to the tropical Americas. Commercial crops are now growing in California, Australia, and South America but the fruit is fragile and, despite increasing demand for its custardy flesh, its availability may remain sketchy.

Cherimoyas are most available in the winter. Harvested when hard, they need to ripen at room temperature and are damaged by cold. Purchase one that is just beginning to soften, but avoid a brown or bruised fruit. They vary in size from one-half to two pounds; size does not affect flavor. To increase its sweetness, allow it to ripen at room temperature just until it begins to brown and before it becomes overly soft. Once ripe they may be refrigerated for up to five days.

Spoon out the inedible black seeds as you would watermelon seeds. When at its prime, this milk-custardlike lush fruit is best savored unembellished by other ingredients.

For a fruit, cherimoyas are high in calories and have a fair amount of iron and vitamin C. They are a cooling and expansive food.

* * *

Cherimoya on the Half Shell

Elizabeth Schneider, author of *Uncommon Fruits and Vegetables,* recommends serving chilled cherimoya in the half shell "to best savor it. Simply halve lengthwise, and offer spoons (I like the tidiness of grapefruit spoons). Although diners will have to wade through the heavy seeds, there is no other way to get the full effect."[7]

* * *

Cherry, Sour Also known as *Pie Cherries.* The parent of cherries, the choke cherry, is a bitter, astringent fruit smaller than a cherry pit. Its traces have been found in Stone Age European and American sites. From this wild cherry, there developed two main commercial types, sour and sweet. (See **Cherry, Sweet,** below.)

Sour cherries are so juicy and perishable that they bruise at a touch and are thus difficult to market. With increased interest in unusual fruits, fresh sour cherries are once again becoming available, but only in regional markets. Look for them in July following the sweet cherry harvest. They are best used within two days of purchase.

Pie cherries are smaller than sweet cherries, and their color is a bright "cherry" red rather than the almost black red of a Bing sweet cherry. *Acid cherries* would be a more apt name than *sour cherries.* By any name, it takes just one to reap a pucker.

The primary commercial use of sour cherries is canned—or frozen—in a thick sugar syrup as pie cherries. In any recipe calling for cooked cherries, the sour cherry performs better than the sweet cherry. Serve them in cold fruit soups, with game, and in any dessert or preserve that calls for cherries.

Pie cherries require added sweeteners. They are remarkably high in vitamin A and folic acid. This tart fruit is low in calories.

Cherry, Sweet Of temperate-zone stone fruits, the sweet cherry has by far the highest sugar content. They are sweet, lush, juicy, and when tree ripened, incomparably superb. Sweet cherries are more difficult to cultivate than sour. Like the peach, they are stone, or drupe, fruits, each containing a single pit.

Just as the Delicious apple is the preferred commercial apple, so the Bing cherry is also favored. It is an excellent fruit, and when ripe, the darkest in color. There are several hundred cherry varieties and each has its own unique flavor and properties. Those most readily available are Lambert, Chapman, and yellow Royal Anne (the last is usually dyed red and processed into maraschino cherries).

Of fresh fruits, commercial cherries and grapes often contain the most toxic chemical residues. Favor organic cherries when possible, and wash the commercial ones well. Select cherries with fresh, green stems. Dry, brittle stems are a sign of overripeness. Sweet cherries should be full-colored, soft, and plump and have a glossy skin. Refrigerate in plastic and use within four days. Enjoy them fresh, dried, juiced, in preserves, and, of course, in pies.

Cherries contain some phosphorus, potassium, and calcium as well as vitamin A. According to Chinese dietary therapy, the cherry is a warming food that removes blood stagnation and is used to treat paralysis, the heart, numbness in the four extremities, and rheumatic pain in the lower half of the body.[8]

Chestnut The aroma of hot roasted chestnuts from a street vendor on a nippy day is irresistible. Chestnuts are available in the United States primarily during the winter holiday season. They are highly valued in Europe and the Orient for the finest gourmet cookery. Conversely, in these same areas they have been a principal food of the poor. They were also an important food to the American Indian. In addition to being delicious alone, chestnuts enhance soups, fritters, stuffings, cookies, cakes, and icings.

The chestnut is a magnificent tree, and vast chestnut forests grew in the United States until a blight in the early 1900s destroyed them all. Today a few Japanese chestnuts grow commercially on the West Coast, but our primary chestnut source is Europe.

Select fresh chestnuts in the shell with clear, silky smooth, brown shells rather than dry or brittle shells. To roast or bake them, first deeply score the shells with a paring knife; otherwise they may explode. When boiled, they need not be scored. Prior to cooking, refrigerate in a paper bag for no more than one week.

Because of their low oil content they are more easily digested than other nuts and yet still offer a rich, nutlike flavor. Chestnuts have only 1.5 grams of fat per 100 grams. By comparison, macadamia nuts have 71.6 grams fat and almonds have 54 grams. As a kitchen remedy, chestnuts are salutary to the kidneys. See **Nuts**.

Dried chestnuts, available year round, are sweeter than fresh (as moisture is lost, the carbohydrate converts to sugar). Dried chestnuts are always shelled and more expensive than fresh, but they are a great convenience. They may be ground into flour or rehydrated and then cooked.

Chestnut Flour Fragrant, sweet-tasting chestnut flour forms a firm and unyielding paste. Generally available in specialty shops, it makes a tasty addition to pastries, cookies, and tarts. See **Flour** for additional information on storage and use.

Chia Seed See **Seeds**.

Chicken Chicken is a cheap food. This fact is telling. Despite a good nutritional profile when compared to other flesh foods, many health care practitioners recommend other meat products (or organic chicken) over commercial chicken because in terms of its energizing properties, it is a shoddy product.

"In 1935 it required 16 to 17 weeks, with five pounds of feed, to produce a pound of poultry meat. Today the same sized broiler is slaughtered when it is six weeks old and has eaten less than two pounds of feed."[9]

The difference in the feed of 1935 and today's feed is—in a word—chemicals. The poultry industry has discovered that corn grits mixed with growth hormones, antibiotics, tranquilizers, and arsenic means a bigger chicken in less time.

Nearly half of all chicken contains salmonella bacteria, which, fortunately, are destroyed in cooking. But the bacteria may contaminate other raw foods. To avoid transferring this bacteria, it is essential to wash your hands, utensils, and cutting board immediately after touching raw poultry.

For maximum flavor and health, organic, free-range chickens are advised. All poultry should be eaten within eight to twenty-four hours of slaughter. Current freezing practices cause flavor loss because the bird is soaked in a water bath before freezing. When defrosted, the water—containing much of the natural flavor and vitamins—seeps out.

Whole chicken is less perishable, and is generally a more economical purchase, than are parts. Always remove the giblets and refrigerate them in a separate package. When selecting chicken look for a plump bird that shows no surface skin defects. The skin should be moist, the legs and feet soft, the breastbone flexible, and the wing tip should yield readily to pressure.

Chickens are classified as follows: Broilers weigh about two and one-half pounds and are slaughtered at six weeks; fryers weigh from two and one-half to three pounds and are eleven weeks old; roasters weigh from three and one-half to five pounds and are twelve weeks old; fowls and capons (castrated males) weigh from six to eight pounds and are as old as eighteen weeks. The smaller the bird, the more tender and expensive.

Chickpea Also known as *Garbanzo.* Chickpeas are a popular legume in many parts of the world. The most common chickpea in the United States is tannish in color, although there are red, white, brown, and black varieties. Other legumes usually contain five or more seeds per pod; the chickpea pod contains only one or two seeds.

The chickpea provides more vitamin C and nearly double the usual amount of iron than most legumes. One of the most nutritious of the legumes, it is also high in calcium, potassium, vitamin A, and unsaturated fats.

Among legumes the chickpea claims more powers than the others for benefitting the heart. In appearance it looks something like a heart and its pod like a pericardium.

Chickpeas form the popular Middle Eastern dishes hummus and falafel. Marinated, they are a standard item in salad bars. Add them to soups, croquettes, vegetables dishes, or enjoy them plain.

See **Beans** for selection, storage, cooking information and nutritional and medicinal highlights.

Chickpea Flour The high-protein flour, made from chickpeas and called gram flour, is a common ingredient in East Indian flatbreads. It cooks dry and powdery, almost chalky, and lends a sweet, rich chickpea flavor. In color chickpea flour is like corn flour; in performance it is more like millet flour. Gram is gluten-free, and thus is used in a small quantities in leavened bread.

Chickpea flour is available in Indian and natural food markets. It is more digestible than is the other common legume flour, soy flour.

Chicory Some varieties of chicory are grown for their large taproots, which are dried, roasted, and blended with coffee for a desired bitter flavor. Dried chicory root and greens are also esteemed as a medicinal herb for liver irregularities, as a blood purifier, and to nourish the heart and circulatory system.

Chicory greens have been used as a popular salad vegetable and potherb since ancient times. There are numerous green and red chicories, which are generally shaped like romaine lettuce. Chicory greens are often blanched to reduce their bitter flavor.

Look for fresh, crisp greens and avoid those with wilt or browning. Refrigerate and use within a day or two. Chicory is an excellent source of potassium and vitamin A and a good source of calcium. See **Belgian Endive, Curly Endive,** and **Escarole.**

Chile Peppers Also known as *Chile* and *Hot peppers.* Peppers originated nine thousand years ago in Mexico, and Columbus initiated their spread throughout the world. When used carefully chile peppers enhance and expand the flavors of foods. Used excessively, they numb the mouth and overpower subtle flavors.

Capsaicin is an oily substance found in fresh chiles that may literally burn the skin, especially the eyes, nose, and lips. It is important to wear plastic or rubber gloves when you handle fresh chiles, or immediately afterwards to wash your hands thoroughly with soap and water.

Nearly 90 percent of the capsaicin is concentrated in the veins of chiles, so, depending on the chile "temperature" you desire, you may wish to exclude or include these parts. The veins of the milder chiles, such as the Anaheim, impart only a mild degree of hotness.

Hundreds of different chile varieties exist, and many have multiple names. New varieties are frequently introduced, and there seems to be little consistency in the names given any of them. They vary in color, size, shape, and pungency. Select those that are firm and unblemished rather than limp or discolored.

Dried chiles are available whole, crushed, or powdered. When crushed or powdered, they are ready to use in recipes. To prepare whole dried chiles, rehydrate by soaking in hot water for an hour or so. Cut and remove seeds and veins. As with fresh chiles, use rubber gloves and work under cold running water to avoid being burned by the capsaicin.

Chiles are excellent sources of vitamins C and A, potassium, and folic acid. They also contain fiber and iron and are extremely low in calories.

The Anaheim is a mildly hot chile pepper that is bright green when young and deepens to red at maturity. It is the longest of the peppers (up to eight inches). Available year round in some regions, this chile pepper is at its peak of freshness when firm and green. The Anaheim is almost always cooked. It may be used fresh to make chiles rellenos and is excellent when stuffed. When dried the Anaheim is used in chili powder.

The ancho is a mildly hot pepper used fresh and dried. When dried it is dark maroon or black in color and is the primary ingredient in most commercial chili powders. The fresh ancho is at its peak in summer and fall and is also available canned. It grows up to six inches long and ranges from dark green to almost black with red spots. The tough skin must be charred and peeled before use. The ancho is the traditional pepper for chiles rellenos, mole, and chili con carne. Cayenne pepper is long and thin and exceedingly hot and grows in Mexico and Central America. Cayenne is used, in either its red or green state, to flavor soups, stews, and vegetable dishes. The red cayenne is the most fiery.

Explosive best describes the fire quotient of the habanero. This small green or red lantern-shaped pepper is most often found in the ethnic cuisines of Caribbean countries.

One of the hottest of peppers, the jalapeño is green, one to three inches long, pointed at the end, and smooth skinned. It is available twelve months of the year. Select jalapeños with shiny, unwrinkled skin.

The poblano is a mildly hot Mexican pepper that is at its peak in the late summer and fall. It is about five inches long and looks like an elogated forest-green bell pepper. Char and peel its unusually tough skin prior to use.

Serranos are searing! This small (from one to two inches long and no more than one inch wide) green-to-orange pepper looks innocuous but is not. It may be used raw or roasted.

See also **Pepper** and **Sweet Pepper**.

★   ★   ★

How to Prepare Fresh Chiles

Chiles are often peeled prior to use. First slit the skin near the stem. Place them in a broiler pan about four inches from the heat source and broil until blistered. Turn frequently. Once they are blistered, immediately place them in a brown paper bag and close the bag to allow the chiles to steam for fifteen minutes. The skins are then easily slipped off the peppers. Remove skins (and, if you wish, seeds and veins) under cold running water to protect your skin from being burned by the capsaicin.

*   *   *

Keep Things Moving

The pungent or spicy flavor typified by hot peppers is energizing to the large intestine. Many people recall their first experience with a "hot" food and how immediately it stimulated their bowels. Traditionally, the pungent flavors were more favored in hot climates than in temperate climates. Within the past decade fiery foods have swept north from the Mexican border at an astonishing pace.

*   *   *

China Bean See **Black-eyed Pea**.

Chinese Broccoli The most delightful thing about Chinese broccoli is its delicate flowers. These yellow or white blossoms perk up any dish. Fresh, use them as a garnish on the side of a plate or float them on a steaming bowl of soup. For stir-fried dishes, cook the blossoms for only the last sixty seconds so they will retain their color.

Chinese broccoli does not look at all like broccoli but tastes something like it. The two may be used interchangeably. Look for Chinese broccoli with solid stems and with flower buds just starting to blossom. Refrigerate and use within three days.

This vegetable is comparable to broccoli in nutritional properties and medicinal uses. See **Cabbage Family**.

Chinese Cabbage Also known as *Celery Cabbage, Michili Cabbage,* and *Napa Cabbage.* Chinese cabbage is described as a cabbage that even cabbage-haters love. It is tenderer, crisper, juicier, and milder than our common cabbage. Rather than forming a round head, its leaves are longer and, in some varieties, narrower.

There are three distinct varieties of Chinese cabbage. Two are compact heads with the leaves at the top curling either out- or inward. The third type is more elongated and narrow, and its leaves curve inward. Any consistency naming the types of Chinese cabbage is regional rather than national. To confuse the matter further, sometimes bok choy varieties are incorrectly classified as Chinese cabbage. In most marketplaces at least one form of Chinese cabbage is consistently available.

Select fresh, light-colored greens with plump stems. Avoid those that have wilted leaves with any rot spots. Chinese cabbage, like our common cabbage, stores well; it holds in a cool cellar or refrigerated for two weeks.

Stir-fried dishes, soups, pickles, and salads are enhanced with Chinese cabbage. A hearty preparation such as a stew would be less suitable. The Chinese cabbage leaf is more flexible than that of our common cabbage and thus is easier to use in cabbage rolls. To use raw in a salad, favor fresh Chinese cabbage rather than greens that are several weeks old.

Cooked Chinese cabbage has only sixteen calories per cup and is very low in sodium. It is an excellent source of folic acid and vitamin A and a good potassium source. It is said to be medicinal to the lungs. See **Cabbage Family.**

*   *   *

Some Like It Hot

This Korean pickle, kimchi, makes salsa seem like ice.

  1 head Chinese cabbage, quartered lengthwise
  2 tablespoons chili powder
  1 tablespoon toasted sesame seeds
  2 tablespoons tiny dried shrimp (optional)

3 garlic cloves
1 knob fresh ginger, peeled and deeply scored
1 tablespoon sea salt

Place cabbage in a crock (ceramic bowl or wide-mouthed jar). With your fingers, mix in the other ingredients. Place a weight (such as a water-filled jar) on a plate atop the ingredients in the crock. Cover loosely with a clean towel to keep dust out. Water will be pressed from the cabbage and rise above the plate's surface. Allow to set for 10 to 14 days at room temperature. Slice into bite-size pieces as you are ready to serve it. If the pickle is too hot, rinse under running water. If it is still too hot, allow to soak in water for 15 minutes. Refrigerate remaining kimchi, or store in the crock (with the weight intact) in a cool place for a week or so.

★　　★　　★

Chinese Chard　See **Bok Choy**.

Chinese Cooking Wine　See **Mirin**.

Chinese Long Bean　See **Yard-Long Bean**.

Chinese Pear　See **Pear, Asian**.

Chinese Winter Melon　Crunch, rather than flavor, is what this large squash is about. The subtly flavored Chinese winter melon takes on the flavors of other foods it is cooked with, yet retains its pleasing crispiness. It is a favorite soup ingredient in Oriental cuisine and is also found in savory concoctions, candied, and pickled.

This large vegetable is most often sold cut, and therefore it should be used within several days of purchase. Its pale green skin has a thick and waxy bloom that looks like frost. It is available throughout the year. Select one that is firm and unblemished.

Nutritionally and medicinally the winter melon is more similar to summer squash than winter; however, it does have a better shelf life.

See **Squash, Summer** for information on selection, storage, and use and for nutritional and medicinal highlights.

Chives　Chives look like slender scallions without swollen bulbs. Their soft springtime flavor is more delicate than that of scallions and also more arresting. They are most used as a garnish or in subtly flavored dishes. Feature their purple pom-pom blossoms in flower arrangements or as a decorative, rather than edible, garnish.

This fragile onion-family member is available year round but must be very fresh to be worth the purchase. Avoid yellowed or wilted chives. Refrigerate in a plastic bag for three or four days, or trim the ends, immerse in a jar of water, and loosely cover with plastic to extend their life.

Chives contain vitamin A, B complex, and calcium. They are energizing to the liver and help to bring energy upward. See **Herbs and Spices** and **Onion Family**.

★　　★　　★

The Cuttable Leek

The German word for chive is *Schnittlauch,* which means the cuttable leek. This aptly names the chive, which actually thrives when the top half is clipped back. The chive also is a common and rewarding kitchen windowbox herb.

★　　★　　★

Chlorella　Chlorella, the first plant form with a true nucleus, has been on earth since the pre-Cambrian period—over 2.5 billion years. This single-celled alga grows in freshwater lakes and ponds.

Today, chlorella is making headlines as one of the most (if not the most) esteemed nutritional supplements. It is one of the highest natural sources of DNA and RNA. This freshwater alga contains more than twenty different vitamins and minerals, plus nineteen amino acids, including all of the essential amino and fatty acids. It is particularly rich in lysine and is one of the highest natural sources of chlorophyll. It is from 50 to 60 percent protein.

Some eight hundred articles on the supplement chlorella have been published in medical journals around the world. It has been indicated for a wide variety of maladies and conditions, including chronic gastritis, high blood pressure, some forms of cancer, diabetes, constipation, anemia, and high cholesterol.[10]

Chocolate   Chocolate, a native of tropical America, was called "food of the Gods" by the Aztecs. Introduced to Europe by Columbus, it took more than one hundred years for chocolate to capture appetites in Europe, but catch on it did and caught-on it remains.

The cacao tree bears fruit pods that contain about forty almond-shaped seeds in each pod. These pods are hand harvested and then cut and placed in fermentation tanks, which draw out some of their excessive bitter flavor. They are then roasted and their shells removed and ground into an oily paste called chocolate liquor. The chocolate liquor is then blended into the following products:

Bitter chocolate consists of pure chocolate liquor in a solid state. From 50 to 58 percent is pure cocoa butter with an optional flavoring such as vanilla. It is used in confections.

Bittersweet chocolate is the most intense-tasting chocolate. It contains at least 35 percent chocolate liquor as well as cocoa butter and a smaller amount of sugar than does semisweet or milk chocolate.

Cocoa butter is primarily used in the cosmetic industry but some is added to other chocolate products.

Cocoa powder is the dry cake that remains after pressing cocoa butter. It is pulverized into a powder form and used as a confection and beverage ingredient.

Couverture is a rich French chocolate characterized by an exceptionally shiny finish. It is highest in cocoa butter. The U.S. Food and Drug Administration (FDA) does not regulate the use of the term *couverture,* so *caveat emptor.*[11]

Dutch cocoa is alkali-processed cocoa powder. The alkali, usually potassium carbonate, is used to neutralize the cocoa's acids.

Milk chocolate is derived by combining chocolate liquor, cocoa butter, sugar, flavorings, and at least 12 percent milk solids. Also called Swiss chocolate, this is the most popular chocolate in the United States.

Semisweet chocolate (also called sweet chocolate) contains at least 35 percent chocolate liquor, 27 percent cocoa butter, sugar, and (optional) flavorings such as vanilla. Semisweet chocolate is used in chocolate chips.

White chocolate—that is, quality white chocolate—contains cocoa butter that may be sweetened with sugar or chestnuts. Cheap imitation white chocolate substitutes vegetable oil for the cocoa butter.

*   *   *

Why Broken-Hearted Lovers Binge on Chocolate

Chocolate is rich in phenylethylamine. The brain manufactures this substance when stimulated by the emotion of love. Thus a box of chocolates eases the edge for the slighted or sets the stage for the suitor.

*   *   *

Choy Sum   See **Broccoli Rabe.**

Cilantro   Also known as *Chinese Parsley, Coriander,* and *Mexican Parsley.* Within the past few years cilantro, with its wild and zesty flavor, has become common-

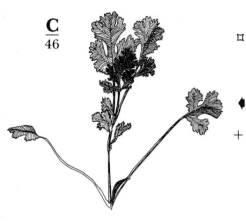

place in our markets. The cilantro leaf is similar in appearance to parsley but is larger and less curled. Cilantro may be used like parsley, as a garnish and as a flavoring herb. It is also used in large quantities in sauces and salsas.

The seeds of cilantro are known as the spice coriander. This fresh herb is basic to Mexican and Indian cookery.

Cilantro is available throughout the year. Select those bunches that are fresh and bright. Old cilantro has a harsh, unpleasant flavor and should be discarded. Cilantro is a good source of vitamin A.

See **Carrot Family** and **Herbs and Spices**.

Citron   This lemonlike citrus fruit has a thick, rough skin and contains little flesh or juice. One of the first citrus fruits to be introduced from the Far East to the Mediterranean region, its rind is used primarily in the preparation of candied peel.

See **Citrus Fruit** for information on selection, storage, and use and for nutritional and medicinal highlights.

Citrus Fruit   One of the largest and most important groups of fruits of the tropical and subtropical regions, citrus originated in China and Southeast Asia. Citrus plants are small trees or shrubs. Most of their fruits are high in sugar, although lemons and limes are high in acids. All species are rich sources of vitamin C, have citric acid, and contain essential oils in their skins. Citrus membranes contain bioflavonoids, needed by the body to absorb vitamin C.

Lemons and grapefruit are used medicinally for certain liver and gallbladder complaints.

Citrus fruits are tree ripened and thus ready to eat from the market. Select heavy fruits with thin skins. Rough skin indicates thick skin, and a light weight indicates an old, dehydrated fruit. Avoid citrus that has brown, bruised, or soft spots. Organic citrus does not have the uniform color of commercial citrus. Store citrus fruits in a cool pantry or in the refrigerator. Do not keep them in plastic bags.

See also **Citron, Grapefruit, Kumquat, Lemon, Lime, Orange, Tangelo, Tangerine,** and **Ugli Fruit**.

Clam   Bivalve shellfish that live in wet sand and are gathered at low tide, clams are sold alive in shells or canned or frozen. Live clam shells should be tightly closed. Any open ones that do not clamp shut when tapped sharply are stale or dead and should not be eaten.

Soft or longneck clams, which come from north of Cape Cod, are best for eating raw or steaming whole. Hard-shell clams are from south of Cape Cod and include butter clams and quahogs. Clams smaller than two inches are called littlenecks. Clams between two and three inches are cherrystones, and larger clams are called chowder clams and are used as such.

The Pacific has many more varieties of clams that are used commercially; the razor and pismo clams are two of the most popular. Clams are in peak season from October to April.

Clams are low in fat and calories and high in protein, iron, calcium, and B vitamins. As with other shellfish, clams are considered energizing to the kidneys and reproductive organs. See **Shellfish**.

★   ★   ★

Happy as a Clam at High Tide

The meaning of this phrase is apparent when one considers the clam harvest. Clams are gathered *only* when the tide is out.

★   ★   ★

Cob Nut   See **Filbert**

Coconut   The largest seed known to man is the coconut, which is native to Malaysia but now grows throughout tropical countries. The buoyant husk is easily waterborne, and coconuts have been carried on the Gulf Stream to places as unlikely as Norway.

The nut is the fruit of the coconut palm, which is an important staple to tropical people. All parts of the plant are used. The fronds are used for roofing material. The hairy outer fiber of the nut is used for matting. The nutmeat itself is eaten either dried or in its limp, wet, "green" stage. And, coconut milk is drunk as a beverage.

Coconut is high in fat (up to 60 percent) and, unlike most other plant foods,   + is primarily saturated fat. Because of its high fat content, it becomes rancid   ▷ quickly. Refrigerate an opened coconut and use within a few days.

To open a coconut, first pierce the "eyes" (three soft spots on the shell) with   ¤ a nut pick and drain the refreshing liquid. Next, place it on pavement and crack it open with a hammer; or place it in a 350-degree oven for 15 minutes, then tap it all over with a hammer and remove the shell as it cracks. The brown skin clinging to the white meat is edible and contains nutrients in addition to fiber.

Commercial shredded coconut may contain propylene glycol and sugar   ☆ added during processing. You may prepare your own by shredding pieces of shelled coconut in a blender or processor.

Coconut is a popular ingredient in curries, confections, and desserts or eaten out of hand. Its oil is easily extracted and is widely used in the tropics. Processed foods containing coconut oil are considered inferior nutritionally because the oil   ✗ is highly saturated.

Coconuts are in season October through December. Buy coconuts that are heavy, have no soft or moldy spots, and that sound full of liquid when shaken.   ▸ Check that the eyes are not wet or pierced. See **Dried Fruit, Nuts,** and **Oil**.

⋆   ⋆   ⋆

Coconut in Your Coffee

Coconut oil, the most common fat found in nondairy creamers, is better at raising blood cholesterol than is cream. Nondairy creamers generally contain sodium caseinate, a protein derived from, believe it or not, milk (so why is it called "nondairy"?).

⋆   ⋆   ⋆

Cocoyam   See **Yautia**.

Cod   Cod is one of the most commercially important ocean fish because of its versatility, cost, and year-round availability. It is a large fish with flaky white flesh and an unremarkable flavor. Although cod is found in the North Pacific, the North Atlantic cod is of principal commercial importance.

Scrod is a term for young cod under three pounds, whose flesh is firmer and sweeter than that of older cod, which attain weights up to eighty pounds. Scrod may also refer to young haddock. Cod is lean fish with as much protein as sirloin steak but half its fat. See **Cod-Liver Oil**.

For information on selection, storage, use, and medicinal and nutritional properties see **Fish**.

Cod-Liver Oil   A supplement long appreciated as the best source for vitamin   ☆ A, cod-liver oil has recently been receiving great attention as one of the richest (and most economical) sources of eicosapentenoic acid (EPA) and docosahexenoic acid (DHA). Research indicates that EPA/DHA are converted into gamma-linolenic acid.

Cod-liver oil is available in capsules and in liquid forms, both flavored and   ▸ unflavored. It is prone to rancidity so purchase in small quantities and refrigerate.   ▷

Coffee   The fruit of a semitropical evergreen, coffee is the most significant single food commodity in the Western Hemisphere. Eighty percent of Americans drink coffee at an annual rate of twenty-eight gallons per capita. Coffee has been called liquid amphetamine, the devil's brew, or simply "power" by the Arabs, who were first to use it some eight hundred years ago.

Coffee stimulates the entire nervous system, increases the pulse rate and blood pressure, raises the blood sugar level, suppresses the appetite, and gives a sense of high energy. A few hours after consumption, the blood sugar level drops, and frequently the coffee drinker can become jittery, irritable, unable to concentrate, and sometimes depressed. Coffee is an addictive drug, even though it is legal and socially acceptable.

Recent scientific studies indicate that as little as three to four cups of coffee a day may pose a threat to the fetuses of pregnant women.[12] Pregnant and lactating women are strongly advised against consuming coffee.

Few would call coffee a health food, yet there are some choices to make in terms of quality. Organic coffee is becoming more frequently available, and though it is costly, many consider it worth the extra price. Commercial coffee is chemically treated and frequently contains traces of pesticides banned in the United States because they are known carcinogens.

Coffee contains caffeine, trigonellin, aromatic oils, acids, and tannin. It also contains B vitamins and some essential minerals. However it is a vitamin and calcium antagonist, meaning that it depletes the body of B-complex vitamins, ascorbic acid, and calcium.

Ground coffee oxidizes quickly and suffers flavor loss in addition to becoming rancid. Buy ground coffee in vacuum cans, and refrigerate it after opening. Better yet, buy whole beans and grind them at home just prior to use.

★   ★   ★

Can't Function Without It

"The only word I can really use to describe coffee is poison. It weakens the kidneys, the intestines, and the entire nervous system. It clouds the memory, reduces sexual vitality, deprives one of deep and proper sleep, and causes irritability and anxiety. A poison, just a simple poison. Do I drink it? Oh yes, I drink it every day. I can't function without it."
—Anonymous student of Oriental medicine as reported to Ronald E. Kotzsch.[13]

★   ★   ★

Coffee, Decaffeinated   Coffee without the caffeine sounds like a healthful substitute, but it is usually of worse quality than regular coffee and is possibly a greater health risk. Solvents are used to remove the caffeine. The most commonly used solvent is methylene chloride, which the FDA has banned in hair sprays and cosmetics because it is a carcinogen.

A solvent considered to be safe is ethyl acetate, which occurs naturally in fruits. Some producers of decaffeinated coffee are using ethyl acetate, which is a slower-acting solvent. The Swiss water process for decaffeinating coffee is chemical free. In place of a solvent, it uses a charcoal or activated carbon filter.[14]

Coffee, Instant   Instant coffee is generally made from inferior, low-grade beans. However, it is lower in caffeine (80 mg. per cup) than freshly ground coffee (100 mg. per cup).

Coffee Substitutes   Several nutritious coffee substitutes are available that approximate the aroma and flavor of coffee but are free of tannin and caffeine. They are often grain based and may be flavored with various vegetables, fruits, sweeteners, or herbs. Check the labels of each to determine contents. Some coffee substitutes are instant; others require steeping or brewing.

Supermarkets generally carry at least one coffee substitute. Natural-food stores carry a selection.

Collard Greens   Possibly the grandaddy of the cabbage family, collards have changed little in four thousand years. This popular "soul food" figures prominently in Southern fare. Early nutritionists attributed the good health of many poor Southerners, who were eating an otherwise insufficient diet, to collard greens.

Collards are a beautiful deep green with large nonheading paddlelike leaves. They are more tender than kale and less pungent than mustard greens. Select collards that are fresh, crisp, and free from insect damage or discoloration. They are available twelve months of the year.

Wrap in damp toweling and refrigerate for up to five days. Collards are delicious steamed, lightly boiled, sautéed, or as a soup and casserole ingredient. They are considered too tough to be used raw in salads.

Collards are nearly twice as high in calcium as broccoli and are also high in vitamins A and C. They are considered medicinal for the liver and an excellent blood cleanser.

Corn   What is *Zea mays* to a botanist, and maize to most of the world, is corn in North America. Corn is the only commonly used native grain of the Western Hemisphere and is unlike other grains in several ways. One is its unique cob structure with multiple grains enclosed in the husk rather than each grain individually contained in a husk.

More than seven thousand years ago the Indians of Mexico began selectively breeding a wild grass called *teosinte*. These early "corn" ears ranged in size from one-half inch to two inches long. In the 1500s corn was introduced throughout the world, following the trade routes of the early Portuguese navigators. With few exceptions, it seemed to adapt to whatever climate it was introduced to.

Most *Zea mays* grown today are hybrid dent varieties (when dried the top of each kernel is indented). About 90 percent of the dent corn produced is fed to livestock. The rest is used for human consumption and in the manufacture and processing of a diverse number of products including paper, textiles, paints, explosives, and plastics. Virtually all commercial food products containing corn, from corn syrup to cornflakes, use dent corn.

The major corn varieties of North American agricultural Indians were flour corn and flint corn. Flint corn, as its name suggests, has very hard kernels whereas flour corn has a soft endosperm that makes it easier to grind and chew.

Indian corn is open pollinated; in other words, unlike hybrids, its seeds produce a crop that resembles the previous generation. Open-pollinated varieties are available through specialized seed companies concerned with saving heirloom seed. Open-pollinated corn has a wider genetic base, is higher in protein, minerals, and cobalt but yields less per acre. Hybridized corn is higher in carbohydrates. As interest in maintaining vital seed supplies increases, we will see greater availability of open-pollinated corn and corn products.

To form a complete protein, combine corn with legumes. Maize is the only grain that contains vitamin A. Yellow corn is higher in vitamin A than is white. Corn, relative to other cereal grains, is cooling, which makes it ideal hot-weather fare. It is good for strengthening the heart and for building strong blood.

See additional corn entries. See **Grain** for information on selection and storage and for cooking chart.

*   *   *

Nutrition from the Ashes

The Indians throughout the Americas added wood ash or lime to cornmeal. This made the precious niacin in the corn available for digestion. Although corn became popular elsewhere in the world the technique of adding wood ash or lime did not. Thus, in impoverished corn-eating populations outside of Latin America, pellagra, a niacin-deficiency disease, occurs frequently.

*   *   *

Corn, Blue   Also known as *Hopi Corn*. Blue corn is literally blue, sweeter, and more delicately flavored than is yellow. This open-pollinated flint corn has been grown continuously by the Indians of the Southwest for centuries. Blue corn products, such as atole, tortillas, chips, and pancake mix, are available in the Southwest and are becoming increasingly available throughout the United States.

Blue contains more complete protein and manganese than does yellow corn. Many people prefer blue (and other open-pollinated varieties) because its energizing properties are superior to those of hybridized corn.

Some people object to eating blue food. A squeeze of lime juice mixed into a blue-corn batter changes it to pink. The Indians, not averse to blue food, combined greasewood ash with their blue-corn meal to enhance its heavenly color.

* * *

The Sacred Colors of Corn

Pueblo Indians grow different colored corn for each of the sacred directions and for different ceremonial uses. These are not the ears of multicolored corn; rather, the kernels of each ear are one pure color. White corn represents the east, and every morning a pinch of white cornmeal is fed to Sun Father and to the family fetishes. Blue corn is for the north, red for the south, yellow for the west, and black for "above."[15]

* * *

Corn, Multicolored   Stunning ears of flint corn are available in the fall for decorative purposes. Their colors range from yellow, black, blue, and violet to red, pink, and white. No two ears are alike in the pattern of their colors. If you have access to a flour mill, buy some for meal. Grind and use this flint corn as you would use other cornmeal.

Corn, Popped   The original corn was "pod" popcorn, in which each seed was enclosed in its own husk. What a fascinating story it would be to determine how early man developed corn varieties with multiple kernels on each cob. Popped corn, carbon dated from 2300 B.C., has been found in New Mexico.[16]

Popcorn is a corn variety unto itself typified by a hard hull and endosperm that seals in moisture content. About 14 percent of the kernel is water. When popcorn is heated the trapped moisture becomes steam, which builds up until the kernel explodes.

Popcorn munching at the movies and at home remains an American pastime that has not significantly caught on elsewhere in the world. One cup of popped corn has 54 calories and two grams of protein. Its nutritional value can be greatly enhanced by sprinkling it with dried, powdered kelp and brewer's yeast.

Today popcorn is hybridized to expand up to forty times the kernel's original size and to have a high percentage of kernels that pop. Some manufacturers guarantee having less than 1 percent duds (unpopped kernels).

If popcorn is dehydrated, it will not pop. To correct this, place popcorn with a sprinkle of water in a sealed jar and allow it to stand for several days to regain its moisture content.

* * *

Popcorn and the Big Apple

Popcorn consumption in the United States is strongest in the Corn Belt region and weakest in New York City.

* * *

Corn, Posole   Parched and then dried white corn, or posole, is a traditional Mexican food that may be cooked whole like other grains. Unparched dried corn is virtually impossible to cook whole. Posole has a delicately sweet flavor and is delicious on its own, cooked with other grains, or ground into meal.

Corn, Sweet On or off the cob, sweet corn is as American as apple pie. Collected from the Iroquois beginning in 1779, sweet corn has been popular for only the past 100 years. This may be because flint corn is easier to grow and, once dried, provides a year-round staple. The characteristic that distinguishes sweet corn from other varieties is a single defective gene that prevents the sugars in the kernel from being completely transformed into starch.

For the sweetest and most delicious corn, fresh and slightly immature (rather than overmature) is best. New hybrid varieties have a more durable sweetness and reportedly hold their sweetness for up to seven days after picking.

Fresh corn has vibrant silk (rather than dry and matted), dark green, compact husks, and firm, full ears. Keep the husks intact until just before cooking.

Corn Flour Corn flour absorbs more water than other flours do and yields a drier, more crumbly product. Corn flour gives a sweet, corny flavor and a beautiful golden color to tempura batter, muffins, and cookies. Because corn has a high oil content, corn flour (or cornmeal) quickly becomes rancid. To avoid rancidity buy it in small quantities. Store corn flour in covered containers in a cool, dry place. See **Flour** for additional information.

Corn Flour, Degerminated Refine the germ and nutrients out of corn, and you'll have a limp, bland flour but one that has an indefinite shelf life. Degerminated corn flour is commonly enriched with artificial B-complex vitamins and iron.

Cornish Game Hen See **Fowl**.

Cornmeal Coarser than flour, meal is most often used in muffins, cornbread, or a cornmeal mush called polenta. See **Corn Flour** for storage tips.

Cornmeal, High-Lysine Agronomists have hybridized a nutritionally "improved" corn. High-lysine cornmeal has 70 percent more lysine than regular cornmeal. It has a better balance of the four limiting amino acids (lysine, tryptophan, methionine, and cystine) than soybeans, milk, or beef. This new cornmeal has a sweet and nutty flavor.

People who eat a wide variety of whole foods from the basic food groups obtain ample lysine. For them, mineral rich, open-pollinated corn is preferable to high-lysine varieties.

Corn Oil One of the most popular of oils, corn oil's domestic use dates back to the American Indians. Expeller-pressed corn oil has a rich corn flavor and heady aroma that some find too strong for delicate dishes. Others prefer it for its buttery taste. It is used in all types of cooking, especially baking, but is *not* suitable for deep-frying. (Highly refined corn oil may be used for deep-frying.)

Most corn oil is extracted from the corn germ, which is a by-product of such corn products as breakfast cereals, cornstarch, and corn syrup. Corn germ oil is yellow in color. Dark orange corn oil with a strong popcornlike aroma has been pressed from whole corn rather than just the germ. At this time domestic corn oil extracted from organically grown corn is not available.

Corn oil is 85 percent unsaturated and is exceptionally high in the essential linoleic acid (59 percent). It also contains a significant amount of vitamin E, which helps to retard oxidation. See **Oil**.

Corn Salad See **Mâche**.

Corn Syrup Chemically purified cornstarch is the basis for corn syrup. This highly refined commercial glucose (a molecule that is one of the components of sucrose) is frequently mixed with sugar to increase its sweetness. Commercial candies, baked goods, and prepared foods commonly contain corn syrup. Whenever possible avoid corn syrup consumption as it has a deleterious effect on the body's blood sugar metabolism. See **Sweeteners**.

Cos Lettuce   See **Romaine**.

✳ **Cottage Cheese**   Cottage cheese has a poor reputation because of the numerous chemical additives it contains. However, a few dairies produce "clean" cottage cheese; select these natural brands.

Almost 100 pounds of skim milk yield 15 pounds of cottage cheese. Creamed cottage cheese and baker's cheese are similar to cottage cheese. See **Dairy**.

Cotton Nuts   A cotton boll contains about fifty seeds. Each seed has a gland containing a substance that is toxic to humans. Thirty years ago, a glandless cotton plant was discovered growing on a Hopi Indian reservation. Genetic research determined that its "gland" chromosome was missing. Researchers at Texas A & M University have been working with this mutant since then to create a "new" food.

+ Edible cotton nuts are the highest source of vegetable protein (38 percent) and high in polyunsaturated fats (37 percent). Cotton nuts are 98 percent digestible.[17] (Some cases of allergic reactions to cotton nuts have been reported.)

✳ **Cottonseed Oil**   Cottonseed oil is not available on the retail level. Cotton, a nonfood crop, contains toxic residues from pesticides, which are heavily used in its cultivation. However, many salad oils, margarines, and other processed foods include cottonseed oil in their ingredients. Food producers who are concerned with quality do *not* use cottonseed oil. See **Oil**.

★   ★   ★

Don't "Jump Down, Turn Around, Pick a Bale of Cotton"!

Don't jump down in cotton fields! Nonfood crops, such as cotton, may be grown with more toxic pesticides than food crops. Cotton is one of the most chemically treated of nonfood crops. If a cotton field is not a healthy place for a bug, it is not a healthy place for you.

★   ★   ★

Couscous   To my palate, the most delectable refined grain product is featherlight couscous. Traditional to North Africa, couscous is the fluffiest and quickest cooking grain. It is easy to digest, delicately flavored, and a food that everyone enjoys.

Couscous is the endosperm particles of refined durum wheat. In North Africa, couscous may also be made of millet. A refined product, it is not considered a medicinal or an exceptionally nutritious food. However, when it is prepared in the traditional Moroccan way, with meat or chicken, couscous is delicious.

See **Grain** and **Wheat** for information on storage and use and for nutritional and medicinal highlights.

Cow Bean   See **Black-eyed Pea**.

Crab   Many varieties of crabs exist throughout the world, all are edible, but only a few have commercial value. Atlantic blue crabs comprise three-fourths of fresh crab sales; Dungeness crabs are a large, flavorful Pacific Coast variety. Large king crabs come from the northern Pacific. Stone crabs are from the Florida coasts.

The words *soft-shell crabs* refer to any crabs that have just molted their shells and whose new shells have not yet hardened. They are eaten whole and considered a great delicacy. Crab flesh is salty and flavorful. The claw meat is white, and the body meat is generally darker. Canned crabmeat, unless marked "white" or "deluxe," is a combination of claw and body meat.

Crabs are extremely high in vitamin A, protein, and calcium and are an excellent source of B vitamins and iron. They have less than 3 percent fat and less cholesterol than lobster or shrimp.

See **Shellfish** for information on selection, storage, and use and for nutritional and medicinal highlights.

Cranberry   Cranberries are one of the few wild fruits commercially available today. Most commercial cranberry production is in bogs in Massachusetts, Washington, Oregon, and Wisconsin. Growth hormones are frequently used on the berries, but they are generally not sprayed with insecticides.

These red, acid berries are at their peak in November and are primarily thought of, and used, as a sauce for the Thanksgiving turkey. However, they are delicious in relishes, cakes, jellies, and juice. Cranberry juice has long been recognized as medicinal for the kidneys and bladder. The Indians combined these tart berries with venison to make pemmican.

Look for cranberries that are bright red, plump, hard, and shiny. Avoid shriveled, soft, or brown fruits. They will keep up to two months refrigerated.

Cream   Cream is thicker than milk because it has more fat globules. All cream products are pasteurized or ultrapasteurized and may be homogenized. Government standards allow certain optional ingredients to be used—emulsifiers, stabilizers, nutritive sweeteners, and characterizing flavoring ingredients (with or without coloring).

Cream is high in saturated fats and should be enjoyed with discretion. Whipped tofu toppings, almond milk, and yogurt are more healthful cream substitutes. Nondairy creams are a manufactured "plastic" food, and their use cannot be justified from a health or a sensory point of view (see **Coconut**). See **Dairy**.

Half-and-half is a mixture of cream and milk. It ranges from 10.5 to 18 percent milk fat.

Light cream, also called coffee cream, contains between 18 and 30 percent milk fat.

Heavy or whipping cream has from 30 to 36 percent milk fat.

Crenshaw   See **Melon Family**.

Crookneck Squash   This thin-skinned, or summer, squash has a yellow bumpy skin and, generally, a crooked neck. Its optimum size is seven inches or under. Some varieties have a straight neck.

See **Squash, Summer** for information on selection, storage, and use and for nutritional and medicinal highlights.

Cucumber   Cultivated cucumber seeds carbon dated from 7750 B.C. have been found near the Burma-Thailand border.[18] The cucumber has been, and remains, a popular vegetable wherever it gets hot. It contains 95.6 percent water (more water than any other food except its relative, the melon) and thus is a cooling food.

Food writers vary in their classifications of cucumbers. The most sensible, to my thinking, is Evelyn Roehl, who observes that be they white, yellow, or green there are two varieties of cucumbers: greenhouse grown or field grown.[19]

Greenhouse-grown cucumbers are relatively new to the market—long, thin, and seedless. Alternative names are English or "burpless." They have a mild flavor.

Field-grown cucumbers may be round or elongated. They are further classified according to their maturity. When immature they are known as pickling cucumbers. When mature they are given the no-nonsense appellation *cucumber*.

A pickling cucumber is spiny and slightly warted. As it matures its skin smooths out, it becomes softer, with larger seeds, and it is less suited for pickling.

Most cucumbers are waxed to increase their shelf life. Discard the skin of any waxed fruit or vegetable. As waxed vegetables do not pickle, favor pickling cucumbers that are available toward summer's end.

⌘ Old field cucumbers are bitter. To eliminate bitterness, cut each end off. Dip the end in salt and rub it against the exposed cucumber until foam appears. Rinse off the foam.

◖ Select cucumbers that are firm, plump, and heavy for their size. Avoid those
◁ that have soft spots or that are withered at the stem end. Refrigerate uncovered for up to five days.

Cucumbers are not remarkable for their nutritive properties. They do, how-
+ ever, contain vitamin E (which may explain their effectiveness for burns and skin care) and—with their skins intact—have a fair amount of vitamin A. See **Gourd Family**.

*   *   *

Cool as a Cucumber

A cucumber is soothing to minor burns—simply rub a slice over the burn.

*   *   *

Curly Endive   The slender, curled leaves of the endive open so widely that it almost looks like a green chrysanthemum. Like escarole, endive is a member of
⌘ the chicory family. Both are bitter and best used in small proportions. A little endive in a salad gives it zing. To lessen its bitterness, it may be lightly sautéed.

◁ Look for crisp, almost prickly leaves. Refrigerate in a plastic bag and use
◆ within five days. Endive is at its peak in the spring and fall. It is said to be
+ medicinal for the heart, and it is high in vitamins A and C, calcium, and magnesium. See **Chicory**.

Currant   Whether black, white, yellow, orange, or red, currants have small commercial value but matchless flavor—they are not exceptionally sweet, juicy, or tart but decidedly enjoyable. This smooth, small berry, from one-quarter to one-half inch wide, is thin skinned and has a number of seeds.

The white currant is the sweetest; the black is the most tart and is favored for preserves. Wild currants grow abundantly throughout the United States and are comparable to the domesticated. It is a more favored fruit in Europe.

The currant is related to the gooseberry, but not to dried currants, which are
◖ raisins made of seedless Corinth grapes. Look for shiny skins and plump berries
◁ beginning in August. Refrigerate and use within three days.

See **Berries** for information on selection, storage, and use and for nutritional and medicinal highlights.

Currant, Dried   See **Dried Fruit**.

Custard Apple   See **Cherimoya**.

Dahlia   The bright, showy dahlia flower has an edible tuber that has been used for centuries as a potato in Central Mexico. In the late 1700s, dahlias were shipped to Spain as a new food, but only its blossom was valued. The flower is popular in backyard gardens and is the city flower of San Francisco. In the mid-eighties the dahlia was introduced to the American natural foods market, but not as a potato.

The dahlia tuber holds potential as a natural sweetener. The sweet elements of the roots are separated from the bitter fibers. The juice is then cooked at low temperatures, which results in 93 percent inulin, a complex carbohydrate based on the fructose chain. Inulin, found in smaller amounts in the Jerusalem artichoke, chicory, and dandelion, has promise for diabetics. Inulin has no calories. Dahlia is high in potassium; it contains 1,215 milligrams per 100 grams.[1]

Roasted dahlia extract is being marketed in tea products as a natural brown colorant and as a coffee substitute. It is also used as a chocolate substitute.

★　　★　　★

A Natural Sweetener for Diabetics

The human body does not have the enzymes to break down and absorb inulin as it does with other forms of sugar. Ingestion of inulin, as found in dahlia tubers, is said not to stress the pancreas or result in an increase in sugar in the urine.

Inulin is not to be confused with insulin. The levulose yielded by inulin is sometimes referred to as "diabetic sugar."[2]

★　　★　　★

Daikon   Daikon is the Japanese name for a long (up to a foot or more), white radish that is becoming increasingly available in American supermarkets. It is more pungent than its common cousin, the small red radish, and it has remarkable medicinal properties.

Cooked, the daikon may be used like carrots or turnips. Its greens, when young and tender, are good in soup. Look for crisp roots that are heavy for their size. When past prime, a daikon is dry and pithy.

Daikon is available year-round. Refrigerated, it holds well for up to ten days. It is a cabbage-family member.

★　　★　　★

Cancer Prevention?

Fresh raw daikon is known to contain diuretics, decongestants, digestive enzymes, and a substance that inhibits the formation of carcinogens in the body.[3] Grated raw daikon commonly accompanies Japanese and macrobiotic dishes as a digestant.

★　　★　　★

Daikon Condiment

1   tablespoon freshly grated raw daikon
½ teaspoon tamari (shoyu)
Dash mirin (optional)
Dash fresh ginger juice (or pinch ginger powder)

Blend all ingredients together. Serve in a small condiment dish. Makes 1 to 3 portions.

★　　★　　★

Daikon Pickle   Pickled daikon, or takuan, is fermented in earthen crocks with rice bran, salt, and sometimes koji. Commonly served at the end of a meal to aid digestion, this fermented vegetable is a favorite macrobiotic and Japanese food.

Koji, or sweet, takuan is especially high in lactobacilli (one ounce contains about 800,000 lactobacilli). A four-ounce serving contains nearly 50 percent of the daily requirement of niacin. It contains linoleic acid and is said to be effective in removing cholesterol from the blood.[4]

◁ Natural takuan (free from chemical preservatives, additives, or coloring) is available in quality food stores. Once the package is opened, place takuan in a closed glass jar and refrigerate.

Dairy The basis of all dairy products is milk. Cow's milk is used most often in the United States; however, milk of goats, sheep, buffalo, camels, mares, and yaks is consumed elsewhere in the world. And, of course, mother's milk is universal.

All humans are born with an enzyme that permits the digestion of milk sugar, or lactose. Many people stop producing this enzyme after the age of three or four and are termed lactose-intolerant.

Milk consumed by lactose-intolerant people leaves the stomach and small intestine still undigested and collects in the colon, where bacteria ferment it, thus producing gas and acid. This results in bloating, diarrhea, cramping, distension, and possibly gastrointestinal bleeding. Lactose-intolerant people who consume milk frequently have pasty white complexions with red blotches on their cheeks.

☆ Dairy foods in which the lactose is predigested by bacteria, such as yogurt, kefir, cheese, sour cream, butter, and buttermilk, are more readily digested by lactose-intolerant people. For some, consumption of acidophilus aids dairy digestion.

Besides the problem of lactose intolerance, other factors influence the quality of milk. Dairy cows' milk concentrates chemical residues from fertilizers, pesticides, environmental pollutants, and antibiotics. Dairy herds are routinely treated with the antibiotics aureomycin and penicillin. If treated cows are not properly segregated these drugs could pass intact, via the milk, into human consumers. And milk is pasteurized.

Pasteurization heats milk to 172 degrees for eighteen seconds. This process kills bacteria and increases shelf life, which enables the mass marketing of milk. However, it is not without a price. Calves given their own mothers' milk that had first been pasteurized perished within six weeks.[5]

Dairy products are the most common allergen. It is possible that the quality of the milk is a key factor, rather than milk itself. Pasteurization of milk causes the loss of 6 percent of calcium and renders the remaining calcium in a form that is difficult to assimilate; it also causes the loss of up to two-thirds of the B vitamins and 50 percent of vitamin C.[6]

☆ Certified raw milk is more nutritious than pasteurized milk. It tastes sweet and vital rather than metallic, waxy, and flat. Dairymen marketing raw milk are generally more conservative in their use of inorganic feed and antibiotics. Some states prohibit the sale of raw milk.

For alternatives that many find more healthful than pasteurized cow's milk see **Almond Milk, Goat's Milk, Soy Milk**, and **Tofu**. And there is always water.

Date Excavations in ancient Mesopotamia show that date palm cultivation was already established in 3000 B.C. Dates thrive in hot, dry areas like northern Africa, Iraq, Iran, and the Coachella Valley in California.

+ The chief nutritional value of dates is their high sugar content, which varies from 60 to 75 percent. They are a good source of nicotinic acid, iron, and potassium. Present in small amounts are calcium, chlorine, magnesium, and vitamins A, B_1 and B_2.

◆ Roasted date pits are used as a coffee substitute. Dates have medicinal properties for the stomach and spleen.

When buying fresh dates select plump, well-colored ones with glossy skins. Dull, shriveled dates are old. When purchasing dried dates, avoid broken ones or those with added corn syrup. See **Dried Fruit**.

Dates are primarily available in the following forms:

Fresh dates are often sold in a pressed mass. Typical varieties include Khadrawi and Barhi.

Semidry dates include the one variety that accounts for 85 percent of domestic production, the deglet noor (also bread date), which is juicy and sweet.

Dry dates are deglet noors that have been dried to yield a long shelf life.

* * *

A Date with Methyl Bromide

At the packing house, all domestic dates are fumigated to kill insect pests. The preferred insecticide is methyl bromide. As all imported dried fruits are fumigated, there are presently no commercially available, unfumigated dates.

* * *

Date Sugar Some quality food stores sell "date sugar," which is 100 percent pitted, dehydrated, pulverized dates. Cosmetically inferior dates are used to produce this sweetener, which is about 65 percent fructose and sucrose. Date sugar contains all the nutrients of dried dates. It tastes sugary and mildly date-flavored.

If consumed in excess, date sugar has the same undesirable effect on blood sugar metabolism as does white sugar. Used in moderation it is a quality sweetener. It is coarse and, unless sprinkled on top of foods, needs to be dissolved or thoroughly mixed with liquids in a blender. Store date sugar in a cool, dark place. See **Sweeteners**.

Dandelion Volunteer dandelions are a gardener's nemesis. Cultivated dandelions fetch a fair price in the market. The cultivated variety has a thicker leaf that is larger, more tender, and less bitter than the wild. Commercial dandelion greens are also lighter in color.

Dandelion is highly reputed in various folk medicines to be a blood cleanser and a rejuvenative plant. It contains more calcium than milk and has diuretic properties.

Select crisp greens and discard any yellowed or wilted leaves. Dandelion is available throughout the year, although it is best, and most abundant, in early spring. It is highly perishable.

Collect wild dandelion greens before the plant blossoms, and from an area that is environmentally clean. Favor the small leaves. For mild dandelions, pick those protected by shade or partially mulched over by leaves. Some people blanch wild dandelions in several boiling water baths to remove their bitterness, but this also lessens their nutritive value. Sauté dandelions with onion and garlic and season with a dash of tamari. Commercial dandelions may be added sparingly to salads.

Delicata Compared to other winter squash, the delicata has (as its name suggests) a more delicate flavor. Its flesh is moist and creamy when steamed and suggests the sweetness of sweet corn. Delicatas are not recommended for soups or baking.

This small squash is the size and shape of a large cucumber. A gourd family member it has a yellow and orange skin and its flesh is a pale yellow. The skin is edible. The delicata is a good source of vitamin A.

See **Squash, Winter** for information on selection, storage, and use and for nutritional and medicinal highlights.

Dill The lacy, delicate umbellifer dill is highly prized in Scandinavian, Russian, and Polish cooking but is used in the United States primarily in pickles, potato salad, and sauerkraut. Both its parsleylike leaf and seed are used; the flavor of the seed is likened to mild caraway.

◆ The name is a derivative of the old Norse word *dilla,* which means "to lull." Dill has a mild soporific effect, and in England a soothing dill water was given to babies. In the 1800s in United States dill seeds were given to children to chew in church to help keep them quiet. Dill seeds were so associated with Sunday meetings that they were called "meetin' seeds."

Fresh dill is available in August and September. Although cucumbers will pickle without dill, the thought of a dill-less pickle is almost sacrilege. See **Herbs and Spices**.

Dried Fruit See also **Date**, **Fig**, and **Raisin**. It is raisins—not grapes—that are essential to oatmeal cookies, and it is prunes—not plums—that are a morning regular for many. Drying food is one of the oldest ways of preserving harvest for lean months, and though this practice is not the necessity it once was, dried foods (especially fruits) are popular.

+ A dried fruit is one that has had enough moisture removed (from 75 to 95 percent) so that it is no longer subject to decay. To dehydrate a food, its moisture is extracted, either naturally or artificially, by air or heat or both. This changes the color and texture and reduces vitamins A and C. Drying concentrates the flavor, sweetness, and some of the nutrients.

☆ Some fruit is still sun-dried, which is certainly the most natural and economical method. However, more nutrients are lost to sun-drying because of greater exposure time. Ovens are used for mechanical drying; this process is faster than sun-drying so more vitamins are retained. A third and superior method, solar drying, has been recently introduced on a commercial level. Solar drying intensifies the sun's heat and is a natural and speedy process. Solar-dried fruit is becoming increasingly available. For maximum flavor, nutrients, and good texture, look for solar-dried fruits.

✣ Sulfured fruits are dipped in a sulfur solution to prevent them from oxidizing and turning dark. Thus a dark raisin is unsulfured, whereas a golden raisin is sulfured. Sulfur compounds destroy all the B vitamins and can cause allergic reactions, sometimes extremely severe, in sensitive individuals. Asthmatics are especially at risk. There is concern that sulfured foods are possible mutagens.[7] The largest volume of dried fruits are sulfured for cosmetic purposes.

✣ Potassium sorbate is often added to prunes and figs to keep them moist and chewy. If a dried fruit has a high moisture content, assume that it has a preservative, otherwise it would be moldy. Fruits for the natural food trade may be dried to a lower moisture content and *not* treated with potassium sorbate.

✣ Coconut frequently contains propylene glycol to retain moisture. Some fruits, especially coconut, papaya, and pineapple, have added corn syrup or sugar.

☆ Since all imported dried fruits must be fumigated with toxic pesticides, domestic dried fruit is preferred over imported. Organic domestic dried fruit is your best choice because it is additive free and lacks the chemical residues found in commercial fruit.

◁ To extend the shelf life of dried fruit, store it in a glass jar in a cool, dry, dark place. For short-term storage a closed plastic bag is acceptable. All dried foods deteriorate to some extent during storage and lose vitamins, flavor, color, and aroma. For this reason they will not retain their appeal indefinitely. Enjoy dried fruits as a good candy alternative, or soak and cook as for a stewed fruit.

The most commonly available dried fruits include apples, apricots, bananas, coconut, currants, dates, figs, mangoes, papayas, peaches, pears, pineapples, prunes, and raisins. The United States is the largest producer of raisins and prunes. Unlike other dried fruits, bananas, papayas and honey-dipped pineapple are not recommended products.

★ ★ ★

Six to One

Dried fruits are a highly concentrated food. When you eat one pound of dried apricots you are eating (the equivalent of) six pounds of fresh apricots.

★ ★ ★

Banana chips are made from bananas that are picked green, before the starch base turns to sugars and deep-fried as for potato chips. Unsweetened chips are a dull product with an oily texture (from the frying) and no banana flavor. Few people would purchase them twice. A product that sells better is sugar-sweetened banana chips.

★ ★ ★

Delicious Dried Bananas

Peel and slice ripened bananas (preferably organic) into quarters and then into eighths. Place in a solar or electric food dryer and proceed per dryer instructions.

Or, for oven drying, arrange sliced fruit in one layer on a cookie sheet. Preheat oven to 140 degrees. Place fruit on the uppermost rack in the oven. According to home preserving expert Ruth Hertzberg, fruit is dry when it is leathery, tough, and pliable and when no wetness can be squeezed from a cut piece.[8]

★ ★ ★

Taiwan is the major producer of the so-called honey-dipped pineapple, which is actually prepared with sugar rather than honey. The slices are not dipped at all, but rather repeatedly immersed in a sugar water solution until the pineapple is saturated to 80 percent sugar. Unsweetened or naturally dried pineapple employs pineapple juice rather than sugar water in the drying process.

Papaya, if it has any flavor at all, has been sugar sweetened. *Honey-sweetened papaya* is as dishonest a term as is *honey-dipped pineapple*.

Duck See **Fowl**.

Dulse Also known as *Dillisk*. Dulse grows from the temperate to the frigid zones of the Atlantic and Pacific. It remains a popular food to eat out of hand in many areas of the world. The Primorskaya Russians ferment dulse into an alcoholic beverage; in Alaska it is used as an inexpensive chewing tobacco; elsewhere it is frequently served with fish or potatoes or sautéed in oil as a side dish.

Dulse is often an immediate favorite of those first tasting seaweed, a claim that may *not* be made for other sea vegetables. American cooks most typically include dulse in soup or salad, where it lends a beautiful rust-purple color, a pleasing texture, and an excellent flavor. Dulse also is featured as a bacon substitute in the DLT sandwich (dulse, lettuce, and tomato).

The organic content of dulse is composed of about 25 percent protein, 45 percent carbohydrate, 4 percent fat, and 26 percent trace elements and mineral salts. Of all foods, dulse is the absolute best source of iron. It is also rich in phosphorus, potassium, magnesium, protein, and vitamin A. Dulse is a good source of vitamins E, C, and B complex (including B_{12}) and numerous trace elements.[9]

Medicinally, dulse is used to strengthen the blood, adrenals, kidneys, and muscles. It is useful in the prevention of scurvy and in the treatment of herpes.

Dulse may be eaten as is, hydrated and used in soups and sandwiches, or cooked. Unlike most seaweeds, dulse as well as nori do not require cooking.

See **Sea Vegetables** for information on selection, storage, and use and for medicinal and nutritional highlights.

★   ★   ★

Salty Snacks

A food that tastes similar to salted nuts and bacon is a likely snack food for barroom counters because salty snacks increase beer sales. Indeed, the seaweed dulse was frequently served in New England taverns through the 1920s. Recently, however, no sightings have been reported.

★   ★   ★

Durum See **Wheat** and **Pasta**.

Echinacea Probably the most effective and best researched herbal antibiotic that supports the natural immune system is echinacea (ek-ken-NAY-she-ah). It is ironic that echinacea is native only to North America and that domestically its use has been rare since the advent of antibiotics. Until the 1930s its use was widespread.

In Germany echinacea is currently listed in over forty pharmaceutical preparations registered for use by physicians. These preparations are employed to stimulate the body's own immune defense system, for hard-to-heal wounds, infections, inflammations, and herpes.

According to herbal expert Steven Foster, USDA researchers have found that a component in the essential oil of the angustifolia variety of echinacea may be useful in certain forms of cancer.[1]

Echinacea is available dried, in tinctures, and in extracts.

Egg The egg is an uncommonly nutritious food. It is a balanced source of all the important vitamins and minerals except vitamin C, and it is an excellent source of protein. Nutritionally its major drawback is that it is high in cholesterol (the only foods higher in cholesterol are organ meats).

Controversy abounds regarding eggs and cholesterol. Current research indicates that egg consumption may lower blood cholesterol levels because eggs contain lecithin, which has an emulsifying effect on fats. Still, the U.S. Dietary Goals for Americans as well as the American Heart Association Dietary Recommendations suggest eating less than 300 milligrams of cholesterol per day. A single egg yolk contains 250 milligrams.

Consider the many egg-enriched foods (like some pastas, pastries, ice cream, bread, cookies, and mayonnaise). Even if you don't have scrambled eggs for breakfast, it is easy to consume more than the recommended one per day.

Nutrition aside, there are two factors worth considering regarding egg consumption—quality and energy. According to Michio Kushi, the foremost living author and teacher of macrobiotics, the egg is an even more contractive food than red meat, for one small shell potentially holds a whole bird. Kushi attributes many degenerative illnesses to overconsumption of this potent food, including prostate cancer and heart disease.[2]

In terms of quality there is much to say about eggs. A commercial, or battery, hen's environment is highly mechanized. She is confined in a one-half square-foot cage and is debeaked so that she won't cannibalize her neighbors. Artificial lights are controlled with timed light flashes to stimulate her ovulation cycle. Her feed is mixed with chemical antibiotics, dyes, hormones, and tranquilizers as well as her own recycled waste.[3]

A free-range chicken, unlike the chicken described above, is one who has freedom of movement. Organic eggs from free-range chickens do not have toxic chemical residues, and nutritionally they contain three to four times the vitamin A of commercial eggs.[4]

Organic eggs cost more. If fertile, the yolk contains a tiny light-brown speck enclosed in a membrane. Unlike sterile eggs, fertile eggs contain beneficial growth and reproductive hormones. Brown eggs are nutritionally equivalent to white but are more costly because chickens that lay brown eggs are larger and require more feed.

Whatever type of eggs you purchase, freshness is important in terms of taste and nutrition. Fresh eggshells are never shiny, and eggs that are cracked should be discarded. U.S. Grade AA (or Fancy Fresh Quality) denotes the freshest and best-quality commercial eggs.

Try to use eggs within one week of purchase. The egg holders inside many refrigerator doors may be convenient, but eggshells are porous and easily allow absorption of odors and flavors. Eggs held in a covered container stay fresh longer.

E

★　★　★

Stressed Foods

When a food is highly commercialized, like battery eggs, is its energizing quality adversely affected? Dr. Saul Miller, dietary therapist for U.S. Olympic athletes, has studied the subtle effects of foods. Dr. Miller remarks, "Psychologically, people regularly eating chemically treated, artificial, and 'stressed' foods may experience alienation, a lack of harmony with the natural order, and the dissatisfaction and unhappiness that [this practice] engenders."[5]

★　★　★

Eggplant　Eggplants, which are actually a berry, are enjoying increasing popularity. Their fleshy texture makes them a favorite in numerous vegetarian dishes, and the new varieties afford increased culinary applications.

The most common eggplant in the United States is large and purple with a shiny, patent-leather-like skin. There is also a slender, elongated purple variety that is generally sweeter than the larger one. Yet another variety is small, white, and looks like an egg. The whites are firmer, creamier, and less bitter than the purple varieties.

Eggplant is available year round but is at its peak in the summer. Purchase only those that are firm and unblemished. Discoloration or dents indicate a bitter fruit. Avoid spongy-to-the-touch or large eggplants.

This highly perishable fruit should be purchased no more than two days before use. Store in a cool, not cold or hot, area. Summer and fall eggplants are grown commercially in the United States. Most of those available in the winter and spring are from Mexico.

A low-calorie food, eggplant is an excellent source of folic acid. See also **Nightshades**.

★　★　★

Grandma Knows Best

The eggplant is extremely acidic and therefore hard to digest. Old cookbooks advise salting prior to use. This step draws out some of the acidity and renders a more digestible dish. Most contemporary recipes do not call for this step. Experiment both ways—salting and not salting—and let your own stomach be the judge.

Slice eggplant and sprinkle generously with salt. Allow to rest on absorbent paper for 30 minutes (the paper will become damp). Rinse off salt and cook per recipe.

★　★　★

Elephant Garlic　Each clove of this jumbo garlic is about as large as 10 regular garlic cloves. Elephant garlic may be substituted for regular garlic when you want a more delicate garlic flavor, or it may be served as a vegetable. Elephant garlic has about thirty calories per clove. See also **Garlic**.

Endive　See **Belgian Endive**, **Chicory**, and **Curly Endive**.

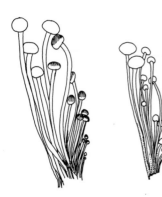

Enoki　Also known as *Snow Puff*. The fanciful, creamy white enoki mushroom has a long slender stem, topped with a diminutive round cap. In size and color it is comparable to a raw bean sprout; in gestalt it evokes fairylike images. Unlike other mushrooms, the enoki is not earthy but fruity.

Enoki come packaged with their root section intact. Purchase those that are firm and white. Refrigerate in the package for up to four days. Prior to use, cut off and discard the bottom root cluster. Rinse, and add enoki raw to salads or steam for 30 seconds for use in a side dish. When cooked for 1 minute in a clear soup broth, enoki lend exquisite eye appeal.

For nutritional and medicinal highlights see **Mushroom Family**.

Escarole   Like endive, escarole is a member of the chicory family and is fairly bitter. Its green leaves are broader and less curly than those of endive. Escarole is the sturdier of the two and is therefore more commonly available.

The inner, more yellow escarole leaves are favored for salads. Both inner and outer leaves may be used as a potherb. Select vibrant heads with no sign of dehydration, and refrigerate in a plastic bag for up to a week. Use sparingly in salads or braise and serve as a hot vegetable.

Escarole is an excellent source of chlorophyll, vitamins A and C, iron, and calcium. As a kitchen remedy it energizes the liver and heart. See also **Chicory**.

Evening Primrose Oil   The delicate primrose unfurls its petals at dusk and is as elusively magical as sunset itself. It is worth seeking out. Look for this yellow blossom in dry soil and along roadsides in the eastern and central states. In the western states, the evening primrose blossoms a rare white-green and is found in dry desert regions or on sage-covered slopes. It blossoms from June to September.

From primrose seeds is extracted an oil that contains gamma-linolenic acid (GLA) and that is used in the successful treatment of a wide range of medical problems including arthritis, premenstrual syndrome, obesity, cardiovascular ailments, hyperactivity, diabetes, skin disease, and allergies.

Supplementation with evening primrose oil or other GLA-containing substances may be appropriate for some. It would be prudent for all to avoid those substances that create biochemical obstacles to the body's own formation of GLA. They include a diet heavy in saturated fats and cholesterol, processed vegetable oil, and alcohol. See **Oil**.

F

Fat Fat is an all-inclusive term for a class of energy-rich food components commonly known as fats and oils. Fat occurs in many plant and animal food products. Typical solid fats are butter, lard, the fat of meat, and the hidden fat in dairy products. Oils are fluid fats, such as salad and cooking oils obtained from the vegetable realm, and the hidden fat in nuts and fish. A nutritionally complete diet must contain fat.

Fat is "visible" in foods like butter, lard, margarine, and vegetable oil. Fat is "invisible" in dairy products, eggs, nuts, chocolate, and—in minute quantities—in fruits, grains, and vegetables. The USDA estimates that roughly 40 percent of the fat in the American diet is visible and about 60 percent is invisible.

Polyunsaturated fatty acids, sometimes called vitamin F, are called essential fatty acids because the body cannot produce them and because they are essential for health. The three essential fatty acids are linoleic, linolenic, and arachidonic. They help maintain healthy blood and circulation and the nervous system. Fatty acids also transport the fat-soluble vitamins, promote normal growth and healthy skin, and contribute to the fatty tissue that surrounds, protects, and holds the organs in place. Essential fatty acids are found in grains, beans, seeds, and to a lesser extent in some animal foods, especially fish. See **Oil**.

Fava Bean Also known as *Broad Bean* and *Horse Bean*. As its alternate names suggest, the fava is substantial in size. It also has a substantial, Old World, hearty quality. The fava is indeed one of the most ancient cultivated vegetables and has been found with Iron Age relics in various parts of Europe. It has remained a favorite throughout the major continents with the exception of North America, where the fava is just now becoming available. It has a pleasing albeit slightly bitter flavor.

Immature pods, up to three inches long, may be cooked whole. The mature fava is more available commercially. Its pods must be shucked to get at the large green seeds. Substitute fresh favas for fresh limas in any recipe. It is advised to double-shell them (the first shell is the pod, the second is the individual skin of each bean). These bitter, tough skins are time-consuming to remove, which probably explains why this bean has had limited popularity. To remove the fava skin, slit it open with your thumbnail or a knife, and peel it off.

Dried fava beans are available regionally. In South America fava flour is available. Soak the beans overnight, remove their leatherlike outer skin, and then prepare as you would lima beans. See **Beans**.

Feijoa Also known as *Pineapple Guava*. This fragrant tropical fruit has a tart, tutti-frutti flavor. Although sometimes called the pineapple guava, the feijoa (fay-JO-a) is not a true guava. It has a slightly bumpy, thin skin, and the color ranges from lime green to olive. Feijoa flesh is tan, soft, but gritty like a pear and filled with tiny seeds. The New Zealand crop of feijoas is available in the spring and early summer. Domestic fruits are available in the fall.

Select a feijoa with a full aroma. Ripen at room temperature until it is soft, then refrigerate and use within a day or two. Immature feijoas are bitter. When mature, their distinctive flavor may dominate more subtly flavored dishes. Use in salads or in any preparation calling for apples.

Feijoas are high in vitamin C and are a cooling, expansive food.

Fennel Also known as *Finocchio* or *Anise*. Fennel, the vegetable variety of the herb, is as common a vegetable in Italian markets as celery is in ours. The enlarged leafstalks form a kind of false bulb, often as big as a fist, which may be cooked or eaten raw in salads. The feathery leaves are used as a garnish and a flavoring agent. When raw, its mild, sweet flavor resembles celery and licorice. Cooked, its flavor becomes more delicate.

Peak season for fennel is fall through spring. Select unblemished fennel that looks crisp, with fresh, green leaves. If the leaves have been cut off, it is probably

because they were old, and this indicates a past-prime vegetable. The bulb should be medium-size, well developed, firm and white. Refrigerate and use within three to five days of purchase. Enjoy it raw or cooked in any dish calling for celery.

Fennel is said to help in weight reduction. This Italian favorite is a good source of vitamin A and is very low in calories. See **Carrot Family** and **Herbs and Spices**.

⯈
¤
◆
+

* * *

The First Marathon Was About a Fight in the Fennel

In 490 B.C. the Greeks defeated the Persians in a battle that was fought in a fennel field. A runner raced 26 miles and 385 yards to carry news of the victory to Athens. The Greek word for fennel happens to be *marathon.*

* * *

Fermented Food   Olives, tea, dill pickles, beer, miso, sauerkraut, yogurt, and most cheeses are just a few fermented foods that may enhance our diet. Every culture ferments foods. Scientists now believe that the first cultivated plants were not grains and vegetables, but rather the microscopic organisms that cause food to ferment. Ancient man surely fermented food to enhance its storage time. He probably appreciated the increased digestibility and variety of fermented foods as well as their new textures and tastes.[1]

Fermentation, simply speaking, is the predigestion of foods before consumption. Molds, yeast, and bacteria break down the complex components of the original ingredients and synergistically create a superior food. This new, living food is more digestible (in some cases it requires no digestion). It contains vitamin B_{12} and is nutritionally superior in its new form. Furthermore, some naturally fermented foods enhance our ability to digest other foods and to eliminate wastes. A cultured product has the same caloric value as its original ingredients.

Lactic acid bacteria are among the principal bacteria active in food fermentation. They produce lactic acid, which contributes to the sour flavor and aroma of fermented foods and inhibits the growth of unfavorable organisms.

Lactic acid bacteria in fermented foods help the body produce natural antibiotics, natural anticarcinogenic compounds, natural anticholesteremic compounds, and even compounds that retard or deactivate toxins and poisons. Lactobacilli completely eliminate an antinutritional factor in soybeans. Undesirable phytates found in grains, beans, and seeds are totally eliminated when fermented.[2]

In utero, a baby has a sterile digestive tract. Within two days of birth, cultures of microorganisms from the mother's milk have established themselves in the infant's intestines. As many as four hundred different species of bacteria live in the adult colon! Consumption of certain fermented foods helps build and maintain our population of intestinal flora.

The foods with the best potential for building intestinal flora include miso; natural, unpasteurized vegetable pickles; and lactobacillus acidophilus. Recent research indicates that the bacteria in most yogurts are not able to colonize in the gut.[3]

Foods and substances that decimate intestinal flora include broad-spectrum antibiotics, antiseptic mouthwashes, alcoholic beverages, and some medications. Colonics, a mechanical high enema, eliminate old fecal matter as well as intestinal flora; for this reason colonics may not be desirable.

When some people start eating whole grains they find that their digestion gets worse rather than better. They forgot the pickle! A daily serving of an unpasteurized, fermented food helps whole grains be digested.

Unfortunately the fermented foods most often found in markets and restaurants are *not* "healthful" for two reasons. First, they are dead foods. The microorganisms they once contained have been killed with heat or additives to create a consistent product with increased shelf life. Second, they often contain preservatives, additives, and excessive amounts of salt. See also **Acidophilus**.

* * *

Eskimo Fermented Delicacy

A great delicacy for the some Eskimos is mattak. Huge flakes of narwhal are cached for several years. In the low temperatures they do not become rancid; rather they ferment until the skin tastes much like walnuts while the blubber turns green and tastes sharp—almost like Roquefort cheese.

* * *

You Are What You Assimilate

What you eat and what you assimilate may be two different stories. Good assimilation requires a vital crew of intestinal flora. The average healthy adult intestine is populated by three and one-half pounds of enzymes, bacteria, and fungi![4]

* * *

Fiddlehead Fern The delicate green shoots of the ostrich fern look like a violin's scroll and taste like asparagus with woodsy tones. They are found in forest land throughout the country. If they grow in your area, forage them. When fresh, their fragile flavor provides a remarkable delicacy. The fiddlehead season is from May to July, and their commercial availability is limited to specialty markets.

Look for small, vital, jade-green young shoots, tightly furled; open shoots are poisonous. Avoid any that are wilted, rotted, or more than two inches in diameter. They lose flavor rapidly, so use within a day. Fiddlehead's flavor is enhanced with light sautéeing or steaming. Season or sauce as you would asparagus.

Fig Plucked from the tree at its peak, a perfect fig can inspire poetry. Botanically, figs are fascinating. Their multiple fruits blossom and mature inside the skin. The tiny "seeds" in the fig's interior are actually hundreds of tiny fruits! Only the female fruits are edible.

The fig is one of the most ancient fruits enjoyed by people and is frequently mentioned in the Bible. A species of fig, the bo, is the tree under which Gautama sat and Buddhism was born.

Figs are enjoyed fresh, dried, or canned. Of the common fruits, they have the highest sugar content. Dried, a fig is about 50 percent sugar. It has a notable amount of protein and abundant calcium, magnesium, phosphorus, and potassium.

Figs are alkaline forming and aid digestion. They have mild laxative properties. In England "Syrup of Figs" is a well known medicinal preparation for constipation that is included in the British Pharmaceutical Codex.

Because figs are so fragile, they are infrequently available fresh, except in California and a few southern states where they are grown. Most figs are grown in the orchard country surrounding Fresno, California, the "Fig Capital of the World."

Select plump, soft figs with intact skins and a fresh aroma. Figs that are starting to dry are acceptable. The new crop is available in late August to early September. Dried figs should smell sweet and be slightly moist. Avoid those preserved with potassium sorbate. See **Dried Fruit.**

The following three types of figs are most commonly grown in the United States. They each represent about 30 percent of the market share.

Adriatic figs are white—actually tan skinned—and good fresh or dried.

Calimyrna figs are similar to the Adriatic, only larger and sweeter. California fig production started with the Turkish smyrna. Combine these two names (California and smyrna) for "Calimyrna."

Mission figs are a dark purple to black sweet fig used fresh or dried. They received their name because they were introduced to California by Spanish missionaries.

* * *

Figs Eat Wasps

Pollination of the interior flowers of the calimyrna fig occurs only with the assistance of a tiny gnat-size fig wasp *(Blastophaga psenes)*. The female wasp hatches from inside an inedible male fig, called a caprifig. As she crawls out the caprifig eye (the small hole at the blossom end) she must pass over numerous, pollen-laden male flowers.[5] The wasp emerges and flies off to search for another caprifig in which to lay her eggs.

The fig wasp apparently cannot distinguish a caprifig from a calimyrna (female fig). She typically ends up inside a calimyrna, where she futilely attempts to lay her eggs but her ovipositor is too short for her to succeed. Up to her death she continually attempts to deposit eggs at the numerous flower styles. The fig becomes pollinated. As the fruit ripens, its enzymes assimilate the dead wasp.[6]

* * *

Filbert   Also known as *Hazelnut* or *Cob Nut*. Filberts and hazelnuts are so closely related that their names are used interchangeably. Both are birch-family members. The hazelnut grows wild on shrubs, and the filbert is cultivated on small trees. They are the sweetest of the nuts and have a mild but distinctive flavor.

Many ancient myths surround this popular native European nut. The Celts characterize the hazel as the tree of knowledge, and in France and Germany young girls danced under the hazelnut tree to attract suitors.

Of the various nuts, filberts are second only to almonds as a good calcium source. They have a pleasant, somewhat toasty flavor and are delicious in stuffings, candies, and cookies.

Filberts grow wild all across the United States and are grown commercially in Oregon and Washington. However, most of our domestic supply comes from England, Turkey, and Spain.

For information on selection, storage, and use and for medicinal and nutritional highlights see **Nuts.**

Finocchio   See **Fennel.**

Fish   A multitude of fish abound in lakes, rivers, and the seven seas. These cold-blooded creatures have always been an important part of our diet, and as problems of world population and hunger are more widely recognized, fish may come to play an increasingly important role in our diets.

In terms of nutrition, fish is excellent. It is easily digested, low in calories and fat, and most of the fat is unsaturated. Fish is high in protein, and many varieties have as much protein as lean meat with only half the calories. Fish is also an excellent source of vitamins and minerals; it contains almost no carbohydrates.

In terms of energy, fish is a warming and contractive food because it is high in protein. However, it is less warming than meat. The expression "in cold blood" describes a state of emotional detachment. Folk wisdom claims that excessive consumption of cold-blooded fish makes one emotionally cold.

Fresh fish smells fresh, has bulging eyes, firm flesh, reddish gills, and glistening scales that adhere firmly to the fish. The flesh of a whole fish, a fillet, or a steak should spring back when pressed lightly with your finger. Fish is at its peak when newly caught and it deteriorates rapidly. Try to purchase fish the day that you will use it.

Most fishing boats go to sea for seven to fourteen days. If the weather holds and the fishing is good, they will not return until they have a boat full of fish. The catch is stored on ice in large pens. Before the fish is unloaded at the dock, it may be two weeks old.[7]

A reputable fishmonger buys the freshest catch from ships that have been out on short, rather than long, trips. With the recent increase of air freighting, it is possible for an inland retailer to receive fish that is less than two days old. It is also possible for him to have fish so old that you would not want to eat it. Shop from the most reputable fish merchant in your area.

☆ Most ocean fish is treated with a preservative on the boat. A few suppliers, upon request, will not add preservatives to whole fish. At the plant, fish is sprayed with chlorinated water to eliminate any surface bacteria. Fish that comes to the market already cut into fillets or steaks most likely is preserved.

For the best flavor and texture, fresh fish is a first choice. It is also gaining an increasing share of the market. Select canned fish that is additive free and packed in water rather than oil. Frozen fish should be solidly frozen with its wrapping intact.

♮ Cooking fish is easy. Start with fresh or thawed fish. If it has been treated with a preservative, soak it for a few minutes in lightly salted water to counteract the preservative. Allow ten minutes cooking time for each inch of thickness; this applies to baked, steamed, poached, and broiled fish. Quality fish is most often enhanced by simple cooking rather than complicated recipes.

There are more than twenty thousand species of fish, and almost all of them are edible. Relatively few appear regularly in our markets. Many other cultures consume a large variety of fish: A Tokyo fishmonger offers more than sixty varieties daily. The fish most commonly available in the domestic market are listed individually. See **Flounder, Halibut, Salmon,** and so on.

Fish, Freshwater and **Shellfish** have specific considerations and are listed as specific categories.

★   ★   ★

Your Nose Knows

Freshness is a must with fish. Smart shoppers ask to smell fish before making a purchase. If it has a fishy odor, especially around the gills or the belly, do not buy it. Old fish smells fishy.

★   ★   ★

Fish, Freshwater   Two of the biggest dietary sources of pesticide residues are ⚡ fish from inland waters and fatty meats. Freshwater fish are particularly laden with pesticide in the late summer because, as water levels drop, pesticide concentration from agricultural runoff increases.

The FDA has restricted fishing in highly polluted waters, but it is still difficult to know precisely how contaminated any fish might be. Saltwater fish is signifi-☆ cantly less polluted than freshwater fish.

Flax Seed   See **Seeds**.

Flounder   Flounder, and related flatfish such as halibut, sole, and sand dab, are similar in that both eyes appear on the same side of the fish. Available year round ◆ from the U.S. Atlantic and Pacific coasts, flounder is best from February to September. It rarely exceeds two pounds in weight or a foot in length.

Most of the fish sold as sole, whether as gray sole or lemon sole, is actually flounder. True sole is from the North Sea, including the English Channel, and is called Dover sole. It has limited availability in the United States.

+ Flounder, sole, and sand dab are low in fat and are good sources of protein and significant amounts of vitamins and minerals. Like other vertebrate fish, they contain no carbohydrates. See **Fish**.

Flour   For the fun of it, as well as for flavor and nutritional variations, there is a whole realm of different flours to play with. Each flour excels in its own way and can transform what might otherwise be a mundane dish into a culinary master-piece.

All the cereal grains as well as amaranth, arrowroot, chestnuts, chickpeas, fava beans, quinoa, and soy are ground into flour or meal. (See individual listings for the properties unique to each.)

The type of mill that grinds the grain has a surprising effect on a flour's performance, flavor, and nutrition. You can easily verify this for yourself by purchasing different flours and testing them in the same recipe.

The best flour comes from stone-ground mills where layers are flaked off the grains. This milling process does not overheat the flour and so nutrients are retained, rather than lost. A number of stone flour mills, either manual or electric, are available for home use. Some are made of a synthetic stone, and others are made of natural stone. For optimum nutrition, flavor, and performance, a stone flour mill is an excellent investment.

The majority of commercial mills are hammer mills or blade mills. Hammer mills smash grains into bits. Blade mills are like a gigantic blender that chops grains into particles. Unless a commercial flour indicates that it is stone ground, you may assume that the flour was milled by the more economical hammer or blade method.

Any whole-grain flour has a limited shelf life. It is ideal to grind your own flour twelve hours prior to use in a hand or an electric mill. Flour used sooner is "green" and performs poorly.

When buying whole-grain flour, purchase it from the retailer in your area who has the quickest turnover and who refrigerates his flour. You will then be most apt to have fresh flour. Once home, store your flour in a covered container in a cool, dark place or refrigerate it.

"Freshen" flour that is a little old or bitter (oat and corn flours tend to be bitter) by lightly dry-toasting or sautéing in a skillet. Stir continuously while it is on the fire, and remove just when the flour emits a pleasant aroma.

Once a grain is ground into meal or flour, it starts to oxidize and become rancid. Light and heat speed the process. Rancid foods are toxic to the liver and are considered carcinogens. If whole-grain flour is over three months old, discard it.

In terms of energy there is a significant difference between eating grain and eating flour. Plant a grain and it grows. Plant flour and it decomposes. Each individual grain is an integral, balanced food. When a grain has been broken down into minute flecks of flour, it has lost its vitality. Make these flecks into a dough, bake it, and each speck gets baked solidly into place. Your digestive enzymes have a hard time getting at these "cemented" flecks. A whole grain that has been broken down by your molars and mixed with digestive enzymes is easier to assimilate.

Healing diets recommend limited use of flour products as they tend to be more mucus forming and difficult to digest than whole grains. Soft flour products, such as noodles, dumplings and hot breakfast cereals, are easier to digest than are baked flour products.

★   ★   ★

Barley Pancakes

The superbly earthy flavor of barley lends itself to pancakes. Top with butter and a natural fruit preserve or pure maple syrup.

1½ cups barley flour (whole wheat pastry flour may be substituted)
¼   teaspoon sea salt
3   tablespoons dried barley malt or rice syrup
1¾ teaspoon baking powder
1 or 2 eggs
3   tablespoons unrefined sesame or olive oil
1 to 1¼ cup water

Sift the dry ingredients together. If using two eggs, separate them. Add the yolks to the water and oil, and mix and blend into dry ingredients. Beat the whites until stiff but not dry, and fold them lightly into the blended batter.

Pour onto a seasoned or lightly oiled griddle heated on a medium flame, and cook until air bubbles pop. Turn and cook several minutes more. Serve hot. Makes about twelve 4-inch cakes.

★   ★   ★

Flower Blossoms, Edible Like faces of children, blossoms of flowers invite the eye and delight the heart. Their fragrances add a heart-warming touch to a meal as well as enhanced nutrition. For instance, violet blossoms contain almost three times as much vitamin C as oranges.

Float violets in a glass of wine for a memorable occasion. Enjoy blossoms in salads or as soup garnishes. If they are large, like nasturtiums or squash blossoms, slice them prior to use. Medium- and small-size blossoms may be used whole.

Flower blossoms that are edible include borage, calendula, chrysanthemum, day lily, geranium, hollyhock, lavender, lobelia, nasturtium, pansy, rose, Scotch broom, and violet.

The flowers of some bulbs, such as daffodils and tulips, may be toxic, and so it is best to avoid flowers from bulbs.[8]

Fruit blossoms are almost too precious to eat, but if there is an abundance then indulge in some. Edible fruits have edible blossoms. Cherry and strawberry blossoms are a special delicacy.

Herb blossoms include chive, dill, garlic, marjoram, oregano, rosemary, savory, tarragon, and thyme.

Vegetable blossoms for the table include arugula, bean, chicory, cucumber, pea, and squash.

Fowl The term *fowl* generally refers to game birds that were traditionally hunted in their natural habitats. Today increasing varieties of fowl are farm bred and available in supermarkets and specialty stores. They include Cornish game hen, duck, grouse, guinea hen, partridge (quail), pheasant, squab (immature pigeon), wild turkey, and woodcock.

Fresh game is preferred over frozen game. It generally *is* fresh if it *looks* fresh. Select birds with a soft, smooth skin and avoid those with mottled or translucent spots. Wild game is "gamier" tasting than farm-raised game.

Of these birds, ducks and geese are the fattiest and the highest in calories. Pheasants and guinea hens are the highest in protein and the most energizing of the various fowl. The fat in fowl is mostly found in its skin and abdomen and may be trimmed before serving.

★   ★   ★

Fair Game

From time immemorial man has gratified his palate with feathered game. We usually think of such game as duck, goose, and pheasant. In other times anything on the wing has been fair game.

Some cultures have sanctions against specific species, such as Jewish law, which forbids consumption of birds of prey. However the flesh of all birds, from sparrows to crows, flamingos to vultures, is edible, and most likely it has been featured in more than one ethnic cuisine.

★   ★   ★

Frozen Desserts See **Ice Cream and Frozen Desserts**.

Fructose Fructose is a natural monosaccharide that occurs in fruits and honey. In whole fruit, it is an excellent energy source. Pure fructose may be derived from fruit, but this is not financially expedient. Commercial fructose is available in either liquid or crystalline form. Liquid fructose is made by splitting the two components of corn syrup. High-fructose corn syrup may contain as much as 55 percent sucrose. Crystalline fructose is made from intensely refined cane and beet sugar.

Commercial fructose contains no nutrients and is about 60 percent sweeter than sugar. As with other highly refined substances (fructose is 90 percent pure), the body reacts to it more like a drug than real food. Some people experience allergic reactions to fructose; it aggravates blood sugar problems and may increase cholesterol buildup.

Food manufacturers who sweeten their products with "natural" fructose are either misinformed, or they simply don't care about its effects. See **Sweeteners**.

*　　*　　*

A Surfeit of Sweet

A surfeit of the sweetest things
The deepest loathing to the stomach brings.

—William Shakespeare, *1 Henry IV,* III, ii

*　　*　　*

Fruit　Sweet, saucy, lush, and (when sun ripened and fresh) utterly irresistible— these are but a few ways to describe fruit. Botanically, a fruit is the ripened ovary of a flowering plant consisting of one or more seeds and surrounding tissue. Grains, legumes, and nuts are dry fruits with skins that become hard and dry when mature. The foods we most often think of as fruits have soft, fleshy skins when mature. By this definition certain vegetables, such as cucumbers, tomatoes, and avocados, are also fruits.

Fruits may be classified as acid, subacid, or sweet. They fall into four botanical categories: aggregate fruits, which grow in clusters like bananas; berries, such as strawberries, which have many seeds throughout the fruit; drupes, such as peaches, which contain a single stone or pit, and pomes, such as apples, which contain cores and small seeds.

Fruits are enjoyed raw, juiced, cooked, and dried. An excellent source of natural sugar (fructose), they provide quick energy and their fiber aids digestion. They are low in protein and fat. Fruits are a source of vitamins A, C, and traces of B complex. They contain potassium, magnesium, calcium, phosphorus, and iron.

Medicinal uses vary according to the fruit; generally they are alkaline, expansive, and cooling. The tropical fruits tend to be higher in vitamin C and more cooling than those that grow in temperate regions. The cooling properties of fruits are reduced when they are cooked.

Because of their high sugar content, fruits are more perishable than other fresh produce. For maximum flavor and sweetness, fruits should be picked when fully ripened. When most fruits reach their peak of ripeness, they start deteriorating. Thus most commercial fruits, by necessity, must be picked before peak maturity. Allow immature fruits to ripen at room temperature; then eat or refrigerate, and use as soon as possible. If a fruit is picked when too green, it will never become sweet. For the most flavor, serve fruit at room temperature.

When selecting fruit, consider smell, touch, and weight. Ripe fruits smell lightly fruity and fresh. If their aroma is dank, or cloyingly sweet, they have started to rot. A gentle press with your thumb will cause ripe fruit to give a bit. Mature fruits are heavy, rather than light, for their size.

Seasonal fruits are always a first choice. A cantaloupe in January will not have the flavor of one in July. Locally grown fruit is preferable because it is harvested closer to maturity than is fruit shipped from several states away.

Organic fruit costs more, but to many it is worth every extra penny. Commercial fruit is subjected to chemical soil fumigants, herbicides, fungicides, and growth regulators. Cherries, pineapples, and grapes are frequently more chemically treated than other fruits.

Commercial fruits have a cosmetic uniformity of size, shape, and color that frequently means a corresponding lack of flavor. Fruits that are waxed or dyed should be peeled before they are eaten.

See also **Dried Fruit, Fruit Conserves**; individual fruit entries, such as **Apple, Banana, Cherry**; and fruit categories such as **Berries** and **Citrus Fruit**.

★   ★   ★

Small Is Flavorful

On a per pound basis, smaller fruits contain more nutrients and flavor than larger ones. This is because in most fruits (and vegetables) the nutrient and flavor components are concentrated in the skin or just under it. The smaller the fruit, the more surface there is in relation to total mass.

★   ★   ★

Fruit Conserves   Life without jam and jelly is hard to imagine. These fruit products delightfully embellish numerous desserts and entrées with nutrition, color, flavor, and pizzazz. However, due to an FDA definition, many people concerned with health turn their spoons down on these products.

The FDA sets specific minimum levels of total sugar concentration for jam, preserves, jelly, and fruit butter. Thus, a fruit "jam" with no added sweetener, or with less than the approved formula, cannot be marketed by one of these terms.

Fortunately, there are several natural-food manufacturers who produce superb fruit toppings. They may be 100 percent fruit or may contain some honey or fruit concentrates. Such products are most commonly labeled as "fruit conserves" to be within FDA regulations.

Fu   Fu is an easily digested vegetable protein made from wheat gluten and water. It has little flavor of its own but takes on the flavor of soups or stews and lends a succulent texture.

It is generally available in Japanese markets and macrobiotic sections of natural-food stores. To prepare fu, soak it in water until it softens. Squeeze out the extra water, add fu to a soup, adjust the seasonings, cook for five minutes, and serve. See **Gluten**.

Garlic   Young garlic contains a strongly antiseptic oil called allyl disulphate, which inhibits the growth of bacilli. This explains its use as the oldest broad-spectrum antibiotic known to man.

Practically every culture uses garlic as a home remedy. It is used in the treatment of all lung ailments, for high and low blood pressure, against parasites and infections, for headaches, and for nervous disorders.[1]

Garlic increases body heat and thus may act as an aphrodisiac. Populations that favor garlic often are described as having "explosive" temperaments. Historically, it was fed to soldiers before a battle.

Select garlic cloves that are plump and firm. Store garlic as you would onions, in a cool, dry place in a basket or container where air can circulate. Ninety percent of our domestic supply of garlic comes from California. It is available year-round with the greatest supply following the fall harvest.

Two varieties of garlic have significant commercial use. One is pure white and the other a pale pink. **Elephant Garlic** has mild-tasting cloves the size of an apricot, which may be used as a vegetable rather than a flavoring agent. See **Onion Family**.

★   ★   ★

The Taste of Garlic

For maximum garlic flavor, press or crush fresh garlic cloves and cook briefly or not at all. For a mild garlic flavor cook whole cloves for a long time. Garlic browned in oil imparts a bitter flavor. To obtain the maximum medicinal properties of garlic, do not heat.

★   ★   ★

Gelatin   See **Agar**.

Ginger   Ginger is a major spice used throughout the world in both dry or fresh form. It originated in Asia, where it is a favorite medicinal preventive and curative herb for "expelling dampness."

Scientific studies show that ginger acts as a general stimulant to boost circulation, respiration, digestion, and nervous-system function. It also helps affect a systemic cleansing through the skin, bowels, and kidneys. It acts as a carminative, expectorant, stomachic, astringent, and diuretic. It eases congestion in the throat and lungs, relieving symptoms of cold and flu, and helps alleviate menstrual discomfort.[2]

Ginger tubers are actually a rhizome that grows in the shape of a palm with fingers, called a "hand" of ginger. Look for firm, plump root stalks with clean, smooth skin. Avoid wrinkled, dehydrated ginger. The young, smaller sprouts appearing on the hand have the most delicate flavor.

Ginger has a peppery, piquant flavor. Its flesh may be grated and the juice extracted, or thin slices may be cooked with a variety of foods. One tablespoon of freshly grated ginger equals one-eighth teaspoon ground ginger spice.

Refrigerate fresh ginger in an airtight container. For long-term storage, bury ginger in a container of dry sand and place in a cool area.

Ginseng   Ginseng, which literally means "man root," is found in many health food products including capsules, tablets, extracts, whole roots, teas, energy bars, and even sodas. The lore around ginseng's amazing properties is abundant and goes clear back to classical Oriental medicine. Western science is now substantiating ginseng's properties.

The main active constituents of ginseng are a group of fifteen ginsenosides, each of which acts differently. Different ginsenosides have opposing actions; for example, some stimulate and some sedate. The effect of ginseng varies depending on the particular metabolic needs of a person.[3] Hence the term *adaptogen* is used to describe ginseng, for it helps the body restore and maintain internal homeostasis.

◆ The effects of ginseng on both animals and humans are increased motor coordination, stamina and endurance, mental alertness, adaptability and agility, sensual perception, and learning ability. It has also been found to afford protective medicinal action against radiation exposure.[4]

Wild American ginseng is the highest priced herb in the world, with a prime root costing up to $200 an ounce. Korean and Chinese ginseng are somewhat less costly. Fraudulent ginseng products have been sold to unknowing consumers. Purchase only ginseng products that have the Ginseng Trade Association seal. This seal, in use since 1986, certifies labeling and manufacturing standards.

◀ * * *

What Herb Do Orbiting Cosmonauts Take?

American astronauts drink the ersatz orange juice Tang while zipping through space. Orbiting Soviet cosmonauts take ginseng because it is an adaptogen and has been shown "to have an anti-fatigue effect and to reduce error ratio."[5]

* * *

Gluten The protein found principally in wheat is called gluten. When made into a dough, this protein becomes glutenous (elastic) and traps gas bubbles released from the yeast. Without gluten, yeast could not perform its leavening function. Hard wheat is higher in gluten than is soft or pastry wheat.

Barley, oats, rye, and triticale contain gluten but in lesser amounts than wheat. Some people are allergic to gluten and so use the gluten-free grains, which are amaranth, corn, millet, quinoa, and rice.

A pale yellow "flour" that contains only gluten protein is marketed as gluten. Most professional bakers, and many home bakers, add it to their bread dough. The addition of 5 to 10 percent gluten significantly increases a dough's leavening power. Unlike whole-grain flours, gluten has an indefinite shelf life because its germ has been refined away.

* * *

The Original Chewing Gum

Wheat gum is worth trying at least once. Chew 1 teaspoon hard wheat berries for several minutes or until all that remains is the water-insoluble wheat protein, gluten. Add a dose of imagination and you've got chewing gum.

* * *

☆ **Goat's Milk** For human consumption, goat's milk is remarkably superior to cow's milk. It has ten times the iron, contains more protein, and has a softer curd and smaller fat globules, which allow easier digestion. Its composition is closer to mother's milk.[6]

◀ Goat's milk has limited commercial availability. It is most often procured by having your own nanny goat, or by having a friend who has one. Its taste is stronger than cow's milk.

Gobo See **Burdock**.

Golden Nugget The tiny winter squash that looks like a pumpkin is a golden nugget. It ranges from tennis ball to grapefruit size. When fully ripe it has a mildly
◀ sweet squash flavor. If picked before maturity it has a shiny rind (rather than dull) and will be bland and tasteless.

¤ The golden nugget is treacherous to cut because of its impervious shell and its size. Bake it whole, then cut into desired shapes, season and serve.

See **Squash**, **Winter** for information on selection, storage, and use and for medicinal and nutritional highlights.

*   *   *

Individual and Edible Soup Tureens

Golden nugget squash make delightful and delicious individual soup tureens. Allow one squash per person. Rub the shell with oil and bake at 350 degrees for 30 minutes. Remove it from the oven and cut off and reserve the top so that it will serve as a lid. Remove its seeds and interior fibers. Add hot soup. A cream of celery or mushroom soup goes well. Replace lids. Return to the oven and bake another 15 to 20 minutes or until the squash is *just* cooked. Watch carefully. Overcooked squash looses its shape and eye appeal. Sprinkle soup with a green garnish such as chives. Serve hot, with or without the lid.

*   *   *

Goose See **Fowl**.

Gooseberry *Tart* describes gooseberries. *Very tart.* They can have a smooth or downy skin, and their color varies from white through shades of green to purple. Domesticated for only about 100 years, gooseberries are not widely used. Sweetened, they may be added to pies, preserves, and sauces. They are available from late spring through August. They are high in vitamin C and a good source of potassium.

*   *   *

To Play Gooseberry

When lovers are together and you are an awkward third, you are "playing gooseberry." This term probably originated when a chaperone marked time by picking gooseberries.

*   *   *

Goosefoot Family The chenopod, or goosefoot, family of plants is found throughout the world. The name is derived from the plants' triangular leaf shape, which looks like the webbed foot of a goose or sometimes more like an arrowhead.

Goosefoot greens are a popular salad ingredient or potherb. They contain oxalic acid, which gives some varieties a piquant tang. Chenopod varieties include beet, chard, lamb's quarters, and the numerous varieties of spinach. In cooking, their green color holds up better than the greens of the cabbage family, which turn a drab olive color if overcooked.

Edible seeds of goosefoot family members include lamb's quarters and quinoa. Although technically not a cereal grain, they are used like a grain.

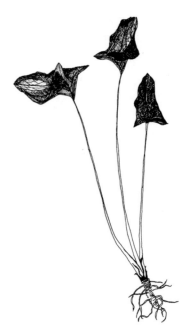

Gourd Family The cucurbit, or gourd, family grows throughout the warm regions of the world and provides numerous and diversified foods. It includes cucumbers, gourds, melons, pumpkins, and squash.

Chayote, squash, and pumpkins evolved in the Americas. Cucumbers, gourds, and melons originated in Africa and Eurasia. The plants are trailing or climbing herbs with tendrils and with large, often palmate-lobed leaves. Cucurbit blossoms are edible.

Grain Whether as a delectable pie crust, a refreshing noodle salad, a hunk of homemade bread, or a bowl of rice, grains are inextricably part of our daily fare. Unlike some newfangled foods, cereal grains have been a primary food staple throughout history. A few exceptions are cultures consuming a predominantly animal-food diet, including subarctic and contemporary Western cultures. These societies, considered against history, are indeed uncommon. It is easy to see why most world religions have a goddess of grain.

Grain-based diets are traditionally supplemented with a variety of legumes, seasonal and regional vegetables and fruits, nuts and seeds, and small amounts of animal foods. With such a variety of supplemental foods, as well as countless preparation methods, grain-based diets are nutritionally sound and aesthetically pleasing.

Grains and beans have a natural affinity for each other. They taste good together, are plentiful, and form a whole protein with superior nutritional properties. This unbeatable duo is part of our heritage: Boston brown bread and baked beans, cornbread and black-eyed peas, chili and sourdough. They also appear in virtually every national cuisine: tortillas and frijoles, pita bread and falafel, pasta and fagioli, rice and dhal.

As with other seeds, grains contain concentrated protein and other nutrients that allow them to burst into life if planted; and if eaten, they provide sustaining energy and regenerative properties. Cereal grains are low on the food chain, and if they contain pesticide residues, these residues are not highly concentrated. The toxic residues in animal foods (meat, fish, poultry, and dairy products) are about thirteen times higher than those found in vegetable foods.

Grains are a complex carbohydrate consisting of bran, germ, and endosperm. They are low in fat and a good source of fiber, minerals, and the B-complex vitamins. To be assimilated they must be cooked with salt (at least ⅛ tsp. salt to 2 cups grain) to reduce their slightly acidic properties. They also require chewing, since the first stage of grain digestion occurs in the mouth. However, chewing well is no hardship, for the longer you chew, the sweeter the grains become.

The advantages of purchasing grain from bulk bins are price and quality. Bulk buying is economical (no packages to pay for) and enables you to see your purchase. Good-quality grain is whole and contains few broken, scratched, or deteriorated grains. It would seem that the presence of grains of the same size and color indicates quality, but actually it indicates hybridized seed, which, although more cosmetic, is less vital than unhybridized grain.

Store grain in a cool, dry place. Any grain, if it sits long enough, will become infested. To prevent this, try to use grain within six months of purchase, store it in glass jars, or keep it in tightly closed sacks. Should it develop bugs or moths, isolate it from other grains and use it up quickly. If it is heavily contaminated, discard it. Place a bay leaf in the container to retard insects from hatching. Although it may not sound tasty, a minuscule amount of insect protein is not harmful or even noticeable in a cooked dish.

See **Barley, Buckwheat, Corn, Job's Tears, Millet, Oats, Quinoa, Rice, Rye, Sorghum, Teff, Triticale, Wheat,** and **Wild Rice**. See also **Flour**.

★   ★   ★

Grain Cooking Chart

The following chart lists water proportions and cooking time for one cup of grain cooked in a pot or pressure cooker. You will rarely cook just one cup of grain, and the water proportion slightly decreases for three or more cups of grain. Also, individual preferences (some like it wet; some like it dry) make this chart a guideline rather than an unalterable given. For a whole-grain breakfast porridge, use up to five cups of water for each cup of grain.

Pressure-cooking is not advised for cereals, porridges, quinoa, teff, amaranth, or buckwheat. However, it is a preferred way to prepare other grains, since it is energy efficient and since grains cooked under pressure are easier to digest and have a sweeter, more delicious taste.

Grain 1 cup dry	Pot-Cooking		Pressure-Cooking	
	Water (cups)	Time (mins.)	Water (cups)	Time (mins.)
Amaranth	3	30		
Barley (whole),	3	60	2½	60
pearled	2½	40	2	30
porridge	5	90		
Buckwheat	2	15		
porridge	3	30		

Grain 1 cup dry	Pot-Cooking		Pressure-Cooking	
	Water (cups)	Time (mins.)	Water (cups)	Time (mins.)
Cornmeal, yellow, white, or blue	4	30		
posole	2½	90	2	60
Job's tears	4	70	3½	60
Millet	3	30	2½	25
porridge	5	60		
Oats	3	60	2½	45
porridge	5	60		
rolled	2½	15		
steel cut	3	40	2½	30
Quinoa	2	20		
Rice (brown)				
short grain	2	60	1½	60
medium grain	1½	50	1¼	50
long grain	1½	50	1¼	50
porridge	5	90		
Rice, sweet (brown)	1½	30	1	20
Rice, white	1½	30	1¼	25
Rye	2½	60	2	50
flakes	3	30		
Sorghum	3	60	2½	50
Teff	2	20		
Triticale	2½	60	2	50
Wheat	3	60	2½	50
couscous	2½	10		
cracked wheat	3	25		
bulgur (red)	2	15		
bulgur (white)	2½	10		
porridge	5½	150		
Wild rice	2½	50	2	.45

★　　★　　★

Grape　The fruit of Bacchus is one of the oldest cultivated plants, and certainly the one most associated with frivolity. Grapes are the basis of the world's largest fruit industry. They are thought to have originated in Asia, but they figure prominently in ancient literature and the art of the Western Hemisphere as well as that of the East. The three most important types are grown for the table, for wine, or for drying as currants and raisins.

Nutritionally, grapes contain vitamins A, B complex, and C. They contain potassium and other trace minerals, including calcium, and are high in natural sugars. Grapes are easily digested and are said to be medicinal for the lungs and to strengthen the internal organs.

Grapes cease ripening when harvested; therefore, select a mature bunch. Examine where the grape attaches to the stem, and if this area looks fresh, the grape will be fresh as well. Gently shake a bunch of grapes and few, if any, should drop. Look for well-colored, plump grapes with a powdery bloom on their skins. Unfortunately, grapes are one of the most chemically treated fruits; therefore, you may wish to limit your consumption of nonorganic grapes.

The volume of U.S. grape production ranks only under that of apples and oranges. California produces 90 percent of table grapes. More than half of all grapes produced are made into juice, wine, or brandy.

Peak season for grapes is September to November, but some are harvested as early as July or well into winter. Grapes stored under controlled atmospheric conditions are available until May. See **Fruit**.

The main varieties of table grapes include the following:

- Concord grapes, dark purple and native American; also popular for jelly, juice, and wine

- Emperor grapes, European by origin, red in color, and with a cherrylike flavor
- Ribier grapes, large, purple-black, and mildly sweet
- Thompson seedless grapes, green (comprise half of California's grape production); most popular for eating and for drying into raisins

Grapefruit   The largest member of the citrus family was so named because its fruits are borne in clusters, somewhat resembling grapes. Grapefruit is the most important citrus that originated outside of Asia; it was hybridized in the West Indies and has been cultivated commercially for one hundred years.

The two types of grapefruit are ruby and white. Rubies have pink flesh and a pink blush to their yellow skin, are grown mainly in Texas, and are generally larger and sweeter than whites. Florida grows 70 percent of the world's supply of grapefruit, which is the white variety.

A popular diet food, grapefruit is an eliminator, is stimulating to the liver, and is helpful in treating jaundice. Its most abundant nutritive property is vitamin C. See **Citrus Fruit**.

Great Northern Bean   This medium-size white bean is similar to a navy bean, only larger. Great northerns or navies are standard in baked beans and pork-and-bean dishes.

See **Beans** for information on selection, storage, and cooking, and for nutritional and medicinal highlights.

Green Bean   Fresh beans are harvested and consumed when the pods are soft and the seeds tender. Select green beans that are firm, whole, and crisp and without rust spots. Fresh beans have ample vitamin A, calcium, potassium, and B-complex vitamins.

New hybrid varieties are stringless; the heirloom varieties have strings that need to be removed prior to cooking. This is a time-consuming process; however, the old varieties are generally more flavorsome.

Some types of green beans include haricot, Italian snap, purple podded, and yellow or green wax beans. A fresh bean snaps crisply and feels velvety to the touch. Old beans are bulging and leathery.

*   *   *

Green Bean Test

Hold a green bean against your shirt. If it sticks when you take your hand away, it is fresh. The surface "fuzz" clings like tiny Velcro fibers do.

*   *   *

Green Foods   Photosynthesis, the conversion of sunlight into food, is possible because of the green pigment chlorophyll. With this miraculous substance the plant kingdom manufactures its food from basic elements and sunlight. All life is thus dependent on the chemical reactions made possible by chlorophyll, which is often referred to as the "blood of plants."

The term *green foods* is applied to supplements and foods that are exceptionally high in chlorophyll. New studies reveal that these foods may have a cleansing, detoxifying and healing effect on our bodies.

Green food supplements include **Barley Grass, Chlorella, Sea Vegetables,** and **Wheat Grass**. Green foods also refers to the leafy green vegetables most commonly found in the goosefoot and cabbage families.

Green Onion   See **Scallion**.

Green Pea   See **Pea, Green**.

Green Tea   See **Tea**.

Grits   The term *grits* refers to any broken cereal grain, especially buckwheat and corn. Because they are no longer a whole food, store them with the same considerations as flour.

Groat   The term *groat* refers to any hulled grain, most often oats and buckwheat.

Ground Cherry   Also known as *Cape Gooseberry, Chinese Lantern, Husk Cherry,* and *Strawberry Tomato.* This small, fanciful fruit that has so many names is not a cherry, gooseberry, or strawberry but rather a fruit of the nightshade family. The ground cherry, native to the Americas, grows all over the United States in open fields and as a roadside weed. As it grows wild in temperate, subtropical, and tropical areas, it was used by almost every South and North American Indian tribe.

The ground cherry is now cultivated throughout the world. Our commercial crop comes primarily from New Zealand and is available in the spring. Immature wild ground cherries are green and may be toxic. Purchase and consume only those that are yellow or yellow-orange.

The golden fruit comes "packaged" inside an inflated, thin-walled covering that looks like a miniature paper lantern. Refrigerate in a single layer for up to a month. Remove the husk prior to eating. The cherry is sweet, attractive, and easy to use. Prepare it as you would a tomato, either raw or cooked.

Grouse   See **Fowl**.

Guava   Originally from the American tropics, the guava is now widely grown throughout the tropical world. The rounded fruits have yellow-green skin with white or pink flesh. There are over one hundred guava species that range in size from a small tangerine to a large orange. Their most distinctive characteristic is an aroma that may be exceptionally sweet or unbelievably foul.

The guava supply is scant but best during the summer. Select a ripe one with a rich aroma. (An immature guava is green and hard.) To ripen, set it out at room temperature until it is slightly soft to the touch. Do not refrigerate until it is fully ripe, and then use it within two days. Hawaii, California, and Florida now produce guavas.

Remove the skin and the numerous seeds, and eat the fruit raw, stewed, or as a preserve. Guava's vitamin C content is several times greater than that of citrus fruits.

Guinea Hen   See **Fowl**.

Gumbo   See **Okra**.

H

Habanero Pepper See **Chile Peppers**.

Haddock A small member of the cod family, haddock is a North Atlantic fish that has been an important food throughout northern Europe from time immemorial. Unfortunately, haddock numbers are rapidly diminishing today.

Found in cold waters, its peak season is fall and winter. Prepare haddock like cod. It has a firmer, drier flesh and a slightly more distinctive flavor. Haddock is remarkable among fish for its high protein and low fat content.

See **Fish** for information on selection, storage, and use and for nutritional and medicinal highlights.

* * *

Finnan Haddie

Smoked haddock, named for the Scottish village of Findon, is called finnan haddie. The story goes that a Findon warehouse of salted haddock caught fire, leading to the inadvertent discovery of smoked haddock.

* * *

Halibut Halibut is the largest of the flatfish and can grow up to five hundred pounds. Smaller halibut, under four pounds, are termed chicken halibut and have finer flesh; their peak season is March to October. Larger halibut are best in fall and winter. The flesh of either is firm and white and has a good flavor.

The halibut is found in all northern seas, but three-quarters of the catch is from the Pacific. Its name means "holy fish" in English and other European languages, probably because it was a popular dish on holy days.

Halibut is high in protein and low in fat with only two grams of fat per ounce of raw flesh. Halibut oil is a good dietary supplement for vitamins A and D.

See **Fish** for selection, storage, use and nutritional and medicinal highlights.

Hato Mugi Barley See **Job's Tears**.

Hazelnut See **Filbert**.

Head Lettuce See **Iceberg**.

Herbal Tea Herbal teas are an infusion of virtually any leaf, twig, root, seed, or flower that is steeped in hot water to produce a beverage. Technically, such a drink is a tisane or ptisan. *Tea* refers specifically to a beverage made from the tea plant. Herbal blends are becoming increasingly popular because they are tasty, economical, and wholesome beverages. Some contain pharmacologically active substances that are beneficial in treating illnesses.

Of the numerous herbal teas marketed, most are blended primarily for flavor; a few are carefully combined for their medicinal effect. Just like food, herbs have different effects on different organs and body processes. The medicinal qualities depend on the freshness of the herb, its maturity at harvest, how well it has been handled, the concentration of the plant's essence, and what it is combined with.

How health promoting any herb or herb blend may be to an individual is relative. For example, someone whose diet is high in animal products and highly processed, inorganic foods will be less sensitive to the subtle properties of herb infusions. Likewise, a medicinal tisane taken on an empty stomach is more effective.

Generally, many herbs in an infusion yield a fuller-bodied drink, and thus most herbal beverages are multiple blends. If you primarily desire the medicinal effect of herbs, they are strongest in simple combinations or even alone. Many people prefer buying individual herbs from bulk containers and combining them to their own specifications. This practice saves money and frequently assures fresher herbs. See **Herbs and Spices**.

Granted, tea bags are a convenience and make brewing a tidier event. However, a tea bag that dangles from a plastic strip—rather than a cotton thread—is a questionable improvement. Infused plastic does *not* enhance the flavor of tea.

A proper cup of tea is made from loose tea so the hot water can better circulate, invite, and coax forth the herbs' maximum flavor. Good tea requires excellent water, a ceramic or glass pot for boiling the water, a ceramic teapot, a quality tea, and a relaxed atmosphere.

Bring ample water to a boil. Rinse out the teapot with some of the boiling water. Into the now-warmed pot put a teaspoon of tea for every cup desired plus one for the pot. Immediately pour in boiling water, cover, and allow to steep for five minutes. To serve, pour through a strainer. Serve, sit back, relax, sip, and savor.

*   *   *

Herbs and Spices   All cultures have used various plant parts for medicinal purposes as well as to enhance and preserve foods. Herbs—the leaves of plants—are subtle and complement the natural flavors of foods. Spices—the bark, roots, fruit, or berries of plants—can give a food such flavor intensity that they give that food a new character.

For maximum spice flavor, buy spices whole and grind them prior to use. For maximum herb flavor, grow your own and "harvest" them just prior to use. A kitchen window herb garden requires minimum space and effort and yields a variety of fresh herbs.

When purchasing herbs and spices, look for those with a fresh color, a strong scent, and a tart "grab-the-tongue" quality. They should feel resilient and have a deep aroma. Stale herbs that crumble easily between your fingers give a bitter, flat taste. Be choosy and purchase herbs from a reliable retailer who you are sure is obtaining the best quality and who has fresh stock. Buy herbs frequently in small quantities rather than occasionally in large quantities.

Ground or cut herbs and spices over a year old are "dead." Do not buy herbs that have been sitting in the direct sun. Ideally, herbs should be packaged in containers that filter light, and they should not be close to a heat source. At home, store your herbs in a cool, dark place.

Custom wildcrafted herbs are the best quality available. They are harvested in their natural habitat, in the right season, and by correct methods. For example, custom wildcrafted goldenseal is harvested from wild plants in the fall, when its medicinal properties are at their peak. Most common goldenseal on the market is harvested in the summertime when it is easier to find.

Over 80 percent, by weight, of all herbs and spices sold on the North American market are imported. All imported herbs and spices are fumigated in accordance with USDA regulations. Usually ethylene oxide, a potentially hazardous substance, is used.[1] Fumigation reduces the oil and denatures the alkaloids in certain plants.

Domestic herbs and spices need not be fumigated, and the pesticides used on them are regulated, which is not the case with imported herbs. According to results from a Canadian study, as reported by author and herbalist Steven Foster, commercial herbs often have higher than allowed levels of DDT and other toxic chemicals in them. Foster reports, "Herbal products are not more free, and are often considerably less free, of unwanted [toxic chemical] ingredients than are the rest of our foods."[2]

All herbs and spices—domestic and imported—may be irradiated with up to 3,000 kilorads of ionizing radiation.

Herbs frequently available fresh are listed individually. See **Basil, Borage, Chives, Cilantro, Dill, Fennel, Lemon Grass, Marjoram, Parsley, Rosemary, Sage, Tarragon,** and **Thyme.**

* ★ ★

700 Percent Markup

According to a report in an herb trade journal, culinary herbs and spices in the supermarket often carry a 700 percent markup. This is from seven to thirty times the average natural-food store markup.[3]

★ ★ ★

Fresh Herbs

Fresh herbs lend a more delicate and refreshing flavor to foods than do dried herbs. When substituting fresh herbs for dried herbs use the following proportions:

$$1 \text{ tablespoon fresh herb} \begin{cases} \text{⅓ teaspoon powdered herb} \\ \text{or} \\ \text{½ teaspoon crushed herb} \end{cases}$$

On arriving home with fresh herbs, trim their stems, immerse in water, loosely cover with a plastic bag, and refrigerate. Every other day cut off ¼ inch of the stem end. This enables you to keep herbs fresh for up to ten days.

★ ★ ★

Herring   Historically, herring is an important food fish and is one of the most abundant sea fishes as well as one of the most economical and nutritious. Herring is taken from northern seas and is available year-round on the Atlantic coast. It is at its peak season on the Pacific coast from May to July. Both hard and soft herring roes are delicacies.

Herrings are among the highest protein fish and, at 6 percent fat, are somewhat fattier than other fish. Because of their fat they are highly perishable and therefore are often smoked, salted, pickled, or dried. Rollmops is a pickled herring; kippers and red herring are smoked herring. Fresh herring has a creamy flavor and a firm texture.

A strongly smoked herring is red and aromatic, and the phrase "to draw a red herring across the path" means to divert one's attention from the main issue, just as a hound would be diverted if a smoked herring were drawn across a fox's path.

See **Fish** for information on selection and storage and for nutritional and medicinal highlights.

Hijiki   Also known as *Hiziki.* The most mineral rich of all foods is the stringy marine alga hijiki. It has a strong taste that, for some, is an acquired one. Hijiki strands are several inches long, bulbous in the middle, and pointed on both ends.

Hijiki is black when dried or when cooked. It is a deep brown when fresh or hydrated. Hijiki expands to more than four times its original volume when soaked, so start with a small quantity. Sautéed, boiled, or simmered with other vegetables, this vegetable has a unique flavor. Cook it for one hour to an al dente texture.

Hijiki is an extremely rich source of calcium. It contains 1,400 mg of calcium per 100 grams dry weight. This is considerably more than milk, which checks in at 100 mg per 100 grams dry weight.[4] It is high in other trace elements, an excellent source of iron, a good source of protein, vitamin A, and the B vitamins. Hijiki, as other seaweeds, is low in calories.

Because of its calcium and iron content, this sea vegetable is a highly recommended food during pregnancy. In the Far East it is esteemed as a food that increases one's beauty and strengthens and adds luster to the hair. It helps stabilize the blood sugar level.

Sea **Sea Vegetables** for nutritional and medicinal highlights.

Hokkaido Pumpkin   See **Kabucha.**

Homeopathy   Homeopathic medicinal preparations are available in most natural-food stores. The Food and Drug Administration recognizes homeopathy as a science, and so homeopathic labels state the purpose of a product. Most other alternative substances used medicinally may not make medicinal claims on their labels.

Honey   Some people exalt honey as an ideal sweetener. Others say it is as harmful as white sugar. The truth lies somewhere in between. Flower nectar, a disaccharide, is processed (through enzymatic action in the stomachs of bees) to form a highly concentrated and refined product. There can be no doubt that this manufacturing process is wholly natural and organic. Even so, honey is classified with other use-in-moderation-only sweeteners.

The total sugar content of honey is higher than that of any other natural sweetener. Seventy-five percent of honey is glucose and fructose. Like white sugar, honey is absorbed quickly into the bloodstream and upsets the blood sugar level. If eaten in large quantities, it can contribute to hypoglycemia and diabetes. It is an empty-calorie food that contributes to tooth decay and can lead to obesity.

All honey is heated to facilitate packaging. Quality honey is processed with low, rather than high, heat. It contains minuscule amounts of enzymes, vitamins, and pollen and therefore is preferable to sugar.

The FDA periodically monitors honey for drug residues, adulteration, and botulism. Bees are subject to a variety of illnesses, and some are treated with fumagillin and oxytetracycline, traces of which may show up in honey. Some producers fraudulently add high-fructose corn syrup or invert sugar to honey. And a form of botulism *(C. botulinum)* is associated with honey consumption and causes some infant botulism deaths.[5]

Dark honey is more mineral rich and also stronger tasting. The best-quality honey, either dark or light, has not been heated to temperatures over 105 degrees and is cloudy due to minimum filtration and clarification.

Crystallization will develop in these more natural honeys with either long or cool storage. To reliquefy, place the honey jar in a saucepan with hot water and heat slowly until all the crystals are dissolved. Store honey in a warm, dry, dark cupboard, and it will stay fresh indefinitely.

Most honey is produced in California, the Midwest, and Florida. The best selection is unpasteurized honey from a local apiary. See **Sweeteners**.

Honeydew Melon   See **Melon Family**.

Honey Leaf   See **Stevia**.

Hopi Corn   See **Corn, Blue**.

Horse Bean   See **Fava Bean**.

Horseradish   Horseradish has by far the strongest kick of cultivated vegetables. Though it is one of the five "bitter herbs" of the Jewish Passover seder, to me its flavor is pungent rather than bitter.

Horseradish is a member of the mustard family, and its characteristic hot flavor is produced by mustard oil. This oil dissipates rapidly after cutting or grating and is destroyed by heat. Thus, horseradish is best when raw and freshly grated.

Look for plump, firm crisp roots, which are available from the fall through the spring. Refrigerate and use within a week.

Horseradish is an excellent source of iron and potassium. As a kitchen remedy it is said to "burn" fat, and so some use it in weight-reduction programs.

Hot Pepper   See **Chile Peppers**.

Hubbard Squash The hubbard is a large (often over twenty-five pounds) winter squash with dark green or reddish orange pebbly skin. It looks something like a gargantuan crookneck squash. Hubbard flesh color is more yellow than orange. See **Squash, Winter**.

★　　★　　★

Hubbard Popularity Decreases

Once regular fare across the United States, Hubbards' declining popularity is not a reflection of their flavor or excellent keeping properties. Few families today can handle twenty-five pounds of squash at one sitting.

★　　★　　★

Husk Cherry See **Ground Cherry**.

Hydrogenation Liquid oil that is treated with hydrogen gas to change its molecular structure is hydrogenated. This process saturates the fatty acids to render a solid or semisolid oil like margarine and shortening. Most processed cheeses and commercial peanut butters also contain hydrogenated oil. Even when such a product is made from polyunsaturates, the result is an unnaturally saturated fat.

As with naturally saturated fats, hydrogenated products are to be avoided. Scientists have determined that they interfer with the body's production of vital nutrients. See **Oil**.

Iceberg Also known as *Imperial* or *Head*. Unfortunately, the most widely consumed lettuce is iceberg. The best thing one can say about iceberg is that its leaves are crisp. Iceberg is nutritionally inferior to other lettuces, and commercial iceberg is one of the most highly chemically treated crops.

Fortunately, the availability of other types of lettuce is growing and cooks are experimenting with a multitude of other leafy greens in their salad bowls. See **Lettuce**.

Ice Cream and Frozen Desserts Floating in soda, scooped into a dish, frozen on a stick, sandwiched between wafers, or packed into cones—ice cream is more American (certainly more commonplace) than apple pie. Originally, ice cream was made from pure cream, milk, fresh eggs, fruit, nuts, and natural flavorings.

In 1927 the air-injection freezer made it possible to make ice cream that was up to 60 percent air. According to Gaylord Willis, "real" ice cream entrepreneur, this was the start of the adulteration of ice cream. To hold the air, stabilizers were added and manufacturers didn't stop with just one or two. Over half of an average ice cream marketed today is synthetic.[1] Stabilizers, improvers, emulsifiers, smoothers, chemical flavorings and artificial color, and synthetic replacements for milk, cream, and eggs is what most ice cream is about today.

Manufacturers of quality ice cream give full product disclosure on their labels. Their price is definitely higher than ersatz frozen dairy varieties, but definitely worth it. See **Dairy**.

Frozen yogurt contains a host of stabilizers and emulsifiers, up to 25 percent sugar, and most often has been pasteurized. (The healthful lactic acid culture is killed in a pasteurized yogurt product.)

Ice milk contains 2 to 7 percent fat. This product often has extra sugar to compensate for the reduced butterfat. Although it has less calories, the amount is insignificant (forty calories less per four-ounce serving).

Rice "ice cream" is a low-fat, no-cholesterol ice cream look-alike. Its texture is remarkably creamy and comparable to high-quality ice milk. It is made of amasake, water, oil, vegetable stabilizers, and natural flavors. Rice cream is sweet without additional sweeteners being added because its carbohydrates are converted into simple sugars through fermentation.

Sherbet usually has about the same calories as ice cream, but one-third the protein and calcium. It contains a small amount of milk or milk solids, but up to 30 percent sugar! Sherbet relies heavily on additives to give it texture, flavor, and color.

Soft ice cream has less air and less sugar than regular ice cream but a lot more emulsifiers and stabilizers for its texture. Soft ice cream is served at a slightly higher temperature than regular ice cream.

Soy or Tofu ice cream exists in as wide a range of quality as does regular ice cream. Some tofu ice creams are shoddy synthetic products that use a minuscule amount of highly refined soy isolates. Other soy ice creams use quality ingredients. Read labels carefully.

★   ★   ★

Real Ice Cream Melts

"Ice cream" may be 80 percent synthetic. A single product may contain as many as fifty-five chemical ingredients. The only artificial ingredient that must be acknowledged is artificial flavoring. These shabby products do not melt, are often gummy, sticky, crumbly, or brittle and have a metallic aftertaste.

A scoop of real ice cream is icy, refreshing, pleasantly flavored, and leaves a sweet aftertaste. It melts to a creamy mixture if left at room temperature for fifteen minutes.

★   ★   ★

Indian Fig See **Prickly Pear**.

Irish Moss   Also known as *Carrageen.* Irish moss provides an excellent, but softer, gel than agar. Its extract, often called carageenan, has numerous culinary uses. An essential ingredient in blancmange, this sea vegetable is used in brewing, ice cream, salad dressings, candy, and puddings, or added to soups and stews as a vegetable.

This red algae, which grows near the low-tide mark, is exceptionally high in vitamin A and iodine. It also contains iron, sodium, copper, and numerous trace minerals, as well as protein and vitamin B_1.

Long noted for its medicinal properties, Irish moss is used in cough preparations; for digestive disorders (including ulcers), kidney ailments, heart disease, and glandular irregularities; and as a bowel regulator.

The high sulfur content of Irish moss gives it a sea odor much stronger than that of other sea vegetables. Rinsing it several times and soaking it reduces this. The domestic sources of this sea gel are Massachusetts and Hawaii. It is also produced in Ireland, Brittany, and the Canadian Maritime Provinces.

See **Sea Vegetables** for nutritional and medicinal highlights.

Ita Wakame   See **Wakame**.

Jalapeño   See **Chile Peppers**.

Japanese Horseradish   See **Wasabi**.

Jerusalem Artichoke   Also known as *Sunchoke.* Jerusalem artichokes are not from Jerusalem, nor are they related to artichokes. This sunflower tuber is a native of North America and its taste has been likened to globe artichokes. It has narrower leaves and smaller heads than the common sunflower, but is widely distributed throughout the United States. This tuber was a popular food staple for numerous Indian tribes.

The crisp flesh is white and sweet, and it looks like a small, knobby potato. During the fall and winter the tuber is at its peak flavor and availability. Select firm vegetables; avoid limp, wilted, or sprouting ones. Refrigerate for up to a week. Jerusalem artichokes may be stir-fried, baked, deep fried, pickled, or served raw in salads. They do not can or freeze well.

Jerusalem artichokes are a superior source of inulin, a natural sugar that is said to be medicinal for diabetics. They also contain vitamin A and B complex, potassium, iron, calcium, and magnesium. Unlike most root vegetables, this sunflower tuber contains no starch.

Jicama   A Central American root vegetable that is gaining increasing popularity in the domestic market is the jicama. This underground tuber of a legume plant looks like a brown, oversize turnip. Jicama has a thick brown skin, and its crisp, slightly sweet flesh is similar to that of water chestnuts, only crisper.

Select roots that are thin skinned, fresh looking, and relatively unblemished. Store a whole jicama unwrapped in the refrigerator, where it will keep for several weeks. Once cut, wrap, refrigerate, and use within several days.

Jicama may be eaten raw or cooked as you would water chestnuts or Jerusalem artichokes. It lends itself well to both fruit and vegetable salads. A popular Latin American preparation is to squeeze raw slices with lime juice and sprinkle with salt.

An excellent dieter's food, jicama is low in sodium and is a good source of potassium.

Jinengo   Also known as *Mountain Yam.* Grated raw jinengo (ge-NEN-jo) is one of the gooiest substances imaginable. Add tamari to this goop and you have got a digestive aid highly esteemed in Japanese and macrobiotic cuisines. It contains even more of the starch-digesting enzyme diatase than does daikon. Like comfrey, it contains allantoin, which is medicinal for stomach ulcers and asthma.

American Indians, as well as Orientals, value this wild mountain yam as a food and for its medicinal properties. It strengthens, increases stamina, rejuvenates, and is used for the treatment of various digestive disorders.[1]

Jinengo may be cooked like potato chips or potato patties, or used as a binder to hold other ingredients together. When cooked it loses its mucilaginous quality.

The buff-colored tuber is slightly hairy and grows to lengths of three feet. When you find it in a specialty market, break off as large a section as you wish to purchase. Refrigerate it. Although the cut end becomes discolored, the yam will keep for a week.

Job's Tears   Also known as *Hato Mugi Barley.* A "new" grain that is a true cereal and looks like a giant pearl barley is Job's tears. This Oriental native is a newcomer to the natural-food scene and is in great demand. American farmers in the Midwest are currently developing seeds in order to provide a domestic crop of Job's tears.

Soak Job's tears prior to use. It requires longer cooking than barley and is less sticky than either rice or barley. Combine with rice or another grain or add to long-cooking soups.

In the Far East its medicinal properties for the stomach and nervous system and for purifying the blood and restoring health are widely reputed. Job's tears' complement of protein, fat, calcium, iron, and the several B vitamins is superior to that of brown rice, and the quality and value of its amino acids is superior to those of the common grains.[2]

Juice, Fruit   Refreshing and wholesome fruit juices are enjoyed straight from the bottle, as a sweetener in natural desserts, or mixed with carbonated water for a delicious soft-drink substitute. Natural fruit juice is nothing but the liquid pressed from a fruit and then pasteurized and bottled. If the juice were not pasteurized, it would become alcoholic or turn to vinegar (see **Apple Cider**).

There are numerous types of fruit juice and various blends. The flavor of any one kind of juice varies greatly according to the variety of fruit used, its quality, ripeness, and how it was handled. Because of the abundance of apples and their superior keeping qualities, apple juice is frequently blended with other fruit juices. The current manufacturers' trend is to use inexpensive grape concentrate from South America as a base for other juices.

In terms of quality the best choice is pure, organic, unfiltered juice. Unfiltered juice has sediment that sinks to the bottom of the bottle. This sediment is composed of proteins, minerals, fibers, and pectins. Unfiltered juice has a richer, fuller taste and a heavier "mouth feel." The sediment of unfiltered grape juice contains a naturally occurring acid (commonly called cream of tartar), which settles to the bottom as small crystals.

Unfortunately, the FDA regulations for labeling fruit juice are poorly defined, and it is difficult to know exactly how a juice is processed. The best juices are pressed from whole fruit. Others may be made from water and fruit pulp that may have been frozen or canned, or from a blend of water and fruit juice solids (concentrates) that are processed by extreme heat or cold. Reputable brand names indicate on their labels precisely how the juice was made.

Fruit nectars, ades, drinks, and punch are sham products that may contain as little as 10 percent juice with added sugar, water, artificial color, flavor, and preservatives. Only 100 percent pure juice can be labeled "juice."

An unopened bottle of fruit juice will keep on the shelf for many months. Once opened it should be refrigerated and used within ten days.

Occasionally, fresh, unpasteurized juices, such as orange juice or apple cider, are locally available. When fresh, these are the best buys in terms of nutrition and flavor. Apple cider made from whole, pressed apples is a seasonal treat. Pasteurized apple juice pales by comparison.

* * *

Inimitable Fresh Juice

Raw juice is undoubtedly the best-tasting juice, and it is a potent source of vital nutrients. The classic is ambrosial carrot juice, but many vegetables and fruits make equally delicious drinks. Many people consider their electric home juicers as indispensable as their kitchen sink.

* * *

Juice Is Potent Stuff!

One apple, juiced, is ingested more than *ten times faster* than if the apple were eaten whole.[3] The natural fiber of whole apples slows the ingestion of nutrients. Because juice is a refined food and is high in sugar, it triggers a rebound fall in blood sugar. For optimum health, choose whole fruit over fruit juice. This is especially applicable to those with hypoglycemia and diabetes.

* * *

Juice, Vegetable   Available primarily at the local level, fresh vegetable juice is not pasteurized and should be consumed within a day or two of purchase. Carrot juice is the most popular vegetable juice, but there are various blends as well.

Vegetable juice is more highly concentrated than fruit juice because fruit contains more water. One cup of carrot juice represents four cups of carrots. Excessive carrot juice consumption can cause the skin to turn orange.

Some imported bottled vegetable juices have interesting flavors although they are not comparable to fresh juice. Acidic vegetable juices (such as tomato juice or blends containing it) should be in fiber cans; otherwise, the acid can leach lead from the can's soldered seams.

K

Kabucha Also known as *Hokkaido Pumpkin.* The kabucha (ka-BOO-cha) pumpkin, which is actually a squash, has the highest sugar content of any squash. One variety has a blue-green skin and another is bright orange. Both have mustard-yellow flesh and are similar to buttercup squash but have a drier texture that crumbles if overcooked. The kabucha is shaped like a ridgeless pumpkin. Even though it originated in the United States, it was reintroduced to us by the Japanese, who named it after their northernmost province.

Prepare kabucha like any winter squash. It may be baked, steamed, sautéed, or—once cooked—puréed for soup. For a flavorful and nutritious pie, try replacing pumpkin with kabucha in a pastry shell.

According to macrobiotic usage, the naturally sweet properties of kabucha make it a medicinal food for people suffering from blood sugar irregularities. When cooked with aduki beans and kombu seaweed, it is said to be especially healing to the pancreas and the kidneys. See **Squash, Winter.**

*   *   *

Price Discrepancy

Because of its reputation as a strengthening food, kabucha is often priced higher than other winter squash. Growing a hokkaido costs no more than growing any winter squash. You might buy seeds and grow your own next year.

*   *   *

Kale Kale is like a curly-leaved collard and is a superior source of calcium, iron, and vitamin A. Whereas collards prefer warmer climes, kale thrives in the cold. In fact, kale's flavor is enhanced by a touch of frost. It still grows wild in northern Europe. Kale is a strong-tasting vegetable but may be cooked in numerous delicious ways. Of the dark leafy-green vegetables, it is exceptionally strengthening and is said to help ease congestion in the lungs.

Depending upon the variety, kale may be green-gray or blue-green in color. Select kale that is uniformly colored. The edges of some varieties are tightly curled. Refrigerate kale in a plastic bag for up to five days.

See **Cabbage Family** for information on selection, storage, and use and for nutritional and medicinal highlights.

Kale, Flowering Also known as *Ornamental Kale* and *Flowering Cole.* Decorative bouquets of ruffly-edged violet-, cream-, or green-leaved kale are becoming a popular ornamental plant. This plant goes by several names, but is most closely related to kale. It is found in food markets, flower shops, backyards, and shopping malls.

Like other cabbage-family members, flowering kale is edible; however, it is not as tender as kale. To best preserve its delicate color, boil in lightly salted water until just tender and then rinse under cold water.

Kanten In common American usage, *kanten* means Jell-O made out of the sea vegetable agar (see accompanying recipe).

Kanten also refers to a product that may be used in place of agar flakes or powder. It is a Japanese blend of eight varieties of agarophytes and is available in a bar form that looks and feels like cellophane. Kanten bars are prepared in a centuries-old traditional method that includes freeze-drying it outside in the winter. In recipes one bar of kanten may be substituted for two slightly rounded tablespoons of agar flakes. See **Agar** and **Sea Vegetables.**

*   *   *

Apple Kanten

4 cups apple juice or fresh apple cider
Small pinch sea salt

    5 tablespoons agar flakes*
    2 cups apples, diced

Pour the juice into a saucepan; add the salt and agar flakes. Bring to a simmer over medium heat and simmer for 3 minutes. Stir several times. Place the apple chunks in a dish and pour the agar over them. Allow to sit, uncovered, in a cool place and it will set within 2 hours.

You may use other varieties and combinations of juices and fruits. When agar is flavored with only apple, it is said to be medicinal for the lungs.

*If substituting kanten bars, follow directions on package.

⋆ ⋆ ⋆

Kasha   See **Buckwheat**.

Kefir   This tasty, yogurtlike beverage is made of milk cultured with several strains of yeast and bacteria. The claim that kefir aids digestion and absorption by increasing the bacterial content of the intestines is in question. However, kefir is unquestionably easier to digest than milk. Some kefir is made of certified raw milk.   ☆

Kefir is available plain or flavored and may be used in cooking. Many natural food stores carry kefir culture, which enables you to make your own.

See **Dairy** and **Fermented Food** for additional information.

⋆ ⋆ ⋆

Homemade Kefir

    1 quart raw or pasteurized milk
    1 packet kefir culture or 3 tablespoons prepared kefir

Scald the milk to 180 degrees and pour it into a sterilized glass jar or bowl. Allow to cool to room temperature. Add the kefir culture, stir, cover with a cotton cloth, and allow to ferment for 24 hours at room temperature. Stir and refrigerate. The first batch of kefir may be thin, but it thickens with repeated preparations of a culture.

⋆ ⋆ ⋆

Kelp   There are nearly nine hundred known varieties of this brown sea vegetable. *Macrocystis,* the largest of marine plants, grows up to sixty yards in length. The kelps grow in frigid to temperate waters throughout the world and have been widely used by different cultures for centuries.

The kelp family includes kombu, wakame, and arame; however, these vegetables are packaged under their own names. Kelp is most commonly sold as powder or in kelp tablets. As a powder it may replace salt in recipes or in your salt shaker to season cooked foods. Kelp has numerous commercial uses as a stabilizer, an emulsifier, a suspending agent, and a thickener.

Kelp is high in calcium and iodine. It contains many trace elements, as well as sugar and starch, and various vitamins including A, B_6, B_{12}, C, D, and K.   +

Medicinally, kelp is used to regulate blood pressure, for weight loss, as a   ◆
digestive aid and colon cleanser, and to alleviate kidney, reproductive, circulation, and nerve problems.[1]

The kelp most widely used is *pleurophycus gardneri,* simply called kelp. It is harvested from both the Pacific and the Atlantic. A light brown alga, its leaves grow to a yard long and a foot wide. See also **Sea Vegetables**.

⋆ ⋆ ⋆

World's Largest Vegetable

Macrocystis pyrifera, a brown Pacific kelp, grows in fronds up to 180 feet long.

⋆ ⋆ ⋆

Kidney Bean   The largest red bean, the kidney bean, gets its name from its shape. The kidney bean family (*Phaseolus*) includes pinto beans, green and wax beans, bolita beans, and great northern beans. This species has been cultivated in the Americas since prehistoric times. It was introduced to Europe, where it was christened the "French bean," in the sixteenth century.

Kidney beans are a common ingredient in chili and a colorful addition to salads.

See **Beans** for information on selection, storage, and use and for nutritional and medicinal highlights.

Kiwi Kiwis are as strange looking as the New Zealand bird for which they are named. They look like furry brown eggs; they have a brilliant green, syrupy flesh; and their tiny edible black seeds surround a creamy yellow center.

Kiwis are eaten raw in salads and desserts. They contain twice the vitamin C of oranges and only 45 calories per fruit. They are a cooling food.

A ripe kiwi feels like a ripe pear—firm, but it gives to gentle pressure. To speed the ripening, place kiwis in a closed bag or fruit-ripening bowl along with another fruit and leave at room temperature. A kiwi will also ripen gradually if it is refrigerated several weeks. A ripe kiwifruit should be refrigerated and kept separate from other fruits, or it will take on their flavor. Kiwi keeps, refrigerated, for several months.

California kiwifruits are harvested in October and are available through May. New Zealand kiwi are imported during the summer months, and thus they are available year-round.

* * *

Kiwi Enzymes

Have you ever added kiwi to Jell-O or kanten? Don't! It contains enzymes that prevent gelatin from setting. These enzymes also change the composition of many dairy dishes and they tenderize meat. Feature kiwi boldly as a garnish rather than incorporated into gelatins and milk dishes.

* * *

Knob Celery See **Celeriac**.

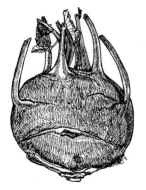

Kohlrabi Kohlrabi is like a turnip in shape and texture but is actually the swollen stem of this cabbage-family plant. It grows as big as an orange but is sweetest when it is smaller. The large ones tend to be pithy or woody. The leaves, when young, may be eaten like other brassica greens, but older greens are too strong in flavor.

Peel the fibrous skin, which may be green or purple, and slice it thin for salads, or cook it as you would a turnip. Kohlorabi is not a widely used vegetable, but it is a fun food and worth getting acquainted with.

Kohlrabi is a good source of vitamin C and calcium. As a kitchen remedy it energizes the stomach.

See **Cabbage Family** for information on selection, storage, and use and for nutritional and medicinal highlights.

Koji Koji is the catalyst that ferments amasake, miso, sake, shoyu, and tamari. Fermentation produces enzymes that break down proteins, starches, and fats into more readily digestible amino acids, simple sugars, and fatty acids. Fermented foods are nutritionally and energetically superior to their original raw ingredients.

To make koji, cooked grain (or beans) is inoculated with spores of the mold *Aspergillus oryzae,* held at specific temperatures and humidity for three days, and then dried. Ready-made koji is available in natural-food stores and is packaged with simple instructions for its use. It is possible to purchase *Aspergillus oryzae* and to make koji.

Kombu Kombu is one of the better known and more versatile sea vegetables. It is used for soup stock, to soften beans, in stews, as a wrap for food morsels, and it stands on its own baked, deep-fried, or boiled. It is tasty and mucilaginous.

Kombu is very high in sugar, potassium, iodine, calcium and vitamins A and C. It also contains appreciable amounts of B-complex vitamins, glutamic acid, starch, and trace minerals. The medicinal properties of kombu are similar to those for kelp.

Our major source of kombu is Japan. New seaweed industries in California and Maine provide some domestic kombu. The most commonly used kombu comes in strips several inches wide and of varying lengths. Other forms of kombu include the following:

- Natto kombu, thin strands of kombu.
- Ne-kombu—the holdfast (root) is a strengthening food that is said to be particularly beneficial in the treatment of cancer and dysfunctions of the intestines, kidneys, and reproductive organs. Ne-kombu is recommended for breaking down fatty acids in the body and reducing cholesterol and high blood pressure.[2] It requires long soaking and cooking.
- Tororo kombu—fine kombu filaments seasoned with rice vinegar. It may be used as a condiment or added to soups just before serving. It is tasty and mucilaginous.

See **Sea Vegetables** for information on selection, storage, use and for nutritional and medicinal highlights.

*   *   *

Natural—and Healthful—MSG

Glutamic acid, a main ingredient of monosodium glutamate (MSG), was originally synthesized from kombu. Glutamic acid has a stimulating effect on the taste buds and thus enhances the flavors of many foods. It is also an effective tenderizer. Laboratory-produced MSG has a deleterious effect on health, but naturally occurring glutamic acid in kombu is healthful. Use kombu to increase the flavor and nutritional value of many foods, especially beans, soups, and soup stock.

*   *   *

Kudzu See **Kuzu**.

Kukicha Also known as *Twig Tea*. The lowest-grade tea from the tea plant, *Camellia sinenis,* is kukicha. Kukicha, which means "twigs" in Japanese, is literally the twigs of the tea plant rather than the leaves. This standard macrobiotic beverage is a digestive aid that helps neutralize an overly acidic digestive system.[3]

The terms *bancha* and *kukicha* are sometimes incorrectly interchanged. Bancha is composed of leaves as well as twigs. Both teas use plant parts that are at least three years old, and both are simmered to increase their flavor and medicinal properties. The caffeine in kukicha is 18.6 milligrams per eight ounces tea compared to 80 milligrams per eight ounces of black tea.

Kumquat This date-size fruit is not a true citrus, but it is closely related. It looks like a miniature orange and may be eaten whole. The spicy skin and tart flesh make it a great taste combination.

Choose kumquats that are heavy for their size, bright, glossy, and not shriveled. They are available from December through May. Kumquats have a thin skin that makes them more perishable than other citrus fruits. Refrigerated they last up to a week. Kumquats are a cooling food and a good source of vitamin C.

See **Citrus Fruit** for information on selection, storage, and use and for medicinal and nutritional highlights.

Kuzu Also known as *Kudzu*. Pronounced KUD-zoo in the Southern states, where this plant is cursed as a noxious weed, it is KOO-zoo in Japan, where its root is praised for its medicinal and culinary properties. Kuzu powder is the concentrated starch of the root, which is absorbed easily into the blood and converts readily into energy in the human metabolism.

Kuzu may be used as a thickener like cornstarch and arrowroot; it serves as a gelling agent like agar and gelatin. As a kitchen remedy it helps develop an alkaline condition and provide relief from intestinal and digestive disorders, headaches, fever, colds, and hangovers.[4]

Currently, kuzu is available only as an expensive Japanese import. Surely someday an industrious individual will harvest and market domestic kuzu. The kuzu available in natural-food stores is a pure product. That available in Oriental markets is frequently blended with potato starch.

This root lends a subtle sweetness and smoothness to sauces, desserts, and confections. To prepare the starch for use, dissolve it in cold water. For suggested uses refer to *The Book of Kudzu* by William Shurtleff and Akiko Aoyagi as well as Japanese and macrobiotic cookbooks.

* * *

Macrobiotic Aspirin

In popular macrobiotic usage the kuzu recipe Ume-shoyu-kuzu replaces the contents of a medicine cabinet.

1¼ cups water
½ to 1 umeboshi, minced
1½ tablespoons kuzu powder
½ to 1 teaspoon shoyu
⅛ teaspoon ginger juice, or ½ teaspoon powdered gingerroot

Place the kuzu in ¼ cup water. Add the remaining ingredients in a saucepan and bring to a boil. Stir the kuzu to dissolve it, and add to the boiling liquid. Stir continuously while returning to a boil. Reduce heat and simmer for 1 minute. Drink hot.

* * *

Kuzu-Kiri A light noodle made from sweet potato starch and kuzu, kuzu-kiri enhances soups, broths, salads, and one-pot cooking preparations.

Lamb   Many consider lamb a superior meat because it is young and tender and can be prepared without additional fat. Also, it is the lowest in fat of the common red meats. This is because its average age at slaughter is six months. The term *spring lamb* refers to an animal under twelve months old.

Because lamb is an immature animal, its flesh is basically muscle (fat marbling in the flesh is a sign of maturity). Nearly all fat in lamb is exterior and may be trimmed off, but although lower in fat content than beef, lamb has a higher percentage of saturated fat.

With the exceptions of fat content and quantity of saturated fat, lamb is nutritionally comparable to beef. Lamb cuts and methods for their selection and storage are also similar to beef. (See **Beef**.)

To recognize high-quality lamb, look for meat that is fine textured, firm, and lean. The meat should be pink and the cross section of bone red, moist, and porous. The fat should be firm, white, and not too thick. If the lamb is grass fed, its flesh is light pink; the grain-fed lamb's flesh is darker.

Lamb's Lettuce   See **Mâche**.

Lamb's Quarters   Also known as *Chinese Spinach, Pigweed, or Red Root*. The hottest and most tedious farm chore when I was a kid was weeding lamb's quarters from the sugar beets. We called it red root and I detested it. Today it is one of my favorite vegetables. Lamb's quarters is one of the world's most ubiquitous weeds; when cultivated and marketed it is called Chinese spinach.

The seeds of some varieties of this goosefoot-family member are used as a grain (see **Quinoa**), and its young leaves may be used in salads or as a spinach substitute. They have a delicate, refreshing flavor. Older leaves are red tinged and should not be consumed.

My resources do not list its nutritive properties, but it is reasonable to assume that it is comparable to spinach. It does contain oxalic acid. From my own observations, lamb's quarters are a good blood cleanser and are healthful to the liver and kidneys.

Leaf Lettuce   The tender and fragile leaf lettuce does not ship well and so has limited availability. It is primarily seen in the spring and the fall. Either red or green varieties are grown. Nutritionally, leaf lettuce is a superior choice to iceberg.

See **Lettuce** for information on selection, storage, and use and for nutritional and medicinal highlights.

Leek   Leeks are fondly called the sweet cousin of onions. They were such an important staple in medieval Europe that the Anglo-Saxon word *leek* once meant any vegetable.

Leeks are often found in the soup pot but may be substituted for onions in many recipes. Some people use just the white bulb and discard the green leaves; however, the leaves are an important source of nutrition and flavor and should be used as well. When preparing leeks, slice the vegetable in half lengthwise before washing. Otherwise the dirt that clings inside the leaves is difficult to remove.

Look for leeks with long, untrimmed leaves. Those with trimmed leaves are assuredly old. Refrigerate in plastic. Leeks are best used within four days of purchase.

In terms of energy the leek assists the liver and brings energy upward. Leeks are a good source of vitamins A, B complex, and C, and the trace minerals calcium and magnesium.

*   *   *

Welsh National Emblem

On Saint David's Day the Welsh wear a piece of leek in their buttonholes in memory of their A.D. 640 victory over the Saxons. At that battle, their forefathers wore a leek in their cap to distinguish themselves from their foes.

*   *   *

Legume Fruits contained within the pods of leguminous plants are beans, peas, peanuts, and lentils. Another family member, which is less recognizable as a legume, is jicama. See **Beans**.

Lemon Lemons have less sugar and more acid, primarily citric acid, than do oranges. They are used for their culinary virtues and medicinal properties. The juice or rind of this small citrus is added to a number of dishes for a refreshing, sour flavor. Lemon juice is one of the best home remedies for treating colds, fever, indigestion, obesity, and neuritis. It is also said effectively to decongest the liver and kidneys.

The two main varieties of domestic lemons are Lisbon, a smooth-skinned winter fruit with a long nipple at its blossom end; and Eureka, a more rounded fruit whose peak season is in the summer.

The lemon's high acidity may have an erosive action on teeth, and therefore sucking on lemons is not advised. All citrus (especially lemons) consumed in excess may deplete the bones and teeth of calcium reserves.

Organic lemons are available seasonally in some markets. For lemon peel, select these since commercial lemon skins are dyed and waxed.

See **Citrus Fruit** for information on selection, storage, and use and for nutritional and medicinal highlights.

*   *   *

Lemon Sole

Lemon sole does not mean sole cooked with lemon. It is rather a flat fish that is more like a dab or flounder than a sole. Its name probably comes from the French term *limande-sole,* which refers to a flat fish.

*   *   *

Lemon Grass The herb lemon grass is becoming increasingly available fresh. This reedlike grass delivers a pleasant lemony flavor, without the harsh lemon aftertaste. It enhances meat and vegetable recipes and is often an ingredient in Thai curries, bouquet garni, and herbal teas.

Peel and discard the fibrous outer layer, and use the tender center section. Or you may wrap the whole chopped herb in cheesecloth for easy removal after cooking. See **Herbs and Spices**.

Lentil One of the first cultivated crops, lentils comprised the "mess of pottage" for which Esau sold his birthright (Genesis 24:34). Lentils are eaten throughout the world as an inexpensive source of protein and have earned the name "poor man's meat." In Catholic countries, lentils were standard Lenten fare for those who could not afford fish.

Unlike other legumes, the lentil is shaped like a disk or lens. The most common lentil in the United States is a tan-brown color. In India, the greatest lentil-consuming country, over fifty varieties of lentils are cultivated. Dhal, an Indian dish, is made from husked and split lentils.

With the exception of soybeans, lentils are richer in protein than any other legume. Lentils are high in calcium, magnesium, sodium, potassium, phosphorus, chlorine, and vitamin A. They cook more quickly than other beans, and are most often used in soups.

Lentils are mild flavored—some would call them bland—and do not have the characteristic "beany" flavor. Thus, they lend themselves well to subtly seasoned soups and patés. Most people think of lentils in terms of soup. Try them in patés, turnovers, combined with vegetables, or alone.

Our domestic supply of lentils comes primarily from eastern Washington and northern Idaho. See **Beans** for information on selection, storage, and use and for medicinal and nutritional highlights.

Lettuce Lettuce accounts for a whopping 25 percent of all fresh vegetables consumed in the United States. Considering the wide variety of available vegetables this is an astounding figure. Lettuce is used almost exclusively raw; however, it may also be lightly cooked.

The five varieties of lettuce are butterhead, celtuce, iceberg, leaf, and romaine. Iceberg is used most widely because of its superior shipping qualities.

Lettuce is a cooling food and acts as a mild diuretic. It has some fiber, is low in calories, and contains no single mineral and vitamin in significant amounts.

Lima Bean Also known as *Butter Bean* and *Sieva Bean.* A newer member of the kidney-bean family, the lima is a favorite South American bean and takes its name from the capital of Peru. Today it is the main legume crop in tropical Africa. It does not thrive in cold climates. Limas are white and come in two sizes—large and small. The large are also known as butter beans and the small are called baby limas or sieva beans.

Limas are pale green and delicious when fresh. Dried, they are popular in succotash, soups, and casseroles or mashed like potatoes. They are starchier than other beans and lower in fats. Limas and other white beans are said to be medicinal to the liver.

Unlike other beans, the lima contains enough of the potentially toxic cyanide compounds that it requires special cooking attention. Boil lima beans in an uncovered pot and the hydrogen cyanide gas will escape with the steam. It is advisable to prepare all lima beans—fresh, dried, or sprouted—in this manner.[1]

See **Beans** for information on selection, storage, use and for nutritional and medicinal highlights.

Lime The citrus with the most fragile shelf life is the lime, and it is primarily grown and used in the tropics. Limes are smaller and rounder than lemons and yellow-green in color. Limes are used in the same way as lemons and are also used to flavor beverages. Select firm limes that are heavy for their size.

See **Citrus Fruit** for information on selection, storage, and use and for medicinal and nutritional highlights.

Lobster The best-flavored lobster comes from cold North Atlantic waters. The spiny rock lobster, or langouste, which is available from Florida, California, Australia, and South Africa, is actually a crawfish. Lobsters are a mottled blue-black when caught and turn a bright red color when cooked.

The shell of cooked lobster should be dry and tight and its tail tight and springy. It should smell fresh and pleasant. A live lobster should be lively, and if you stretch the tail out flat, it should snap back. Lobsters are most plentiful in the summer, when they live in shallow waters where they are more easily caught.

Although lobsters are high in cholesterol, they contain only half as much as eggs. They are the least fatty of fish and an excellent source of protein, calcium, iron, and B vitamins. See **Shellfish** for additional information.

Loganberry A hybrid cross between a blackberry and a raspberry, the loganberry is grown commercially for canning. It looks like a large but dull red raspberry, and it is more acidic than are blackberries.

See **Berries** for information on selection, storage, and use and for nutritional and medicinal highlights.

Lotus Root   Also known as *Renkon.* The beautiful lotus blossom, featured in Indian and Oriental art, is edible as well as its leaves, roots (rhizome), and seeds. The seeds and roots are available domestically in specialty shops. Lotus grows in tropical paddies with its sausage-shaped roots submerged in the mud. The leaves and blossoms float on top of the water.

The lotus rhizome is highly valued in Oriental cookery. Its crunchy texture and mild flavor enhance many dishes. Slice it thin and add to soups, stews, sautéed vegetable combinations, stir-fried, or deep-fried dishes. When sliced into rounds, it forms a beautiful floral pattern because of the air tunnels that run lengthwise through the root.

Lotus is in season in the fall and winter. Select firm, cream-colored roots free of bruises, soft spots, or discoloration. Uncut, the root stores well in the refrigerator for up to a week. Once cut it should be used within three days.

The medicinal properties of the root are well known in Oriental medicine. It is a warming food and is prescribed for lung-related ailments, to increase energy, control blood pressure, neutralize toxins, and help digestion. The linking part between two roots is considered to be the most medicinal.

Dried lotus root is available in specialty shops. It is packaged sliced into rounds. Reconstitute it by soaking it in water for two hours prior to use. It may be substituted for fresh lotus in most dishes.

Lotus Seed   The cream-colored lotus seed, which looks like a cooked chickpea, is known as a powerful medicinal food. This costly seed increases energy, promotes vitality, and aids digestion. The lotus seed contains 20 percent protein and so is highly nourishing.[2] It has a pleasant nutty flavor.

Lotus seeds require cooking. First soak them for several hours, and then boil them alone, as you would cook beans, for an hour. They may then be added to or cooked with other vegetable dishes.

Lotus Tea   Also known as *Kohren.* Packaged lotus tea, available in specialty shops, is made from crushed, dried, and powdered lotus root. It may also be made by finely grating a fresh root. The regular use of lotus tea is thought to build overall strength, and specifically to strengthen the heart, lungs, kidneys, and digestive system.

To make lotus-root tea, mix 2 teaspoons of dried lotus powder (or 2 tablespoons of freshly grated lotus root) into one cup of water. Add a pinch of salt, and heat over a low flame just to the boiling point. Drink hot. When ginger is added to this tea, it is said to be specifically medicinal for enteritis and digestive disorders.

Lychee   This bright red, rough-skinned fruit is similar to the plum in size and shape. The edible portion is between the skin and the large interior seed. The consistency of lychee flesh is similar to that of a grape and has a sweet acid flavor that makes it a popular last course of a traditional Chinese meal.

The lychee, long appreciated in its native China, is now also being grown commercially in Florida. The fruit is a good source of vitamins B and C. Its high presence of vitamin C indicates that it is a cooling and expansive fruit.

Lychees are most usually eaten fresh alone or in a fruit dish, but some are canned in syrup. Lychee "nuts" are made by drying the fruit, which takes on a nutty, raisinlike flavor. The lychee kernel is not edible.

Macadamia Nut   Of nuts, the fat macadamia is the most ravishingly rich in oil and flavor. This lush dessert and cocktail nut is especially difficult to crack, and so it is usually sold shelled, as well as roasted and salted.

Macadamias originated in Australia, but Hawaii has been the main producer of our domestic supply. California is developing a commercial crop. The supply of this tree nut currently does not meet the demand, and the costly macadamia is not always available.

See **Nuts** for information on selection, storage, and use and for medicinal and nutritional highlights.

Mâche   Also known as *Corn Salad* and *Lamb's Lettuce.* An attractive blue-green, this European salad herb is once again appearing in domestic markets but this time with a different moniker. What was available at the turn of the century as corn salad is back again as mâche. Its flavor is bland and lettucelike, and its texture is slightly chewy and firm. This hardy valerian-family member thrives in cold, wet regions and grows even through frost and snow.

Mâche usually has a spoon-shaped leaf that lends itself beautifully to arranged salads. It may also be used as a potherb.

Select very fresh heads with unblemished leaves. Most often sold with its roots attached, mâche is available in specialty-food stores throughout the year. Avoid mâche that has wilted or is dry. Use immediately.

Mackerel   A fish is classified as "fatty" if it has more than 1 percent fat. The mackerel contains from 6 to 13 percent fat. This economical, smooth-scaled fish has iridescent coloring when fresh. A mature mackerel averages fourteen inches long. Fresh mackerel is rich and gamy tasting. It may also be smoked, kippered, salted, and canned.

Mackerel is available during the spring and summer months. There are several varieties of mackerel, which are found throughout northern waters and in the Mediterranean. It is a high-protein fish.

See **Fish** for information on selection, storage, and use and for nutritional and medicinal highlights.

★   ★   ★

The Hibernating Fish

The mackerel hibernates. Huge schools clump together in deep-water troughs along the ocean floor during the winter months. Its high fat content enables hibernation.

★   ★   ★

Ma-Huang   Also known as *Ephedra.* An Oriental herb currently attracting much attention in the West is ma-huang *(Ephedra sinensis).* Its primary active ingredient, ephedrine, effects the human body as does adrenaline. However, this herb is chemically different; it is nontoxic, nonaddicting, and free of caffeine. Some people are using it as a healthful coffee replacement.

Specialty products containing high concentrations of ma-huang are being used as energy stimulants to improve stamina and endurance, stimulate perspiration, and significantly increase breathing capacity. It is also being used to relieve arthritis and to treat sinus and lung congestion. See **Herbs and Spices** for selection and storage information.

Maize   See **Corn**.

Malanga   See **Yautia**.

Malt   See **Barley Malt**.

Mango   The mango's sticky, sweet, lush flesh makes it a popular tropical fruit. A cashew relative, it normally has a smooth outer skin that ranges through green, yellow, and red. As the mango ripens, the skin color intensifies (green-skinned mangos excepted). The thick, leatherlike skin is inedible. Mangoes are generally round to oval and vary in weight from six ounces to one and a half pounds.

The juicy orange-colored flesh surrounds a large single stone. A mango contains from 10 to 20 percent sugar and has a rich and pleasing flavor. Its aroma is spicy. Mangoes are primarily eaten fresh but are also used in preserves or canned. Serve in fresh fruit salad or with ice cream. Chutney is made of unripened mangoes.

Select mangoes that are firm, plump, and fresh-looking and that have a pleasant aroma at the stem end. If there is no scent, the fruit is flavorless. Ripen at room temperature until soft, and then use or refrigerate. Most of our mangoes are imported, but some are grown in Florida. The Florida crop is in season during the summer.

This delectable fruit is a superior source of vitamins A and C and provides a good source of potassium. It is moderately high in calories. The mango is said to be a cooling and expansive food.

Mannitol The powdery dust on sticks of chewing gum is mannitol, and this powder is the most common use of mannitol. Natural mannitol is derived from seaweed or other plants. Inexpensive commercial mannitol is synthesized from sugar. When used in excess, mannitol has been implicated in kidney and gastrointestinal disturbances. See **Sweeteners**.

Maple Sugar The buff-colored maple sugar is made by evaporating the water from maple syrup. It is nearly 100 percent sucrose, with a subtle maple flavor. The human body reacts to it in essentially the same ways as it does to white sugar. See **Sugar** and **Sweeteners**.

Maple Syrup A prized and pricy sweetener, maple syrup rates a qualified endorsement as a healthful food. It undergoes a simple refining process—boiling or reverse osmosis. However, because maple sap contains only 3 percent sucrose it takes forty gallons of sap to yield one gallon of syrup! That is highly concentrated. And its sucrose content is 65 percent, which means that it is best used—and savored—in moderation. It causes insulin and adrenaline reactions—albeit less intense ones—like those brought on by white sugar.

There are four grades of maple syrup: Fancy, which comes from the first sap of the season; and Grades A, B, and C, which come from subsequent tappings. Fancy is the lightest colored syrup and has the highest sugar content. Grade C is the darkest syrup and has the highest mineral content. This is because the lower grades are more concentrated and are boiled longer and at higher temperatures.

There are some problems associated with the quality of pure maple syrup. One is that profit-oriented producers sometimes place a paraformaldehyde pellet in the tree's taphole to prolong sap flow. This contaminates the sap. The Canadian government prohibits use of these pellets, and so Canadian maple syrup is free of formaldehyde. Vermont producers reportedly refrain from using the pellets as well.

Maple syrup may be contaminated with very high levels of lead. This may be from the lead seams in the metal cans it is marketed in or from the homemade evaporating pans used by most producers. As the FDA limits the lead content of imported maple syrup, Canadian brands can be considered safe. There is no easy way to determine if domestic supplies have toxic quantities of lead without visiting the producers. Syrup processed only in stainless steel buckets, evaporating pans, and storage tanks, and marketed only in glass or plastic containers, would be lead free. Few producers can afford expensive stainless steel equipment.

Maple syrup adds moisture and denseness to baked goods. It is less sweet than honey and white sugar. Store maple syrup in a cool cupboard during cool months, but refrigerate during the summer. See **Sweeteners**.

★ ★ ★

Snow Candy

"Grandma stood by the brass kettle and with the big wooden spoon she poured hot syrup on each plate of snow. It cooled into soft candy, and as fast as it cooled they ate it. . . . There was plenty of syrup in the kettle, and plenty of snow outdoors. As soon as they ate one plateful, they filled their plates with snow again, and Grandma poured more syrup on it." (Laura Ingalls Wilder, *Little House in the Big Woods*.)[1]

★ ★ ★

Margarine   Margarine is made by bonding hydrogen molecules onto oil molecules (hydrogenation) to produce a solid, saturated kind of "plastic." Indeed, hydrogenation makes the molecular structure of oil the same as a plastic.[2] Regardless of its original source—petroleum or corn oil—our digestive enzymes do not assimilate plastic.

The "mouth feel" of margarine is reminiscent of petroleum jelly, and its flavor and aftertaste are pleasurable. Cottonseed oil is frequently present in margarine, and is one oil best to assiduously avoid. Margarine contains a host of additives such as preservatives, emulsifiers, plasticizers, artificial color and flavors, and synthetic vitamins. Its fats may be of animal or vegetable origin or a combination of both. If the margarine is of animal fat, it is as saturated as butter.

Saturated or not, margarine is hydrogenated, and hydrogenated foods are becoming increasingly suspect in the scientific community. They are implicated in heart disease[3] and interfere with the body's production of gamma-linolenic acid.

★ ★ ★

Bugs Are Smart!

"I placed a cube of margarine on a saucer on a windowsill that caught afternoon sun. I knew what would happen if it were butter: The heat of the sun through the glass would melt it down, it would begin to stink, mold would grow, bugs would find it—it would be an ugly mess until the forces of nature could manage to draw all the life from it. If margarine is really food, I reasoned, it will get attacked in the same way.

"Two years later I gave up waiting for anything alive to attack that margarine. It had only about half melted in all that time, it was quite dusty, but no stink, no mold, no bugs, *no sign of life.*"[4]—Fred Rohé

★ ★ ★

Marjoram   This favorite culinary herb is becoming increasingly available fresh. With its mild oregano flavor, marjoram adds an assertive pungency to fish, vegetable, and meat dishes. See **Herbs and Spices**.

Maté   Also known as *Yerba de Maté* An important beverage throughout South America, maté is readily available in the United States. Some people who desire a mild caffeine beverage prefer maté over coffee. It is available either green or roasted. The green has a mildly astringent flavor and the roasted has a more musky, earthy flavor.

Meat   See **Beef, Buffalo, Chicken, Fowl, Lamb, Pork, Rabbit**, and **Turkey**.

Mediterranean Squash   The Mediterranean is a winter squash that looks like a large butternut squash but internally has the texture of a spaghetti squash. It is sweet enough to use in pies and lends itself well to stuffing with vegetable, meat, or cheese combinations.

For information on selection, storage, and use and for medicinal and nutritional highlights see **Squash, Winter**.

Mekabu   See **Wakame**.

Melon Family   The gourd-family members known as melons are the most cooling and refreshing fruit and are fondly equated with lazy summer days. Watermelon is botanically unrelated to the melons listed below, which may be subdivided into three classes: cantaloupe, muskmelon, and winter melon. These three varieties do *not* interbreed with watermelon, but they do interbreed among themselves so readily that there are many varieties, with many new ones likely, and endless confusion about nomenclature.

To add to the muddle, what we in the United States call a cantaloupe is not. Rather it is a muskmelon. True cantaloupes have warty or scaly rinds (not netted) like the casaba or crenshaw. The muskmelon has a netted rind. Melons from both the muskmelon and cantaloupe family usually have orange, aromatic flesh and are best used within a few days after becoming fully ripe.

The winter melons, typified by the honeydew, are more readily recognized. They have green and mildly scented flesh with skin that is either smooth or shallowly corrugated, but not netted. Winter melons ripen late, and their hard rind enables them to be stored for a month or more. They are not to be confused with the squash called Chinese winter melon.

A melon's sugar content does not increase after picking so select ripe ones. Choose one that is heavy for its size and has a firm rind with no soft spots. Melons are grown in many southern states and in California. Off-season melons are imported from Mexico.

All melons are low in sodium. They are a good source of vitamins C and A, with the darker orange-fleshed melons being higher in vitamin A. A cooling and expansive fruit, melon are a fun food. (See also **Watermelon**.)

Technically a muskmelon, the golden-fleshed, lush cantaloupe is at its best from June through September. For a ripe cantaloupe, pick one with the most pronounced, coarse netting and the most even, dull color. Its stem should be completely gone. It should have a yellowish cast to the rind and a pleasant cantaloupe odor when held to the nose. Light thumb pressure applied to the blossom end of the melon should cause it to give slightly. Uncut, a ripe cantaloupe keeps for up to a week.

The casaba is round like a pumpkin but pointed slightly at the stem end. Its rind has deep wrinkles running from end to end. Some have a pale green rind and pale yellow flesh; others have a light orange to dark green rind with golden flesh. Look for a slight softening at the blossom end. A ripe casaba has no aroma until cut. Avoid a melon with dark, sunken spots.

Crenshaw melon rinds are smooth, golden, slightly corrugated, and unnetted. Their thick flesh is a bright salmon color. A crenshaw is ripe when it has a sweet smell.

The honeydew has a smooth, pale green skin and a very sweet, lime-green flesh. A slight "bloom," faint netting, and a slightly sticky feeling on its skin indicate a ripe honeydew. If it is very hard and has a white or green-white rind, the honeydew was picked prematurely and will not be sweet.

The Persian melon is esteemed as having the thickest and richest-tasting flesh. This globe-shaped fruit has a finely netted, dark green rind and orange flesh.

Michili Cabbage   See **Chinese Cabbage**.

Milk   Milk and milk-derived products are the number-one cause of food allergies. They are also among the most popular foods. Fermented dairy products are more digestible than are nonfermented ones. See **Dairy**.

Fresh milk forms include the following:

- Whole milk—has a minimum fat content of 3.25 percent.
- 2 percent and 1 percent—have, respectively, 2 or 1 percent fat.
- Skim milk—is essentially fat free.

- Unhomogenized milk—in which the cream floats at the top.
- Chocolate-flavored milk—flavored with 1 percent cocoa and 5 to 7 percent sugar.

Milk is available canned in two forms. Evaporated milk has had 60 percent of the water removed. Sweetened condensed milk is evaporated milk containing 40 to 45 percent added sugar.

Virtually all dried (or powdered) milk prepared for retail sales is spray dried by a low-heat process. It is called low-heat, nonfat dry milk and it may be further processed into instant nonfat dry milk. There is little difference in nutrient value between noninstant and instant dry milk. There is concern among nutritionists that the drying process damages the cholesterol in dried milk.

Millet   Millet is one of the first cereals used by man and is still an important staple in Asia and northern Africa. This small, yellow grain grows well in depleted soil and with insufficient water, so it is often thought of as food for the poor. Of the numerous varieties grown today, only one type, called pearl millet, is available for domestic consumption. It has a pleasing nutty flavor.

Of the true cereal grains, millet has the most complete protein and significantly more iron. It is gluten free. Due to its high alkaline ash content, it is the easiest grain to digest. Millet is the only grain that may be cooked without salt and be alkaline rather than acidic.

The smallest of common grains, millet is said to be good for the stomach and spleen and has some healing action in cases of gastrointestinal irregularities. When cooked with winter squash its medicinal value to the stomach and spleen is increased. Millet is the preferred grain in the treatment of blood-sugar imbalances.

Millet is delicious by itself, with condiments, sauces, vegetables, or beans, or in croquettes, soups, or casseroles. See **Grain**.

★   ★   ★

For the Birds

In North America, most corn is fed to cattle, most barley is brewed for beer, and most millet is used as birdseed. The primary claim to fame of the eastern Colorado town of Otis (population 700) is its reputation as the "Birdseed Capital of America."

★   ★   ★

Millet Flour   Millet flour gives a dry, delicate, cakelike crumb and a yellow color to baked goods. Fresh millet flour has a distinctive sweet flavor. When old, it is bitter and should be discarded. If millet flour is between sweet and bitter, you may revitalize it by pan-toasting it until it darkens one shade and emits a pleasing aroma.

Because millet has no gluten, its flour is best combined with wheat flour in baked goods. Try up to 20 percent millet flour in bread, and up to 50 percent for cookies and muffins. For sauces or a flat bread, it may be used alone. See **Flour**.

Mirin   Also known as *Chinese Cooking Wine*. Quality mirin is an ambrosial cooking wine that is, like sake, naturally brewed and fermented from sweet brown rice, rice koji, and water. The 13 to 14 percent alcohol in mirin evaporates quickly when heated but imparts a mild sweetness and rounds out the flavor of many dishes. In Asian cookery it is a basic seasoning.

Most of the mirin available in Oriental markets has not been naturally brewed and is sweetened with sugar or corn syrup. The sweet rice wine found in natural food stores is generally a natural and high-quality product. Still, it is important to read the label and to select naturally fermented mirin made only of sweet rice, rice koji, and water.

⛝ Use mirin for a glaze on piecrusts, pastries, and barbecued dishes. It is excellent in vinaigrettes, fish or vegetable dishes, sauces, and dips.

Miso Miso is a purée made of fermented soybeans, a grain, and salt. Prior to the 1970s *miso* was an unknown word—and taste experience—to most Americans. Today this traditional Japanese food is fast becoming an important staple for health-conscious people.

Miso's range of flavors and versatility endear it to simple home-style cooking as well as to sophisticated preparations. From sweet and light to meaty and hearty, miso complements a wide range of foods. Its most typical use is in soup, where it serves as a rich and flavorful bouillon.

Miso is a superior source of usable whole protein because it contains the eight essential amino acids. Its protein content ranges from 12 to 20 percent, depending upon the variety. It is also low in fat, neutralizes environmental pollutants, and is reputed in the Far East to promote health and longevity.[5]

Probably miso's most remarkable quality is as a digestive aid. This living food is "predigested" and actually helps digest other foods! Here is how. Whole populations of natural digestive enzymes, lactic acid bacteria, yeasts, and mold that thrive in miso help digest other foods in the large and small intestines. The living organisms in miso break down complex proteins, carbohydrates, and fats into more easily assimilable molecules.

Miso is made by fermenting a cooked grain with a starter to make *koji*. The koji is then blended with salt and cooked beans and allowed to ferment naturally for one month to several years. Making your own miso is a simple, enjoyable process.

Several varieties of miso are available. The preferred choice is unpasteurized and naturally fermented (rather than chemically processed) miso. If miso is a new taste experience, you may wish to start with a light colored variety that also has a lighter flavor. "Sweet" miso contains 6 percent salt and has a straw-yellow color; "mellow" miso contains up to 9 percent salt and is amber or reddish brown; and "country" miso contains 12 percent salt and is colored deep brown. Miso may be made from a variety of grains and legumes. The most common types are rice and barley. See also **Fermented Food**.

Barley (mugi) miso is made of soy, pearled barley, and salt. It is considered a good all-purpose miso. Natural barley miso requires up to one year of fermentation and is more strengthening than most rice varieties, which generally ferment for a shorter time. Barley miso is available in "mellow" and "country" styles.

Chickpea miso is a sensational American adaptation of an Oriental basic. In place of soy beans, chickpeas and a grain (barley or rice) are fermented. The rich result is a delectable, light-colored, light-flavored miso. It lacks the characteristic soy flavor. For a milklike cream soup, use chickpea miso and a soup stock in place of milk and other seasonings. Chickpea miso is available in "sweet" and "mellow" styles.

Instant miso is a popular ingredient in the ubiquitous ramen noodle soups. It is also available as an instant soup sans noodles. Controlled freeze-dried methods are used that do not destroy the lactobacillus in miso. Rather, instant miso is more concentrated and has 8,000 lactobacillus cells per gram, which is higher than in fresh miso.[6] Currently all instant miso is imported.

Natto miso, unlike other miso, is used not as a flavoring for soups but rather as a zippy condiment. Its base is barley miso, and it is flavored with ginger, kombu, and barley malt. Because of the added sweetener, natto miso has a short fermentation period of two months. It is high in sodium, but even a dab spiffs up a meal.

Rice (kome) miso ferments more quickly than barley miso and is, therefore, said not to be as strengthening. Rice miso is sweet and light and is traditionally used for summer cooking or in dressings. Rice miso is most typically a "sweet" miso. A brown rice miso (called genmai) has some availability and is heartier, darker in color, and higher in salt than that made of refined rice.

Soy (hatcho) miso is unique among misos, for it is grain-free. Hatcho consists only of soy and salt. Thus, it requires longer fermentation and is the heartiest, strongest flavored, darkest colored, and saltiest miso.

*   *   *

Miso May Prevent Radiation Sickness

William Shurtleff and Akiko Aoyagi, authors of *The Book of Miso* report that Japanese scientists "discovered a substance in miso which they called Zybicolin. Produced by miso and *natto* yeasts, it has the ability to attract, absorb, and discharge from the body radioactive elements such as strontium."[7]

*   *   *

Mochi   One of the best "instant" natural foods on the market is mochi. Mochi is a fun food and a favorite of all ages. Pounded sweet rice, unadorned or flavored with a variety of ingredients, spells *mochi* and mochi spells *more.*

To make mochi, cook sweet rice and then pound it with a baseball bat until it becomes so glutenous that it takes all your strength to pull the bat from the rice. Or, buy it ready prepared, either fresh or frozen, from a natural or Asian food market. To prepare ready-made mochi, brown both sides in a skillet (with or without oil), bake or deep fry until it puffs, or cook it in a waffle iron. Eat it out of hand for a snack, as a grain entrée, or as a dumpling in a soup.

Mochi is sticky. It is satisfying and energizing. The Japanese traditionally celebrate New Year's Day with mochi and also consider it especially beneficial for pregnant and lactating women and for those with anemia and blood-sugar irregularities. See **Rice**.

Molasses   The positive thing to be said about molasses is that it contains all the minerals that have been refined out of white sugar. It is a fine source of minerals.

However, it is a by-product of sugarcane manufacture. Thus, molasses is also processed and it has an adverse effect on the blood-sugar level. Molasses differs from sugar in flavor, texture, color, and mineral content. Its calcium and iron content are significant. It also contains magnesium, potassium, zinc, copper, and chromium. Less desirable substances in molasses are the concentrated amounts of pesticides and industrial toxins, which may include sulfur.

There are three types of molasses. Light molasses is the residue from the first extraction of sugar and is quite sweet. Dark, or blackstrap, molasses is slightly sweet and strongly aromatic; it comes from the third extraction. Medium molasses is from the second extraction and in color and flavor is between the others. Unsulfured molasses indicates that sulfur was not employed in the refining process.

Blackstrap molasses is an excellent source of calcium, with 116 milligrams per tablespoon. Light and medium molasses have 33 and 58 milligrams per tablespoon respectively.

Monukka Raisins   See **Raisin**.

Morel   Fresh morels offer an unusual taste experience. Their flavor is hard to describe, but the eminent food expert, Elizabeth Schneider, comes closest: "The flavor of morels varies; it may suggest warm autumn leaves, hazelnuts, or even nutmeg. As with truffles and caviar, tasting is believing."[8]

Morels are the most esteemed of edible mushrooms. They are crisscrossed with irregular pale brown ridges that produce a spongelike appearance. A favorite in French cuisine, morels are available fresh and dried. Look for fresh morels in the spring in specialty markets. They are costly. Select those that smell sweet and look fresh. Refrigerate and use within two days.

See **Mushroom Family** for information on selection, storage, and use and for medicinal and nutritional properties.

Muesli A European variation of granola, muesli (mews-lee) is a combination of grains, flakes, seeds, nuts, and raisins. Cook muesli for a hot breakfast cereal, or add water, let it sit overnight, then serve.

Mugi Miso See **Miso**.

Mung Bean In the United States, most people think of mung beans in terms of sprouting. More people are delighting in mung pasta, which looks like cellophane (see **Pasta**). This small green member of the kidney bean family originated in India and plays an important part in the national cuisine of China.

Mung bean flour is widely used in India, and the beans also may be cooked like other dried beans. Of dried legumes, mung beans and chickpeas have the highest amount of vitamin A. The mung bean is considered a cooling food and is good for the liver.

See **Beans** for information on selection, storage, and use and for nutritional and medicinal highlights.

Mushroom Family Mushrooms, a fungus, are one of the most primitive of plants. They do not contain chlorophyll (as do vegetables), so instead of converting sunlight into food they must receive their nourishment from other organic matter, as do scavengers or parasites. The mushroom is actually the fruit of the fungus, which remains underground.

Although "fruit of the fungus" does not sound appetizing, these fruits are indeed among the most costly, exotic, and delectable of foods. Like a sponge, they soak up the essence of whatever they are cooked in; thus, the more finely they are sliced, the more flavor they absorb. In a sauce or sautéed, they add a meatlike flavor and color.

Mushrooms, Commercial Relatives of the wild field mushroom, the common, or supermarket, mushrooms are bred for their shipping and keeping properties, not their taste. Their primitive reproductive process is very difficult to simulate; thus commercial mushrooms require high technology to grow and are one of the most chemically treated crops. As a result, commercial mushrooms lack the vitality, medicinal properties, and flavor of wild mushrooms. Natural food buffs who favor energizing foods frequently disdain this type of mushroom.

Select buttons rather than open caps, as the open ones tend to have a musty flavor. Refrigerate unwashed in paper towels (not plastic bags) for up to four days. See **Mushroom Family**.

Muskmelon See **Melon Family**.

Mussel Called the poor man's oysters because of their relative cheapness, mussels are tender and sweet. They deteriorate rapidly, so extra care must be taken that their shells are tightly closed before cooking. Never eat mussels from contaminated waters. Mussels live in all oceans of the world, but those from colder waters have the best flavor.

Mussels are available year-round. They yield more food per pound than oysters or clams because their shells are thin. This shellfish is low in fat, calories, and carbohydrates; it is a good source of protein, iron, calcium, and vitamins. Mussels are said to energize the reproductive organs.

See **Shellfish** for information on selection, storage, and use and for nutritional and medicinal highlights.

Mustard Greens Mustard greens are a pungent, bright green plant with curly leaves that grows wild throughout the world. Its seeds are used as a spice or ground and mixed into a paste with water or wine.

Mustard greens, as well as the seed, are said to have medicinal properties for the lungs and colon. Like collards and kale, mustard greens are a superior source of calcium, iron, and vitamin A.

The greens are available all year long but are at their peak in the winter and spring. Select young, fresh-looking greens. They are extremely perishable and should be used within a day or so. If their pungent flavor is too strong when raw or steamed, you may prefer to boil or sauté them lightly. They are especially delicious when sautéed with garlic.

N

Napa   See **Chinese Cabbage**.

Natto   Fondly called the Limburger of soy, powerful-tasting natto is a most unusual food. It looks like innocuous brown soybeans until you dip a spoon into it and pull the spoon away. Then hundreds of hair-fine strands stretch up to ten inches in length. These strands contain countless enzymes, bacteria, and fungi. For some, natto is an acquired taste, while others love it and its mozzarellalike stringiness from the first.

Natto, which contains no salt, is an excellent source of protein. It is a digestive aid said to be medicinal for the regenerative organs and to help regulate blood sugar.

It is available frozen in some natural food stores and in Oriental markets. To serve, thaw the natto and mix it with a little mustard or shoyu. Allow one tablespoon per serving. It is also added to soups and noodles.

Natto Miso   See **Miso**.

Navy Bean   See **Great Northern Bean**.

Nectarine   The nectarine is like a smooth-skinned peach only it has a sweeter and richer flavor, brighter color, and is generally smaller in size. Both peaches and nectarines are either freestone or clingstone. Nectarines are most frequently eaten out of hand. They are more costly and fragile and generally less available than peaches.

The majority of nectarines are produced in California and are in season from late summer through September. Out-of-season nectarines are imported from South America or the Mideast.

Like all stone fruit (cherries excepted), commercial nectarines are picked while still hard and therefore not fully sweet. Once picked, their sweetness will not increase, but they do soften when kept at room temperature. Tree-ripened nectarines, available seasonally at farmer's markets, are incomparably superior. Use nectarines interchangeably with peaches and apricots in fruit salads, preserves, and cooked desserts.

Nectarines are high in vitamin A and low in calories. They are said to be medicinal to the lungs.

New Zealand Spinach   As its name suggests, this vegetable originated in New Zealand. Like spinach, it is a member of the goosefoot family, and it is an excellent spinach alternative. Its leaves are more porous and smaller than those of spinach.

For home gardeners the major endearing property of New Zealand spinach is that it is impervious to heat. When the hot summer sun wilts spinach, lettuce, and other salad greens, this vegetable thrives.

New Zealand spinach is available from the spring through the fall. Favor the young leaves and shoots. Refrigerate for up to five days. Use as you would spinach, either cooked or raw in salads.

With the exception of potassium, spinach is a richer source of vitamins and micronutrients than is New Zealand spinach. New Zealand spinach is high in oxalic acid. See **Goosefoot Family**.

Nigari   Extract salt from seawater and the residue that remains is primarily magnesium chloride with additional trace minerals. This residue is called nigari and is the traditional coagulant used in making tofu. A tofu label that lists magnesium chloride as an ingredient is not recommended, for it is highly refined nigari.

Tofu may be made with other coagulants such as vinegar, lemon juice, or calcium sulfate. The latter is prefered nutritionally because it increases the calcium content by three and a half times more than if other coagulants are used.

However, for flavor, fresh nigari-made tofu is unsurpassable. Nigari is available in natural-food stores and in Oriental markets.

Nightshades (*Solaraceae*) The nightshade family, whose member belladonna is known as "deadly nightshade," includes plants that literally grow during the night. Other plants grow during the day only. The nightshades originated in subtropical areas and were long considered poisonous by Europeans.

Today the nightshades figure importantly in the diets of people throughout the world. Have we adapted to their toxic substances or were these substances bred out? Traditional uses of nightshades often suggest long cooking or special preparations to make their flavorful flesh more balanced fare.

See entries for individual nightshade members: **Eggplant, Ground Cherry, Pepper, Potato, Tomatillo,** and **Tomato**.

*   *   *

Nightshades and Arthritis

In his book *Childers' Diet to Stop Arthritis: The Nightshades and Ill Health,* Norman F. Childers, Ph.D., professor of horticulture at Rutgers, reveals a correlation between arthritis and rheumatism and nightshade consumption. According to Dr. Childers' studies, when some people eliminate these foods from their diet their arthritis or rheumatism symptoms are alleviated or even disappear.[1]

*   *   *

Noodles See **Pasta**.

Nopale Also known as *Cactus Pad.* The prickly pear cactus pad is a popular Mexican vegetable called nopale. Its mucilaginous quality does not appeal to some, but its soft crunchy texture and pleasant flavor make this vegetable worth experimenting with at least once.

Look for pads that are stiff, firm, and around eight inches long. Much larger pads are available but tend to be fibrous. Nopales may be refrigerated in plastic for several weeks.

Cultivated nopales are without spines and may be easily peeled with a vegetable peeler. Wild prickly pear pads have their thorns intact. Grasp such a pad with tongs and cut off the prickers with a sharp knife. Then peel and discard the skin.

Nopale enhances egg, tomato, and cheese dishes. Add to soups and stews ten minutes prior to serving, and it serves as a thickener and imparts a pleasing flavor.

Nori Also known as *Laver.* Several years ago in the Saturday market of the small British coastal town Barnstaple, I purchased freshly harvested laver (nori), cooked and seasoned with vinegar. Despite its black color and sludgelike texture it was absolutely exquisite, with a fresh sea essence and full range of flavors. Traditionally, the British incorporate laver into in a variety of dishes, including a popular laver-oat bread.

Wild Maine nori is sold dried and requires long cooking to soften it. The superb flavor and energetic properties of wild nori, like the Barnstaple laver, make it worth seeking out. It is becoming increasingly available in specialty shops. (See the packages or traditional British cookbooks for recipes.)

The bulk of our commercial nori is dried, imported from Japan, and, unlike other sea vegetables, cultivated. Nori spores are scattered over shallow inlets into which bamboo poles supporting nets have been sunk. Months later, mature nori is hand harvested, washed, chopped, and spread over bamboo mats to dry into paper-thin sheets.

Sheets of nori are used to wrap sushi and rice balls or can be cut or torn and used as a garnish or in soups. Nori may be used as is or lightly toasted by slowly waving it over an open flame or the burner of an electric stove. It has a delicious, delicate, nutlike flavor and is a favorite finger food for the very young.

In Hawaii a different variety of nori, called limu eleele, is salted, chopped, and used as a relish. It is an essential ingredient in the Japanese condiment called seven-spice seasoning.

Nori is remarkable in that it contains more vitamin A than carrots. It has an incredible 35.6 percent protein, which makes it higher than soybeans, meat, milk, fish, or poultry. It is also high in B vitamins and vitamins C and D, and it is a good source of calcium, iron, potassium, iodine, and many trace elements.

Nori is a natural complement to fatty foods, for it emulsifies fat and aids digestion. The enzyme cholesterase, which breaks down cholesterol, is found in large amounts in nori.[2]

See **Sea Vegetables** for nutritional and medicinal highlights.

Nut and Seed Butters   Seeds and nuts ground into a paste are called butters. The all-American favorite is, of course, peanut butter, which is also the most economical. About 700 million pounds of peanut butter are produced annually. Other butters include almond, cashew, sunflower, and sesame (from whole sesame seeds) and tahini (from hulled sesame seeds).

Nut and seed butters become rancid when stored for a long time, especially in warm weather. It's best to purchase butters in small quantities, and if they are used infrequently, to refrigerate them.

Homemade butters are easily made from a variety of nuts (or seeds), or a combination of them. Grind roasted nuts in a blender, meat grinder (use the finest attachment), steel (not a stone) grain mill, or nut-butter machine. Add salt (optional), and if the paste seems dry, a little oil.

Nut and seed butters provide healthful alternatives to butter when used moderately. In excess, they are hard to digest. Add them to sauces, cookies, icings, salad dressings, candies, dips, and spreads. They are high in fat and protein and are thus warming foods. Tahini is 25 percent protein! Nut butters are rich in fiber, highly unsaturated, and low in cholesterol.

See also **Almond Butter, Peanut Butter, Sesame Butter,** and **Tahini**.

NutraSweet   See **Aspartame**.

Nuts   Nuts were an important staple for early humans, and over the eons their popularity has not waned. They are easily cultivated and exceptionally nourishing. Nuts left in their shells ship well; almonds have been used as currency; and the lowly peanut, thanks to George Washington Carver, changed the public health and economy of the Deep South.

Generally, nuts grow on trees and have a hard, removable outer shell and a soft, edible inner seed. Not everything we call a nut is a nut. Almonds are a fruit, peanuts a legume, and pine and Brazil nuts are seeds. They are, however, all nutritionally similar to nuts and so are conveniently categorized with them.

From a nutritional standpoint, nuts are an excellent source of protein; some are nearly as protein rich as meat. Most nuts are good sources of calcium, phosphorus, magnesium, and potassium and contain some of the B vitamins. Some have vitamin E, and a few contain vitamins A and D. They are high in unsaturated fats, which makes them an important food for strict vegetarians. Because of their oil content, nuts are high in calories and take longer to digest than other plant foods.

Fatty foods, such as nuts, are particularly hard on the liver and gall bladder and may congest the intestines. Clogged intestines are said to correlate with cloudy thinking.

The oil content of nuts makes them easily prone to rancidity once they are shelled. The shell shields the kernel from spoilage, fumigants, and other chemical treatments. Therefore buy unshelled, unroasted nuts for freshness, economy, and health. Nuts in unbroken shells keep for about a year if stored in a cool, dry place.

For convenience, purchase shelled nuts in small quantities and refrigerate them. They will keep for several months. If rubbery, moldy, or acrid tasting, they are rancid and should be discarded. Sliced, broken, roasted, flavored, and blanched nuts are more prone to rancidity than are whole nuts.

Most dry-roasted nuts contain sugar, salt, starch, monosodium glutamate, vegetable gums, spices, and preservatives. Avoid packaged nuts as the packaging frequently has been chemically treated. See also **Almond, Brazil Nut, Cashew, Chestnut, Filbert, Hazelnut, Macadamia Nut, Peanut, Pecan, Pine Nut, Pistachio, Seeds,** and **Walnut.**

★   ★   ★

When You Want Nuts, But Not Fat, Go for Chestnuts

Grams fat per 100 grams edible portion

Macadamia nuts	71.6
Pecans	71.2
Brazil nuts	66.9
English walnuts	64.8
Almonds	54.0
Sesame seeds, whole	53.4
Peanuts	48.4
Cashews	45.7
Chestnuts	1.5

★   ★   ★

O

Oat Bran Cooked oatmeal is sticky because its bran contains a fibrous, water-soluble oat "gum." This oat gum is high in beta glucan. Beta glucan is currently receiving rave reviews for its ability to reduce serum cholesterol levels. Not only does it reduce the levels of low-density lipoproteins (undesirable cholesterol), but it maintains the desirable high-density lipoproteins.

Currently, the studies differ as to whether oat bran or oatmeal is the most effective blood cleanser. Both work. Experiment with each—in baking and for hot cereal—and see which you prefer. Oat bran is a more refined food product and it is not as filling or warming as oatmeal. However, as with wheat bran, it does aid in elimination.

The flavor of oat bran is satisfyingly sweet and almost reminiscent of mother's milk. Unlike rolled oats, it is not sticky. See also **Oats**.

Oat Flour There are several excellent reasons to experiment with oat flour. Oats have a natural antioxidant that enables baked products to retain their freshness longer than wheat flour products. Oat flour is sweet and produces a cakelike crumb that makes it an excellent addition to cookies, piecrusts, yeast breads, and muffins. Oats contain very little gluten; thus their flour is combined with wheat in leavened breads.

For a dairy-free but milklike base, use oat flour in soups and sauces. In Scotland oat flour is used in everything from bannocks to breading fish. Oat flour is easy to make. Place oats—rolled or whole—in a blender and whizz into flour. A nut grinder or coffee mill works equally well.

Oats Wild oats, native to Europe and the United States, were long considered a weed before being cultivated. As the Romans conquered Europe they sowed their cultivated oats. Oats do best in cold, damp climates, and they thrive in the northern part of the British Isles, where they are still a staple grain. Our domestic supply of oats is grown in the northern Midwest.

Oats contain the highest percentage of sodium and unsaturated fat of any grain, and also an antioxidant that delays rancidity. High in protein, they have an amino-acid content similar to that of wheat. Only the outer husk is removed during milling, so oat products retain more of their original nutrients than do processed wheat products.

Oats are good for digestion and can act as a mild laxative. They are said to help regulate the thyroid and blood sugar. People who are allergic to wheat find oats a delicious replacement. Oats are most often used as breakfast food but are certainly more versatile. The whole groat may be cooked like brown rice.

Unlike other grains, oats must be steamed before their two inedible outer hulls can be removed. They are then rolled to reduce cooking time. Instant oats vary in that they are thinner, less hearty, and require shorter cooking time. They make a delicious creamlike base for soup and may be added to breads, cookies, casseroles, croquettes, and, of course, granola.

Coarsely cut oat groats require more cooking time than rolled oats but less than whole oats. They are termed steel cut. See **Grain, Oat Bran,** and **Oat Flour**.

Oil The seed is the embryonic plant, which contains all the nourishment required to propagate a new plant. One of the most significant components of the seed is its oil. Or as the anthroposophists aptly put it, "The tremendous condensation of the plant process that occurs in the seed very much needs the fine envelope of warmth provided by the oil."[1] Our vegetable oils come not from the root, stalk, leaf, or flower but rather from the reproductive part, from the nut, grain, seed, or, in the case of the olive, the fruit.

Consider a corn plant. The total weight of an eight-foot-tall plant including its root system is measured in pounds. The weight of the oil pressed from the corn of that same plant is measured in grams. Oil is a highly concentrated food, a warming food, and one best used in moderation.

We are going to be hearing more, not less, about oils and fats. Since the 1960s numerous health problems have been associated with overconsumption of fatty foods and specifically with saturated fats. New studies indicate that poor-quality polyunsaturated fatty acids (PUFAs) may be *equally* responsible for degenerative health problems.

For health, we daily require about one teaspoon of PUFAs. These essential acids naturally occur in vegetable and fish oils and human milk. The problem is that PUFAs easily become rancid and form free radicals, which may accelerate aging and weaken the immune system. Furthermore, overprocessed or rancid oils and fats interfere with the body's utilization of PUFAs.

Fortunately, it is easy to tell if a vegetable oil is overprocessed or rancid. A rancid oil tastes acrid and burns the tongue and throat. If an oil is solid at room temperature or has no flavor or food aroma, it is highly processed. Or in the words of natural-food expert Phil Levy, "Your nose will easily distinguish between heavily processed oil and natural oil: the first one smells like a breeze that just passed over a parking lot. The second one carries with it the true bouquet of olives, corn, sesame seeds, peanuts, soybeans or safflower. Where there is strong natural flavor and aroma, there is always an equal amount of nutritional value."[2]

A description of how the majority of oils are processed, or refined, is sobering. The oil is separated from its food source with hexane or other petroleum solvents and then boiled to drive off the solvents. This technique significantly reduces vitamin E content. The oil is next refined, bleached, and deodorized, which involves heating it to over 400 degrees. Antioxidants such as BHA or BHT are then frequently added. The resulting product lacks flavor, aroma, pigments, and nutrients. All that can be said for such an oil is that it has an extended shelf life, a clear, uniform color, and an oily texture.

Hydrogenated oils are made from PUFAs but are highly processed. Hydrogenation saturates the fatty acids with hydrogen gas to change the molecular structure. A natural saturated fat such as butter or lard is preferable to a hydrogenated vegetable oil such as margarine or shortening. (See **Margarine** for more details.)

Fractionated oil, such as palm kernel oil, is highly processed to duplicate the melt-in-your-mouth property of cocoa butter. Real chocolate is a more healthful choice than a food containing fractionated palm kernel oil. It is also more satisfying and tasty.

Fortunately, quality oils are available that are 100 percent expeller pressed. An expeller press is a large screwlike device that presses the seeds against walls of a slotted steel barrel and forces the oil out. The oil is then filtered and bottled.

An expeller-pressed oil has a shelf life of four to six months if stored in a cool, dark place. It should be purchased in small quantities and refrigerated. This superior oil will taste and smell like the food from which it was extracted. Such an oil contains minerals, phosphatides, and vitamin E and is high in trace nutrients. It enhances the flavors of foods it is cooked with.

Three vegetable oils *not* recommended are cottonseed oil, because it may be chemically contaminated, and highly saturated palm kernel and coconut oils.

See **Fat, Margarine,** and individual oils: **Canola (Rapeseed), Coconut, Corn Oil, Cottonseed Oil, Olive Oil, Palm Kernel Oil, Peanut Oil, Safflower Oil, Sesame Oil, Soy Oil,** and **Sunflower Oil**.

* * *

The "Cold-Pressed" Hype

The term *cold-pressed* is (with the exception of olive oil) a marketing term. Cold-pressed oils can be alkali washed, bleached, deodorized, and degummed. Such oils are labeled cold-pressed to give the false appearance of a wholesome product.

Your nose and taste buds can immediately recognize a quality 100 percent expeller-

pressed oil, for such an oil will smell and taste like the food from which it was made. A highly refined oil, even if called cold-pressed, has *zero* food aroma and flavor.

* * *

Okra   Also known as *Gumbo.* A vegetable that is becoming chic, thanks to the interest in regional cuisine, is okra. The size and shape of okra suggest their alternate, descriptive name, *lady's fingers.* In Southern food dishes it is called gumbo. A relative of cotton, mature okra pods are used for rope making, and the seeds are pressed for edible oil. Okra seeds are also roasted and used as a coffee substitute.

Okra is a hot-weather food and is available from middle summer into Indian summer. Select small okra, preferably under four inches. Okra above seven inches becomes fibrous. This mildly sweet vegetable does not store well and is best used within three days of purchase.

Some people are put off by the sticky, mucilaginous texture of okra, whereas others enjoy it. Garden-fresh okra is delicious lightly steamed and seasoned and eaten like green beans. Sliced into rounds, it looks like fanciful little wheels. Okra goes well with tomatoes and highly seasoned vegetable dishes and serves as an excellent thickener in soups and stews. Do not cook it in aluminum or cast iron.

Okra is high in carotene and contains B-complex vitamins and vitamin C. In terms of energy, it is an expansive food.

Olive Oil   Like fine wines, different olives and processing techniques produce a wide range of subtle oil flavors. Have at least one superior-quality olive oil on hand to complement your most delicately flavored foods.

Sweet and nutty-flavored olive oil is esteemed not only for its taste but its nutrition as well. It is high in vitamin E and so resists rancidity. Olive oil is also high in monounsaturated fats, which appear to effectively lower the undesirable low-density lipoproteins.

The best olive oil comes from hand-picked fruit that is crushed, stone or hydraulic pressed, separated from the olive water, and then filtered. It is termed *virgin olive oil,* and (unlike other oils) is accurately described as cold-pressed.

Compared to other natural oils, olive oil is low in linoleic acid and both saturated and polyunsaturated fats. Most of its fat is monounsaturated, which results in a heavier, more fatty oil that becomes semisolid at cold temperatures. Olive oil contains small amounts of iron, copper, and calcium.

Almost all olive oil is imported from the Mediterranean area, although olives are grown commercially in California. See also **Oil**.

* * *

Grades of Olive Oil

There are five grades of olive oil. The best are termed *virgin* and are cold pressed and greenish tinted. The lesser two grades are extracted, rather than cold pressed, and are straw yellow in color.

- Extra virgin comes from the low-yield first pressing.
- Fine virgin comes from the second pressing and is more acidic.
- Virgin is the third pressing, the most acidic and least costly of cold-pressed olive oils.
- Pure olive oil is solvent extracted from the pulp and pits remaining after virgin oil is pressed.
- Natural pure olive oil is extracted without solvents from olive pulp and pits.

* * *

Onion   Called the "rose of the roots," the onion is not even a root vegetable (it's a bulb), but its perfume is as distinctive as the rose's.

Like garlic, the onion is valued for its alleged medicinal properties, which include improving kidney function, lowering cholesterol, and serving as an antibacterial agent. The onion and its relatives are prohibited in yogic diets because they increase body heat and the appetites.

Select firm onions that have papery, dry skin, little or no neck, and no soot. It is best to store them in a cool dry place with air circulation, such as a pantry. If you must refrigerate them, place them in a tightly closed plastic bag to prevent moisture accumulation. Do not store onions close to potatoes or other moist foods.

Onions contain about 90 percent water and are low in calories. They have vitamins A, B complex, and C. Most commercial onions come from California, Texas, New York, Oregon, and Idaho. Regardless of the variety, the farther south an onion is grown, the milder it is.

Globe onions are also called yellow or white onions depending upon their skin color. Globes are the best-keeping onions and are available year-round. They are a good all-purpose onion. Small- and medium-size globes are pungent, whereas larger globes tend to be more sweet.

Pearl or pickling onions are radish size and may be layered like miniature onions or have a single flesh layer like a garlic clove. The small size of this pungent onion affords great eye appeal in fancy dishes. They are time consuming to peel; expedite peeling by parboiling first.

Spanish and Bermuda onions are sweeter and milder tasting than globes. They are favored for raw use but may also be used in cooking. These onions are higher in moisture and do not store as well as globes.

*   *   *

Crying over Onions

There are as many techniques for preventing tears while peeling onions as there are cures for hiccups. Some people tear just looking at a raw onion, and others can chop for hours and stay dry. Freshly harvested and past-prime onions are the most irritating.

To lessen the tears, try peeling onions under running water or chilling the onion first. People who wear contact lenses are not bothered, so if you do not wear lenses, you might try goggles.

*   *   *

Onion Family   Unequivocally the most outstanding characteristic of the onion, or Alliaceae, family is a characteristic strong taste and smell. Onions and related crops have been used by humans for more than six thousand years and probably originated in Asia Minor. They grow throughout the world and are the most universally used vegetable and flavoring agent.

Although many cuisines and individuals find the onion family indispensable, there are cultures and individuals who disdain the whole clan or specific members. Onions and garlic are the most potent of this group.

See also **Chive, Elephant Garlic, Garlic, Leek, Onion, Scallion,** and **Shallot.**

Orange   An orange is an orange is a berry. Yes, the subtropical, orange-colored citrus is botanically considered a berry.

There are two main types of oranges—the sweet or China orange, and the bitter or Seville orange. Bitter oranges are primarily used in marmalade and for the aromatic and tonic properties of their peel. They are not readily available in the United States but are worth seeking out for their superior cooking properties.

Color is not a useful guideline when purchasing oranges. Unlike other fruits, all citrus fruit is tree ripened, but temperature variation may cause a color change. Some oranges are gassed with ethylene to decompose the chlorophyll and render the fruit a cosmetic orange color. Many oranges are routinely colored with red dye.[3] Under current FDA regulations fresh produce with colors, waxes, and chemical additives must be identified with a sign at the retail level. This regulation is currently not being enforced.

Avoid oranges that have dark brown spots, soft spots, or have a puffy-looking or thick peel. Select those that are heavy for their size. Store loose in a dry and cool, but not cold, place.

Oranges are famed for their high vitamin C content. They also contain potassium and some calcium. The interior white membrane is a superior source of bioflavonoids (vitamin P).

Nearly 80 percent of sweet oranges are grown for juice; the remainder are eaten fresh. The two main varieties grown domestically are navel and Valencia. Prepared orange juice imported from South American countries is becoming increasingly available in the United States.

Navel oranges are seedless and named for the bellybutton-like spot at their blossom end. Native to Brazil and favored for eating, their bumpy skin indicates a thick rind that is easy to peel. Their peak season is from November to May.

Valencia oranges are favored for juicing. They have numerous pips (seeds) and a sweet and juicy pulp. Their skin is thin and smooth; they are primarily available in spring and summer.

Blood oranges have a dramatic red-orange flesh and are exceptionally sweet and juicy. (The flesh color may be spotted or totally colored with a flamboyant red.) The skin color may be uniformly orange or a combination of orange and red. This delightful pipless orange is imported from southern Spain, Italy, or Israel, although domestic orchards are now being developed. It will undoubtedly be more widely consumed in the United States. See **Citrus Fruit**.

★　　★　　★

Bridal Bouquet

The tradition of brides wearing orange blossoms may come from the story of Jupiter giving an orange to Juno when they were wed. Whatever the myth, orange blossoms are so fragrant and beautiful that they naturally invite inclusion in special bouquets.

★　　★　　★

Orange Juice　See **Juice, Fruit**.

Organic　When used by a chemist, the term *organic* refers to any carbon-containing compound. When used to describe a food, *organic* refers to one grown without the use of synthetically compounded fertilizers, pesticides, growth regulators, and livestock feed additives.

An organic farmer is one who uses practices that are in harmony with nature. His major aim is to preserve and increase the humus in the topsoil. Humus is a complex living organism full of bacterial, microbial, and insect life. Health—be it human, animal, or plant—is directly related to the health of the soil.

Chemically treated soil becomes dead. It yields inferior food, contaminates the environment, and is implicated in the increasingly prevalent phenomenon of "desertification."

There is a groundswell of enthusiasm for organic food products even though they are more expensive than commercial foods. California was the first state with guidelines to certify organically grown foods, and some other states are following suit.

Oriental Brassicas　See **Bok Choy** and **Chinese Cabbage**.

Oxalic Acid　A popular belief is that foods containing oxalates decrease calcium absorption and may contribute to the formation of kidney stones. The vegetables highest in oxalic acid are spinach, New Zealand spinach, rhubarb, beet greens, lamb's quarters, purslane, and Swiss chard. Other foods high in oxalics are whole sesame seeds, coffee, and chocolate.

Nutritional educator and author Jeffrey Bland mantains that the oxalic acid controversy is overblown. Although some people have kidney-stone problems that may be associated with excessive oxalates, he maintains that "these problems are more the exception than the rule—spinach, beet tops and all those products are good sources of dietary calcium."[4]

Columnist and author Robert McDougal concurs that even daily servings of oxalate-containing vegetables do not influence calcium retention. However, they may be implicated in kidney-stone formation if the diet is also high in animal proteins and fats.[5]

Oyster For centuries the oyster has been a gastronomic favorite. The first known oyster farm was in Italy in 102 B.C. This exquisite delicacy is at its best in cold weather when it is not spawning. Oysters from southern waters spawn throughout the year; they are not as flavorful and so are often served highly condimented.

As with other bivalve shellfish, fresh oysters should be tightly closed, or if open, should snap shut if tapped. Oysters are also available without their shells (be certain to remove any bits of shell before serving), either frozen, shucked, prebreaded, canned, or smoked.

All oysters are gathered from commercial beds where they breed and are husbanded. Pearl-producing oysters are bred in tropical waters specifically for pearls. There are many varieties of edible oysters throughout the world. Blue-point, Cotuit, and Olympia are some of the more common domestic varieties.

Oysters are vitamin rich and contain a high proportion of iodine and other minerals. Six oysters surpass the recommended daily allowance (RDA) for iron and supply more protein than milk. Shellfish does contain cholesterol, but oysters have less than meat.

Oysters, like mussels, are a contractive and warming food and are considered an aphrodisiac by many. See **Shellfish**.

Oyster Plant See **Salsify**.

P

Palm Kernel Oil   One of the world's most important sources of edible oil is extracted from the fruit of the—appropriately enough—oil palm. This palm, which looks similar to a coconut tree, originated in western tropical Africa and is now grown commercially throughout the tropical world. Rain forests are burned off to clear land for palm plantations.

Two oils (palm oil and palm kernel oil) are extracted from two different parts of the fruit. Palm oil comes from the fibrous pulp (mesocarp) and is used in commerce, for soap making, and—when ultrarefined—for margarine. Palm kernel oil is extracted from the nut that is contained within the fruit. Both oils are liquid when warm and are solid at room temperature. Two other highly saturated oils with this property are coconut and cocoa butter.

Ubiquitous palm kernel oil is the oil of choice in many processed foods including crackers, cookies, cakes, candies, baked goods, and dairy substitutes such as margarine, processed cheese, and coffee creamers. It is the *primary* ingredient in carob confections.

Palm kernel oil is a whopping 85 percent saturated fat. It is a highly processed oil. These two factors render this product one that—at the least—is highly suspect.

* * *

Oil with(out) a Future

The Oxford Book of Plants notes that "as it [palm oil] yields more per acre per year than can be obtained from any other vegetable oil or from animal fat, its importance is not likely to decline."[1]

* * *

Panocha   See **Wheat Flour**.

Papaya   The papaya, called a tree melon by Columbus, is almost cloyingly sweet and meaty. It can weigh from one to twenty pounds. A papaya is shaped something like an elongated melon or pear. Although some varieties remain green when ripe, the skin of most turns yellow or orange. Its lush pink-to-orange flesh contains many black seeds that look like oversize caviar in a central cavity.

A ripe papaya is slightly soft to the touch. If green it will ripen at room temperature. Domestic papayas are grown in Hawaii and, to a lesser extent, southern Florida. Imported papayas come from Puerto Rico and Mexico. Their peak season is from January to April, but they may be found year-round.

Enjoy the mellow juiciness of papayas sliced with a squeeze of lemon or lime juice. Dice and add to fruit salads or skewer for a kebab. When cooked they remain firm and lend themselves to savory dishes.

Papayas are an excellent source of vitamins A and C, potassium, and phosphorus. They are low in calories and contain about 8 percent sugar.

* * *

Vegetable Pepsin

Papain is an enzyme found in unripe papayas, which, like the animal enzyme pepsin, breaks down protein. Papain is used medicinally as a digestive aid. It is also used in chewing gum and toothpaste and as a meat tenderizer.

* * *

Papaya, Dried   See **Dried Fruit**.

Parsley   There are more than thirty-seven different parsley varieties of varying strength. And *strength* is an apt word for this herb. Parsley contains as much vitamin A as cod-liver oil, three times as much vitamin C as oranges, and twice as much iron as spinach. It is held to be especially strengthening to the adrenal glands, aids digestion, and is probably the best natural breath freshener.

All too often parsley is used only as garnish. Try serving it as a main ingredient in a vegetable side dish and use it generously in soups and casseroles. When steaming vegetables include several parsley sprigs and enjoy their firm chewy texture and bright, unfading green. Parsley stems are more strongly scented than the leaves and are preferred for flavoring white stocks and sauces, for they do not impart their color.

Look for bunches of clean, dark green parsley with no signs of yellowing or wilting. It is readily available twelve months of the year. See **Carrot Family**, and for information on optimum storage see **Herbs and Spices**.

* * *

Peter's Parsley

When Peter Rabbit had overindulged in Mr. McGregor's vegetables and was "feeling rather sick, he went to look for some parsley." Parsley, as little rabbits seem to know, is a digestive aid.

* * *

Parsley Root An Old World vegetable with increasing availability in the United States is a variety of parsley grown specifically for its root. Parsley root resembles a small parsnip in appearance and tastes similar to celeriac and carrots. It is most often used to flavor soups.

Select parsley roots that are firm and preferably have their greens intact. Store refrigerated in plastic for up to a week. Parsley root is a good source of vitamin C and is rather high in sodium. See **Carrot Family**.

Parsnip Parsnips look like oversize albino carrots, but they are much sweeter than carrots. Wild parsnip is abundant in Europe and the Caucasus region and has enjoyed more widespread use in the past than it presently does. Its lack of popularity is certainly no reason to not experiment with it. The odds are that of the vegetables in your market, this is one of the least apt to be a hybrid.

The high sugar content of parsnips increases if it is allowed to remain in the ground past the first frost. Parsnips are at peak flavor and availability in the late fall and winter. Look for straight, smooth-skinned roots that are firm and fresh looking. Large roots tend to be woody. Refrigerate in plastic for up to two weeks.

Because of its strong, dominating flavor, use parsnips with discretion in soups and stews. They may be boiled, steamed, baked, or used in puddings or in making wine.

Parsnips are high in fiber and offer some vitamin A and C, calcium, and potassium. They are said to be medicinal for the stomach and spleen. See **Carrot Family**.

Partridge See **Fowl**.

Pasilla See **Chile Peppers**.

Passion Fruit One easily develops a passion for the wonderfully intense tropical sweetness of the passion fruit and might assume that herein lies the origin of its name. Not so; this fruit is named for the passion (crucifixion) of Christ. The twelve white petals are for the apostles, the bright red stamens look like the wounds, and the nails and crown of thorns are discerned in the disc floret.

This purple fruit has the shape and the size of an egg or larger. It has a punchy flavor, sweet, golden flesh, and many black edible seeds that cannot be separated from the flesh unless it is strained. Passion fruit may be eaten like a melon, made into juice, or puréed and used as a sauce to decorate and flavor desserts.

Ripe passion fruit has a little "give," like a pear. Look for one with a firm, smooth shell. Hold at room temperature until it becomes wrinkled, appears old

◁ and sounds liquidy when shaken next to your ear. Then refrigerate for up to a week.

Passion fruit is a fair source of vitamins A and C.

☆ **Pasta**   Pasta is an upbeat dish that is quick to prepare, nutritious, and readily digestible. It is fun, satisfying, and versatile. The old and incorrect accusation that noodles are fattening and starchy has been discarded. Pasta is as nutritious as the grains it is made from.

☆ Quality American and European pasta is made from a variety of hard wheat, durum, grown specifically for pasta making. Natural noodles made from whole flour are more filling and have more fiber and a nutty flavor. Because they are a whole-grain product, they should be used within a few months of purchase so that the oil in the germ does not become rancid.

Semolina pasta is made from refined durum wheat. Like white flour, which also lacks germ and bran, it has a long shelf life. If a pasta label includes *farina,* the Italian word for *flour,* it refers to the less expensive, common wheat flour. The cooking water of such noodles clouds with starch and the cooked pasta turns soggy.[2]

✳ The taste and texture of different noodles varies incredibly. Unfortunately *some* whole wheat pasta performs poorly and if overcooked may disintegrate in the pot! Ask your retailer to direct you to the best of the whole-grain pastas—they are available and are worth seeking out.

According to FDA labeling regulations, a noodle, by definition, must contain eggs; if egg free, it must be termed *pasta.* Oriental imports are excepted and may be sold as noodles even when egg free.

¤ Pasta may be an entrée or a side dish and is tasty in soups, casseroles, salads, and desserts or alone with a sauce. There are hundreds of types and shapes to choose from. New varieties contain vegetable flavoring, and some are wheat free.

Asian noodles include a panoply of Oriental-style pastas available in supermarkets and specialty-food markets in the United States. Available fresh, precooked, and dried, many—but not all—are imported. Their characteristics are as varied as Asian cuisines. Fortunately, Linda Burum, in *Asian Pasta,* brings a manageable order to them all. This excellent book includes descriptions of all the pastas with ethnic recipes for each.

Buckwheat noodles are among the more familiar of the Asian pastas, due to the popularity of Japanese soba (buckwheat). This brownish gray noodle may be made of 100 percent buckwheat or may contain varying amounts of wheat flour. It may also be flavored with other foods such as green tea, egg, jinengo, or lotus. Soba is often thought of as a cold-weather dish, but it may be enjoyed in any season. The Korean pasta, naeng myun, is made of buckwheat and potato starch.

Corn noodles are a wheat-free pasta with a beautiful golden color. This noodle lends itself to summer fare or is a light grain complement to an otherwise heavy meal. Watch cooking carefully, for if overcooked it tends to disintegrate.

Quinoa noodles are made of durum wheat and quinoa. They are a pleasantly flavored, whole-protein noodle.

Ramen noodles are available prepackaged with instant soup mix. Within the past few years they have gained immense popularity as a tasty yet quick and easy food to prepare. Their accompanying soup mixes come in a variety of flavors, and the noodles themselves may be made of wheat, rice, or buckwheat. Unlike other Oriental grain pastas, ramen noodles are extruded rather than cut. They are also pre-steamed to reduce their at-home preparation time. Ramen quality varies widely. Commercial brands contain highly refined ingredients, whereas those found in natural-food stores or the natural-food section of supermarkets use whole flours and quality ingredients.

Rice pasta is available in many shapes and guises, from fragile vermicelli to flat, moist sheets. In its manufacture it has been cooked, and so preparation time is short. Presoaking is advised. In Southeast Asia rice is the most common pasta ingredient. Rice vermicelli, which varies greatly in width, may be called mai fun in China, maifun in Japan, sen mee in Thailand, bun in Vietnam, pancit bihon in the Philippines, beehoon in Malaysia, and bihun in Indonesia.

Sesame noodles have a nutty flavor and yield a whole protein. The sesame most often used in this product is the meal that remains after the oil is pressed from sesame seeds.

Vegetable noodles are wheat pasta flavored with one or more dehydrated vegetables such as spinach, tomato, parsley, onions, celery, artichoke, carrots, beets, garlic, or spirulina. They impart their own unique flavor, a festive color and additional nutrients.

Vegetable starch pastas are gluten free and may be made of mung beans, yams, potatoes, or cornstarch. They are clear and springy when cooked. As they have been cooked during manufacture, they need only rehydrating and heating. The better-known Chinese and Japanese bean-thread pastas are called fen si and saifun respectively.

Wheat-free noodles are composed of corn, soy and rice flour. They are favored by those on a restricted wheat diet.

Wheat pasta in the Orient is made of a soft white wheat flour rather than durum, which means it must be cut rather than extruded. For these two reasons, its flavor and texture differ greatly from American and Italian pasta. As with domestic wheat noodles, Asian varieties may be made with or without eggs. *Mian, mein, men,* and *mee* are generic terms for wheat noodles in most Asian countries.

*   *   *

Labeling Laws

"Such unappetizing terms as 'alimentary paste' or 'imitation noodles' are used to describe package contents [of Asian pasta]." Linda Burum also observes that "this is because, until very recently, the United States Food and Drug Administration required that all products labeled 'noodles' contain wheat flour and eggs . . . a recent ruling in favor of Asian-American noodle manufacturers gave them the right to call their nonwheat products 'Oriental noodles.' Still, many of the old packaging terms persist."[3]

*   *   *

Passion for Pasta

The taste difference between a superior pasta and a mediocre one is vast. Pasta imported from Italy, where there remains a tradition of craftsmanship and pride in the quality of a product, are generally superior. They are more costly and definitely more sensually satisfying than domestic varieties, in which, unfortunately, cost effectiveness is often the bottom line. A quality pasta tastes "quality" because of these factors:

- Flour is milled fresh.
- *Only* semolina flour is used, and different flour varieties are carefully blended to achieve a precise texture.
- Kneading is slower and longer.
- Noodles are extruded through brass (rather than Teflon) dies, which yields a superior texture.
- Noodles are extruded at low pressure (high pressure creates high temperatures that denature the flour and, when cooked, will produce a too-soft noodle).
- Drying is at low temperatures in closets (rather than fast drying in tunnels).
- If used, eggs are fresh (rather than frozen or dried).

*   *   *

Pattypan   Also known as *Scallop Squash.* Among vegetables with fanciful shapes, as well as names, the pattypan ranks high. The fruit, technically a berry, of this summer squash plant looks like a thick round cushion with scalloped edges. When immature, it has a pale green skin that turns white or cream. Some varieties have green speckles. The pattypan is at its best when its diameter does not exceed four inches.

See **Squash, Summer** for information on selection, storage, and use and for nutritional and medicinal highlights.

Pea, Dried Peas are an ancient legume used in Europe and Asia since prehistory. Several varieties are popular as a fresh vegetable eaten with or without the pod. As a dried food, peas are generally yellow or green and may be whole, or they may be split and have their outer seed coat removed.

Split peas, which are primarily used in soups, have less vitality (they can't sprout and grow) but are more common than whole dried peas. Split peas have the advantage of being the quickest-cooking legume. They are lower in protein than are other legumes. Our main producers of dried peas are Wisconsin and Washington.

See **Beans** for information on selection, storage, and use and for nutritional and medicinal highlights.

Pea, Green Like corn on the cob, peas are a vegetable unsurpassed in delicacy of flavor when brought straight from the garden to the table. Once picked, the sugar content decreases and the starch content increases.

In the market look for small, crisp, shiny pods that squeak when rubbed together. Refrigerate and try to use within three days. Shuck peas just prior to cooking. The pods are an excellent stock ingredient.

Green peas are high in vitamins A and B complex and are a good source of calcium and potassium.

*   *   *

Pease Porridge

Pease is the old singular English word for pea, as is evident in this children's clapping rhyme:

Pease porridge hot,
Pease porridge cold,
Pease porridge in the pot
Nine days old.

*   *   *

Peach *Peach* has become synonymous with something that is unusually fine and particularly good in its class. Indeed this fleshy, sweet and yet tart fruit evokes positive symbolism.

Like their relatives, apricots, peaches originated in China, then moved along caravan routes to Persia and eventually to Europe and the Americas. They were originally called Persian apples; the name *peach* comes from the Latin word for *Persian.*

This delectable dessert fruit needs great care in handling, transporting, and storing. In the United States the peach is among the most popular fruits for eating out of hand, and it's also good canned, dried, or made into preserves, confections, and liqueurs.

There are two main types of peaches: clingstone and freestone. These names denote whether the flesh adheres to or breaks free of the pit. Freestones are preferred for eating fresh, and most clingstones are used in commercial processing and never sold in the market. Peaches vary greatly in ripening, from early summer to fall. Unlike many fruits, peaches are available in most of the continental states.

Buying seasonally locally grown fruit is your best bet for getting good peaches. Imported, out-of-season peaches and those with greenish skins do not ripen or become sweet. Its red blush indicates variety and not ripeness. A peachy aroma also indicates ripeness. The fuzz of the peach skin is often considered undesirable, and commercial peaches may be defuzzed (some are even waxed).

Store fully ripe peaches in the refrigerator in a single layer and use within ▷
a week. Allow the firm ones to ripen at room temperature out of direct sunlight.

Peaches contain fewer calories than apples or pears, and they aid in elimina- +
tion. They are high in vitamins A and C and, unlike most fruits, contain calcium.

A close relative of almonds, peach seeds are used as an almond oil substitute
in cosmetic preparations. Their leaves and bark are used as a medicinal tea for ◆
chronic bronchitis, coughs, and gastritis.

Peanut This all-American favorite snack food was cultivated by the Aztecs and
Maya, then introduced to Africa, Europe, and North America. Technically a
legume, the peanut is unusual in that after the flower is pollinated, the flower-
bearing stalk elongates and forces the young pod down into the soil, where it
matures.

Like other legumes, the peanut is a good source of protein (more than 26 +
percent); but unlike other legumes, it is high in fat (nearly 50 percent). It is most
often used as a nut, but it may also be boiled like other beans. Peanuts are the ¤
second highest source of pantothenic acid. They are high in the B vitamins
thiamine and niacin and in vitamin E and iron.

Fifty percent of the domestic crop is made into peanut butter; the remainder
is used primarily for oil and industrial purposes. Peanuts are an excellent soil
enricher. You can bury a few ground shells in your houseplants as fertilizer.

The most popular domestic varieties are the small Spanish and Valencias,
which are primarily used for peanut butter, and the larger Virginia, which is used
mostly for roasting.

See **Nuts** for information on selection, storage, and use and for nutritional
and medicinal highlights.

*   *   *

A Possible Explanation for Peanut Allergies?

Peanuts are a leading crop in the United States, and unfortunately they are one of the
most chemically adulterated crops. Most peanut fields are crop rotated with cotton. Because cotton is a nonfood crop it is treated with chemicals too toxic to be allowed on food
crops. A field of cotton may receive up to sixteen applications of various pesticides annually. These chemical residues affect the next peanut crop. Some people who are allergic
to commercial peanuts find that they are able to enjoy organic peanuts.

Furthermore, the USDA allows a low percentage of the carcinogenic mold aflatoxin
in peanut products. Peanuts grown in the humid South invariably develop some mold
while drying in the field. Peanuts grown in arid areas, like eastern New Mexico, are free
of aflatoxins because there is not enough moisture to support mold formation.

*   *   *

Peanut Butter Try a taste comparison of a natural peanut butter with a commercial variety. Most commercial peanut butter contains 10 percent sweeteners, ✳
emulsifiers (hydrogenated oil), and salt. It is amazing how much more flavor the ☆
natural butter has.

Natural peanut butter (as well as other nut and seed butters) contains only
ground nuts and sometimes sea salt. Its oil may separate to the top, but is
easily—albeit messily—stirred back in. The hydrogenated oil in commercial peanut butter prevents oil separation.

Natural peanut butters may be classified according to quality. Some are made
with commercial peanuts; others are made with organic peanuts. Favor the organic. Due to its fat content, peanut butter will become rancid if stored long
enough. After opening, refrigerate and plan to use within a few months. ▷

The problem with chilled peanut butter is that it is unspreadable. Remove
from the refrigerator ahead of time. Or if peanut butter is used in quantity in your
home, keep a small jar at room temperature and refrigerate the rest. See **Nut and
Seed Butters**.

* * *

Which Is More Digestible—Peanuts or Peanut Butter?

Despite popular opinion, peanut butter is *harder* to digest than peanuts! Recall how a spoonful of peanut butter sticks to the roof of your mouth. Imagine that same oily puttylike glob in your stomach with microscopic digestive enzymes attempting to penetrate it in order to assimilate the nutrients.

Now imagine a spoonful of peanuts broken into bits by your molars and lubricated with your saliva. Once in your stomach your digestive enzymes easily surround these bits and get right to work digesting them.

* * *

Peanut Oil The peanut is an excellent oil food, for it is about half oil. However, the quality of commercial peanuts is doubtful. Twenty percent of peanut oil is saturated, which is higher than other natural oils. It is low in linoleic acid and vitamin E and high in mono-unsaturated fats. Its trace mineral content is low.

When highly refined, this inexpensive oil is unobtrusive in cooking. Relatively stable, it is excellent for frying and may be heated to 450 degrees without smoking. At the time of this writing, at least one company produces a 100 percent expeller-pressed peanut oil. Due to its strong flavor its applications are limited.

See **Oil** for guidelines for determining oil quality, and for storage information.

Pear When properly ripened, pears are so tender they were once called the "butter fruit." This fall fruit is an apple relative and has a similar seed core. It is native to temperate Europe and Asia.

Unlike most tree fruits, pears are best ripened *off* the tree. Select firm—not hard—pears with a noticeable pear aroma. Allow to ripen at room temperature until the flesh at the stem end yields to gentle thumb pressure. Once ripe, refrigerate in a plastic bag and use within five days.

Sweet, melting, and *juicy* are terms that best describe pears preferred for eating out of hand. Varieties that are more firm and crisp, almost like apples, are canned or pickled. Pears may also be juiced, puréed, made into preserves, brandied, frozen, dried, or distilled into liqueur or wine. Some are the distinctive pear shape, others are elongated, and some are round.

The tender pear skin is a good source of fiber. The flesh is low in sodium and has small amounts of phosphorus and vitamin A.

In *Prince Wen Hui's Cook,* Bob Flaws and Honora Wolfe describe the medicinal properties of the pear as clearing and energizing the stomach and lungs. They also indicate that the pear is commonly used in the treatment of diabetes, hot cough, and constipation.[4]

Anjou pears are green to yellow-green and rounded with almost no neck. A winter variety, they are spicy-sweet, juicy, and favored fresh.

Asian pears include numerous Far Eastern pear varieties marketed under the same name. Their size and appearance vary greatly. These fruits are generally round with a skin color that ranges from yellow-green to brown. They are a mildly sweet-flavored fruit, both juicier and crisper than our common pears.

Bartlett pears, the most common variety, are available from mid-July through September. They are good for eating fresh and also for canning. Bartletts are large, golden yellow, and when fully ripe they have a red blush. A red-skinned Bartlett pear is becoming increasingly available.

Bosc pears are dark yellow with russet-brown skins. Their necks are long and narrow. Boscs are a medium-size pear and are available from the fall to early spring. They are excellent baked, broiled, poached, or preserved.

Comice pears are similar in size and color to Anjous but are distinguished by their pink blush. They are especially good in cooked desserts.

Seckels are small, often bite-size pears with sweet flesh. Poached or pickled whole, they are eye-catchers.

Winter Nelis is a green pear used mostly in desserts and available during fall, winter, and early spring.

*   *   *

The Duke Was into Pears

A sixteenth-century Italian manuscript lists 209 different pear varieties that were served during one year at the table of the Grand Duke Cosimo III!

*   *   *

Pecan   Pecans are the most important native American nut crop. Best characterized as rich, their fat content of 70 percent is second only to macadamia nuts. Pecans are indigenous to the Mississippi River basin and are an essential ingredient in Southern cookery. As their appearance suggests, they are closely related to walnuts.

This oblong nut has a smooth brown shell. If the shell is red, it has been dyed. Because of their high fat content, shelled pecans have a shorter shelf life than other nuts. Ideally they are consumed shortly after they are shelled; if this is not possible, refrigerate shelled nutmeats in tightly closed plastic containers.

High in iron, calcium, phosphorous, and potassium, pecans contain vitamins A, C, E, and B complex. Like other nuts, seeds, and high-protein foods, the pecan is a warming food.

See **Nuts** for information on selection, storage, and use and for nutritional and medicinal highlights.

Pepito   See **Pumpkin Seed**.

Pepper   Columbus voyaged to find black pepper, which grows in India. Unsuccessful but undaunted, he named the most pungent New World food "pepper" and the people who cultivated it, Indians. Peppers native to this hemisphere are not related to black pepper. Even though pepper varieties are legion, they neatly fall into two categories.

Chile peppers and sweet peppers are both members of the Capsicum family; *capsicum* comes from the Latin word for *box*, which aptly describes their hollow, boxlike interior. The difference between the chiles and the sweets is that the former are pungent and used as a spice; the latter are sweet and used as a vegetable.

For a comprehensive listing of individual varieties of peppers see **Chile Peppers** and **Sweet Pepper**. See also **Nightshade**.

Perch, Freshwater   Perch is considered one of the best tasting of all small freshwater fish and is found throughout the world. It may be cooked simply, like trout or catfish. This delicate fish has many bones, which discourage some from preparing or eating it. Perch are typically a pound in weight and about a foot in length.

This freshwater game fish is an excellent source of protein and is low in fat and calories. Perch is easily digested and is a fair source of calcium, vitamins, and other trace nutrients. See **Fish, Freshwater** for additional information.

Perch, Sea   There are many varieties of sea perch, which are closely related to bass. The Atlantic "white perch" is actually a bass, and the Pacific black perch is more precisely a black sea bass. Their flavor is less delectable than that of freshwater perch but is comparable nutritionally. Sea perch flesh is white, flaky, and delicately flavored, albeit extremely boney. See **Fish**.

Persian Melon   See **Melon Family**.

Persimmon   The bright orange fruit that looks like a plastic tomato is a persimmon. When fully ripe it is so sweet that it is almost cloying. There are two main

P
126

varieties. One is tomato shaped, American in origin, and tends to be astringent if immature. The other is smaller, pointed like an acorn, and comes from the Orient. Persimmons grow abundantly in the southeastern and Gulf areas of the United States and in California.

Available in late fall or winter, the persimmon is best after a frost. Select plump fruits with their green cap intact. Persimmons are fragile and easily broken, so handle with extreme care. Allow to ripen at room temperature until they are past the soft stage and mushy. The mushier a persimmon, the sweeter it is.

Persimmons are eaten out of hand, sliced and peeled for salads, or used in puddings or cakes. They are an exceptional source of vitamin A and have significant vitamin C, as well as calcium, potassium, and phosphorus. They are a low-calorie fruit and are considered cooling.

Pheasant See **Fowl**.

Pickles Traditionally, pickling was a method of preserving food for the winter months. But due to their high salt content and numerous additives, pickles have earned a bad reputation and rightfully so. There are pickles from natural-food manufacturers, which, although pasteurized, are tasty, additive free, and lower in salt than commercial varieties.

Naturally fermented, unpasteurized, low-salt pickles are a quality fermented food that aids digestion. Such pickles, cottage-crafted or from a local pickle maker, are occasionally available in natural-food stores. Seek them out and enjoy them. Or make them yourself. Sauerkraut, dill pickles, and corn relish are a few traditional pickles that add variety, texture, and flavor to any cuisine.

The kimchi recipe listed in the **Chinese Cabbage** entry is a naturally fermented pickle.

Pineapple The pineapple, which is native to South America, is not a fruit in the ordinary sense of the word. It is a multiple organ that forms when the fruits of a hundred or more separate flowers coalesce. Its high sugar content and lush flavor make it one of the most popular tropical fruits.

Fresh pineapple is at its peak for just a day, and it doesn't ripen or sweeten after harvesting. A fragrant aroma is a key to selecting a ripe pineapple. Also look for glossy, golden orange skin; a small, compact, and fresh (rather than dehydrated) leaf crown; and a fruit that is heavy for its size. An overmature pineapple is soft and mushy. It is available throughout the year with peak supplies in the spring.

Pineapple contains an enzyme called bromeline that is a digestant and tenderizes meat. If pineapple is allowed to sit in a fruit salad, the bromeline causes it to become soggy. Pineapple contains vitamins A, B complex, and C. Its mineral content is small, and it is high in carbohydrates and fiber.

Pineapple, Dried See **Dried Fruit**.

Pine Nut Also known as *Piñon, Pignoli*. Pine nuts are a sensuously flavored seed rich both in taste and price. As their name suggests, they come from pine trees, specifically those that have seeds large enough to be edible. Varieties with large seeds—orange-pip to sunflower-seed size—grow in various parts of the world. Our domestic supply comes from the Mediterranean stone pine and the piñon of the southwestern states.

When lightly roasted, their flavor is a delicate combination of almond and pine. The stone pine nuts are much higher in protein than any other nut or seed (over 30 percent), and they are lower in vitamins and fat than the domestic piñon. The piñon seed is richer in vitamin A and the B-complex vitamins and minerals, and it contains 14 percent protein.

Whole pine nuts are eaten as a snack either raw or roasted and salted. They are a main ingredient in pesto and may be used in soups, cakes, candies, casseroles, and numerous other dishes. Because of their high price and limited availability, they are used sparingly.

The shell of the seed is thin and is easily removed by cracking it between your teeth. When purchasing pine seeds in the shell, look for dark-colored shells. Light-colored shells contain undeveloped seeds. When purchasing shelled nuts, look for creamy white, plump kernels.

See **Nuts** for information on selection, storage, and use and for nutritional and medicinal highlights.

* * *

Wash up with Mayonnaise

If you are in the piñon country of the southwestern states in mid-fall, watch the pine jays. When they cluster in the piñons and start pecking at cones, it is time. Wearing old clothes, shake piñon branches with a rake or long stick until the cones fall to the ground. Collect the cones. At home, place the tightly closed cones on a foil-lined cookie sheet and bake at 350 degrees for 10 minutes or until the cones open and the house is filled with a heady pine fragrance. Shake or pick out the pine seeds from each cone, crack them individually, and savor.

To clean your clothing and hands of the pine pitch that gums up *everything* it touches, wash with salad oil or mayonnaise and then soap and water. Once the cones have been baked, the sap hardens to a varnishlike sheen and is no longer sticky.

* * *

Pink Bean   See **Bolita**.

Pinto   What bean is associated with tacos? The pinto. Indeed, pintos are nearly synonymous with southwestern-style cooking. This kidney bean–family member is identified by its buff-to-pink color, which is splotched like a pinto pony. Next to soy, pintos are the most common bean grown in the United States. They are a highly hybridized crop.

See **Beans** for information on selection, storage, and use and for nutritional and medicinal highlights.

Pistachio   The seed of an evergreen and a relative of the cashew, the pistachio originated in Asia Minor and has been used throughout recorded time. This nut is so prized for its pleasant, mild flavor and fetching green color that consumers are willing to pay exorbitant prices for it.

Iran, Turkey, and Afghanistan are the largest producers of pistachios, and Americans consume nearly 90 percent of the world's supply. Commercial crops were planted in California in 1968. California pistachios are generally larger. Pistachios in storage are fumigated with pesticides such as methyl bromide.

Almost all pistachios are sold roasted and salted. Because the shell of pistachios splits during its drying process, they do not have as lengthy a shelf life as do other whole nuts. Store in a cool place and plan to use within three months.

Pistachios are an essential ingredient in Turkish delight, pistachio ice cream, and nougat, and they also make an exquisite halvah. They may be substituted for other nuts in recipes; however, their green color will suffuse any food they are mixed with.

Among nuts, the pistachio is one of the best sources of protein, calcium, and vitamin A, and the best source of iron and potassium. See **Nuts**.

* * *

Plain-Jane or Day-Glo Red

The preferred Afghan pistachio shell has a natural pink tint; other varieties are tan. American pistachio importers and growers, trying to make a good thing better, dye this hapless nut a shocking red. As the shells naturally split during drying, kernels of dyed nuts are exposed to the chemical dyes. Favor plain-Jane pistachios over Day-Glo reds.

★   ★   ★

Plantain   The oversize green banana called the plantain figures prominently in Latin American and Asian cookery where it is used as a starchy vegetable. It is served sautéed, baked, fried, or mashed; unlike the ubiquitous sweet banana, the plantain is never eaten raw.

Do not be intimidated by a black- or brown-colored peel, for as the plaintain ripens, it darkens. Avoid any that are cracked or overly soft. Store at room temperature, and do not refrigerate unless absolutely soft.

The starchy and bland green plantain may be used like a potato. As it ripens it develops more of a banana flavor and becomes sweeter, but it still holds its shape when cooked.

Plantains are available year-round. They contain a fair amount of vitamin C, are an excellent source of potassium, and are high in calories.

Plum   The juicy sweet-tart plum is a cousin to peaches and cherries and grows on every continent except Antarctica. Of the thousands of plum varieties in existence, the twenty or so grown commercially are usually classified as European or Japanese. The European plums have purple or blue skins and are small and firm. The Japanese varieties are generally larger and juicier and are red, yellow, or green.

Plums are characterized by a tart flavor and are enjoyed fresh or in preserves, desserts, cordials, wines, and liqueurs. A wild domestic plum, the sloe, is used to make sloe gin. A prune is a dried plum.

Purchase plums that are plump and firm but not hard, shriveled, split, overly soft, or bruised. They should have a powdery bloom on their skin. If not fully ripened, leave out at room temperature for a few days. Then refrigerate for three to five days.

Plums provide carbohydrates, some minerals and vitamins, and a fair amount of silicone.

California supplies 90 percent of our commercial plum crop. The most popular variety is the Santa Rosa; others are damsons, gages, monarch, Victoria, el dorado, casselman, and nubiana.

★   ★   ★

This Is Just to Say

I have eaten
the plums
that were in
the icebox

and which you were probably
saving
for breakfast

Forgive me
they were delicious
so sweet
and so cold

—William Carlos Williams[5]

★   ★   ★

Poblano   See **Chile Peppers**.

Pollock   A relative of the cod, the pollock is from Atlantic waters. Its use and nutritional value are comparable to cod, but it is held in less esteem. Pollock is especially suited to soups and stews.

See **Fish** for information on selection, storage, and use and for nutritional and medicinal highlights.

Pomegranate The word *pomegranate* means "grained apple." This unusual fruit figures in biblical literature and Greek mythology. A western and south Asian native, the pomegranate is now widely cultivated in the tropics, subtropics, the Mediterranean region, and southern California.

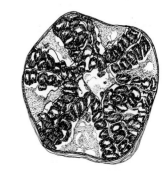

The flavor and flesh of this ruby-colored fruit is both unusual and sweet. A hard brown-red or purplish skin encloses hundreds of juicy seeds. Look for a fresh-looking, plump, heavy fruit with a hard skin. Favor large fruits over small fruits. Pomegranates are at peak supply in the fall. Store at room temperature out of direct sunlight or refrigerate for up to two weeks.

Extracting the seeds is a sticky and time-consuming process. To obtain its refreshing juice easily, bruise the fruit by rolling it on a hard surface, then puncture the end of it, insert a straw, and drink up its piquantly sweet juice.

The fruit is primarily eaten raw, but it may be used in jelled desserts, sauces, conserves, and syrups. A few of its ruby red seeds sprinkled in a fruit cup add dramatic flare. Grenadine is a pomegranate syrup.

Pomegranates are a superior source of potassium and high in citric acid. Medicinally they have been used to expel tapeworms, to strengthen the gums, and soothe ulcers in the mouth and throat. The peel is used as a home remedy for treating chronic dysentery.

★   ★   ★

Fertility Prediction

Among Chinese, Greek, Hebrew, and Persian peoples, the many-seeded pomegranate symbolizes fecundity. A Turkish bride throws the fruit to the ground and however many seeds pop out are said to indicate the number of children she will bear.

★   ★   ★

Pompano Considered by many as the finest of all eating fish, the pompano is chiefly found in the southern Pacific and Atlantic, the Gulf of Florida, and the Caribbean. Its flesh is rich and moist with a delicate flavor. Available throughout the year, its peak season is from April to November.

The Pacific pompano is a relative of the butterfish, whereas the Atlantic pompano is related to the mackerel. Both types of pompano are high in fat compared to other fish.

See **Fish** for information on selection, storage, and use and nutritional and medicinal highlights.

Popcorn See **Corn, Popped**.

Poppy Seed See **Seeds**.

Porcino See **Bolete Mushroom**.

Pork Pork has long played an important role in the human diet. Today's pork is quite different from the pork available twenty-five years ago. It has been bred to be leaner, lower in calories, and to contain more nutrients.

Select fresh pork that is light pink. The lean should be firm, fine-grained, and free from excess moisture. Look for some but not excessive marbling. The fat cover should be firm and white.

Favor fresh pork over cured, cured and smoked, canned, and processed cuts unless the preserving processes used are natural and nitrate free. Natural pork and pork products are available at quality meat stores.

Pork purchases need prompt refrigeration in the coldest part of the refrigerator. Use within three days. Pork is a valuable source of several B vitamins including thiamin, riboflavin, niacin, and B_{12}. It is high in iron and zinc.

Posole See **Corn, Posole**.

Potato I recently feasted on potatoes in the Peruvian Andes, which is where our potatoes originated. These tiny little papas were like taro potatoes or Jerusalem artichokes in shape and size. Their colors were stupendous—black skinned with bright yellow flesh, rose-colored skin and flesh, and all the shades of purple and blue. But even more memorable were their sweet, sweet flavors. Each variety had a different and full flavor. Only in texture were they comparable to our common potatoes.

The potato is one of the most important food plants of the world. It has been used in South America for two thousand years and was introduced into Europe some four hundred years ago. Let's hope that some of these heirloom varieties will be introduced into our market.

Select firm potatoes that are free from soft spots or darkened areas. Potatoes store best at 50 degrees in a cool and dark area. Do not store next to apples or the apples will become musty. Refrigeration is not advised, for the potatoes darken and their starch converts to sugar.

Potatoes have an undeserved reputation for being high in calories. What makes potatoes fattening is the butter or sour cream that goes on them. They are almost 78 percent water; they are high in carbohydrates and have 2 percent protein. Just beneath the potato skin are significant quantities of manganese, chromium, selenium, and molybdenum. Peel a potato, and you lose these nutrients and fiber. Every potato preparation, from mashed to salad, works well with the skin intact. Do not consume the sprouts or any green-colored flesh or skin, for they contain poisonous alkaloids.

There are several types of potatoes, each of which is best suited to certain types of cooking.

New potatoes are not a specific variety but rather any freshly harvested potatoes with thin, flaking skins and a sweet flavor. They require less cooking than do mature potatoes, they need to be prepared within two weeks of purchase, and they are best when boiled or steamed.

Purple potatoes are a potato new to our markets that yield violet mashed potatoes. Their skins and flesh are indeed purple, and in flavor and shape they are similar to a russet. When fried, they turn a dingy gray color, so boiling or baking is recommended.

Red potatoes have thin reddish skins ranging from pink to dark red. Their flesh is white and crisp. They are best roasted, steamed, or boiled and are the standard ingredient in potato salad.

Russets (or Idahos) are elongated cylinders with a yellowish-brown skin. They have a dry floury or mealy texture and are best for baking, frying, or making potato pancakes or dumplings.

Yellowfins are waxy, yellow-fleshed potatoes that perform best in salads. They are also called Finnish yellow wax.

White potatoes are either round or long with smooth, tan-colored skins and a firm inside texture. Use these all-purpose potatoes for cooking, baking, steaming, mashing, or frying. See also **Nightshades**.

    ★   ★   ★

Life Without Lumps

Mashing potatoes in a food processor or electric mixer does not work. Rather, it does not work well. To mix them enough to eliminate the lumps causes the starch to break down. The gummy result is reminiscent of packaged instant mashed potatoes.

A potato masher, plus ample elbow grease, will delump boiled potatoes. Best of all is a ricer, which yields long, silky, and light potato strands.

    ★   ★   ★

Poultry See **Chicken, Fowl**, and **Turkey**.

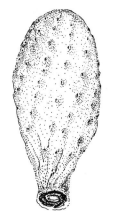

Prickly Pear Also known as *Indian Fig* or *Tuna*. Fruits of the Opuntia cactus varieties are popular in many national cuisines. The elongated "pears" are plum size. A firm, prickly green-to-purple skin, which is not eaten, encloses a juicy, soft, and lightly refreshing pulp. The pulp is a brilliant ruby color and it contains many hard seeds. Domestic availability of prickly pears is increasing.

Prickly pears are available except during the summer. Select those that are tender and fresh looking. Refrigerate for up to a week. To serve, peel, slice, and serve raw. Prickly pears may also be puréed, and their color will dramatize ices and beverages.

Prickly Pear Cactus Pad See **Nopale**.

Propolis A supplement said to strengthen the human immune system is propolis. The sap from certain trees is rich in natural antibacterial agents. Bees collect this sap and mix it with their own secretions to make propolis. They spread the propolis inside the hive, and it prevents bacteria, virus, and fungi development. This bee product is available in herbal formulas for external and internal antibacterial use.

Protein How much protein do we need to maintain health? The average American consumes more than 100 grams of protein daily, and yet studies reveal that as little as 20 grams daily for an adult male is adequate to maintain health. Excessive protein consumption—of which most Americans are guilty—is implicated in a wide range of health problems.[6]

Furthermore, quality, rather than quantity, is a crucial consideration. As protein from animal foods is high in fat, moderate quantities are recommended. Protein from vegetable sources, which has been processed at high temperatures, is also far from ideal. High technology food processing denatures some amino acids, which are the protein components. This immediately makes one question the quality of a popular health food item—protein supplements.

In her landmark book *Diet for a Small Planet*, Frances Moore Lappé soundly demonstrates that ample protein is readily available from vegetable sources if one "balances" the amino acids with each meal.[7] Since then, Lappé and other scientists have demonstrated that a person who consumes adequate calories from a varied diet obtains ample protein and that one need not be concerned with balancing amino acids.[8] See **Amino Acids**.

Prune See **Dried Fruit** and **Plum**.

Pumpkin Along with its cousins the squashes and its second cousins the melons and cucumbers, the pumpkin is a kind of berry. This native American "fruit" was a staple of the Indians, who dried it and made it into flour. Today its use is primarily limited to making pies and jack-o'-lanterns.

Pumpkins can weigh as much as three hundred pounds. For eating, rather than for carving, buy the "pie" pumpkin variety. The jack-o'-lantern variety is not suitable for cooking. Pie pumpkins are round or oblong in shape, and new varieties may be buff or white in color. Look for a firm rind without soft spots.

Store whole in a cool place. Do not refrigerate. The major nutrient supplied by pumpkins is vitamin A. See **Squash, Winter** for additional information.

＊　　＊　　＊

Endearment and Confinement

Pumpkin is a term of endearment, but it can also represent female servitude and confinement, as in the Cinderella tale and the following:

Peter, Peter Pumpkin-Eater
Had a wife and couldn't keep her.

He put her in a pumpkin shell,
And there he kept her very well.

*   *   *

Pumpkin Seed   Also known as *Pepito*. The largest and most costly of seeds, the pumpkin seed is not from the jack-o'-lantern variety of pumpkin. Rather it is from a South and Central American squash that is specifically grown for its seeds. Seeds from our domestic pumpkin may be hulled and eaten like pepitos but are smaller and not available commercially.

Pepitos have a slight crunch, an interesting green color, and a mildly nutty flavor. Few snack foods are more delicious. Pumpkin seeds are available raw or roasted and salted.

Pumpkin seeds are higher in protein (29 percent) than many other seeds and nuts, and they are higher in fat than most nuts. An excellent source of iron, phosphorus, and vitamin A, they also contain calcium and some of the B vitamins.

*   *   *

Kitchen Pinworm Remedy

Raw pumpkin seeds are recommended by some to expel pinworms or other intestinal parasites. Eat one handful raw in the morning and eat no other food until lunch. As the fibrous seed particles pass through the intestine, they are said to "scrub out" any unwelcome guests. Depending on the severity of infestation, this may need to be repeated for up to a week.

*   *   *

Purple-Podded Bean   See **Green Bean**.

Quince   The quince was once a staple in many homes throughout the world for its usefulness in preserving fruits and jellies. As home preserving has become unfashionable, so has the quince. Happily, the current interest in "exotic" produce has brought it back into the market. The quince has numerous culinary uses in addition to home canning.

This green- to golden-colored pome is unusual among fruits in that it is always eaten cooked, as it is exceedingly hard and somewhat bland when raw. The quince resembles a misshapen apple or pear. It has a musky aroma and tastes almost like a puckery pear or banana. According to my palate, quince outshines apples and pears in fruit compotes.

Availability of the quince is greatest in the fall. Select firm fruits that are smooth skinned. Handle carefully because, despite their hardness, they do bruise easily. Quinces store well and may be refrigerated for a month or more.

Stewing, baking, or braising brings out the unique quince flavor, which complements meat, savory, or sweet dishes. The fruit maintains its shape beautifully even with long cooking and so it affords grandiose experimentation. Some food writers recommend removing the quince peel as it tends toward bitterness. This has not been my experience.

This high-pectin fruit provides a fair amount of vitamins A and C and potassium and is a good source of fiber.

Quinoa   Native to the high valleys of the Andes, the grainlike quinoa (prounced KEEN-wha) was a staple of the Incas and is still used by traditional Indians. Its survival ability is impressive. The plant flourishes under extreme ecological conditions including high altitude, thin cold air, hot sun, radiation, drought, frost, and poor soil. Although most quinoa varieties grow best at ten thousand feet and above, some varieties grow as low as sea level.[1]

Its domestic availability began in 1984, and it is rapidly gaining popularity. At this time quinoa is imported from South America; however, commercial crops are being developed in several western states. It is strengthening, easily digested, light, delicious, and as versatile as rice. Athletes eat quinoa as a stamina-enhancing food.

Quinoa, a goosefoot-family member, is not a true cereal grain but is used as one. This Andean staple is the size of sesame seeds, and in taste is reminiscent of couscous and peanuts. It has the highest protein of any grain (16 percent) and, unlike other grains, is a nearly complete protein with an essential amino acid profile like that of milk. It is high in lysine. (Lysine is an amino acid that is scarce in the vegetable kingdom.) Quinoa is a rich and balanced source of many other vital nutrients, including starch, sugars, oil, fiber, minerals (especially calcium), vitamin E, and the B-complex vitamins.[2]

The conquering Spaniards brutally destroyed the Incan civilization in one short year. Of the three major altiplano staples (quinoa, corn, and potatoes) the invaders determinedly squelched quinoa cultivation. The "mother grain" figured so prominently in the Incan socioreligous structure that it was eliminated in order to establish colonialism and Catholicism. Quinoa barely survived in remote areas.

I was recently in Peru and Bolivia and saw quinoa interspersed in the corn fields. Today's Indians are growing quinoa; however, they are embarrassed to admit eating it and believe that quinoa makes their children mentally dull. Pasta and bread made of refined flour are more socially acceptable foods.

See **Grain** for information on selection, storage, and use and for nutritional highlights.

Quinoa Flour   Whole-grain flours have ample flavor but yield heavy products. White flour imparts a light delicate crumb, but is short on flavor and nutrients. Quinoa flour happily combines the best features of both. It is a preferred flour for fine pastries and increases the flavor range and depth of the finished product.

Cakes, cookies, pancakes, and waffles are improved by using up to 100 percent quinoa flour. Because it is gluten-free, quinoa flour is best combined with wheat for leavened bread, biscuits, pie crust, crepes, tortillas, and pasta.

Quinoa flour has some commercial availability. Fortunately, this flour is quick and easy to make at home in your blender. The quinoa, much softer than wheat or corn, pulverizes within a few minutes. It yields a slightly beady flour that is finer than cornmeal. To make one cup of quinoa flour, place ¾ cup quinoa in a blender and whizz for several minutes.

See **Flour** for additional information.

*   *   *

Curried Quinoa and Pistacho Pilaf

4   cups vegetable stock
2   cups quinoa, washed
½ teaspoon salt
1   teaspoon clarified butter
3   shallots, diced
1   onion, diced
½ cup carrots, diced
1   tablespoon garam masala (or allspice)
2   teaspoons coriander
1   teaspoon cumin
½ teaspoon turmeric
¼ cup raisins
⅔ cup pistachios
Curry to taste

Bring the broth to a boil in a 2½-quart pot. Add the salt and quinoa, cover, and simmer for 15 to 20 minutes or until the liquid is absorbed. Meanwhile place the oil in a wok and sauté the shallots, onion, and carrots. Stir in the garam masala, coriander, cumin, turmeric, raisins, and all but 2 tablespoons of the pistachios. Cook for two to three minutes.

Add curry to the pot of just-cooked quinoa. Heat, stirring—or bake, covered—until heated through. Garnish with the remaining pistachios. Serves 4 to 6.

*   *   *

Rabbit The animal with the greatest reputation for proliferation has been prolific in the cookery of almost every clan, tribe, nation, and people from time immemorial. Called a coney by the English, the rabbit was found in such abundance on the southwest end of Long Island that it was named Coney Island.

The hare (jack rabbit) is red fleshed, has a gamy flavor and is not commercially available. Domesticated rabbit, once again enjoying popularity, is white fleshed, lushly tender, mild flavored, and easy to digest. Some compare the taste of domestic rabbit to chicken. To this comparison, my local rabbit producer, Martin Shellabarger, retorts that rabbit tastes just like rabbit.

Rabbit is a labor-intensive product and thus is more expensive than chicken. Natural as well as commercial rabbit is available. Its flesh is close-textured and not fatty. Cook slowly and keep moist, or it will become tough. Rabbit stock is a good base for almost any soup.

Rabbit is higher in protein and lower in fat than chicken, veal, turkey, beef, lamb, and pork. Its moisture content is also lower than that of other meat and so it is a more concentrated food. Because of its low cholesterol factor and low sodium content it has been endorsed by the American Heart Association for low sodium diets. As with other flesh foods, rabbit is considered a warming food.

Radicchio Also known as *Red Chicory*. The brash magenta radicchio (rah-DEEK-ee-o) is now flourishing in American cuisine. This member of the chicory family has firm crisp leaves and an arresting flavor that boarders on sweet and bitter.

This vegetable is available throughout the year, and, as it gains in popularity and availability, its price is dropping into the reasonable range. Select radicchio that has a firm white core and that looks garden fresh rather than travel weary. This small-headed green keeps surprisingly well, but becomes bitter—decidedly bitter—as it ages. It is best when used within seven days.

Radicchio is most commonly thought of as a salad green, but its sturdy leaves afford much wider use. Freely substitute this red-leafed chicory in any chicory or endive recipe. Braise, add to soups, or grill. Individual leaves may be used as cups for containing a salad, or as wrappers for morsels of food.

Radicchio is a cooling food, and its bitter properties are said to energize the heart. This green is a good source of vitamins A and C and is also high in calcium.

Radish Radishes, believed to be Oriental in origin, are a mustard relative and belong to the cabbage family. Their pungent, peppery taste makes them a popular salad ingredient. Cooking transforms their tangy bite into a delicate sweet kiss. Radish greens add flavor and nutrition to soups; however, they do not lend themselves to steaming or boiling.

Select firm, crisp radishes with bright, fresh-looking greens. Avoid large radishes, for they tend to be pithy. Cut green tops from radishes; otherwise the leaves will dehydrate the root. Wrap in plastic and refrigerate for up to five days.

Radishes contain vitamin C, potassium, and other trace minerals. Although often used as an hors d'oeuvre to stimulate the appetite, they excel as a digestive aid with which to end the meal.

See **Cabbage Family** for nutritional and medicinal highlights.

The black radish looks like a black-skinned turnip. Its dry white flesh may be as hot as horseradish.

An icicle radish is white and several inches long. Its bite may be mild or hot.

The daikon, a large, long, and very hot white radish, is technically a separate species. See **Daikon**.

The red radish, which is the size and shape of a cherry, is our most common variety. Some markets now offer elongated red radishes that are more pungent than the round ones.

★   ★   ★

Radish Solitaire

The bright green leaf on a perky pink radish and a few shimmery strands of translucent noodles renders this clear soup a work of art.

1 4-inch strip kombu (sea vegetable)
1 medium-size dried shiitake mushroom
5 cups water
4 small red radishes with greens
½ ounce fine bean-thread noodles
Tamari to season

Place the kombu, shiitake, and water in a soup pot and allow to sit for 30 to 60 minutes. Bring to a boil and immediately remove from heat. Remove the shiitake and kombu (you may reserve the kombu to use for making a second soup stock). Trim and discard the shiitake's fibrous stem tip; thinly slice the remaining mushroom. Add the mushroom slices and bean-thread noodles to water. Trim away all but the innermost leaf from each radish. Return soup to a simmer, add radishes, and simmer for two minutes or just until the radishes turn from red to pink. Adjust seasoning. Place one radish, a few mushroom slices, and several strands of noodles in individual soup bowls. Serve immediately or the radish color fades. Serves 4.

★   ★   ★

Raisin   Remove the water from a grape and you have a raisin. The other constituents of the grape, particularly the sugar, remain intact. It is the high sugar content of raisins that have made them a popular food since the days when all food was foraged. Until cane sugar was imported into Europe in the medieval period, raisins were used as a sweetener second only to honey.

Almost all domestic raisins are produced in California, and 95 percent are made from Thompson seedless grapes. Golden raisins (called sultanas in Europe) are sulfured Thompsons. Muscats and monukka are two less common varieties.

The new raisin crop is available in September. Look for plump raisins. These fruits are past their prime when very dry or sugary. Store raisins cold to prolong their shelf life and prevent flavor and texture deterioration.

Esteemed as a high-energy food, raisins are rich in potassium, phosphorus, magnesium, iron, and calcium. They are a good source of vitamins A and B complex. See **Dried Fruit** and **Grape**.

★   ★   ★

Raisin Relativity

The wholesome image of our most popular dried fruit, the raisin, is relative. Unfortunately grapes are grown with more chemical fertilizers, pesticides, and growth hormones than most food crops. A raisin is simply a concentrated grape. Thus, toxic chemical residues are more concentrated in raisins than in grapes.

Organic raisins are free of toxic residues. Instead of being fumigated with methyl bromide, organic raisins are frozen to −5 degrees Fahrenheit to achieve insect kill.[1]

★   ★   ★

Rapeseed   See **Canola**.

Rappini   See **Broccoli Rabe**.

Raspberry   As fate would have it, the most delicious fruit of the temperate climate is also the worst traveler. The exotic, almost musky raspberry is so fragile that it turns to pulp if simply held in the hand too long. This renders fresh raspberries an expensive and rare summer fruit.

The most common raspberry is red, but there are yellow and black varieties. The black one is known as a black cap. The yellow-colored raspberry is called a white and is rarely available commercially because it is particularly soft. Raspberries are not a true berry but rather a cluster of drupelets with numerous round one-seeded fruits.

Select raspberries that are fresh, brightly colored, and plump. Refrigerate and use within twenty-four hours. Most raspberries ripen in July; however, some varieties ripen in September. Raspberries are high in pectin and therefore will thicken homemade jam. They provide vitamins A and C and some B-complex vitamins and minerals.

A sprinkling of fresh raspberries makes an artful garnish for desserts and fruit dishes. Among jam connoisseurs, raspberry remains an unsurpassed favorite.

See **Berries** for information on selection, storage, and use and for nutritional and medicinal highlights.

Raw Sugar   See **Sugar**.

Red Bean   Red beans are comparable to kidney beans in color and use but are smaller in size. See **Beans** and **Kidney Bean**.

Red Chicory   See **Radicchio**.

Red Snapper   One of the most important U.S. food fishes, the red snapper is considered the finest by many. Red snapper flesh is creamy, lean, white, and delicate. This sea bass relative is found in deep, warm waters from New England to the Gulf of Mexico.

The average length of a red snapper is two feet. In season throughout the year, the snapper keeps better than many fish. Several other snapper varieties are available, such as the gray and pargo; however, their flesh is less delicate than that of the red.

Red snapper is very low in fat and is a good source of protein. It contains numerous minerals, vitamins, and trace nutrients.

See **Fish** for information on selection, storage, and use and for medicinal and nutritional highlights.

Renkon   See **Lotus Root**.

Rhubarb   Tightly furled and scarlet, the primitive-looking rhubarb sprouting in the garden heralds spring. It is not ready to eat until its large, celerylike reddish stalks are a foot in length and its forest green leaves seem the size of elephant ears.

Rhubarb leaves are poisonous and not to be eaten. The fleshy stalks are extremely high in oxalic acid, making it a food that is automatically eaten in moderation. This certainly allows for the spring ritual of at least one slice of strawberry-rhubarb pie.

Select fresh stalks, trim off dehydrated ends, and stew or boil until tender. To be edible, this tart vegetable, which is used like a fruit, requires ample added sweetener.

* * *

Rhubarb on the Diamond

A rhubarb on the baseball field is a vehement affair that may occur when a player disagrees with an umpire. A juicy rhubarb involves players from both teams—plus the ump—and raucous vocalization from the grandstands.

* * *

Rice

Grain upon grain
Fresh and delightful as frost

A dazzling jewel
To what can I compare this treasure?

—Yang Ji (Ming Dynasty)

Rice remains the staple food for more than half the world's population! The word *meal* is synonymous with rice in both Chinese and Japanese languages. Likewise, in English *meal* originally referred to what was our staple food—ground grain. As grain no longer enjoys this prominence in the United States, it is difficult to realize the importance of rice to cultures where it is *the* staple.

Americans eat less than 10 pounds of rice per year per person, compared to more than 100 pounds per year per person in the Far East. According to the National Academy of Sciences, the United States grows about 1 percent of the world's crop; about 60 percent of the U.S. harvest is exported.

Unlike the other true cereal grains, rice is easy to eat whole and may be relished day after day without becoming boring. Feature it in haute cuisine or serve it in everyday cooking. Serve rice with a protein complement, and enjoy it plain or fried in soup, croquettes, breads, casseroles, salads, and sushi.

Rice is said to calm the nervous system, relieve mental depression, and strengthen the internal organs.

There once were thousands of rice varieties, many of which have been irretrievably lost because of the promulgation of hybrid seed. However, in the past few years, some old varieties are resurfacing as specialty items.

Basmati rice smells like buttered peanuts and has a memorable nutty flavor and fluffy texture. The cooked grain almost doubles in length yet changes little in thickness. This prized rice variety originated in the foothills of the Himalayas. It is available either refined or whole.

Brown rice is the whole rice kernel from which only the hull has been removed; it is therefore nutrient rich. Brown rice is highest of all grains in B vitamins, but somewhat lower in protein than the others. It is chewy and has a sweet, nutty flavor. Brown rice also contains iron, vitamin E, amino acids, and linoleic acid.

Brown rice is available in three sizes: short, medium, and long grain. Short grain contains less protein but more minerals and is heartier and more strengthening than long grain. Cooked day-old short grain holds moisture well. Long grain yields a fluffy and light rice. Day-old long grain becomes hard and is less palatable. Medium grain is closer to long in appearance and performance.

Parboiled rice is a refined white rice that undergoes a steam-pressure process prior to milling. This process modifies the starch and fosters the retention of some of its natural vitamins and minerals. The bulk of its nutrients are lost during processing.

Sweet rice is somewhat sweeter and decidedly stickier than other rice varieties. It is higher in protein, more easily digested, and considered a more warming food. In the Orient sweet rice is esteemed for its strengthening properties, especially for lactating and pregnant women. Sweet rice is a favorite food of children. In the United States, sweet rice is most often found in mochi and amasake products.

Sweet rice has been called "glutenous" rice because it is superbly sticky when cooked. However, the protein gluten, which is found in wheat and some other grains, is not contained in any variety of rice. Gluten-intolerant people may safely enjoy rice and rice products.

Texmati rice is a hybrid of long grain and basmati that is grown primarily in Texas. Its rich flavor and aroma is similar to basmati.

Wehani rice is a rust-colored variety developed by the Lundberg brothers, the California farmers who pioneered the cultivation of organic rice. When cooked it smells like corn popping. Its taste is reminiscent of fresh-roasted chestnuts.

Wild rice is not a true rice. (See **Wild Rice**.)

White rice has had its hull, bran, and germ removed in the refining process. It has less protein and has lost 100 percent of its vitamin E as well as other vitamins and minerals. Premium white rice is talc free and has not been enriched with synthetic vitamins. White rice is available primarily in long and short grain varieties.

See **Grain** for information on selection, storage, and use and for nutritional and medicinal highlights.

Rice Cake   One of the most popular natural-food items is the rice cake. This crunchy wafer is short on flavor but is a great medium for anything spreadable. The fact that it is also low in calories (around 35 per cake) makes it an in-demand snack food.

A full taste marks a good-quality rice cake. It should not crumble (much) when you eat it, and its top and bottom should be smooth. There are a number of commercial brands, and each one has its own flavor and texture. A crisp rice-cake variety is puffed from raw rice, whereas a softer variety is puffed from precooked rice. The more rice a cake contains, the more flavor and calories it will have. Likewise, a rice cake with more air is shorter on flavor and calories.

The standard rice cake is a round disk about four inches in diameter; small rounds are also available and some varieties are square. Puffed rice, with or without other grains or salt, is the usual ingredient. Some varieties are made of rice bran and seconds (broken grains) rather than whole-grain rice, and their texture and flavor suffer.

Rice Flour   This gluten-free flour has a granular texture and imparts a lively, seedlike flavor to baked goods. One of its best applications is in breadings, coatings, cookies, and crackers, for it makes them crispy. It is excellent for dusting bread dough when shaping it into loaves, for it dries the dough's surface without adhering to it so that any excess may be brushed off. Possibly its showiest use is in sauces, for unlike whole wheat flour, rice flour—be it brown or white—yields a spankingly white béchamel.

Because rice has no gluten, its flour alone cannot make a bread dough. However, when combined with wheat, it yields a light crumb. Sweet brown rice flour yields a gummy texture that is unsurpassable in dumplings and brownies.

Brown rice flour, as with all whole-grain flours, starts to oxidize as soon as it is milled and so should be used fresh. An old flour is rancid if it tastes or smells strong and acerbic. Discard such a flour. See **Flour** for additional information.

*   *   *

Lemon Drop Cookies (wheat free)

This sunshine-colored cookie has a refreshing lemon flavor. The rice flour gives it an airy, delectable crumb.

    3   cups brown rice flour
    1   teaspoon baking soda
    ¾   teaspoon sea salt
    ½   cup butter
    ½   cup sweetener (honey, maple syrup, or rice syrup)
    2   teaspoons pure vanilla
    Juice and rind of one organic* lemon
    30 pine nuts, or pecan or almond halves

Heat oven to 375 degrees. Sift the flour, soda, and salt together. With your fingertips, cut in the butter. Combine the sweetener, vanilla, lemon rind, and juice. Mix wet and dry ingredients. With your fingers, form the dough into small rounds. Place on an oiled cookie sheet and press each round down with moistened fork tines (or with damp fingers) to a

2½-inch diameter and ⅓-inch thickness. Press one nutmeat into the center of each cookie. Bake for 10 to 12 minutes or until the bottom is lightly browned. Makes thirty 2½-inch cookies.

*Commercial lemon rind (which is waxed and dyed) will not color these cookies yellow and is not recommended. If an organic lemon is not available, you may prefer to substitute ½ teaspoon lemon extract for the lemon juice and rind.

* * *

☆ **Rice Syrup** One of the most healthful sweeteners is rice syrup. It is predominantly slow-digesting carbohydrates that enter the bloodstream steadily over a
◆ two-hour period. This protects against problematic rapid fluctuations in blood-sugar levels caused by ingestion of simple sugars (fructose, glucose, and sucrose) found in sugar, corn syrup, honey, and maple syrup.[2]

Best of all, rice syrup is sweet but so mild that it does not overpower other
◆+ flavors. It is hypoallergenic and has little free glucose and no fructose or sucrose. The pH of the finished syrup is 6.3, very close to that of our blood.

¤ You can make rice syrup in your own kitchen. Mix cracked rice with enzymes obtained from sprouted barley. Incubate this mixture until the enzymes break the rice starches down into simple sugars. Then filter the syrup through cloth and cook down to reach a syruplike consistency. Powdered rice syrup is also available.

Currently, there are about six different domestic brands of rice syrup on the market, most of which are produced by California Natural Products of Manteca, California. This company's food chemist and co-owner, Dr. Cheryl Mitchell, informed me that each syrup is formulated and produced to different specifications and thus the flavor of each varies remarkably. When made from white rice the syrup has a lighter color and flavor. Brown rice syrup is full-bodied and contains more B vitamins and minerals. Those made from organic brown rice have a slightly butterscotch flavor.[3]

All rice syrups have about 50 percent complex carbohydrates, but their glucose-to-maltose proportion differs. The one with the highest glucose is the sweetest and performs more like honey in baking. One with a higher maltose content is milder flavored and would be more appropriate for diabetics.

◁ Rice syrup is available in natural-food stores. It has a long shelf life and requires no refrigeration. Unlike honey, it does not crystallize. If the syrup hardens in cold weather, set the jar in warm water until it softens. Should condensation occur in the container, the syrup is subject to surface molds. If this occurs, remove the mold and then refrigerate the syrup.

* * *

Candied Popcorn

½ cup rice syrup
2 quarts popped corn (lightly salted, optional)
1 cup almonds, toasted

Preheat oven to 350 degrees. Place the rice syrup in a saucepan and bring just to a simmer. Place the popcorn and almonds in a large bowl and stir in the syrup. Spread on an oiled baking sheet and bake for 10 minutes.

* * *

Rocket See **Arugula**.

Romaine Also known as *Cos.* The second most popular lettuce after iceberg is romaine. This tall lettuce with crisp, bright green outside leaves has a strong molecular structure and so withstands shipping better than other lettuces. An overly large or mature romaine is unpleasantly tough.

Romaine is available throughout the year, but at its best during colder sea-sons. Some red-leaved romaines are becoming available. Romaine is a cooling
◆ vegetable and in Oriental medicine is used in the treatment of alcoholism.

See **Lettuce** for information on selection and storage and for nutritional and medicinal highlights.

Romanesque Broccoli   The fanciful Romanesque broccoli is a veritable vegetable mandala. In overall shape and color it is similar to a large artichoke. Its florets look like the spiraling onion domes of a Russian Orthodox church. Each floret is part of a spiral, and each tiny spiral is part of a larger spiral yet.

The zippy, sweet flavor of Romanesque broccoli lends itself to crudités or light steaming. Its shapes are so commanding that they are complemented by simple, rather than complex, presentations.

Availability of this cabbage-family member is growing. It withstands severe frost and the frost makes it sweeter. Favor Romanesque in the late fall. Select one that has fresh green outer leaves and florets of uniform color. Wrap in plastic and refrigerate stem side up so that condensation does not occur on the florets and discolor them. Use within a week.

The nutritional properties of the Romanesque are not available at this time, but it is reasonable to assume that they are similar to those of broccoli.

See **Cabbage Family** for medicinal and nutritional properties.

Root Vegetables   Leafy green and stalk vegetables are said to be good for the lungs and for bringing energy up into the body. Root vegetables are said to be helpful in grounding or bringing energy down into our "roots"—that is intestines, bladder, kidneys, and sexual organs. Some believe that the more vigorously a root vegetable penetrates the earth, the more potential it has to invigorate those who eat it. Thus a carrot is more strengthening than a turnip, and a turnip is more strengthening than a potato.

Root vegetables often contain higher concentrations of minerals than those above ground. These earthy vegetables enhance our diet with important color, flavor, and texture variations. Include root vegetables in your daily fare.

★   ★   ★

Root Strength

Aveline Tomoko Kushi, the doyenne of macrobiotic cooking, writing, and teaching, uses scallion roots. In a cooking class Mrs. Kushi typically holds up a scallion and asks which is the strongest part (green leaves, bulbs, or rootlets). "The roots," she says. "These tiny rootlets hold up this big plant. The roots are the most mineral rich and have the greatest strengthening potential. Wash the roots well, mince them, and use them in stews and sautéed dishes. They add minerals, fiber, and flavor." [5]

★   ★   ★

Rutabaga   Also known as *Swede*. A turniplike vegetable, the rutabaga is commonly thought of as a turnip hybrid developed in the seventeenth century. Food historian Waverly Root disagrees: The rutabaga "is almost certainly a mutant, not a hybrid, for it has thirty-eight chromosomes while the common turnip has twenty." [6]

In Europe there are two main rutabaga varieties; the large one is used for animal feed and the turnip-size one is for human consumption. The rutabaga's skin, which may be purple, white, or yellow, has been maligned by many who advise to peel and discard the skin. I second the suggestion but only if the skin has been waxed or is untowardly thick. The yellow-fleshed rutabaga is firmer and sweeter than a turnip and lacks a turnip's pungency. Unlike a turnip, it has a swollen "neck," bearing ridges or scars from leaf bases.

Select rutabagas that are firm and fresh looking with a smooth, unblemished skin. Avoid withered specimens. Turnips and rutabagas are similar in appearance, flavor, use, and nutrition; however, rutabagas also have some vitamin A.

Like other root vegetables, rutabagas are a warming food and are said to strengthen the digestive organs. See also **Cabbage Family**.

Rye Rye is a feisty, scrappy survivor that is able to sustain itself in severe climates. Rye is like wheat in color, shape, and flavor, but it has blue-gray overtones, is more slender, and has a more robust and tangy flavor. This cereal grain was a staple in Europe during the Middle Ages and is still consumed in much of Eastern Europe and Russia. The main use of rye in the United States is in rye whiskey. Compared to other grains, its domestic use is minimal and is most often thought of as a bread ingredient. We produce only 2 percent of the world's rye crop.

Nutritionally, rye is similar to wheat but contains less gluten. Of the common grains, rye has the highest percentage of the amino acid lysine. It contains eleven B vitamins, vitamin E, protein, iron, and various minerals and trace elements.

Rye's strong flavor seems to match its strong, weedlike hardiness. Rye is said to build muscles and promote energy and endurance.

Rye, like wheat, is rarely cooked whole by itself. For a pot of brown rice with pizzazz, add a handful of toasted rye. Crack rye in a mill or blender, and blend it with any cracked-wheat dish. Flaked rye is used like rolled oats for a breakfast cereal and in granola.

See **Grain** for information on selection, storage, and use and for nutritional and medicinal highlights.

> Between the acres of the rye
>   With a hey, and a ho, and a hey nonino,
> These pretty country folks would lie,
>   In spring time, the only pretty ring time,
> When birds do sing, hey ding a ding, ding,
> Sweet lovers love the spring.
>
> —WILLIAM SHAKESPEARE, *As You Like It,* V:III

Rye Flour Rye flour, as with wheat, may be whole or refined. Nutritious whole rye flour is a little darker than the refined (which may also be bleached). With the rare exception of specialty pumpernickels, bread is rarely made entirely of rye flour because its gluten is not a variety that leavens well. An all-rye loaf tends to crack and spread. However, a bread of rye and wheat flour is robust and filling.

Sourdough rye bread is popular, and it is the sourdough starter—*not* the rye—that gives it a characteristic sour taste. Rye flour is sweet and tangy rather than sour. Rye bread is also commonly flavored with caraway or dill seed. Bread containing rye stays moist longer than an all-wheat loaf and slices thinner. Traditional gingerbread desserts were made of rye flour.

* * *

Color Me Artificial

Rye bread of the deep, rich color of chocolate is commonplace. This hue has nothing to do with rye! Rye flour is only slightly darker than whole wheat flour. Caramel (burnt sugar) colors commercial rye bread.

* * *

Saccharin   What is four hundred times sweeter than sugar, a coal-tar derivative, and known to cause cancer in laboratory animals?[1] Saccharin. Because of industry pressure, it has not been banned for human consumption. However, most health-concerned individuals ban it from their shelves.

Unfortunately, some diabetics feel that saccharin is a necessity. There are others who prefer the moderate use of natural sweeteners such as dried fruit, fruit juices, and rice syrup over synthetic sweeteners. See **Sweeteners**.

Safflower Oil   The safflower, a thistlelike sunflower relative, is an excellent oil-bearing plant. The flavor of expeller-pressed, or natural, safflower oil is almost corny but with a nutty overtone. It is an excellent all-purpose oil, fairly light in weight and color, and the preferred choice for deep frying. Safflower oil is high in vitamin E and highest of all oils in linoleic acid. Of natural oils it is the least stable because it has the highest percentage of unsaturated fats.

Most high-quality processed natural foods that have added oil use safflower oil. Of the quality oils, it is the least expensive and mild. The safflower prefers a semiarid climate; California and Arizona are our principal safflower growers.

See **Oil** for information on selection, storage, and use and for medicinal and nutritional highlights.

Salmon   Sweetly rich and tender, the salmon is universally regarded as the finest and most palatable of all fish. Unlike other fish, which is primarily served hot, salmon is delicious cold or hot. Like the eel, the salmon is a migratory fish; it lives in the ocean but spawns in fresh water. Some salmon are landlocked (they live in large lakes and spawn in rivers). The flesh of landlocked salmon is considered inferior to that of ocean-dwelling salmon.

Peak salmon season is spring and summer. Atlantic salmon, which contains 17 percent fat, is the most valued. Of the several varieties of Pacific salmon there are two types, king (or chinook) and sockeye, which are nearly as fatty as Atlantic salmon. Less fatty varieties of Pacific salmon are coho, dog, and humpback (or pink salmon).

Salmon flesh varies from a deep red to pink. Its texture is firm and its flavor rich and meaty. Salmon is high in protein and, relative to other fish, high in fat. Its fat, which is primarily unsaturated, is less than that in chicken and is a superior source of EPA/DHA.

Lox is smoked and salted salmon. Salmon eggs, called roe or red caviar, are exceptionally delicious. Salmon milt is the male's sperm and is called soft roe. A vein running through salmon milt is removed before use.

Red-fleshed fish, like salmon, are considered to be more energizing than white- or blue-fleshed fish.

See **Fish** for information on selection, storage, and use and for medicinal and nutritional highlights.

Salsify   Also known as *Oyster Plant.* Salsify is said to have an oysterlike flavor, which accounts for its alias. My hunch is that the oyster association comes from the milky fluid present in the fresh greens. To me, salsify tastes like a tame burdock. This long, buff-skinned taproot, which looks like an undernourished and hairy parsnip, has white, mild-tasting flesh.

Salsify is occasionally available commercially and is readily available wild. Look for it along roadsides and as a sturdy weed in gardens. Its tender young leaves are a good salad ingredient, and the root is delicious boiled, sautéed, baked, deep fried, or in soups and stews. The immature purple bud is reminiscent of asparagus in flavor.

Its flavor is best following a frost, so look for salsify in the late fall or winter. Select roots that are firm and crisp rather than soft. The root will be up to eight inches long and will have many tiny protruding rootlets. Large roots tend to be pithy.

◁

◆

+

Store in plastic in the refrigerator for up to ten days. Salsify skin is edible, but needs a good scrubbing before cooking. It tends to become overly soft if cooked too long or if peeled. In European traditions it is considered strengthening for the digestion. Salsify is a good source of calcium and iron.

See **Scorzonera**. Scorzonera is a black-skinned vegetable similar to, and interchangeable with, salsify.

Salt Historically, salt that was shared created a sacred bond between host and guest as the story of Ali Baba and the Forty Thieves demonstrates. (The robber chief would not eat any of Ali Baba's food containing salt, for the chief planned to murder his host.) Jesus said, "Ye are the salt of the earth." Often salt was literally worth its weight in gold.

Overconsumption of any food is deleterious to one's health. Salt has been particularly abused, primarily because of processed foods. The watchdog food publication *Nutrition Action* estimates that roughly 75 percent of America's sodium intake comes from processed foods.[2] Most prepared foods lack the flavor of fresh foods; their blandness is masked by adding salt. Salt also serves as a preservative in prepared foods.

Excessive salt intake was apparently not a problem when foods were made from scratch. In 1977 the Senate Select Committee on Nutrition and Human Needs recommended salt consumption be reduced by about 50 to 85 percent to approximately three grams NaCl.[3] In the decade since then many people have reduced their sodium intake. The food industry has followed suit with low-sodium items; unfortunately many of them are low-sodium in name only.

According to numerous health-care practitioners, it is not only the amount of sodium that presents a problem, but the quality. Table salt is refined to 99.99 percent sodium chloride. Any substance this pure may no longer be considered a food but rather a chemical. In the interest of long-term health, it is advised to avoid the use of highly refined salt.

Only 14 percent of our domestic salt supply comes directly from the sea. The remaining land salt is, however, technically sea salt, for it was deposited by the great ocean that covered the earth 300 million years ago.[4] Salt is extracted from the earth or sea by three methods: shaft mining, solution mining, and solar evaporation. Next, it is processed to meet the standards of the Food Chemicals Codex, which specifies that food-grade sodium chloride should not be less than 97.5 percent NaCl.

The processing includes treatment by various chemicals to remove mineral "impurities" as well as dirt. It is made of uniformly fine crystals by being subjected to a heat of 1200 degrees Fahrenheit.[5] Once the salt is reduced to almost pure sodium chloride, additional chemicals are added for cosmetic purposes.

In the last decade, salt-free diets flourished because of the association of salt with hypertension and other diseases. Today more moderate low-salt diets are generally preferred, and recognition of salt quality is increasing. See **Sea Salt**.

*   *   *

Sugar in the Salt!

Have you read a salt label recently? If iodine is added, then it includes dextrose to stabilize the iodine and sodium bicarbonate to prevent it from turning purple. Salt also contains magnesium carbonate or sodium silicoaluminate to keep it free-flowing.

*   *   *

Sapote The semitropical sapote looks like a green pippin apple. This coreless fruit has an ambrosial aroma and a soft and juicy texture. Commercial crops are being developed in California and Florida and, of the many new and exotic fruits, this is one that is destined to gain in popularity.

◀   Look for sapote during the winter months. Choose firm fruits than are free of bruises and green or yellowish green in color. Allow sapote to ripen and soften at room temperature, then refrigerate. Enjoy out of hand or use in preserves or fruit sauces. Its skin tends to be bitter and is best discarded. Sapote contains a fair amount of vitamins A and C.

Sardine   True sardines are abundant on the Mediterranean coast. Because of their high fat content, they deteriorate quickly and so are not available fresh in the United States. Sardines are a popular canned fish.

Domestic sardines are actually immature herrings and anchovies, but the name applies to any soft-boned, tiny fish that can be preserved whole in oil, salted, or smoked.

Sardines are among the fish highest in protein and are an excellent source of calcium. They contain vitamin C as well as some B vitamins.   +

Scallion   Also known as *Green Onion*. Scallions, often used as garnish, serve an important function. Not only do they add color and texture, but their zippy bite affords a counterpoint to heavier soups and entrees. Scallions are also used as a vegetable.

This onion-family member is available throughout the year but is more perishable than its cousins. Look for bright green onions with their long rootlets   ▶ intact and that show no signs of withering or slime. Wrap in plastic and use within five days.

The green part of a scallion is high in vitamin A. Its bulb contains vitamins   + A, B complex, and C and some calcium, magnesium, and potassium. In addition to serving as a digestive aid, scallion bulbs are used as a kitchen remedy for   ◆ relieving earaches. Slice the rootlets and their connecting base from a scallion bulb and place the bulb in the affected ear. See **Onion Family**.

★   ★   ★

How Many Ways Can You Skin a Scallion?

Portugese natural-foods chef, Carlos Fierriara, who now wields his knife in Denver, Colorado, can cut scallions. He turns them into flowers, leaves, trees, tiny O's, pieces of confetti, thin shreds, curlicues, fans, long diagonal wedges, and other fanciful shapes to enhance the texture and appearance of many dishes.

★   ★   ★

Scallop   This extremely delicate bivalve mollusk has firm and succulent flesh, which makes it a sensory delight. It comes primarily from the Atlantic. The two domestic varieties are the bay scallop and the sea scallop. The bay is creamy pink or tan and is the smaller and more tender of the two. The sea scallop is larger, firmer, whiter, and less expensive. Sometimes sea scallops are cut into smaller pieces and sold as the more expensive bay scallops.

Fresh scallops have a sweetish aroma. If purchased in bulk, they should be   ▶ free of liquid. They are at their fattest and best from September to April but are available twelve months of the year.

Like other shellfish, scallops are an excellent source of protein, minerals, and   + vitamins and they have often been considered an aphrodisiac.   ◆

See **Shellfish** for information on selection, storage, use and for medicinal and nutritional highlights.

Scallop Squash   See **Pattypan**.

Scorzonera   Also known as *Black Salsify*. The scorzonera (skort-soh-NAIR-a) is similar to the salsify in shape, use, and flavor; however, it has a chocolate brown skin and is more carrotlike in shape. Food writers attribute it with more flavor than the salsify.

Current supplies of scorzonera are imported from Belgium during the colder months. Select roots that are firm and smooth. Wrap in plastic and refrigerate for up to a week.

As with a carrot, the scorzonera skin needs only a light scrubbing rather than peeling. The skin offers interesting color relief and also increases the scorzonera's flavor and nutrition. For additional information see **Salsify**.

Sea Salt   There are forty-four minerals and trace elements in seawater. Historically, salt was simply concentrated ocean with its water evaporated and impurities removed. It contained all trace elements and minerals (except for light, unstable iodine) balanced in the same ratio as seawater.

Before salt became highly processed, it enjoyed great esteem. Pliny called salt the foremost among remedies for disease. The Roman legions were paid their salary in salt. In prehistoric times regions with salt deposits became centers for developing civilizations. London was originally a stopping place for salt traders.

Today's commercial salt is refined to about 39 percent sodium (Na) and about 60 percent chloride (Cl) by weight. It is essentially void of trace elements. According to macrobiotic teacher Linio Stanchich, "Over-refined salt has a similar effect on the body as white sugar. It apparently drains minerals from the body in an attempt to be metabolized. In my experience, over-refined salt may contribute to over-eating, irritability, and cravings for sweets, alcohol, and coffee."[6]

The normal saline count in body fluids is about 1 percent. If this falls lower, it can lead to poor intestinal muscle tone, diarrhea, or thin and weak blood, which may be manifested as organ, gland, or nervous-system disorders. Thus, some salt is essential. Commercial salt is not recommended. Fortunately quality natural sea salt is available. Here are some guidelines for selecting it:

- Taste salt to determine its quality. A highly refined salt tastes harsh and abrasive and burns the tongue. More natural salt has a mellow salty taste. It is smooth, rather than harsh, and actually delicious.
- Buy salt without iodine because iodized salt includes the presence of other chemicals.
- Favor solar-dried sea salt over kiln-dried sea salt. One intuitively questions ingesting any substance that has been heated to 1200 degrees Fahrenheit.
- Prefer sea salt over land-mined salt. Oftentimes rain will have leached out some important minerals and trace elements in land salt deposits.
- Buy lumpy salt. If it is free flowing it is almost pure NaCl and contains chemical additives.

Most of the sea salt sold in natural-food stores and speciality shops is highly refined. There are several small companies who manufacture quality natural sea salt. According to laboratory analysis some natural sea salt varieties were high in trace minerals and as low as 93.98 percent sodium chloride. See **Salt**.

* * *

Housewarming Gift

A traditional Eastern European housewarming gift was the most esteemed and most basic staples . . . rye bread and salt. Such a gift proffered a symbolic blessing that the new household enjoy abundance. Charm your host or hostess at a contemporary housewarming with the incomparable gift of homemade bread and a quality natural sea salt.

* * *

Sea Vegetables   Also known as *Seaweed.* Vegetables from the sea, usually called seaweed, are the most singularly nutritious food. Among the most ancient life forms, they have been consumed throughout the world for centuries. Their use is gaining popularity among those expanding their culinary horizons for sheer sensorial as well as health reasons.

Sea vegetables supply all the minerals needed for human health, with the most significant elements being calcium, iodine, phosphorus, sodium, and iron.

They are one of the few complete protein sources in the vegetable realm, and they contain up to 38 percent protein. Seaweed is a better-than-average source of vitamins, including the one vitamin that is hard to find in a strict vegetarian diet, B_{12}.[7]

The researched medicinal properties of sea vegetables are voluminous. Benefits include reducing blood cholesterol, removing metallic and radioactive elements from the body, and preventing goiter. They also have antibiotic properties known to be effective against penicillin-resistant bacteria. In the Oriental medical traditions seaweed is also reputed to counteract obesity and to strengthen bones, teeth, nerve transmission, and digestion.[8]

Additionally, sea vegetables have long been acclaimed as beauty aids. It is said that they help maintain beautiful, healthy skin and lustrous hair, and they are also credited with anti-aging properties.

A highly versatile food, sea vegetables are easily incorporated into numerous styles of cuisine. They enhance and complement grain, vegetable, bean, dairy, fish, and meat dishes.

Seaweed is harvested throughout the year; however, some varieties are of preferred quality during specific seasons. Reputable distributors carry the top grades, which are generally more costly. In some areas fresh seaweed is commercially available, but most is sold dried. Dehydrated seaweed keeps for several years when stored in a cool, dry place.

As our seas become more polluted, some people question whether or not sea vegetables are contaminated. According to laboratory analysis, pollutants are not concentrated in marine vegetables.[9]

The sea garden contains hundreds of nutritious sea vegetables, all edible. The three that most invite beginners' use are **Kanten, Kombu**, and **Nori**. See also **Agar, Arame, Dulse, Hijiki, Irish Moss, Kelp**, and **Wakame**.

★   ★   ★

Radioactive Detox

Seaweeds have an astounding ability to detoxify radioactive elements, according to increasing scientific studies. Alginic acid in sea vegetables binds certain metallic ions to itself and is impervious to digestion. "Heavy metals taken into the human body are rendered insoluble by alginic acid in the intestines and cannot, therefore, be absorbed into body tissues."[10]

Studies at the Gastrointestinal Research Laboratory of McGill University, Montreal, indicate that alginates bond toxic metals like lead and carry them out of the body. Alginates even remove radioactive strontium 90 that has already been absorbed into body tissues.[11]

★   ★   ★

Maximum Minerals

Land plants absorb nutrients from the soil, and so their nutritional content reflects their immediate environment. A carrot grown in deficient soil is nutritionally deficient. One grown in good soil is nutritionally superior.

Sea vegetables, on the other hand, are continuously bathed in the mineral-rich sea brine. They are a direct transformation of seawater and their mineral content is from 7 to 38 percent of their dry weight.

★   ★   ★

Seaweed See **Sea Vegetables**.

Seeds A seed, like an egg, a grain, or a nut, is the self-contained embryonic plant that holds the potential for propagation of the species. Such potency is reflected in a seed's nutritional and energetic properties. They hold concentrated nutrition and flavor, and it is no coincidence that they are a mountaineer's staple.

Seeds are an excellent protein and mineral source and are higher in iron than nuts. They contain vitamins A, B complex, E, and D and are outstanding calcium sources. Seeds are high in unsaturated fats, and, if eaten raw or lightly cooked, they are a superior source of fatty acids. Because of their oil content, seeds are high in calories.

Select seeds that are free of debris and that look vital. Hulled seeds that have many broken, rubbery, or discolored pieces are best avoided. Some sunflower samples always have dingy seeds amongst them. If this is the case, cull through and discard imperfect specimens. Taste is the best way to determine the quality of small seeds like poppy seeds and sesame seeds. The seeds should taste fresh and full bodied with no off flavor. Purchase whole, unroasted, unadulterated seeds and store them in a cool, dark place.

The seeds most used in appreciable quantities are sesame, sunflower, and pumpkin seeds. These are substituted for nuts in recipes and eaten as snack foods. The small seeds that are esteemed for medicinal purposes include alfalfa, chia, flax, poppy, and psyllium. These seeds are commonly available in natural-food stores.

Alfalfa seeds are a legume valued for their root system, which penetrates twenty feet into the ground and greatly enriches the soil with nitrogen. They are most commonly sprouted.

Chia seeds are considered a high-energy food and are used as a laxative.

Flax and psyllium seeds are used to regulate the bowels.

Poppy seeds are the best source of calcium, with 1,448 milligrams of calcium per 100 grams edible portion!

See also **Canola, Sesame Seed, Sunflower Seed**, and **Pumpkin Seed**.

★   ★   ★

Apache Endurance Food

The tiny seed that looks like a flattened, washed-out poppy seed is the chia, which grows in the Mexican and southwestern desert. Fred Rohé, the natural foods author who in the 1960s established the prototype natural-foods store, comments on the chia in his *Complete Book of Natural Foods.*

"Folklore calls it 'Indian running food' and tells us that Apache Indians took to the warpath for weeks at a time with only a small sack of chia seeds for food, exhibiting endurance that astonished their enemies. Whatever may have been the case, some contemporary reporters have touted chia seeds as an 'energy food,' saying they have noticed an energizing effect about an hour after eating them."[12]

★   ★   ★

Seitan   Also known as *Kofu.* A chic meat substitute that is versatile, succulent, hearty, wholesome, and strengthening is seitan (say-TAN), or wheat gluten. Except among Seventh-Day Adventist and Latter-day Saint populations, "wheat meat" has not been widely used in the West. It was traditionally eaten in China, Korea, Russia, and the Middle East. The Chinese call this high-protein food *kofu* and the Japanese call it *seitan;* they flavor it with shoyu and spices.

Seitan is easily made at home by water-extracting the gluten from wheat flour. This is accomplished by making flour and water into a bread dough and then, under running water, kneading out the wheat starch and bran until only gluten remains. It is then seasoned and ready for use in a variety of dishes, most often as a meat replacement. The complete method is described in multiple natural-food cookbooks, including a book about gluten by Barbara and Leonard Jacobs entitled *Cooking with Seitan.*

Natural-food stores may stock imported Japanese seitan, which is exorbitantly expensive and salty. Cottage-crafted seitan and seitan products are becoming increasingly available in different parts of the United States.

Seitan has 118 calories, 18 grams of protein, and, of course, no saturated fat per 100 grams edible portion. The same amount of beef (ground sirloin) has 207 calories and 32.2 grams of protein and is high in saturated fats.[13]

As gluten is the protein component of wheat, seitan is concentrated wheat protein. It is highly esteemed in natural foods circles for its strengthening and energizing properties as well as its hearty "meatlike" texture and flavor.

Semolina   See **Pasta** and **Wheat**.

Serrano   See **Chile Peppers**.

Sesame Butter   Sesame butter is made of whole roasted sesame seeds and may be used interchangeably with peanut butter. It differs from tahini, a better-known product, which is made of hulled raw sesame seeds. Sesame butter is thus a heavier and a more wholesome product. However, tahini, lighter in flavor and color, has more culinary applications.

Sesame butter may be with or without salt. As with any natural nut or seed butter, oil may separate to the top of the jar. If this occurs, simply stir it back into the butter.

Sesame is high in vitamin E and therefore has a longer shelf life than other nut butters. Unopened sesame butter may be stored for up to six months. Once opened it should be refrigerated, and it will hold another six months. If it causes a harsh or slight burning sensation in the back of the throat, it is rancid and should be discarded. See **Nut and Seed Butters** for additional information.

Sesame Butter, Black   A high-priced sesame butter made of black sesame seeds has a richly intense sesame flavor. It has recently become available in some specialty-food stores and is worth experimenting with at least once. This black, gooey spread has no comparable match in our culinary tradition, and my hunch is that it poses no threat to the peanut butter industry. See **Sesame Butter** and **Sesame Seed, Black**.

Sesame Oil   The use of sesame oil dates way back into antiquity, and many people consider it the most healthful of all oils. It is light, mild, and nutty flavored, with excellent stability and resistance to oxidation. The seed and its oil are superior sources of nutrients. Sesame oil contains 87 percent unsaturated fats, 42 percent of which is linoleic acid.

Sesame seeds are a staple protein among many peoples, especially in Africa, the Mideast, and the Orient. The oil as well as the seed is important in these areas.

The best-known sesame oil is light in color. A richer, flavorful dark oil is made by roasting the seeds before oil extraction. Dark or roasted sesame oil costs more than light, and in the Orient it is considered more strengthening and digestible. Sesame oil is suitable for sautéing, baking, and use in sauces and dressings.

See **Oil** for information on selection, storage, and use and for nutritional and medicinal highlights.

Sesame Seed   All it takes are a few hulled sesame seeds topping the crust of a loaf of bread to lend a lively sesame flavor and add winsome eye appeal. No wonder this minute seed has been an important food since prehistory. It is the oldest known herb grown for its seeds and oil and was especially valued in Mediterranean and Eastern civilizations.

Sesame seeds contain over 35 percent protein, more than any nut. They are about 50 percent oil and are high in vitamin E, which renders sesame oil highly stable and resistant to oxidization. Sesame seeds contain as much iron as liver and are rich in potassium, phosphorus, niacin, and thiamine. Sesame has a unique surplus of the two amino acids, methionine and tryptophan, that are most commonly lacking in popular vegetable protein foods.

The sesame seed is available either hulled or unhulled. Some refrain from using whole sesame seeds because the calcium is bound with oxalic acid, and it has been reported that this substance might adversely affect one's calcium reserves. Current scientific thought, and certainly years of gastronomical experience, indicate that whole sesame seeds enjoyed in moderation do not interfere with calcium absorption. (See **Oxalic Acid**.)

Sesame seeds are hulled in a lye or a salt brine solution or are mechanically hulled. Hulled sesame seeds lose their fiber and calcium oxalate, and much of their potassium and vitamin A, iron, and thiamine. The calcium content of hulled sesame seeds is 4 milligrams per 100 grams, whereas it is 1,160 milligrams for whole sesame seeds.

Sesame seeds are used in baking, in tahini, halvah, gomashio (sesame salt), and as a sprinkle for hamburger buns. They are also used in candies, soups, salads, and vegetable dishes. They must be well chewed to be assimilated, and toasting enhances their flavor.

Because sesame seeds are so small, thorough commercial cleaning is difficult; therefore, home washing is advised. Place seeds in a large bowl and fill with water. Pour into a strainer those seeds that float to the top of the bowl. Add more water and repeat the process until all are washed; be careful not to pour out any of the sand or grit that has settled to the bowl's bottom.

Sesame Seed, Black   The most common sesame seed is buff colored. A black variety has limited availability but is worth seeking out. As a garnish, a sprinkle of black can be stunningly dramatic. This seed tastes and smells like the more prosaic variety, only several times more so.

According to Oriental medicine, black sesame seeds, as with other black foods, are strengthening to the regenerative organs. Their stronger flavor indicates that they are higher in minerals and trace nutrients than the buff sesame seed; however, their nutritional data is not available.

See **Seeds** for information on selection, storage, and use and for nutritional and medicinal highlights.

⋆   ⋆   ⋆

The Black Sheep

Unfortunately the "black" sesame seeds frequently found in Asian markets have been dyed. They are shiny and monochromatic. The genuine black variety has a dull, matte finish and ranges in color from coal-black to gray-black with an occasional rust-colored seed. Natural black seeds, imported from the Orient, are available in some quality food stores. Unlike the buff varieties, they generally are preroasted.

⋆   ⋆   ⋆

Shallot   The aromatic shallot has a rich, complex flavor that is sweet, mild, and elusive. It is a cross between onions and garlic. A favorite ingredient in French and New Orleans cuisine, the shallot lends itself especially well to sauces, for it cooks down and serves as a thickener.

Fresh shallots are available year-round. Look for firm bulbs with no signs of rust. Store as for onions. Shallots are also available dried. See **Onion Family**.

Shellfish   All edible marine and freshwater animals with a calcium-based shell rather than a calcium-based skeletal system, are termed shellfish, and they are prized for their tender, fine-textured flesh. Shellfish are nutritionally remarkable. They are high in protein and minerals and are less fatty than other fish.

All shellfish are notorious for rapid spoilage and, without exception, should be eaten only when very fresh or directly after thawing. Also, because they have a tendency to concentrate harmful bacteria, shellfish from polluted waters should never be consumed. Paralytic shellfish poisoning is associated with the "red tide" phenomenon, and the hepatitis virus may be in oysters, clams, and other mollusks that are eaten raw or only partially cooked.

It is prudent not to give shellfish to very young children because they are sometimes not able to digest it. Such children may develop a condition termed anaphylaxis, which can cause severe sickness, when shellfish (as well as other food substances) are consumed. This reaction may continue into adulthood.

The folklores of numerous cultures regards shellfish, especially the mollusks, as aphrodisiacs.

See **Abalone, Clam, Crab, Lobster, Mussel, Oyster, Scallop**, and **Shrimp**.

*   *   *

Dead or Alive

Sound tells if a shellfish is living or dead according to macrobiotic author and teacher, Cornelia Aihara. " . . . take one shellfish in each hand and knock them together. If the sound is 'katchi-katchi' then this sound tells you they are living. If the sound is 'boke-boke' this means the shellfish is dead. So be careful when you choose and cook shellfish; one dead one will make the whole batch taste bad."[14]

*   *   *

Shiitake   Also known as *Japanese Forest Mushroom.* Fresh shiitake (she-TAK-ay) are succulent, meltingly tender, and high-priced mushrooms that enhance almost any dish. Their shape is similar to the common commercial mushroom, only the cap is peaked at the center, and they are larger and darker in color.

The shiitake spores contain a substance called eritadenin, which apparently reduces blood cholesterol. Thus, medicinal potential is highest when the mushroom is still a cap with intact spores. Caps are also the most costly.

Several shiitake farms are in production in the United States, which is making this meaty mushroom increasingly available. When purchasing fresh shiitake, look for firm, fleshy mushrooms that are still a little closed rather than open, flat, and dark. The more aroma it has, the more flavor. Wrap loosely in plastic and refrigerate. A shiitake will hold without spoiling for up to a week, but it loses flavor rapidly.

Dried shiitake are readily available in natural-, Asian-, and gourmet-food markets. Select the thick mushrooms with caps somewhat intact over flat, dark-colored, or broken mushrooms. Store dried shiitake in an airtight container in a cool dry cupboard. To reconstitute prior to use, submerge in water for at least two to three hours or, preferably, overnight.

The shiitake is rich in vitamins D_2, B_2, and B_{12}.

*   *   *

Ultimate Panacea?

The Chinese, Japanese, and Korean folklore and medicinal attributions for shiitake make it sound like the ultimate panacea. Interestingly enough, contemporary scientific research is substantiating many of these claims. According to Jan and John Belleme, authors of *Cooking with Japanese Foods,* shiitake is effective in the treatment of cancer, high blood pressure, sexual problems, excess cholesterol, gallstones, hyperacidity, and stomach ulcers, diabetes, vitamin deficiencies, anemia, and the common cold.[15]

*   *   *

Shiso   See **Beefsteak Leaf**.

Shrimp   Several varieties of shrimp are abundant in both fresh and salt waters. This lobster relative deteriorates quickly, and most are frozen on the shrimp boats immediately on being caught. Some are cooked on board. Fresh farmed shrimp are becoming increasingly available.

Good shrimp are dry and firm with a shell that fits tightly around the body. Shrimp with an aroma of ammonia have been chemically treated.

Shrimp are high in protein, calcium, and phosphorus and are extremely low in fat. Shrimp are very high in iron, with a three-ounce portion having three times the RDA for iron.

See **Shellfish** for information on selection, storage, and use and for medicinal and nutritional highlights.

Sieva Bean See **Lima Bean**.

Smelt A smelt is a small, silvery, migratory, troutlike fish that lives in the ocean but spawns in fresh water. When freshly caught it has a curious smell reminiscent of violets and a sweet flavor something like cucumbers. This extremely bony fish is most often fried or baked. Canned smelts are available kippered, smoked, and boned.

Smelts are available throughout the world; however, the Pacific smelt doesn't keep as well as others. Their seasons are fall and winter. Smelts are an excellent source of protein and, among fish, are extremely low in fat.

See **Fish** for information on selection, storage, and use and for nutritional and medicinal highlights.

Snow Pea The tender-crisp, jade-colored snow pea, with its sweet, edible pod and succulent peas is a vegetable par excellence. The sooner it is consumed after it has been picked, the higher its sugar content and delectability. Purchase snow peas that look squeaky fresh. When withered at the tips, or when the peas are large and round (rather than small and in a flat pod), the vegetable is past its prime.

Snow peas are available year-round in some markets but are the least costly in the spring. Refrigerate wrapped in plastic. For maximum flavor, use as soon after purchase as possible.

This delicacy is a popular ingredient in Chinese-style cooking. When split open and spread with a delectable tofu or cheese filling, snow peas make showy hors d'oeuvres.

Snow peas are a good source of vitamin A and have a fair amount of B-complex vitamins, iron, phosphorus, potassium, and calcium. See **Pea** and **Sugar Snap Pea**.

Snow Puff See **Enoki**.

Soba See **Buckwheat** and **Pasta**.

Sole The sea fish sole is particularly scarce in the United States. What is often sold as sole is actually flounder. See **Flounder**.

Sorbitol A naturally occurring substance, sorbitol is present in many fruits, algae, and seaweed. It is about 40 percent less sweet than sugar and is absorbed slowly by the body. Sound like the ideal sweetener? Yes, when it is naturally occurring.

Although sorbitol may be isolated from whole foods, it is a costly process. Commercial quantities are inexpensively processed from potentially harmful sugar substitutes. Health problems, especially of the digestive tract, have been reported by those who have used sorbitol in quantity. Claims that sorbitol is healthful are farfetched.

Quality sweeteners are available. You can have your cake and eat it, too, without resorting to highly processed sugar substitutes. See **Sweeteners**.

*   *   *

Sweet or Metallic?

Taste, really taste, a candy containing an artificial sweetener like sorbitol. The initial impact is knock-your-socks-off sweet. The lingering aftertaste is harsh, unpleasant, and metallic. A naturally sweetened food has a pleasing sweetness, from the initial taste through—and including—the aftertaste.

*   *   *

Sorghum This milletlike grain is the staple grain of Africa and was cultivated in Egypt as far back as 2200 B.C. Brought to the American colonies by slave ships, sorghum has primarily remained a southeastern crop. The grain is used for cattle feed; the stalks are used to make sorghum molasses.

Sorghum may be cooked whole, or ground and cooked as a porridge. To prepare whole, add one cup sorghum and a pinch of sea salt to four cups water and cook for an hour. Sorghum is nutritionally similar to corn.

Sorghum Molasses Not to be confused with molasses made of sugarcane, sorghum molasses is made from the stalks of a plant that looks like a thin-bladed corn but is related to millet. It is comparable to blackstrap molasses nutritionally. Both taste smoky and bittersweet, have thick textures, and are from 65 to 70 percent sucrose.

Sorghum molasses was a chief sweetener in American homes during the eighteenth and early nineteenth centuries. It currently has greater demand in southeastern states. Store sorghum in a cool, dry place, preferably in a jar. If it crystallizes or becomes gelatinous, gently heat the uncovered jar in a pan of water.

Sorghum is high in iron and is a fair source of calcium. See **Sweeteners** for additional information.

Sour Cherry See **Cherry, Sour**.

Sour Cream Rich and sensuous, sour cream is made by inoculating cream with a lactic acid culture and allowing it to ferment. Until about 1916, all the sour cream used in the United States was homemade from heavy cream. The mechanical cream separator enabled commercial production of sour cream.

Sour cream is comparable to yogurt except that cream, rather than milk, is used. It is high in saturated fats and often contains stabilizers. Light cream and sour cream share practically the same nutrient values.

See **Dairy** for information on selection, storage, and use and for nutritional highlights.

Soybean The first record of the soybean was in 2800 B.C., when it was described as one of the most important crops in China. Termed the "vegetable cow" or the "meat of the earth," soy is the least expensive source of protein in virtually every country in the world. It is a complete protein, high in lecithin, low in calories and saturated fats, and cholesterol free.

Soy is a versatile food. Quality soyfood products retain the excellent nutritional properties of the bean and are easy to digest. Traditional soy products include tempeh, tofu, miso, natto, soy milk, and shoyu.

Soy is also highly refined into food products with questionable health value, such as texturized vegetable protein (TVP) and soy isolates. Additionally, soy has industrial uses in the paint, plywood, pharmaceutical, and cosmetics industries. The United States produces two-thirds of the world's crop of soy, with Brazil and China the other major producers.

The just-harvested green soy may be eaten fresh, and occasionally the dry bean is used whole. However, because soy contains certain enzymes, such as the trypsin inhibitors, it is difficult to digest. Therefore the largest and most healthful use of soy is in traditional products in which the trypsin inhibitors are eliminated primarily through the fermentation process.

Soy grits are made from raw or partially cooked soybeans that have been cracked into eight or ten pieces.

Defatted soy grits (also granules) are made from soybean meal, the byproduct of soy oil manufacture. An advantage of using grits is their short cooking time. However, they are not a whole food and have not been processed to eliminate the enzymes that inhibit digestion.

See **Beans** for information on selection, storage, and use and for nutritional and medicinal highlights. For soy products not listed immediately below, see also **Miso, Natto, Tofu**, and **TVP**.

* * *

Optimum Land Utilization

An acre of land planted in soybeans produces over *twenty times* more usable protein than if that land were used to raise beef cattle or grow their fodder. As over half the world's population has a protein-deficient diet, the importance of soybeans is apt to increase rather than diminish.

* * *

Soybean, Black   Most varieties of soy are a cream or buff color, but one type has a glossy black skin. It is easy to distinguish from the black turtle bean. The black soy is round, plump, and glossy while the turtle is shaped like a small pinto and has a matte black skin. Like other soy, the black requires long cooking. It has rich, deep flavor and is wonderfully palatable.

◆   Nutritionally black soy is comparable to other soy varieties. It is said to be especially medicinal to the sexual organs.

⌑   Cook as for whole soybeans or with rice as follows: In a skillet, roast ¼ cup black soybeans until their skins pop. Place roasted beans in a pressure cooker with 2 cups of rice, 2½ cups water, and 1 teaspoon tamari. Pressure-cook for one hour.

* * *

Black for Endurance

Prior to arduous journeys the Chinese fed black soybeans to their horses to increase their endurance.

* * *

Soybean Paste   See **Miso**.

Soy Cheese   See **Cheese**.

Soy Flour   Yellow-colored soy flour, although believed to be a nutritious additive to baked goods, still contains those pesky trypsin inhibitors and so is hard to digest. Additionally, soy flour has an overpowering flavor. It is thus toasted to improve its digestibility and flavor.

Since soy flour provides moisture to baked goods, it extends their keeping ability. It also inhibits fat absorption and so is excellent to include in breadings and batter for fried foods.

✺   Low-fat and defatted soy flours are by-products of soybean oil extraction. They are an incomplete food derived from a highly refined process.

Of the soy flours available, full-fat soy is preferable because it is made from whole soybeans that have been dehulled, cracked, and toasted with radiant heat. Like other whole-grain flours it has a limited shelf life.

Soy Ice Cream   See **Ice Cream and Frozen Desserts**.

✺   **Soy Isolate**   Whenever soy isolate is included in an ingredient listing, it is best to exclude that product from your diet. After the oil is pressed from soybeans, the remaining meal is bathed in acid, base, and alcohol solutions to eliminate all the carbohydrates. The remaining soy isolate is commonly used in imitation cheese and ice cream. It may be further processed to make TVP or other highly processed soy products.

Soy Milk   Concurrent with the increasing incidence of milk allergies is the gaining popularity and availability of soy milk. In terms of flavor, milk from the bean is a fair approximation of milk from the cow, but, of course, is not an exact duplication. Soy milk is enjoyed by the glassful, over cereal, and in cooking.

☆   In terms of nutrition, the vegetable source is superior. This milk substitute has the same amount of protein as cow's milk, approximately one-third the fat, fewer calories, no cholesterol, many essential B vitamins, and fifteen times the iron. Because it is lower on the food chain, it contains one-tenth the chemical residues.[16] Soy milk is nutritionally better than cow's milk in all respects except one—it is lower in calcium.

Fresh soy milk, manufactured by some small regional soy dairies, is superior to packaged soy milk because it is minimally processed. It has a shorter shelf life than cow's milk or highly processed soy milk. If fresh milk is purchased in a plastic container, transfer it at home into a glass container and refrigerate to increase its storage time. If it does "clabber" (become sour and separate), use it like buttermilk or yogurt in cooking and baking.

Both domestic and imported large-scale commercial soy milk is available in aseptic cartons or foil packs that have a shelf life of a year. It is available in a variety of flavors as well as dried. Once opened it holds for several weeks refrigerated.

Soy milk is packaged as a nutritious noncarbonated soft drink in many Third World countries. This beverage is economical and nutritious, and many health claims are made for it. Indeed, soy milk will continue to gain popularity.

In *The Book of Tofu*, Bill Shurtleff, fondly called the Johnny Appleseed of Soy, and Akiko Aoyagi say this about soy milk: "Many Japanese doctors view it as an effective natural medicine and prescribe it as a regular part of the diet for diabetes . . . heart disease, high blood pressure, and hardening of the arteries . . . and anemia. It is also used to strengthen the digestive system . . . and alkalize—hence fortify—the bloodstream."[17]

* * *

Rule of Thumb

An apt rule of thumb is that a long shelf life (for processed foods) reflects a higher degree of processing. This is applicable to soy milk packaged in aseptic containers. To create a milk with a twelve-month shelf life, the beans undergo up to fourteen mechanical steps in production, some of which include the use of high temperatures. (Homemade soy milk, which lasts four days only, is a low-technology process requiring simply boiling and straining.)

Nutritionally, soy milk has an impeccable profile. However, from an energy point of view, nutrition is not the whole story. A highly processed food with a lengthy shelf life is less energizing and strengthening than one that is prepared by simple technology.

* * *

Soynut   Those oversalted, beggarly little crunches found in everything from trail mix to salads are soynuts. Soybeans trying to pass as a dessert nut! I will pass. True, they are an excellent protein source, but most Americans suffer from too much protein. Soynuts are hard to digest and exorbitantly high in sodium.

If you must, you might try making them at home to limit the amount of salt. Soak soybeans overnight. Drain and spread on an oiled cookie sheet and roast in a moderate oven for about half an hour. Stir occasionally. Remove from heat when they are golden brown. Sprinkle lightly with tamari.

Soy Oil   Natural soy oil is not a big seller for two reasons: (1) It is highly inefficient to extract soy oil by expeller press; and (2) many people find its taste offensive and describe the aroma as fishy or paintlike.

When these objectionable traits are refined away with hexane solvents, soy oil is highly versatile. Highly refined soy oil currently accounts for over 80 percent of all oil used in commercial food production in the United States.[18] Almost any product labeled vegetable oil is apt to contain soy oil.

Natural soy oil is dark yellow and, due to its chlorophyll content, has a green tinge. It contains about 3 percent phosphatides (lecithin), which act as an antioxidant and emulsifier, rendering it well suited to baked goods. It is high in polyunsaturates and linoleic acid. Soy oil is more susceptible to oxidation than sesame, olive, or corn oil.

See **Oil** for information on selection, storage, and use and for nutritional and medicinal highlights.

Soy Sauce   Also known as *Shoyu* and *Tamari*. The seasoning agent indispensable to Oriental cookery is a fermented product of soy, salt, water, and generally wheat, which is known by three different names and refers to three different products. Tamari and shoyu are naturally fermented seasonings that enhance the flavor of food because they contain glutamic acid.

A brief description of how these products are made clarifies the differences between them. However, the ultimate test, and the one that really matters, is the taste test.

Soy sauce is commonly made by reacting hydrolized vegetable protein (from extruded soybeans) with hydrochloric acid. In twenty-four hours the acid has broken down the soybeans and it is removed. The remaining soy substance is mixed with caramel coloring, salt, corn syrup, and water. A preservative is usually added. Soy sauce is cheaply priced and its flavor is harsh, abrasively salty, sweet, and bitter, and it has a metallic aftertaste.

Shoyu is fermented from whole soy beans, salt, water and wheat koji. It has aged for a year or two and has a wide range of flavors. Just as countless factors influence the bouquet and flavor of a fine wine, so too do innumerable factors influence the quality of shoyu. A superior shoyu has a round, full flavor and a mellow aftertaste. Much of the sweet aroma and flavor of shoyu is lost during long cooking, so it is best used to season toward the end of cooking.

Tamari is a term around which there is much confusion. It originally referred to the liquid that rises to the surface of aging hatcho miso. This product is not commercially available in the United States. Today the term tamari most often means a wheat-free shoyu; however, it is sometimes incorrectly applied to a manufacturer's top-of-the-line shoyu.

Real tamari contains only soy, salt, and water. (It is fermented with soy koji rather than wheat koji.) Tamari is higher in amino acids, contains more glutamic acid, and has a stronger flavor than shoyu. Long cooking enhances and rounds out its flavor.

★   ★   ★

Enhance Flavor with Minimum Sodium

In low-sodium circles, shoyu (and tamari) has a bad name because of its high salt content. This reputation would be warranted only if it were consumed by the glassful. Shoyu's wide range of flavors enable richer seasoning with less salt than if straight salt were added to a dish. Indeed, shoyu and tamari are flavor enhancers, and minute quantities bring out the natural flavor of foods to which they are added.

Plain salt contains two grams of sodium per teaspoon while the same amount of natural soy sauce contains 286 milligrams of sodium—or about one-seventh as much.

★   ★   ★

Soy Yogurt   As delicious and versatile as yogurt is yogurt made of soy. "Soygurt," a lactose- and cholesterol-free product, is available commercially and is also easy to make. Nondairy cultures are available in health food stores, or any regular unpasteurized dairy yogurt may be used as a starter.

Prepare, store, and use soy yogurt as you would dairy yogurt. Soygurt has a comparable nutritional profile to soy milk's with enhanced digestibility because it is fermented.

Spaghetti Squash   The spaghetti squash is pale-fleshed and mildly flavored like a summer squash; but it has the storage capabilities of winter squash. Its memorable property is that when cooked its flesh may be coaxed into spaghetti-like strands that some people adore. Others find the vegetable too neutral and stringy.

See **Squash, Summer** for information on selection, storage, and use and for nutritional and medicinal properties.

Spinach   Spinach is one of the most popular greens for cooking, and it is also enjoyed raw in salads. This goosefoot-family member is a superior source of vitamin A and iron and is higher in protein than most vegetables.

Spinach is available throughout the year. Look for crisp, bright green leaves with short stems. Avoid spinach that is yellow, wilted, slimy, or whose stem ends show dehydration. Refrigerate in plastic for up to five days. Spinach grows in sandy soil, and so it needs several thorough washings prior to cooking.

Savoy spinach, with wrinkly, crinkled leaves, is most commonly available. There are also flat-leafed varieties. See **Goosefoot Family**.

*   *   *

Popeye's Spinach Passé; Olive Oyl Still Prime

Popeye was on a good track endorsing spinach, but that it was canned does date the promotion. Today's consumers go for maximum flavor and sensory appear, which precludes canned spinach. Spinach in the 1980s is more apt to appear in a salad bowl tossed with olive oil.

*   *   *

Sprouts   Over the past few decades sprouts have been the fall guy for anyone poking fun at vegetarianism. Admittedly, a diet based on sprouts is bound to raise eyebrows. Ten years ago alfalfa and mung bean sprouts were not a supermarket item. Today sprouts are an "all-American" food.

Sprouts are one of the most economical and nutritious foods. Sprouted seeds add flavor, versatility, and interest to numerous dishes. In the process of sprouting, seeds attain higher levels of protein, sugar, hormones, and vitamin C and some B vitamins. Sprouts are low in fat and calories.

A limited selection of sprouts is available in most markets, but they are easy and inexpensive to make at home. All that's needed is a wide-mouthed glass jar (either quart, half-gallon, or gallon), a piece of cheesecloth, nylon, or fine mesh to cover the jar's mouth, a rubber band or screw-on jar ring, some seeds, and a warm counter.

Use seeds that are whole and preservative free. Soak seeds overnight in water to cover. Secure the cheesecloth covering over the jar's mouth. The next morning strain out the water, rinse the seeds, and strain again. Repeat, if necessary, until the water runs clear. Turn the jar upside down into a bowl and set out on the counter. You may speed the sprouting process by holding the jar in the dark; however, sprouting in the light increases their chlorophyll. Rinse and drain the seeds twice a day (or more often if the weather is very hot and humid). When ready, refrigerate, and use with a flourish. Sprouts will keep fresh for up to a week.

Sprouts may be made of legume, grain, vegetable, herb, and oil seeds. Any legume will sprout, but unlike other sprouts, they require cooking prior to consumption (alfalfa sprouts excepted). Buckwheat must have its hull intact for sprouting. Quinoa must be untoasted with its saponin intact. The carbohydrates in grain convert to sugar, which may become alcoholic and develop an unpleasant sweetness if allowed to grow too long.

Alfalfa is sprout queen and ubiquitous in every salad bar. This tiny sprout is high in minerals, protein, and vitamins A, B complex, C, D, E, and K. Alfalfa requires the shortest soaking time—only five hours. Two tablespoons yield one quart; at harvest their length should be one to two inches. Growing time is from four to six days, depending upon temperature.

One cup of black-eyed peas yields a quart of sprouts. They take up to four days' growing time and are ready to eat when the sprouts are three-quarters of an inch long. Black-eyed peas are a good source of protein, minerals, and vitamins A and C.

Flavorful cabbage sprouts are ready to eat when the sprout is an inch long. Sprouting may take up to five days. Place in indirect sun long enough for chlorophyll to develop. Cabbage sprouts are rich in vitamins A and C and various minerals.

Chickpeas require up to sixteen hours' soaking. Three-quarters of a cup yields one quart of sprouts. They are ready in about four days and are best when the sprout is just under one inch long. Like other legumes, chickpea sprouts provide complete protein.

Clover is a popular seed for sprouting, and, of the numerous varieties, red clover is favored. Sprouting instructions are the same as for alfalfa. Clover sprouts are high in protein, calcium, iron, B vitamins, and vitamin C.

Fenugreek sprouts are ready when they're an inch long. They have an aggressive flavor that some do not enjoy. One tablespoon yields about a quart. Fenugreek takes approximately four days to sprout.

Lentil sprouts are most nutritious if sprouted to only one-half inch but are tastier if allowed to grow longer. Three-fourths of a cup yields one quart of sprouts, and they require only four hours of soaking. Lentils are a good source of B vitamins as well as protein.

Mung beans are a popular sprout and a mainstay of Chinese cookery. Soak one-half cup of mungs overnight to yield one quart of sprouts. They require up to five days' growing time in a dark, warm place. Mung sprouts are rich in iron and calcium as well as protein and vitamins A and C.

Peanuts require longer soaking, with one and one-half cups yielding one quart of sprouts. Sprouting time is three to four days, and they are ready when the sprout is one-quarter of an inch long. Peanuts are an excellent source of niacin as well as the nutrients of other sprouted legumes.

Radish sprouts are produced in the same manner as cabbage sprouts but may take a day longer. They have a zesty flavor and are delicious in salads.

Soybean sprouts require extra rinsing. Soak overnight, allow to sprout for three to five days, and use when the sprouts are under one inch in length. Soybean sprouts are hard to digest when raw, and so are best cooked. They contain whole protein and vitamins A, B complex, C, and E.

Sunflower seed sprouts develop a bitter taste if allowed to sprout over one-fourth inch long. Soak two cups of seeds overnight to produce one quart of sprouts. These seeds are ready in the shortest amount of time, from two to three days. Sunflower sprouts provide minerals, proteins, unsaturated fatty acids, and vitamins D and E.

Wheat is sprouted like black-eyed peas. Length, however, may be from one-quarter of an inch to one inch, depending on how you will use the sprouts. Their flavor is sweetest if the sprout does not exceed the length of the grain. Wheat sprouts are a good source of protein and vitamins.

★　　★　　★

Cheap Food

The retail cost of organic wheat berries is thirty cents a pound. Sprouted to their green stage, their weight increases fourfold. Thus you can grow four pounds of wheat berries for a thirty-cent investment. Wheat sprouts, when compared to the wheat berry, provide three times more vitamin E and up to six times more of some B vitamins.[19]

★　　★　　★

Squab　See **Fowl.**

Squash　Squash is a logical abbreviation the Pilgrims used for the Narragansett and Iroquois words *askutasquash* and *isquoutersquash,* respectively. Squashes are members of the gourd or Cucurbitaceae family and relatives of cucumbers and melons. Squashes conveniently fall into two categories, summer and winter.

Squash, Summer　A welcome summer vegetable is the tender, brightly colored summer squash, which comes in a variety of fanciful shapes. Soft-skinned summer squashes are mild but charmingly flavorful when they are small and garden fresh. Their flavor rapidly diminishes as their size or time past harvest increases.

The prolific summer squash plants produce continuously throughout the growing season. Even though hothouse zucchini is available during the winter months, it is not as flavorful.

Squash blossoms are delicious sliced and tossed in salads or batter coated and deep fried. Fresh baby summer squashes are served as crudités or finely sliced in salads. Cooking and seasoning enhances their flavor. An overly mature summer squash has a tough skin, hard seeds, and dry flesh, which makes it well suited to stuffing and baking. The spaghetti squash has the storage capabilities of the winter squash; however, its pale, bland flesh indicates that it is actually an overly mature summer squash.

These gourd-family members are a popular ingredient in stir-fried vegetable dishes, deep fried, and in casseroles and soups. They contain a fair amount of vitamins A and C, potassium, and calcium. Select a squash that is firm and has a shiny skin with no brown or bruised spots. Do not refrigerate in plastic. See also **Chayote, Chinese Winter Melon, Crookneck Squash, Pattypan, Spaghetti Squash**, and **Zucchini**.

★　　★　　★

Energetic Difference Between Winter and Summer Squash

Summer squashes move from bud to table in a matter of days. They are speedy! Months pass from the blossoming of a winter squash until it reaches maturation. The dense sweet flesh of a winter squash reflects a whole summer, plus Indian summer, of accumulating energy from sun and soil. They have concentrated nutrients, are substantially filling, and are said to be a strengthening food. The winter varieties are apt fare for cold winter days.

This is not to say that summer squashes are less desirable. Their zippy energy is perfect for a hot summer day when we want light, rather than concentrated, food.

★　　★　　★

Squash, Winter　The word *squash* aptly describes its cooked texture but does not hint at its sweetness. A good winter squash packs a sweet wallop of flavor. Winter squashes have a dark yellow to orange flesh and a thick rind. The sweetest squashes are generally those with the deepest colored flesh. Of the vegetable realm they are exceptionally high in complex carbohydrates and are said to be medicinal for diabetics and for those with digestive problems.

This gourd relative provides vitamins A and C, potassium, and magnesium and is very low in sodium. It is an excellent source of provitamin A, or carotenoids.

Select a squash that is heavy for its size and has a hard rind with mottled markings. The rind should be free of soft spots, cracks, and bore holes. An intact stem indicates better storage properties. When stored in a dry, cool place, a winter squash keeps into the spring. If you do not have a cool storage area, hold the squash at room temperature, rather than refrigerate, but then plan to use within a week.

Squashes are delicious baked, boiled, or fried. Puréed, it makes a sweet soup or pie, a sensational spread for waffles or toast, or it may be added to cookies, puddings, and cakes. Squash seeds afford a chewy and tasty high-fiber snack. (See recipe accompanying **Acorn Squash**.)

See **Acorn Squash, Banana Squash, Buttercup Squash, Butternut Squash, Delicata, Golden Nugget, Hubbard Squash, Kabucha, Pumpkin**, and **Turban**.

Winter squash and many other orange-colored foods are high in carotenoids. Some carotenoids are antioxidants and protect against carcinogenic cell damage as well as blood vessel cell damage.

According to Marcy Barbour, R.D., "Carotenoids have a remarkable ability to attach to potentially destructive oxygen free radicals (OFR) and render them harmless. OFRs, implicated in aging, are created by natural metabolic processes—but also by dietary toxins like rancid fat or environmental ones like pollution. Left unchecked, OFRs can randomly attach themselves to parts of cells, including DNA, and cause damage that many scientists believe may eventually initiate cancer."[20]

Foods highest in the antioxidant carotenoids are winter squash, sweet potatoes, carrots, cantaloupes, apricots, and papayas.

* * *

Stalk Vegetables   The stalk of a vegetable is the part that carries nutrients and energy up from the earth. Oriental medicine teaches that stalk vegetables are good for bringing our energy upward. A wide selection of all types of vegetables is recommended for optimum health; and an emphasis on stalk vegetables may be recommended for one whose energy is down, who is too materialistic, or who lacks an expansive nature.

Star Fruit   Also known as *Carambola.* The star fruit is a Walt Disney–like creation. Slice this banana-yellow fruit and you have perfectly shaped stars that delight the eye and lighten the spirit. A native of Indonesia, the carambola is now being grown in Florida, and so we are seeing it with increasing frequency in our markets.

The star fruit is a deeply ribbed fruit from three to five inches long. The thin, waxlike skin is edible, and its juicy flesh is almost translucent. It is eaten out of hand, used in salads, seafoods, and desserts, as a garnish or to float in punch bowls. Dried star fruit is available in some natural-food stores.

Look for fruits that are evenly colored and without brown spots. Leave at room temperature until their full fruity aroma is apparent and then refrigerate for up to one week. They are available in late summer and early fall.

The juicy star fruit ranges from sweet to sour in taste. If sweet, it may be eaten without cooking in salads. It is also good in jams and chutney.

Star fruit is a good source of vitamin C and potassium and is low in calories. According to Oriental medicine, it is highly cooling to the body and is thus useful in clearing excess heat.

Stem Lettuce   See **Celtuce**.

Stevia   Also known as *Honey Leaf.* Current interest in a South American plant called stevia is high. Stevia availability is sketchy, but in all likelihood this will change. *Honey leaf* is the English translation of the Paraguayan name *stevia.* The extract from this plant is intensely sweet and similar to molasses in color, flavor, and use but with a suggestion of anise flavor.

Its sweetness is said to come from a glucoside found in the leaf that our bodies cannot metabolize.[21] Thus, honey leaf is essentially nonnutritive and noncaloric. The leaf is 30 times sweeter than sugar. The extract is generally 100 times sweeter than sugar.

The stevia is used extensively in South America and Japan as a sweetener. The Japanese have concentrated it to be 450 times sweeter than sugar. Studies in these countries indicate that it is safe for persons having blood-sugar-related problems, and reputedly it is even medicinal to those with pancreas irregularities.

The FDA has banned the use of stevia extract because it has not yet been adequately tested for use as an approved food additive. The stevia leaf is available as an herb and in herbal tea mixtures. See **Sweeteners**.

Strawberry   I would hope that everyone knows of at least one wooded path that promises wild strawberries. It takes time to get down on your knees and ferret out these ruby, pea-sized jewels. The payoff, in volume, is negligible but this does not in the least detract from the pleasure of the hunt.

The strawberry is an ancient plant that grows wild throughout Europe and North America. It is an unusual fruit in that its seeds are embedded in its surface. At their best, strawberries have a musky aroma and are sweet but acid, almost pineapplelike, in flavor. They are plump, juicy, and soft as a baby's cheek.

Select fully red, slightly soft berries with intact hulls. Do not remove the green caps until after washing the fruit. The strawberry's peak season is from late spring through summer. Those with the most flavor are vine ripened. The odds of purchasing a vine-ripened strawberry are greatest for regional fruits. Out-of-season strawberries look like strawberries but rarely taste like the real thing.

Strawberries provide vitamins A and C, and some B-complex vitamins as well as some minerals. In the Far East they are considered a warming food and may be used medicinally to expell cold from the body's extremities.

* * *

Walton on Strawberries

"God could doubtless have made a better berry, but doubtless he never did."

—Izaak Walton, *The Compleat Angler*

* * *

Strawberry Tomato   See **Ground Cherry**.

String Bean   See **Green Bean**.

Sugar   Sugarcane or sugar beets refined to 99.9 percent sucrose equals sugar. This leaves little room for the fiber, vitamins, minerals, and any trace nutrients of the original plant. Sucrose acts like a chemical (rather than a food, which needs digesting) and is immediately absorbed into the bloodstream, which upsets the blood-sugar balance.

Many unwitting shoppers purchase turbinado sugar, brown sugar, and raw sugar believing that it is lightly refined and, therefore, a more wholesome product. They have been duped. In accordance with the 1948 sugar law, *raw* sugar sold in the United States must be refined to 96 percent purity.

Cane sugar that does not meet the FDA purity code cannot be called "sugar." There are several sweeteners on the market that have their mineral content intact and are therefore less than 96 percent sucrose. These products are indeed natural and they impart a superb flavor and crumb to baked goods.

One is made from organic cane and is termed "dehydrated cane juice." It is used in select natural foods. Piloncillo, a similar Mexican cane product, is available in southwestern markets. Jaggery is an unrefined cane imported from India and is available in Middle Eastern grocery stores.

Consumption of refined sugar is implicated in degenerative diseases as well as behavioral abnormalities. The less you insult your body with sugar, the better. However, sugar is a preferred choice over artificial sweeteners. Some natural health-care practitioners recommend sugar-sweetened tea to help relieve a dry cough. Sugar is not advised in the case of a productive cough. See **Sweeteners** for additional information.

* * *

Sugar is Sugar

" 'Raw,' 'turbinado,' or 'yellow-D' sugar is hardly more nutritious than white sugar; it is still 96 percent sucrose, compared with the 99.9 percent sucrose count in white sugar. If a man strips off all his clothing except his socks you could argue that he was still dressed, and you might win on a technicality. Likewise raw sugar is, by a technicality, raw sugar. Brown sugar is not much different; it is white sugar to which a small amount of molasses has been added for coloring."[22]

*   *   *

Sugar Snap Pea   The cross between the snow pea and the green pea has the best of both pods. As its name suggests, it is sugary and snappy. This legume, like the snow pea, has an edible pod and lends itself to salads and pickles. Cooked, it stars in stir-fried dishes but may be equally enjoyed in steamed and grilled preparations.

The sugar snap pea is available primarily in the fall and spring. Look for bright green pods that contain plump peas. The seeds are best when larger than snow peas and smaller than green peas. Refrigerated in plastic they hold for a couple of days but deteriorate rapidly.

Sugar snap peas are a good source of vitamin A and have a fair amount of B-complex vitamins, iron, phosphorus, potassium, and calcium. See **Pea, Green** and **Snow Pea**.

Sunchoke   See **Jerusalem Artichoke**.

Sunflower Oil   The two oil crops indigenous to North America are corn oil and sunflower oil. The sunflower is one of the few vegetable oil crops that grows in cold climates and it, as well as its oil, is widely used in Canada and Russia. It is relatively new to our market and, as people discover its superior qualities, it may become more readily available.

The sunflower is related to the safflower, and both are high in unsaturated fats and linoleic acid. The flavor of sunflower is more distinctive, and the oil has a better resistance to rancidity. Sunflower oil is an excellent all-purpose oil; however, some people find its flavor too strong for baked goods and salads. See **Sunflower Seed**.

Sunflower Seed   More than any other flower, the sunflower proclaims summer. Wild, it bedecks roadways and gilds whole fields with sun-colored mandalas. Cultivated in home gardens it towers to impressive heights of fifteen feet or more and boasts a flower up to two feet in diameter. A showy plant indeed, but it's more than just show.

This daisy relative originated in western North America, and its seeds were an important food of American Indians. Sunflowers were introduced into Europe in the 1500s and have become a Russian staple. However, until the popularization of health foods in the 1960s, its domestic use was primarily for bird feed; hence its once-common name *polly seed.* Today sunflower seeds are fondly called "sunnies."

The seeds are actually the fruit of the flower. They may be white, brown, black, or black with white stripes. The edible tubers of a smaller variety of sunflower are called Jerusalem artichokes.

Sunflower seeds are nutritionally remarkable. They contain more protein than beef and 20 percent fat, most of which is unsaturated. A good source of calcium, phosphorus, and iron, as well as vitamins A, D, E, and several of the B complex, they also contain a trace of fluorine, which may explain the Russians' claim that they are good for the teeth.

Sunnies are available hulled or unhulled and raw or roasted and salted. Because of their vitamin E content even the hulled seeds have a good shelf life. Look for unbroken, even-colored seeds. Avoid if discolored or rubbery. Most of our commercial supply comes from the Red River Valley of Minnesota. North Dakota and California also produce sunnies.

As a concentrated energy source, sunflower seeds are considered to have medicinal properties for the regenerative organs. See **Seeds** for information on selection, storage, and use and for nutritional and medicinal highlights.

Swede See **Rutabaga**.

Sweet Brown Rice See **Rice**.

Sweeteners Mother's milk is sweet, and maybe this is where it all starts, for most everyone loves sweets. This doesn't have to be a problem as long as attention is paid to quality and quantity. Moderation is a good guideline. An excess of any food, especially sweetners, is not healthful. Sweetening agents are concentrated simple sugars and are refined in some way. Even if labeled natural, none may be considered a whole food.

Two sweeteners, used in moderation, are the most healthful: barley malt and   ☆
rice syrup. Their mellow sweetness comes from maltose. Other sweeteners contain sucrose, are frequently highly refined, and are not recommended. (Honey and fructose are sucrose-free; however, other factors limit their healthfulness.)

Sucrose, like a drug, is quickly absorbed into the bloodstream whereas food must be first digested. Sucrose consumption puts stress on the whole metabolism and supresses the immune system. It causes the pancreas to secrete more insulin to monitor the amount of sugar going into the blood, and extra adrenaline is mobilized to monitor the blood-sugar level. Sucrose provides a few hours of increased energy that are followed by energy depletion and an emotional low aptly referred to by William Dufty as the "sugar blues."[23] Thus sweeteners that contain sucrose are best avoided or used occasionally and with discretion.

For additional information, see **Aspartame, Barley Malt, Carob, Date Sugar, Fructose, Honey, Mannitol, Maple Syrup, Molasses, Rice Syrup, Saccharin, Sorbitol, Sorghum Molasses, Sugar**, and **Xylitol**.

*   *   *

Ranking the Sweeties

Sweeteners run the gamut of quality. Below they are ranked according to healthfulness.

Five-star sweeteners derive their flavor from maltose and have a gentler, slower, more balanced effect on the body's metabolism. They include barley malt and rice syrup.

Three-star sweeteners include carob, date sugar, fruit juice concentrate, honey, maple syrup, and sorghum molasses. They are more stressful to the body's metabolism than barley malt or rice syrup. However, they are decidedly preferable to any of the following sweeteners:

One-star sweeteners are superrefined but at least actually grew in a field and were recognizable as cane, corn, or sugar beets. They are Barbados sugar, brown sugar, cane syrup, corn syrup, dextrose, fructose, invert sugar, molasses, sugar, raw sugar, and turbinado sugar.

The zeros are chemical compounds created in a laboratory and are frequently derived from petroleum products. They are, unfortunately, promoted as healthful sweetener alternatives. Avoid aspartame (also called Nutrasweet and Equal), mannitol, saccharin, sorbitol, and xylitol. Also plan to avoid any new "natural" sweeteners that taste more intensely sweet than sugar. Like a recurring nightmare, a new one hits the market as soon as the current artificial sweetener loses credibility.

*   *   *

Sweet Pepper The produce sections of markets are most festive in late summer and early fall at the peak of the pepper season. The flashy and multicolored peppers range from delicately sweet and peppery to very sweet. They come in a variety of shapes as well as colors. The pepper is so adept at new varieties that we are apt to have more shapes, colors, and flavors available in the future.

The old standard green bell is most consistently available throughout the year. It was named because of its bell-like shape.

Select firm, glossy peppers with stems intact. Avoid those with soft spots or   ▶
shriveled, pale skin, for they are past their prime. In general, those with the thinnest skins are the most peppery whereas the thicker-skinned varieties are

more sweet. Store peppers in a paper bag in the refrigerator and use within five days.

Florida, California, and Texas supply most of our peppers except during the winter months, when they are imported from Europe and South America. Served raw in salads and as finger food, peppers are also stuffed, sautéed, or added to soups and stews. This native American food now figures prominently in ethnic cuisines throughout Europe and the Middle East. See also **Chile Peppers, Nightshades**, and **Pepper**.

Banana pepper (also Hungarian) is a long, tapered pepper that is primarily bright-yellow but also green or orange-red. It has a thick wall, is sweet, and is preferred by many over the bell. The banana pepper may be fried or served raw.

The green bell pepper is crisp with a refreshing peppery taste. It is equally good cooked or raw.

European sweets are similar to the bells in shape but are larger and have tapered ends. These delicious and very thick-fleshed peppers may be green, red, yellow, purple, and even brown.

The pimento is a small, richly sweet, dark-red pepper, bits of which are frequently stuffed into green olives. Now becoming available fresh, the thick-fleshed pimento is superb for roasting.

The purple bell pepper is eggplant colored on the outside and green inside. Its taste is fresh and snappy. Cooking may render purple an unpalatable gray, and so it is most often enjoyed raw.

The red bell pepper is a fully mature green bell and it stores for only a few days. It is the sweetest of the bells and excellent raw or cooked.

Yellow bell peppers are pleasantly sweet but less sweet than the banana pepper. They are delicious raw or cooked.

Sweet Potato   Also known as *Boniato* and *Yam*. Sweet potatoes are sweet. This genre is native to the Americas, a member of the morning-glory family, and is not related to potatoes. Neither are they a yam, although the sweetest sweet potatoes are called yams, which adds further confusion. True yams are native to Africa and are not commercially available in the United States.

Higher in sugar than the potato, the sweet potato is an excellent source of carotenoid antioxidants. They are also high in vitamins A and C and have a fair amount of thiamine.

Select smooth-skinned sweet potatoes without bruises or harvesting scars. They bruise easily, so handle with care. Store in a cool, dry area rather than in the refrigerator and use within four days. Sweet potatoes are at their peak in late fall. This tuber is more dense than the white potato, so allow a somewhat smaller serving per person.

The Jersey or boniato sweet potato has a buff skin with a yellow, firm flesh. When cooked it has a fluffy dry texture and a delicate (rather than domineering) sweetness. The boniato is a Cuban variety.

The yam is a purple-skinned sweet potato with soft, moist, flamboyant orange flesh. This sugar-sweet tuber is highly suitable as a dessert.

Sweet Rice   See **Rice**.

Sweet Rice Wine   See **Mirin**.

Swiss Chard   See **Chard**.

Swordfish   Imagine eating a fish so meaty that energetically it is almost like eating veal. The swordfish is not a lightweight fish. This mackerel relative is found in both cool and warm waters throughout the world. Swordfish may weigh up to six hundred pounds.

Prepare swordfish like tuna. It may be grilled or baked with a generous addition of oil. Sometimes it is available smoked. Atlantic swordfish is available during the spring and fall. Pacific swordfish is available from the fall through the winter.

See **Fish** for information on selection, storage, and use and for nutritional and medicinal highlights.

T

Table Queen Squash See **Acorn Squash**.

Tahini Imagine a meltingly rich and lightly sweet halvah—that's the flavor of tahini at its best. This smooth and creamy spread is nothing but hulled sesame seeds ground into a paste. Tahini is lighter flavored than sesame butter (which is made from whole seeds) and is favored in dressings, sauces, and desserts. It has fewer nutrients than sesame butter.

Commercial tahini is made from seeds that are hulled in caustic chemical baths, neutralized, and bleached. These tahinis tend to be bitter and have a faintly soapy taste. The chemicals reduce some of the nutrition and nutrient absorbability. Quality tahini is made from mechanically hulled seeds.

Tahini may or may not include salt. If roasted it tastes nuttier; if unroasted it is sweeter. Tahini has the same nutrition as hulled sesame seeds; however, if roasted it has less moisture and has slightly more concentrated nutrients.

This high-protein spread is a staple in Mideast and Oriental cookery. Tahini is an excellent base for numerous salad dressings. It may serve as an oil, egg, or milk replacement in many recipes.

Unopened, a jar of quality tahini holds for six or seven months. After opening, it should be refrigerated and will last four to five months. If oil separates to the top, simply stir it back in.

★   ★   ★

Multiuse Tahini Base*

Natural-foods author and chef Mary Estella recommends preparing an all-purpose miso-tahini base that is excellent for making sandwiches or spreading on crackers. It may also be thinned to make a dressing or sauce for grain, noodles, steamed vegetables, tofu, and salads. In her *Natural Foods Cookbook* Estella observes, "Miso-Tahini can keep up to one week refrigerated, but it never lasts that long in my house."[1]

    1 cup tahini
    2 to 3 tablespoons miso
    1 lemon, juiced
    Water to thin

Pour the tahini into a pan; stir over a low flame with a wooden spoon for three to five minutes or until it emits a nutty aroma and turns slightly darker in color. Cool. Blend with miso, lemon juice, and water until creamy.

*Variations:
Tahini-Basil: Add 1 to 2 tablespoons chopped fresh basil.
Tahini-Garlic: Add 2 to 3 cloves minced garlic to tahini while it roasts.
Herbal Dressing: Add 1 teaspoon of favorite herbs—oregano, dill, thyme, and so on.

★   ★   ★

Tai Sai See **Bok Choy**.

Takuan See **Daikon Pickle**.

Tamari See **Soy Sauce**.

Tamarillo The tamarillo is the size and shape of an egg and has a patent-leather-like red or yellow skin. Its copper-colored flesh is pleasantly bitter and contains a number of small magenta-colored seeds. In appearance, it is a stunning fruit. It has a tomato-like aroma and is a tomato relative.

The aromatic tamarillo requires peeling. It is best when cooked in relishes, chutneys, and sweet and savory sauces. It is primarily available as a New Zealand import from early summer through the fall. Select firm fruits and allow to soften at room temperature. Then refrigerate for up to a week. See **Nightshades** for additional information.

Tangelo   Cross a tangerine and the pomelo (a grapefruitlike citrus) and you have a tangelo, which tastes like a blend of orange and tangerine. Tangelos contain many pips and a nipple at their stem end.

See **Citrus Fruit** for information on selection and storage and for nutritional and medicinal highlights.

Tangerine   The tangerine is smaller than an orange, and its deep red-orange peel easily detaches from the fruit. The juicy tangerine flesh contains many seeds. Tangerines are available from November to May.

Tangerines are nutritionally similar to oranges. This cooling and refreshing   +
fruit is used as a kitchen remedy in the treatment of chest congestion.   ◆

See **Citrus Fruit** for information on selection and storage and for nutritional and medicinal highlights.

Taro   Also known as *Albi* or *Eddo.* A tuber with widespread use throughout the tropics is a potatolike plant, the taro. This plant produces two types of tubers. One is a large turnip-shaped and -size corm, from which the leaf stalks grow. There are smaller, subsidiary tubers (called "cormels"), which are the size of a plump Brazil nut and which grow attached to the main corm by rootlets. The taro skin is rough, shaggy, and brown. Its whitish flesh turns violet when cooked.

As a food, taro may be substituted for potatoes, but expect a drier, sweeter,   ⌑
and nuttier flavor. It lends itself well to stews and fried dishes. Select corms that   ▷
are moist and plump and have no sign of withering. Do not refrigerate, but use
at or before the time it starts to become soft.

High in potassium and a fair source of iron, the taro is used medicinally to   +
prepare external plasters for the treatment of cysts, tumors, and boils.   ◆

The taro has been available commercially in both large supermarkets and specialty stores that cater to Asian populations.

Tarragon   The long, delicate, polished gray-green leaves of the perennial herb tarragon are a favorite in French cuisine. Tarragon is classic in tartar and béarnaise sauces. Add the leaves to salads, dressings, and sauces and to vegetable,   ⌑
poultry, and fish dishes. It is especially compatible with beans, mushrooms, squash, and eggs.

Tarragon is frequently available fresh. Its flavor is slightly reminiscent of anise but is more briskly tart. Unlike most herbs, dried tarragon has less flavor than fresh.

See **Herbs and Spices** for information on selection, storage, and use and for nutritional and medicinal highlights.

Tea   One of the world's most widely consumed beverages comes from a small evergreen tree *(Camellia sinensis)* that is related to the camellia family and is native to China. Tea has played a significant role in the histories of many nations. Its leaves and, to a lesser extent, its blossoms and twigs are used to make a wide variety of refreshing infusions. Many factors influence tea flavor including the manner in which the leaves are processed, the age of the leaves, the age of the tea plant, the season in which the leaves are harvested, and the geographical area it is grown in. Various flavorings may also be added.

Tea affects the central nervous system with two stimulants, caffeine and   ◆
theophylline. A cup of tea has 40 to 50 mg of caffeine, about half that in a cup of coffee. Tea also contains tannin, which gives tea its body and is a growth depressant. Tea is about as acid as coffee.

Tea loses its flavor with age and improper storage; it keeps best in a covered   ▷
tin or glass jar in a cool cupboard. Fresh tea leaves should be resilient, not stale and brittle. Organic tea has limited availability but is worth seeking out in terms of flavor and quality.

To brew an excellent cup of tea see **Herbal Tea**. For medicinal teas see

Bancha Tea and **Kukicha**. There are hundreds of tea varieties; some of the major classifications are listed here.

Black tea is allowed to ferment naturally (through enzymatic oxidation), which causes the leaves to darken and release their bitter-tasting properties called catechins. This enables the tea's flavor to emerge. The manner in which a black tea is withered, rolled, dried, and sifted during fermentation determines the flavor and color of the final product.

Decaffeinated tea is a popular beverage for those who enjoy the inimitable black tea flavor but do not want the caffeine stimulation. The increasing concern about the quality of decaf beverages is justified. Tea may be decaffeinated with ethyl acetate or by a water process. Favor decaf tea processed by water.

Tea leaves that are sun-dried or heated immediately after harvesting yield green tea. When infused it has a thin, bitter flavor and a pale color. The best-quality green tea is the hand-harvested first two new leaves that appear on each shoot of young plants in the spring.

A third type of tea, oolong, is a partially fermented tea with characteristics of both green and black tea. Oolong and black teas yield yellow, gold, or red infusions. Oolongs are richer and more full-flavored than green tea.

*   *   *

The Agony of the Leaves

At the end of April, the prime harvest time for tea, traditional Chinese families climbed high into the mountains to pick the new, still-furled tea leaves. They had already collected spring rains to be used for brewing. Karen MacNeil, in her thoughtful and thorough book, *Whole Foods: Nutrition and Cuisine,* describes this tradition:

"A place of 'great tranquility' would be chosen; then, with presence of mind, the tea would be made. The moment the steaming rainwater was poured, the tightly clasped leaves would twist and unwind their contorted bodies in a dance that the Chinese called the 'agony of the leaves.' "[2]

*   *   *

Teff   Also known as *T'ef.* Teff (*Eragrostis tef*) is about as big as the period that ends this sentence. Despite its size, it is the staple cereal grain in Ethiopia, and it is exciting interest in U.S. specialty-food markets.

As with other grains, in antiquity teff was a foraged wild grass that eventually became cultivated. Seeds of teff have been found in a brick of the Dassur Egyptian pyramid built in 3359 B.C. Today teff straw is still used to make adobe in Ethiopia, and it is cultivated for its hay in Kenya and Australia. Commercial teff food crops are growing in Idaho.

Until recently, teff use in the United States was limited to Ethopian cuisine. Because of its excellent nutrition and pleasing flavor it is no longer an ethnic secret. The overall nutrition of this milletlike seed is superior to all other cereal grains. Teff is especially high in calcium and iron. It has 182 mg calcium and 55 mg iron in 100 grams edible portion. Only high-gluten wheat is richer in protein than teff, which boasts 12 percent protein. Like other cereals, it is low in the amino acid lysine.

The reason teff is packed with nutrients is because it is so tiny that it has proportionally more endocarp (hull) than other grains. Also, because it is too small to hull, its nutrients remain intact.

Teff is available in three varieties: white, red, and brown. Each has a pleasing, almost nutty flavor. The mild white teff is chestnutlike in taste; the darker colors are more earthy and taste like hazlenuts.

Brown or red teff makes a rich, rustic breakfast porridge, whereas white teff makes a more delicate creamy cereal. When cooked into a soup or stew for thirty minutes or more, teff bursts open and provides body and flavor. As a pilaf, its texture is granular.

Teff Flour   The Ethiopians use teff flour to make their staple bread, injera. The batter is fermented for several days and then cooked into large flat rounds. Injera's sour flavor and spongelike consistency endear it to some, but not to all. It is a highly digestible bread because it is fermented.

White, red, and brown teff flour are domestically available. Teff flour makes tasty quick breads, pancakes, and waffles. The white is more suited to cakes and pastries. For leavened bread, use predominately wheat flour with up to 20 percent teff flour. See **Flour** for storage techniques.

Tempeh   *Prevention Magazine* publisher Robert Rodale is one of the many who predict that tempeh (tem-PAY) will become an important American food. "Tempeh is on its way up. Before long it will be eaten widely and lovingly across this land . . . I'm convinced that tempeh is just sitting there waiting for lightning to strike, the way it hit yogurt. All the signs point to that happening, and soon."[3]

What is so remarkable about this ancient Indonesian soy food? It is versatile, heartier than tofu, and very adaptable to Western cuisine. Fried tempeh is reminiscent of Southern fried chicken or fish fillets. Steamed, grilled, or fried, tempeh is easily prepared to appeal to all palates. Assertive seasonings like garlic, ginger, and coriander compliment it; souring agents such as wine, lemon juice, or vinegar enhance it.

Tempeh contains 50 percent more protein than hamburger and is cholesterol free. One of the world's richest known sources of vitamin B_{12}, tempeh is highly digestible. Available fresh or frozen in natural-food stores and some supermarkets in North America, it is reasonably priced and it may be made at home for pennies a pound.

Roughly the size and shape of a waffle, a fermented tempeh cake is bound together with a nappy white mycelium of branching, threadlike enzymes. This mycelium makes the soy easily digestible and provides many valuable B vitamins. To make tempeh, soybeans are split, cooked, innoculated with tempeh starter, and incubated. Grains such as rice, mixed grains, and quinoa may be used along with soy for different flavors.

Like miso, tempeh is a fermented and a whole soy food, and it is more strengthening than tofu (which is neither whole nor fermented). Fresh tempeh is preferable to frozen tempeh, but freezing does not impair its bacterial content. See **Soybean** and **Fermented Food**.

Texturized Vegetable Protein   See **TVP**.

Thyme   The balmy aromatic thyme was valued by the ancient Greeks and Romans as an aphrodisiac and for instilling bravery and courage. Medieval knights wore scarves upon which their ladies had embroidered sprigs of thyme. Euell Gibbons observes:

"According to ancient tradition, if a girl wears a corsage of wild thyme flowers it means that she is looking for a sweetheart, and according to another tradition, if a bashful boy drinks enough wild thyme tea it will give him courage to take her up on it."[4]

Culinary uses of thyme place it among the most popular herbs for flavoring soups, stews, stuffings, and sauces, either alone or in a bouquet garni. There are many different varieties of thyme, including lemon-scented and caraway-scented. See **Herbs and Spices** for additional information.

Tofu   In one decade tofu has moved from an obscurity to a common staple in American cuisine—and with good reason. Combined with grains, this soyfood yields easily digested, high-quality protein. Tofu is a fantastic diet food (a one-ounce serving contains only 147 calories) that is cholesterol free and low in saturated fats. Tofu is an excellent source of calcium and a good source of other minerals such as iron, phosphorus, potassium, and sodium. It also contains essential B vitamins, choline, and fat-soluble vitamin E.

Unlike high-protein foods from animal products, tofu is relatively free of toxic chemical residues. It is much less expensive than protein from animal products. Tofu is highly versatile and may be used as a cheese substitute and in countless food preparations.

Soybeans, water, and a curdling agent are tofu's ingredients. The flavor varies greatly from manufacturer to manufacturer, depending on the water and processing techniques and the type of coagulant. Nigari, a mineral-rich seawater precipitate, is a traditional coagulant and is preferred by many. Another coagulant, calcium sulfate, is gaining in popularity because it increases tofu's calcium content significantly.

Tofu is marketed according to its water content as soft, firm, or extra firm. Soft tofu is more delicate and delicious in soups and desserts. Harder tofu lends itself better to frying and pickling. Specially processed tofu, which varies greatly in flavor and texture from regular tofu, includes tofu cutlets, age (deep-fried tofu pouches), freeze-dried tofu, and dried tofu.

Fresh-packed tofu is best used within a few days. Vacuum-packed tofu keeps longer. Once opened, refrigerate tofu submerged in water in a covered container. Change the water daily, and though it will hold for five days or longer, its flavor does deteriorate with each passing day.

*   *   *

Cold Tofu

Foods that are cooling, like tofu, tend to reduce the fire in the lower organs. This explains why tofu was eaten by Buddhist monks to abate their sexual desires.

This is not a prescription against tofu. Well-cooked tofu is less cooling. For optimum health, we need a balance of warming as well as cooling foods. However, if you are feeling cold, or if it is a cold day, or if you have strenuous activities planned, then you may opt for salmon over tofu.

*   *   *

Tomatillo   The tomatillo, like a ground cherry, comes wrapped in a fanciful hull. The enclosed fruit, which is the size of a cherry tomato, varies from yellow-green to purple in color. This Mexican import and nightshade-family member is increasingly featured in southwestern and Mexican cuisine.

In texture and flavor the tomatillo is reminiscent of a green plum. It is sweet and sour, but not as sour as a lemon, and has a delightful aroma of fresh-mown hay. Their lemon balm plus gelatinous texture lends body and flavor to a variety of sauces.

Look for tomatillos throughout the year. Select those that are firm with intact husks. They hold refrigerated for several weeks. Husk just prior to use.

Tomatillos are high in vitamins A and C and are a cooling food. See **Nightshades**.

Tomato   A native of South America, the tomato is widely grown throughout the world. It is valued for its high vitamin content and for its versatility. There are thousands of known varieties, which differ greatly in color and shape. The most common are round and red and vary in size from an apple to a cherry.

Tomatoes are fragile when ripe; so this commercial fruit is picked and shipped when green and then artificially ripened in ethylene gas chambers. Hydroponically grown tomatoes are cosmetically perfect but lack flavor. Vine-ripened tomatoes, available locally and seasonally, are the most flavorful.

Purchase tomatoes that are firm, well-shaped, and have a rich, tomato aroma. Avoid those with bruises, cracks, and dark spots. To ripen immature tomatoes, place them upside down on a sunny windowsill. When ripened they keep up to ten days refrigerated. Serve raw tomatoes at room temperature to maximize their flavor.

An excellent source of vitamin C, especially when vine ripened, tomatoes are also a good source of vitamins A and B complex, and of potassium and phosphorus. Tomatoes are a cooling food and are used as a kitchen remedy for quenching thirst.

+

◆

There have been reported cases of metal poisoning from canned foods. Foods may dissolve tin from the can, from its solder sealer, or from the lacquer lining.[5] Acidic foods such as tomatoes are more apt to leach metals from cans. You may prefer purchasing tomato products in glass jars rather than in tin cans.

◆

Sun-dried tomatoes are a trendy food. Their explosive concentrated flavor lends a new tomato essence to dishes they are used in. In *The Silver Palate Good Times Cookbook,* authors Rosso and Lukins recommend only those "packed in oil and bright red rather than brownish." They warn that those that are not oil-packed tend to be tough.[6] Yes, dry-packed sun-dried tomatoes are tough; however, rehydrated and then added to a sauce or soup, they provide a tremendous flavor boost.

Domestic organic sun-dried tomatoes are available in quality food stores. At the time of this writing, sun-dried tomatoes packed in olive oil are imported. Tomatoes may be sun-dried at home, but they are not among the easiest of vegetables to dry.

Triticale   The world's first human-made grain is triticale (trit-uh-KA-lee) and it's considered by its developers to be "science's gift to the world." It is an amphidiploid hybrid of several different species of wheat (*triticum*) and rye (*secale*). Triticale is slightly higher in lysine than wheat, lower in gluten, and often has a higher total protein. The mature grain is twice the size of wheat, and it has a slightly nutty flavor resembling whole wheat and pecans. In the bowl or in a loaf of bread, it's enjoyable.

+

Triticale was developed in the late 1800s in Sweden, but it has only recently received much attention. Today most triticale is grown in the Dakotas, Nebraska, and Minnesota.

Use triticale as you would use wheat or rye. It is most generally available in flakes or flour form. See **Grain** for information on selection, storage, and use and for nutritional and medicinal highlights.

¤

Triticale Flour   Flour made from the cross of rye and wheat, triticale, is high in protein but low in gluten. It offers a new and pleasing flavor to quick bread, drop biscuits, cookies, and pancakes. When used in a yeast bread, combine with wheat flour, knead dough gently, and allow only a single rising.

Trout   Trout is closely related to salmon. Most of the several varieties of trout favor cold rivers or large lakes, although some are migratory. The rainbow trout has slightly pink flesh whereas lake and brown trout are white fleshed. The flesh of all varieties is delicate, firm, and delicious.

Commercial trout farms produce a large supply that enables yearlong availability. Relative to a native brook or lake trout, the farmed fish have large heads and lack flavor. Trout loses its flavor more quickly than do other fish, and it is best when cooked straight out of the stream.

Trout is fatty, but less so than salmon. It is a good source of protein as well as trace minerals. In Oriental medicine it is considered a hot food, good for expelling cold.

+◆

See also **Fish, Freshwater** for information on selection, storage, use, and nutritional and medicinal properties.

Tubers   Although tubers grow below ground, they are not a root, but rather the thickened, fleshy part of an underground stem. Potatoes, Jerusalem artichokes, sweet potatoes, jicama, and peanuts are common tubers. Traditional medical systems recommend tubers for those wishing to gain weight and do not recommend tubers for those with tumors.

Tuna   The largest and most popular of the mackerel family, tuna can weigh more than thousand pounds. Several species are abundant in warm seas throughout the world. Albacore is considered the finest and has the whitest flesh. Other varieties include bluefin, yellowfin, bonito, and longfin.

Tuna is most often available canned but fresh is a tastier choice. Tuna packed in water rather than oil is of better quality. Canned albacore is labeled white meat, and other varieties are designated as light-meat tuna. Tinned tuna is graded according to the size of the pieces in the can. Fancy or solid pack contains large, white chunks of albacore. Chunk style is second best, and tuna flake is grated from darker-fleshed tunas.

Fresh tuna is available summer, fall, and winter. It has the highest protein of all fish at 25.2 percent per 100 grams, and it is one of the lowest in fat. Energetically tuna is considered a warming food.

Tuna   See **Prickly Pear**.

Turban   Also known as *Warren Turban*. A larger variation of the buttercup squash, the turban has a bright orange-red rind. The turbanlike swirl on its blossom end is a fanciful variegated orange, red, and white. Its flesh and storage ability are comparable to the buttercup's.

See **Squash, Winter** for information on selection, storage, and use and for medicinal and nutritional highlights.

Turbinado Sugar   See **Sugar**.

Turkey   Compared to the wild game that the Pilgrims ate, today's turkey is three times larger. Though its size has changed, it remains a denigrated bird. Benjamin Franklin lamented the choice of the eagle to symbolize our country: "The turkey is a much more respectable bird, and withal a true original native of America."

Wild turkey flocks are still found throughout America. They are a smaller bird and their flesh has a gamey flavor that, according to your taste, is pleasurable or not. Wild turkey has limited availability in specialty shops.

Turkey is rated as the best lean meat available on the market today. A serving, without the skin, yields 81 percent protein to 19 percent fat. The ratio for lean ground beef is 41 percent protein to 59 percent fat. This fowl is also high in niacin, vitamin B_6, zinc, and iron.

The presence of the amino acid tryptophan in turkey indicates that it may have a more calming effect than other flesh foods. It is a warming food.

Turkey is more perishable than chicken. Look for a plump bird free of skin defects that is moist and soft to the touch. If purchased fresh, cook within twenty-four hours. Choose organic turkey whenever possible.

*   *   *

Dated Domestic Turkey

Early explorers of the Americas did not find chicken, but they found turkeys, both wild and domestic. In 1539 the first Spaniards to reach what is now New Mexico observed that each Pueblo Indian home had a turkey hutch: "[We] came to a pueblo of many houses three stories high, but found no inhabitants. They had left the night before because they had noticed our approach. In the houses we found many turkeys and much cotton and corn."[7]

*   *   *

Turnip   The turnip has a rustic character, and for those who have not tasted it at its prime, a low reputation. This inexpensive white root grows in impoverished soils and keeps well—all factors that have endeared it to the poor and given cause for some to scorn it.

Turnips originated in Asia and have been used throughout Asia and Europe since prehistoric times. A member of the *Brassica* family, turnip greens (see **Broccoli Rabe**) are exceptionally nutritious; however, this plant is chiefly cultivated for its root.

A past-prime turnip is bitter, pithy, and has nothing to recommend it. A fresh turnip grown in the spring or fall has a pleasant radishlike bite when raw and is sweet when cooked. Turnips grown in the hot months are decidedly pungent but mellow somewhat with cooking. Baby turnips are exquisitely sweet and refreshing. When cooked with other foods, turnips have the remarkable ability to absorb their flavors, which makes them succulent and rich.

If you have a choice, select turnips whose root end and stem base are intact. If these parts are trimmed away and yellowed at the incision, the turnip will be singularly lacking in flavor. Look for smooth, firm roots; favor small or medium-small turnips as large ones are often pithy and lack flavor. Refrigerated in a paper bag, they store for several weeks; in a cold cellar turnips hold reasonably well for several months.

Turnips contain vitamin C, potassium, calcium, and other trace nutrients. Raw grated turnip serves as a digestive aid; cooked, they are a warming food and are said to energize the stomach and intestines.

* * *

Greengrocers' Compulsive Addiction

Greengrocers persist in the fatuous addiction of overtrimming vegetables to remove "unsightly" root ends, leaf bases, or leaf tops. They assume their customers want tidy (rather than more flavorful) vegetables. When enough of us demand intact vegetables this addiction will disappear.

Broken or trimmed vegetables (fruits also) age more rapidly and have less flavor and nutrients than if intact. However, greens left on a root vegetable draw moisture from the root. Remove the greens at the root base, but do *not* cut into the root.

* * *

Turnip Tops   See **Broccoli Rabe**.

Turtle Bean   See **Black Turtle Bean**.

TVP (Texturized Vegetable Protein).   The meat analog TVP is a highly processed fibrous soy product resembling meat in texture and protein content. Everything but the protein is stripped from the soy, then synthetic nutrients, flavorings, and colorings are added to simulate meat.

To perform this technological marvel the carbohydrates are removed from defatted soybeans by thermoplastic extrusion (which employs high pressure, heat, and chemicals). The remaining soy protein isolate is fiber-spun. This sophisticated spinning process is similar to that used in spinning rayon. Even though the original ingredient in TVP, the soybean, is unobjectionable, the finished product is comparable to plastic.[8]

One good thing to say about TVP is that some people wanting to reduce or eliminate their meat consumption have found it helpful. Usually, as people become more familiar with the inimitable flavors and textures of real food, their TVP use diminishes.

Twig Tea   See **Kukicha**.

U

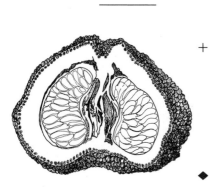

Ugli Fruit   Like the tangelo, the ugli fruit is another tangerine and grapefruit cross, so named because it looks like a puffy, misshapen, ugly grapefruit. Rough on the outside, its inside is similar to a tangerine's in appearance; but in flavor and use it is more like a grapefruit, only juicier. Although not commonly available, look for this Jamaican import in the winter and early spring months.

The ugli is a good source of vitamin C and is a cooling food. See **Citrus Fruit** for information on selection, storage, and use and for nutritional and medicinal highlights.

Umeboshi   Also known as *Salt Plum.* A Japanese seasoning agent that ranks right under shoyu and miso in use and versatility is a pickled plum called umeboshi. Actually, the translation is *dried salt plum,* but the sour, immature fruit is more like an apricot. It is fermented in salt with the herb beefsteak leaf (shiso) for up to a year.

Umeboshi has remarkable healing properties. Traditional Japanese claim that it can replace just about everything in your medicine cabinet. High in citric acid, umeboshi eliminates lactic acid from the body, which contributes to fatigue, colds, flu, viruses, diseases, and chronic illnesses. Umeboshi alkalizes the digestive system, helps strengthen blood quality, and relieves indigestion due to overeating, alcohol overindulgence, or morning sickness.[1]

Umeboshi may replace salt in salad dressings, spreads, seasonings, and sauces, or it may be cooked with grains, beans, and vegetables. This pickle enhances digestion and imparts a refreshing, sour flavor. As a medicine, umeboshi is eaten as is, added to hot tea, or cooked in a variety of foods. (See Umeshoyo-kuzu recipe accompanying **Kuzu** entry.)

Whole umeboshi plums contain the fruit's pit and sometimes the purple beefsteak leaf. Beefsteak is high in iron, acts as a natural preservative, and imparts the characteristic pink color. Use the leaf in cooking for its flavor and color.

Purchase umeboshi from Oriental or natural-food markets. Quality umeboshi contains only ume, salt, and beefsteak. In paste form or whole, umeboshi keeps for several years at room temperature. Hold in glass jar with a tight-fitting lid to prevent dehydration. If old, salt crystals may form on the plums, which may be rinsed off prior to use.

Umeboshi paste is puréed umeboshi minus pits and beefsteak. The purée is less expensive than whole umeboshi and is more convenient to use.

Umeboshi Vinegar   The pink liquid with a deep, cherry aroma and fruity sour flavor that salt draws from fermenting umeboshi is called umeboshi vinegar. Technically, it is not a vinegar, for it contains salt; nevertheless, it may be substituted for vinegar and salt in any recipe. Umeboshi vinegar imparts a light, refreshing citrus flavor that especially enhances salad dressings and steamed vegetables. Its medicinal properties are comparable to those of umeboshi.

Vanilla When the Aztecs defeated the Totonaco Indians of the eastern coastal area of Mexico, one of the most important tributes they demanded was the pod of the indigenous orchid, *Vanilla planifolia.* The vanilla was combined with cacao beans to make a drink called "chocolatl." Hernán Cortés then conquered the Aztecs and introduced both cacao beans and vanilla pods to Spain. Chocolate soon became a luxury beverage for the nobility and by 1602 was used as a flavoring for confections.

Today vanilla is produced throughout moist tropical areas within twenty degrees of the equator. Although the orchid will flower elsewhere, it will not produce pods. In its natural environment, a tiny bee, the melipone, pollinated the vanilla orchid, but this insect is now extinct due to pesticide usage. Currently all vanilla must be hand-pollinated, and pollination must occur within a few hours of the flower's opening.

The green vanilla beans are fermented and cured through steam and sun-drying processes. The flavor and aroma of pure vanilla varies greatly depending on the variety of plant used and how it is processed. A superior-flavored vanilla takes up to six months to cure and is cold extracted as heat damages its delicate essence. Due to labor-intensive growing and processing techniques, vanilla is a costly product.

Vanilla is available in pods or extract. When purchasing a pod look for one coal black in color and frosted with a light crystal coating. Pure vanilla extract contains 35 percent alcohol by volume. Pure vanilla flavor contains less alcohol, has the same taste components, but is less concentrated. The alcohol is used for extracting and holding the flavoring matter in suspension.

Imitation vanilla is—at best—made from vanillin, a sulfite waste by-product of the paper industry. At worst, vanillin is a totally synthetic product. Neither is recommended. Vanillin does simulate the flavor of pure vanilla but is harsh, abrasive, and lacks the well-rounded, sweet real vanilla flavor and aroma. By law, any product containing vanillin must be labeled as imitation.

Vegetables Can you imagine a Christmas tree without ornaments, a bat without a ball, a dinner without vegetables? Even a burger needs its vegetables—lettuce, fries, a dill pickle, onion slice, and catsup. Vegetables enhance a meal with color, texture, and flavor variations. They complement the entree with a wealth of vitamins, minerals, fiber, and micronutrients, and they may be simple, fun, exotic, or commonplace.

Any edible part of a plant—leaves, stems, tubers, roots, bulbs, berries, and seeds—may be called a vegetable. This realm includes grains, legumes, fruits, and sea vegetables; it excludes mushrooms, which are a fungus.

When purchasing vegetables, take enough time to examine them for quality. Young vegetables are often the tenderest, the best tasting, and the most energizing. As nutrients tend to be concentrated in and just under the skin, small vegetables have more nutrients because they have a larger surface-to-mass ratio.

Select vibrant-looking vegetables with no signs of decay, bruises, wilting, or major insect damage. Freshness is important to both flavor and quality in all vegetables, so buy fresh produce in small quantities frequently rather than in large quantities infrequently. Fresh produce is higher in beta-carotene, vitamin C, and folic acid than stale produce.

For optimum nutrition, flavor, and healing potential, favor vegetables that are seasonal, local, and organic. *Seasonal* means vegetables that could be growing right now in your backyard or, during winter months, local foods that have been stored from harvest time.

Local produce is preferable because it is fresher. Energetically, many contend that eating regional foods helps one to be more "attuned" to his environment. Also, it makes more sense to eat a carrot grown nearby than to indulge in the ecological waste of purchasing food that has been shipped for hundreds of miles. Lastly, favoring local supplies strengthens the local economy.

☆ Organic vegetables are nutritionally better for us and better for the ecological well-being of our earth and all its creatures. When we purchase chemically treated foods, we directly support and participate in those agribusiness practices that are damaging our soil.

◁ Store most vegetables in the refrigerator in a closed plastic bag, or in the crisper (without a bag) to prevent moisture loss. Fall squashes, potatoes, onions, and garlic are best stored in a cool, dark cellar or utility room. Keep onions in a basket or loosely woven bag, and keep potatoes in the dark. The vegetables that store well in a cool (45- to 50-degree) pantry rather than a cold refrigerator are avocados, cucumbers, eggplants, okra, peppers, summer squashes, tomatoes, and turnips. If you must store these items in the refrigerator, they do better when not in plastic bags. Remove the tops from root vegetables, for the greens draw moisture from (and thus dehydrate) their roots.

⚡ Supermarket produce is commonly treated with waxes, fungicides, and other preservatives to guard against deterioration and to inhibit natural ripening. Peel the skins of treated produce. Some chemical-sensitive individuals wash fresh produce in soap (not detergent) prior to consumption. Items commonly waxed include apples, avocados, bell peppers, cucumbers, eggplants, grapefruits, lemons, limes, melons, oranges, passion fruit, pineapples, pumpkins, rutabagas, squashes, and tomatoes.

★　　★　　★

For Those Needing Impetus to Grow Their Own . . .

Sounding a sobering note, David Wollner, coauthor of the *Shopper's Guide to Natural Foods,* observes that there is no such thing as "fresh" produce for most of the country, much of the year. ". . . local produce cases are filled with old produce which thanks to modern chemistry and technology is well preserved."[1]

★　　★　　★

American Cancer Society Backs Fresh Veggies

For cancer prevention the 1985 American Cancer Society brochure lists five "protective factors," which emphasize vegetables:

1. Eat more cabbage-family vegetables.
2. Add more high-fiber foods . . . Fiber occurs in whole grains, fruits and vegetables . . .
3. Choose foods with Vitamin A . . . Fresh foods with beta-carotene like carrots, peaches, apricots, squash and broccoli are the best source, not vitamin pills.
4. Do the same for Vitamin C . . . You'll find it naturally in lots of fresh fruits and vegetables . . .
5. Add weight control.[2]

★　　★　　★

Vinegar Distilled vinegar is good for washing windows and little else. It is a synthetic made from a petroleum product, glacial acetic acid. Many prepared food products contain vinegar. Unless a label specifies a natural vinegar, it most likely refers to an inexpensive distilled vinegar.

Happily there is an array of enticing natural vinegars, from modestly priced apple cider and malt vinegars to superb basalmic, champagne, or raspberry vinegars. As with other fine foods, vinegars made from fresh, wholesome ingredients have a wide range of flavors and are not harsh to the taste.

The pricey vinegar made of brown rice, koji, and water is fermented for a year. It has a significant amino acid content that, it is claimed, helps to neutralize lactic acid, alkalinize the blood, and promote health.[3]

Wakame Wakame is a versatile and sweet-flavored variety of the sea vegetable kombu. Most of the U.S. supply of wakame comes from northern Japan; however, our domestic equivalent, alaria (which requires longer cooking as it is tougher), is harvested in Maine and northern California.

The best quality wakame has a thin rather than wide stipe. When dried it is impossible to determine the stipe size, so purchasing reputable brand names is the best way to obtain quality wakame. Once hydrated, the stipe is generally cut out and reserved for soup stock.

A popular soup ingredient, wakame may also be used as a vegetable or salad. When roasted and crumbled, it makes a tasty condiment. Wakame lends itself superbly to miso soup to form a most nutritious and strengthening dish.

Wakame is high in protein, iron, calcium, and some B vitamins. It also contains numerous trace minerals and vitamins A and C. Alaria contains a remarkable 60 milligrams of vitamin B_{12} per 100 grams.

As with other sea vegetables, wakame contains alginic acid, a polysaccharide component. When alginic acid is released by gastric acids during digestion, it enters the intestine where it combines with sodium and is eliminated from the system. As a result, hypertension caused by excessive sodium consumption can be alleviated by eating wakame. In addition, studies indicate that alginic acid also helps eliminate such heavy metals as strontium-90 in the same manner.[1]

Available in Asian and natural-food markets, dried wakame keeps well for a year or more stored in a cool, dry pantry. Fresh wakame, found in Asian markets, requires refrigeration and prompt use.

Ita wakame is the finest grade of wakame, which is dried in large, flat sheets. Toast and crumble it to form a delicious condiment.

Mekabu is the mineral-concentrated wakame holdfast. It grows in a spiral fashion on a thick stipe and is highly mucilaginous. Mekabu is delicious deep-fried or cooked with vegetables.

*   *   *

Wakame-Cucumber Salad

Cucumber provides an exquisite counterpoint to wakame in this salad. You may serve it to someone who would otherwise say no to seaweed and have him back for seconds. It is especially refreshing on a summer day.

   1 ounce wakame
   1 cucumber, sliced thin
   ½ teaspoon sea salt
   1 tablespoon rice vinegar or lemon juice
   1 teaspoon shoyu
   2 teaspoons mirin
   3 radishes, sliced thin

Soak the wakame in water to cover for 10 minutes. Toss the cucumber with salt and gently squeeze for a minute. Set aside. Drop the wakame into boiling water and then immediately plunge into cold water. Drain. Cut out the stem (stipe), and reserve for soup stock. Lightly squeeze the cucumber to rid it of excess water and place it in a bowl. Add the wakame and remaining ingredients. Toss together and serve.

*   *   *

Walnut The Persian walnut is probably the most popular and widely used nut throughout the world. Though everyone else calls it the Persian, we call it the English because of who shipped it here during our colonial period.

Unlike the native American black walnut, the English is easy to shell and does not stain. The English walnut is fatty (over 60 percent) and contains fair amounts of protein, zinc, calcium, and potassium. The walnut is a warming food and is used as a kitchen remedy to strengthen the kidneys and lungs and to lubricate the large intestine.

Commercial walnuts sold in the shell have been washed and polished with bleach to render them a uniform tan color. Organic walnuts have darker brown shells, and their color varies depending on how much sun they were exposed to while growing.

Shelled commercial walnuts are frequently treated with ethylene gas, fumigated with methyl bromide, blanched in hot dye or glycerine and sodium carbonate, and then rinsed in citric acid. The result is a uniform, pale nut that is obviously less healthful than an organic nut. Because the availability of organic walnuts is limited, most natural-food stores sell a lower baking-grade commercial walnut that has not been excessively processed and that has more flavor than the more expensive grades.

Most of our domestic supply, and a significant percentage of the world's supply of English walnuts, comes from California. For the freshest nut with the most flavor, purchase walnuts in the shell and crack just prior to use. For expediency, purchase shelled but favor the "whole" nuts over broken or chopped walnuts, as they will be more apt to be fresh. Refrigerate shelled nuts. If the nuts impart an acrid or bitter flavor, they are rancid and should be discarded.

See **Nuts** for information on selection, storage, and use and for nutritional and medicinal highlights.

* * *

Brain Food

"For the ancient Romans, the walnut was a portrait of the human brain. The outer green husk (which many walnut eaters have never seen) was the scalp. The hard shell of the kernel was the protective skull. The thin envelope inside, with its paperlike partitions between the two halves of the nut, was the membrane. And the convoluted nut itself represented the two hemispheres of the brain."[2]

* * *

Walnut, Black   The native American walnut, the black walnut, is related to the English variety. This nut, with limited availability and commercial use, is prized for its potent, richly sweet flavor. It is difficult to crack, requiring a cement floor, heavy hammer, and a hefty swing. Once split, each morsel of nutmeat needs to be coaxed from the still-unyielding shell. In this process the black walnut oil leaves a lasting brown stain on fingers, fabric, and even on the cement. The amount of meat per nut is small; its flavor is great.

The black walnut is lower in fat and higher in protein and iron than is the English walnut. It contains more vitamin A than any other nut. A bit of black walnut marvelously flavors quality chocolate and ice cream.

See **Walnut** for comparable information on selection, storage, and use and for medicinal and nutritional highlights.

Warren Turban   See **Turban**.

Wasabi   Also known as *Japanese Horseradish.* Peel the gnarled, warty wasabi root, and its flesh is a pale, soft green that packs a furious wallop. Although not related to horseradish, it is often called the Japanese horseradish because its kick is nearly as potent as that of horseradish. Wasabi is the more fragrant of the two and has a "cleansing" taste.

This aromatic root does more than bite, according to Jan and John Belleme, Japanese food experts: "Its abundance of protein-digesting enzymes make it a perfect condiment with raw fish dishes such as sashimi and sushi. Japanese sushi connoisseurs use wasabi to complement the flavor of red-fleshed and oily fish, such as tuna, yellowtail, and salmon, that live close to the surface. . . . Though wasabi can also be used with white-fleshed bottom fish such as snapper and grouper, grated ginger is often preferred with them."[3]

If available at all, fresh wasabi is found in Asian markets in water-filled pans (its natural habitat is in marshy land). Look for a plump and fresh-looking root. Avoid one that is withered and preferably not sprouting. Refrigerate in plastic and use within three or four days.

Powdered wasabi is more frequently available in convenient small tins or foil envelopes. Store in a cool, dry place and mix with water to make a paste just prior to use. If the "wasabi" is bright green (rather than a greenish-gray), it is not wasabi.

Once grated, its flavor and digestive enzymes quickly dissipate, so grate just prior to use.

Water Bottled water and water filters are a growing business . . . and a business with a future. As increasing numbers of studies reveal that additives and environmental pollutants in municipal water are not healthful, more people are using tap water only for washing.

Reputable bottled-water companies provide data sheets about their product. If more than one brand is available in your area, and their data sheets are comparable, then rely on your taste to determine which is best. In general, avoid water with low, or excessive, mineral content.

Water in glass bottles is preferable to water in plastic containers. One reason is that it tastes more like water and less like plastic. Another reason is that a cancer-causing chemical, methylene chloride, has been found in water stored in polycarbonate resin bottles, as is reported by the California Department of Health Services.[4]

*   *   *

I Wonder Why . . .

Do you know anybody who refuses to use tap water for their beloved goldfish or houseplants but serves it up to their own flesh and blood?

Some advocates distill water for cooking and drinking because it is pure H_2O, others disdain it for the same reason. In stripping distilled water of its pollutants, the minerals get stripped as well. Water without pollutants is desirable; water devoid of minerals is unnatural. Food cooked in distilled water is said to loose a much higher percentage of minerals to the water due to osmosis. It is the minerals in water that provide taste and character. Distilled water is wet, but its taste is flat.

Technically, any natural water is mineral water because all water in its natural state contains minerals. But in common usage, *mineral water* most often refers to water containing carbonation. The effervescence may be natural, or it may be created mechanically through injection with a gas. In the latter case the label indicates that carbonation is added. Domestic or imported varieties are available, and their flavors, mouth feel, mineral content, and alkalinity differ greatly.

*   *   *

Water Bar

Trend-setting Beverly Hills, California, has not only a sushi bar and a caviar bar, but as of November 1986, a water bar. It is aptly called the Water Bar and serves fifty-two of "the world's best waters" plus featuring a "water of the month." A serving of bottled water ranges from $1 to $2.

Water that naturally springs up from deep underground aquifers is generally recognized as the superior water in terms of health and flavor. It originates as rain or snow that seeps through rock and sand and then percolates up as a natural spring. Its passage through the earth removes impurities, such as bacteria, while enriching it with minerals. The flavor of springwater varies greatly from source to source and is determined by the water's mineral content and its degree of acidity or alkalinity. Water from some springs varies in flavor according to the season of the year.

Deep well water is the second-best choice after spring water. If the well is shallow the water is apt to contain environmental pollutants. Well water varies greatly depending on the water table from which it comes and its mineral composition.

*   *   *

Water Chestnut   The most memorable property of the water chestnut is its crunch. Although jicama and Asian pears come close to the refreshing crisp texture of this Oriental water vegetable, they do not match its refreshing delicacy or its juicy sweet flavor. As its name suggests, the water chestnut is a water plant. Its edible part, which looks like a grubby chestnut in size and shape, grows in the mud; it is the plant's regenerative part.

This famed Oriental vegetable has been used as a food since Neolithic times. Like a tree chestnut, it may be boiled, roasted, or made into flour. Some eat it raw; however, cooking enhances its flavor and does not detract from its texture.

Currently, the water chestnut is not grown commercially in the United States; however, attempts are being made to cultivate it. They are readily available canned and have somewhat limited availability fresh. Look for them in Asian markets or specialty food stores. Select corms that are hard and free of withering or soft spots. Refrigerate in a paper bag for up to ten days.

The water chestnut is a low-calorie food and high in potassium. It is a cold and sweet food and is used medicinally in the Orient for dispersing excess heat from the body and for treating diabetes and jaundice.

Watercress   Equally as delightful as chancing upon a pure stream boasting watercress is munching this lively, peppery plant. Eurasian in origin, watercress was probably introduced to America in the 1600s. Weedlike in its hardiness, it has spread and now thrives in each of the fifty states. Cultivated and wild watercress are the same variety, but the domesticated plant is generally larger—up to seven inches—and has a thicker stem.

Watercress, a member of the famed cabbage family, has a mustardlike bite and aroma but surprises the palate with a cooling, refreshing effect rather than a fiery one. Nutritionally it is a superb source of minerals with double the calcium of broccoli and significant amounts of iron. In vitamin A, it is comparable to the vegetable famed for its vitamin A content, the carrot.

In kitchen remedies watercress is appreciated for its ability to energize the internal organs, including the stomach, lungs, colon, liver, and kidneys. It is said to help in the treatment of edema.

Forage watercress only from pure water sources. Look for it in ponds or in gently flowing streams. In the store it is bunched like parsley and costly. Purchase that which looks fresh and has no yellowed leaves.

Whether foraged or commercial, wash watercress with extra care and then wash it once again to remove any aquatic insects. At home, trim ends and submerge stems in a water-filled glass. Loosely cover this watercress bouquet with a plastic bag and refrigerate. Use within four days.

Raw watercress perks up salads and sandwiches and is an attractive garnish. Cooking eliminates its bite and leaves a piquantly sweet vegetable. However, when cooked its volume is reduced by three-fourths, so plan accordingly.

*   *   *

Sturdy Watercress

In cold winter regions watercress is the only leafy green that grows throughout the year. In the mountain town where I live the creeks freeze solid in the winter, but my neighbor's artesian well still flows freely. In its run-off thrive verdant carpets of cress. I regularly harvest this welcome green. This winter we've had a generous share of snow cover, below-zero temperatures, *and* the watercress continues to grow. What a sturdy food.

*   *   *

Watermelon   Most everyone loves watermelon because it is refreshingly sweet. Surprisingly, watermelon has only half the sugar (5 percent) of an apple. It tastes much sweeter because sugar is its main taste-producing element and the rest is primarily water. Watermelon is a whopping 92 percent water. This makes it a popular diet food and a unexcelled hot-weather food.

Watermelon originated in Africa and is botanically different from the melon group. Some new varieties are yellow-fleshed but have the characteristic watermelon seeds, rind, and flavor. Watermelons range from small to as large as forty pounds.

As the melon ripens, the white spot where it rests on the ground turns to yellow, which indicates its maturity. A dry, brown stem is another sign of ripeness. Heft a melon and choose one that is heavy for its size. Also hold the melon in one hand and thump it with the other. If it sounds hollow with a slight ring (rather than dull), it is probably ripe. If purchasing a cut watermelon, avoid one with white seeds and any signs of white flesh.

Watermelon is a good source of vitamin C and is low in sodium. As a kitchen remedy it is used as a cooling food, for treatment of thirst, and to relieve mental depression. Watermelon is more cooling than other melon types.

Wax Bean   See **Green Bean**.

Wheat   Wheat is no spring chicken. The common ancestor of all wheats is believed to be a species called einkorn, which has been cultivated for at least 8,700 years. Samples of both wild and cultivated einkorn were found in the excavated ruins of a village known as Jarmo, situated in present-day Iraq.[5]

Because of contemporary man's preference for bread, wheat is the world's most widely distributed cereal grain and is grown in nearly every country and in each of the states. In many cultures wheat has replaced corn, buckwheat, rye, barley, quinoa, teff, and millet as the grain staple.

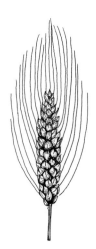

A relatively recent phenomenon is allergic reactions to the staff of life. Some people have found that they are allergic to commercial wheat and yet not to organic. Natural foods expert Annemarie Colbin suggests, "If wheat is consumed with sugar, as it would be in the case of cakes, cookies, or pastries, it would make sense to eliminate the sugar first—and dairy too, if used—before the wheat is accused and found guilty."[6]

Wheat allergies, according to Oriental medicine, are associated with a hardened and swollen liver, which is caused by overconsumption of animal fats and chemical or alcohol abuse. Wheat energetically stimulates the liver. If the liver is full of toxins, wheat triggers the liver to cleanse itself of toxins, which may then be experienced as "allergies." Once the liver has regained its healthful state, wheat consumption does not produce allergic reactions.

★   ★   ★

Allergic to the Staff of Life?

Following mother's milk, wheat was—in the fullest sense of the word—the principle food, the veritable staff of life for people of European and Mideastern ancestry. That many of these people today are allergic to wheat is indeed curious. Rather than blame it on wheat per se, one might consider the quality of the wheat and the quality of one's own health.

Whole wheat contains thirteen B vitamins, vitamin E, protein, essential fatty acids, and important trace minerals such as zinc, iron, copper, manganese, magnesium, and phosphorus. Like rye, wheat is good for the musculature. It is also stimulating to the liver.

Wheat berry is the term applied to whole wheat with just the outer hull removed. Cooked whole wheat berries provide more jaw exercise than other grains and are thus rarely eaten whole.

Wheat that is broken into small pieces by very coarse milling is termed cracked wheat. It is a popular breakfast cereal and may be served as a grain dish for dinner or formed into croquettes. For better flavor and greater nutritional value, purchase whole wheat and coarsely grind it in a flour mill or blender rather than purchasing cracked wheat.

Thousands of wheat varieties exist, but only three types are used for human consumption—hard, soft, and durum.

Hard wheat has a higher protein (gluten) content and is used for bread. It is bronze colored. This wheat is further classified according to growing season as either spring or winter wheat.

Spring wheat is a fast-growing hard wheat sown in the spring and harvested in the fall. It is cultivated where the winters are severe. Spring wheat is the grain of choice for bread making as it generally has the highest protein content.

Winter wheat is normally higher in minerals because it has a longer growing season and so establishes a more extensive root system. This hard wheat is sown in the fall where winters are mild; it germinates, then lies dormant through the winter and starts growing again in the spring. Winter wheat is harvested in the late spring or early summer.

Soft wheat contains more carbohydrates and less gluten than hard wheat so it is not suited to bread making. Soft wheat, which may also be called white wheat because of its light, golden color, is primarily used for pastries. If cooking whole wheat berries, soft wheat yields a softer dish. As with hard wheat, soft wheat may be a winter or spring variety.

Durum wheat is used exclusively for pasta. It contains hard starch granules, which enable pasta to hold together while cooking in boiling water. Semolina is refined durum flour. Couscous is made of either drum wheat or millet. See **Bulgur, Couscous, Flour, Grain**, and **Pasta** for additional information.

*   *   *

Wheat Bran   Probably the most esteemed food for its bowel-regulating abilities is bran. Bran is composed of six fibrous protective layers of the wheat berry. It is resistant to digestion. Thus bran adds bulk and fiber to the diet. For those eating refined wheat products, it makes sense to supplement with wheat bran.

Bran accounts for about 15 percent of the wheat kernel. In addition to it being composed of indigestible cellulose, it is also a rich reserve of nutrients. In a wheat berry, the bran contains 86 percent of the niacin, 73 percent of the pyridoxine, and 50 percent of the pantothenic acid, 42 percent of the riboflavin, 33 percent of the thiamine, and 19 percent of the protein.

Wheat Flour   Wheat berries are milled to separate the endosperm from the bran and germ. The endosperm is then ground into flour-sized particles. There are billions of wheat endosperm particles per cup of flour. The major types of wheat flour are listed below. Also see **Flour** for information on selection, storage, use, and nutritional and medicinal highlights.

All-purpose flour has its germ and bran removed. Then it is processed with up to thirty chemicals to make it whiter and fluffier and to improve its workability as dough. Four synthetic nutrients are added (whole wheat flour contains over forty natural nutrients) and it is called "enriched." All-purpose flour is blended from soft wheat flours for general home use. It does not perform as well as flour made from specialized wheat. Self-rising all-purpose flour contains leavening and salt.

Bolted wheat flour was produced through a refining technique developed by the Romans. Ground flour was sifted through bolts of cloth to remove hulls and a large portion of the bran and germ. Bolted flour, which retains between 25 to 50 percent of the bran and all of the germ, has limited availability today. It yields a bread with a higher volume than a 100 percent whole wheat flour.

Panocha is a flour ground from sprouted wheat. The sprouting process changes the carbohydrates into simple sugars. Subtle yet satisfyingly sweet, panocha is a popular ingredient in Mexican holiday baked goods. It is available in the southwest and in Latin markets.

Whole wheat flour is made of the hard whole wheat berry, contains more than forty nutrients, and has a rich, full taste. However, once milled, the oil in the wheat germ starts to oxidize and become rancid. To retard oxidization store whole wheat flour in a cool, dark place (preferably refrigerated), and use within a month of milling. Flour with a bitter taste is rancid, so discard it. Rancid foods are carcinogens, toxic to the liver, and inhibit the digestion of oils.

Whole wheat pastry flour is made from whole soft wheat berries and is preferred for pastries, cakes, cookies, piecrusts, and other delicate baked goods. Because it is low in gluten, it is unsuitable for bread. This flour requires the same care as whole wheat flour.

Unbleached wheat flour is the same as enriched flour except that it has been spared the bleaching process. Bleaching eliminates various carotenoid pigments and destroys vitamin E. For the health conscious who find 100 percent whole wheat products too heavy, including some unbleached wheat flour yields a lighter product. Unbleached flour is superior to bleached and enriched white flour.

* * *

Flowers of Wheat

Our word *flour* literally means the *flower* or best part of a ground grain. Mill a grain into a meal, sift out the larger bran and germ particles, and the remaining endosperm is the flower. The medieval English would find the term *whole wheat flour* nonsensical.

* * *

Wheat Germ Wheat germ is the heart or embryo of the wheat. It comprises only 2 to 3 percent of the whole wheat berry, but is nutritionally the richest part. An excellent source of vitamin E, wheat germ is also highly susceptible to rancidity. Some people maintain that wheat germ must be used immediately after milling to obtain its vitamin E.

Toasted wheat germ has a delicious nutty flavor, but some nutrients are destroyed by toasting. If you eat whole wheat products, then you are automatically obtaining the rich nutrients found in the germ.

In the whole wheat berry, the germ contains 64 percent of the thiamine, 26 percent of the riboflavin, and 8 percent of the proteins and other important nutrients.

* * *

Different Strokes

Some folks disdain whole wheat flour products because they are more dense. Other folks prefer whole wheat flour products because they have a hearty, full-bodied flavor.

White flour has little, if any, flavor. In order to have taste appeal, a white flour food product relies on other ingredients. A naturally leavened bread made of fresh, stone-ground whole wheat flour, pure water, and sea salt is incomparable to any other bread. It has multiple nuances of flavor and is fundamentally satisfying.

* * *

Wheat Grass Juice Available fresh in some natural food stores, the juice from young wheat grass is high in chlorophyll, potassium, calcium, and magnesium. Imagine a flavor so aggressively sweet that it boarders on astringency, this is seven inch long wheat that has been juiced. Its flavor is one few people claim to enjoy and so they generally mix it with another juice. Wheat grass is also available in a tablet form.

As research continues to stress the positive correlation of chlorophyll-rich foods and human health, we are apt to hear more about wheat grass. For additional information see **Green Foods**.

White Bean Great northern and navy beans are two white beans related to the kidney bean family. They are primarily distinguished by their size (navy beans are the smaller of the two) and are interchangeable. See **Beans** for selection, storage, use and nutritional and medicinal highlights.

Whitefish Whitefish is named for its white skin. It is herringlike with sweet, lean, and mild-flavored flesh. Its major habitat is the Great Lakes region, but it is also found in the Rocky Mountains from Utah north to British Columbia.

Available year-round, whitefish is frequently smoked and, when fresh, may be prepared like trout. Whitefish is low in fat and calories and high in protein. It is an excellent source of vitamin A and has significant amounts of phosphorus, iron, and B vitamins.

See **Fish, Freshwater** for information on selection, storage, and use and for nutritional and medicinal highlights.

Wild Rice   Three seeds native to the Americas that are used like grains but are not true cereals are amaranth, quinoa, and the aquatic plant wild rice. A staple food for the Ojibway, who called it manomen, wild rice has a wondrously wild flavor and essence. Even a small amount imparts its distinctive character to other ingredients. Its quality, as well as its high price, make wild rice a favorite gourmet food.

Almost all wild rice was grown in Minnesota. By state law, lake rice (as opposed to cultivated wild rice) may only be harvested using the traditional harvesting sticks, which are about three feet in length. One person navigates a canoe while a second person bends the rice stalks into the canoe and, with the other stick, threshes out the grain.

Since the 1970s, wild rice has been commercially produced and harvested in domesticated paddies. This rice now comprises over 80 percent of the total crop.

After harvest the rice is fermented for one to two weeks to develop its flavor and to make hulling easier. It is then heated, which gelatinizes the starch and deepens its color.

Properly cooked wild rice splits and is fluffy. It takes from thirty to forty minutes to cook. If you wish to serve it with brown rice (which requires longer cooking) it is best to prepare the two grains separately and then combine them.

+
◆   Wild rice is richer in protein, minerals, and B vitamins and higher in carbohydrates than wheat, barley, oats or rye. Wild rice is a warming food and is said to strengthen the kidneys. Energetically, "wild" wild rice is preferred over the commercial crop.

See **Grain** for information on selection, storage, and use and for nutritional and medicinal highlights.

Winter Melon   See **Melon Family**.

Woodcock   See **Fowl**.

Xylitol A by-product of the plywood industry, xylitol is extracted from birch cellulose by an energy-intensive chemical process. It may also be made from other hardwood chips, almond and pecan shells, cornstalks, and corncobs. It costs about ten times as much as white sugar, but otherwise is comparable to white sugar in almost every way.

Xylitol is used in sugar-free gum, candy, and jam. In animal studies it is linked to cancer, urinary bladder stones, and bladder inflammation. As with other highly refined sugar substitutes, xylitol is not recommended.

See **Sweeteners** for additional information.

Y

Yam   The true yam, native to Africa, is not available commercially in the United States, although it does grow in the Southern states. The vegetable commonly called "yam" denotes the sweetest variety of sweet potato. See **Sweet Potato**.

Yard-Long Bean   Also known as *Asparagus Bean.* The cowpea, a close relative of the black-eyed pea, has a long pod that reaches up to a literal yard in length. When immature, this green vegetable is a staple throughout Asia and in other semitropical regions.

There are several varieties of yard-long beans; the two most common ones contain black or red beans. Purchase pods that are pencil-thin and firm. They are not as flavorful or as crisp as green beans; however, sautéing most enhances their flavor.

Yard-long beans are a good source of vitamin A and fiber. Energetically they are considered an expansive food.

Yautia   Also known as *Cocoyam.* A root crop that food experts predict holds great promise as a nutritious food of the future is the funny-looking, potatolike yautia. When cooked, this tropical tuber has an earthy, almost nutty, flavor and a lush and creamy flesh. It originated in the Americas in dry and swampy soils at various tropical altitudes. Like the taro potato, the yautia is thin skinned and shaggy. Both are the cormels that surround a larger rootlike cormel. The yautia tends to be larger than the taro and is frequently club shaped.

Many supermarkets as well as Hispanic markets now carry the yautia. Select firm specimens. Store at room temperature and try to use within a few days of purchase. Do not consume raw, but use as you would taro or a potato. A common ethnic use of yautia is to peel, boil—like potatoes—and serve with savory dishes. It is also baked, fried, or ground into flour. In a stew it flavors, thickens, and adds creaminess.

Cocoyam has a moderate amount of thiamine and riboflavin and a modest amount of vitamin C and iron. It is high in calories. As a kitchen remedy it may be used to regulate energy and disperse congestion.

Yeast   Nutritional yeast (also called food yeast or primary-grown yeast) is grown on mineral enriched molasses or wood pulp to be used as a food supplement. At the end of the growth period, the culture is pasteurized to kill the yeast.

Yeast is considered by many to be the most valuable supplement available. It is a complete protein and contains more protein than meat. Yeast is an excellent source of B vitamins including B_{12} and it contains the glucose tolerance factor that helps in the regulation of blood sugar.

Brewer's yeast is a by-product of the beer-brewing industry and has the characteristic bitter hops flavor. Nutritional yeast is sometimes incorrectly called brewer's yeast.

*   *   *

Noisy Nourishment

The one food better (or worse) than beans for causing flatulence is nutritional yeast. Yeast aficionados recommend to start taking one-quarter teaspoon daily and then, if there is no objectionable effect, to gradually increase the amount to up to two tablespoons daily.

*   *   *

Yellow Wax Bean   See **Green Bean**.

Yogurt   What food was relatively unknown in the United States twenty-five years ago, then became the fastest-growing food category, and now has a per capita consumption estimated to surpass that of milk? Yogurt.

Like kefir, yogurt is milk that has been inoculated with lactobacillus strains and then incubated. During this process the bacteria convert the milk sugar (lactose) to lactic acid, and the milk thickens and becomes tart.

Numerous health claims including longevity are made for yogurt. The bacteria present in yogurt make it more digestible. However, claims that these bacteria increase the population of intestinal flora are incorrect.

The quality of yogurt varies greatly. To increase shelf life some yogurts are pasteurized, which destroys the culture. Prefer yogurt containing live bacterial cultures. Purchase yogurt that is free of preservatives, stabilizers, and refined sugar. Fruit preserves, by FDA definition, contain sugar, and thus many fruit-flavored yogurts contain sugar. Flavored yogurts may also contain preservatives, stabilizers, artificial flavors, and artificial colors.

Yogurt is an excellent source of riboflavin and protein. Although dairy products have been considered to be superior sources of calcium, this information is currently being challenged. See also **Dairy** and **Fermented Food**.

★　　★　　★

Position Challenged

Yogurt's position as a healthy food is under attack by increasing numbers. Fifty percent of its calories are derived from fat, primarily saturated fat. Even low-fat yogurt is still 31 percent fat.

Author and columnist John A. McDougall, M.D., observes: "Rather than being considered a food that supports health, yogurt should be classified as a delicacy (at best) or even as a health hazard for some people." McDougall cites studies showing that the lactobacillus strain used in yogurt will not grow in the human intestine. He points out that it is "high in animal protein which causes the body to lose minerals—including calcium—through protein-induced changes in kidney physiology. Milk-derived proteins are the No. 1 cause of food allergy."[1]

★　　★　　★

Z

Zucchini   The best-known summer squash is called a marrow by the British, a courgette by the French, and in the United States we call it by its Italian name, zucchini. This squash is generally dark green when small but may develop yellow stripes as it becomes larger. A variety of yellow zucchini is also available.

Zucchini is best when less than six inches long. If allowed to grow it can reach the size of a baseball bat . . . and would have comparable flavor. Select those that are firm and shiny. Refrigerate in plastic and, for maximum flavor, use immediately.

A vegetable of great versatility, the zucchini may be stuffed and baked, puréed, fried, broiled, or used in soups. Some include raw zucchini in salads or serve it as a crudité. I find that cooking is the best way to coax flavor from a zucchini. Its blossoms, when batter dipped and deep fried or tossed in a salad, are a delicacy.

As with other summer squash, zucchini has a fair amount of vitamin A and C and is low in calories.

See **Squash, Summer** for information on selection, storage, and use and for medicinal and nutritional highlights.

Appendixes
Notes
Bibliography

Appendix 1
Personal-Care Products

BODY-CARE PRODUCTS

The personal empowerment a person gains by opting for better-quality products is applicable to cosmetics as well as food. In response to public interest in unadulterated products, more manufacturers of body-care products are waving the back-to-nature banner.

If we were to judge natural body-care products by the same criteria that we judge natural foods, few would qualify. Nevertheless, many natural cosmetics are superior to cosmetics purchased from a mass merchandiser. Let's explore what body-care products contain in order to make more healthful choices. Because these items are so refined, this exploration involves some detail.

Unfortunately, neither the government nor the cosmetics industry has established a standard guideline delineating exactly what "natural" means. At what point does an ingredient, once natural, yet synthetically refined and combined with unnatural ones, cease to be natural? And truly, how different is an originally natural derivative from one completely produced in a laboratory? Why would organic hydrocarbon chains from coal mines or tar pits be less natural than animal or vegetable fatty acids?

Cosmetics have always been used to enhance physical attractiveness. At their best, natural cosmetics complement that quality of winsomeness, called natural beauty, that radiates from within a person. Hair that shines and skin that glows with life depend first and foremost on good health.

Our skin is a porous organ with absorbing capabilities. Ingredients that nourish people internally would be valuable when used externally to achieve the same result. Some body-care products contain natural ingredients such as vegetable oils, herbs, and nutritive substances. Granted, these ingredients exist in the same bottle with laboratory compounds, but better that partnership than a product composed of nothing but synthetic chemical compounds.

The FDA requires that ingredients be listed in decreasing order of prevalence. All substances except fragrances and trade secrets must be listed by standardized names. Manufacturers need not state which ingredients are of animal, vegetable, or synthetic origin. Some companies indicate on the label if a compound is of natural or vegetable origin; others expressly state the absence of animal ingredients in their products.

Laboratories can duplicate just about any molecule. Their decision to synthesize or not usually depends on cost-effectiveness. Some compounds that were once derived from plants or animals (such as the stearyl or cetyl groups from whales) are today more apt to be artificial. As labels generally do not indicate this, you may write to the company directly. They are usually willing to supply the information on request.

Product Safety

Since the Food, Drug, and Cosmetic Act of 1938, the FDA has sought to manage the safety of a product prior to its marketing. Any products whose safety does not meet these standards through proper substantiation must bear the label, "WARNING—the safety of this product has not been determined."

How is such evidence attained? The FDA has no authority to require safety tests, much less regulate the kinds of tests. The cosmetics industry itself assumes the burden of safety control. One can question the objectivity of tests conducted by a manufacturer whose primary interest is sales.

Another controversial aspect of testing is that millions of experimental animals suffer cruel deaths annually in research laboratories. Without going into the horrors of such testing, the validity of these experiments is questionable. The evidence measures fatal or severely damaging doses of a substance rather than doses that place the substance within the safety margin. One wonders about the accuracy of information about toxicity gained from experimental mice, guinea pigs, and rabbits when applied to human beings.

As a result of public outcry, several research labs and universities are exploring humane alternatives to animal experiments. For example, some pharmaceutical and industrial companies use computer models of physiological systems. These models are designed to recognize complex molecules that are potentially toxic to people. They are based on the tremendous accumulation of data on chemicals found to be toxic to laboratory animals.

Unless otherwise noted on the product label, assume that the product was tested on animals. A significant number of natural-cosmetics companies do not use animal testing. Your local humane society may have a list of those companies using animal tests; or you may request this information directly from the manufacturer.

Despite all tests to ensure product safety, there is probably always someone somewhere who is sensitive to any given ingredient in a product. This includes naturally occurring plant or food ingredients.

Homemade Cosmetics

In light of the above information, some people may choose to make cosmetics at home that will cost less and be purer. Various how-to books are available, and most of the ingredients are found in natural-food stores. The do-it-yourselfer's conscience can rest assured that no innocent animals were sacrificed along the way.

Cosmetic Technology

Manufacturers process the basic ingredients in various ways to yield a product that is consistent in its form, texture, workability, and level of moisture or dryness and that is safely pH-balanced and adequately preserved. To assure a cosmetic's attractiveness to the buyer, companies dress up their products with enticing colors, fragrances, flavors, and packaging.

Most commercial products require a host of processing aids to assure a proper blend, texture, and consistency. Those that lather need one agent to create bubbles and another to control the bubble size and tightness. Those that are moist require a humectant to keep them moist, and those that are dry require something to maintain their dryness. Preservatives are a must to maintain shelf life, colorings are added for eye appeal, and scents mask the aroma of what all of the above must smell like.

Immediately following is a list of quality ingredients that appear in cosmetics, after which are inferior ingredients. You may chose to avoid purchasing body-care products that include such ingredients.

☆ Ingredients to Favor

Aloe vera has renowned healing and softening abilities. It is widely used in almost every sort of natural skin-care product, and it is healing to burns.

All the *B-complex vitamins* are valuable in hair care. They stimulate the scalp, thicken hair, and aid in the prevention of baldness by stimulating hair growth. Panthenol, inositol, choline, and folic acid have emollient (soothing to the skin) properties. PABA (para-aminobenzoic acid) is used as a sunscreen and for hair pigmentation.

Bee products, which have natural immune and antibiotic properties, include bee pollen, propolis, and royal jelly. Bee pollen is a complete protein, mineral rich, and it contains B-complex vitamins and vitamin C. Royal jelly, a secretion of female worker bees, is fed to workers, queen larvae, and possibly the adult queen bee. A small percentage of this jelly consists of growth hormones, which no doubt contribute to its reputation as a rejuvenator.

Clay is an especially effective cleanser. Its negatively charged particles give it a strong receptive quality that pulls and attracts substances to it. When used on the face in a mask, it exerts a deeply absorbing action that effectively draws out grime, oil, and toxins that may otherwise have been missed by other forms of cleansing. Clay has a high mineral content with smaller amounts of trace elements, so it is nourishing, as well as cleansing, to the skin.

Different kinds of clay have different sizes of particles and therefore varying degrees of drawing ability. A white cosmetic clay has the largest particles and is softer and more porous. It would be more appropriate for a delicate or drier complexion. Rose clay particles are of medium size and absorbency and work well with normal skin. Problem skin that is oily, rough, and broken out fares best with a strongly astringent green clay, which has the smallest-size particles.

Henna has been used cosmetically for thousands of years in the Middle East. It conditions hair, brings out its natural luster, and adds reddish highlights.

Inorganic colors are powdered minerals naturally occurring in nature. They are not known to be harmful and are decidedly preferable to coal-tar colorings. Inorganic colors include iron oxides, ultramarines, and manganese violet. Bismuth oxychloride is synthesized from bismuth, which occurs naturally in the earth. It gives a pearly effect to cosmetics. Titanium dioxide is a naturally occurring crystal that is powdered to form white pigment.

Jojoba oil deserves special mention in that it is an increasingly popular ingredient in hair care. It is an effective cleaning and conditioning aid. By helping to remove the oil that gathers at the base of the hair strand, jojoba controls dry scalp conditions. It is a valuable substance that, coincidentally, has a molecular structure identical to that of whale oil. Naturally purer than most oils, it needs little refining and does not easily become rancid.

Olive oil castile soap is a good soap—it is gentle and has a close-to-neutral pH.

Protein. Hair consists of a structural protein called keratin. Once a hair strand grows beyond the scalp it is dead. Still, cosmetic companies frequently include protein in their hair-care products. They advertise that their protein products penetrate the hair shafts and resurrect them. It is unknown whether added protein actually reconstructs hair; however, it does add luster and body.

The protein and protein components used for hair care include amino acids (like cysteine), nucleic acids (RNA and DNA), collagen (hydrolyzed animal proteins), and casein (a milk component). Two favored proteins are keratin and elastin. Keratin, which is processed from horns, hooves, feathers, and hair, allegedly strengthens hair. Elastin, a polypeptide amino acid, is located in the skin and helps maintain the skin's elasticity. After the age of thirty the body slows down elastin production; therefore manufacturers frequently include this protein component in facial moisturizers and hair-care products.

Vitamins are now included in many beauty products. Vitamins A and D reputedly maintain soft skin and repair body tissues. Vitamin E allegedly retards the aging process and serves as an antioxidant. These three fat-soluble vitamins, when combined with vegetable oils, are absorbed through the skin and released internally.

Vitamin C as citric acid or ascorbic acid is used in cosmetics as a preservative, antioxidant, and a pH adjuster. It is one of the most prevalent acids used in the cosmetics industry.

✩ Common Body-Care Ingredients to Be Avoided

Coal-tar colors are highly controversial. They are easily recognized by their labels: for example, "f d & c red no. 3" or "f d & c blue no. 1." There are more than eighty coal-tar colors, and only six are considered safe. Almost all the rest have been shown to cause cancer in mice.

Detergent-based soaps contain alkyl sulfate or alkyl sulfonate and are harsh to the skin.

Mineral oil is one cosmetic ingredient to avoid. It depletes the body of vitamins A, D, and E.

COSMETICS

The following is a description, in alphabetical order, of natural cosmetics and the minimum ingredients each needs to be effective. You will find few cosmetics containing just the essentials. Comparing a product against this description will help you determine whether its contents meet your specifications.

Astringent Splashes

An astringent splash is useful in temporarily closing the skin's pores and restoring its slightly acid pH following cleansing. Rose water and witch hazel are excellent natural astringents. Herbal infusions that have astringent properties are elder, mint, and yarrow.

Cleansers

Following good nourishment of the skin in importance is proper cleansing. A deep, thorough cleansing allows an individual's inherent beauty to shine through. When selecting products for skin (as well as hair), a general guideline is, the simpler the better. Natural ingredients clean gently and thoroughly. Skin should not be subjected to detergents and other harsh products.

Facial cleansing involves cleansing, conditioning, and moisturizing. If you choose to wash your face with soap, use a neutral nondetergent soap. Soaps are more alkaline in nature and can be drying. Therefore many use facial cleansers as an alternative. Some cleansers combine soap with softening vegetables. Others are soap free. Some natural skin-care specialists recommend eliminating any soapy washing of the face. They suggest cleansing the face with a weekly herbal facial steam followed by a facial scrub. A basic herbal steaming mixture for dry skin contains comfrey root and leaf, camomile, licorice, and Irish moss. A good herbal steam for oily skin is lemon peel, lemongrass, lavender, and witch hazel.

Conditioners

An effective homemade hair conditioner would be a herbal infusion and simple astringent. Some of the more prevalent herbs for conditioners are the same ones used in shampoos. Other highly effective ones are burdock and wild cherry bark. Herbs that are healing for the scalp and also stimulate hair growth are rosemary, nettles, lavender, basil, yarrow, and horsetail.

Commercial hair conditioners include herbal extracts, nutritional adjuncts (such as vitamins and proteins), processing aids, humectants, finishing agents, fragrances, and preservatives.

Deodorants

Standard commercial deodorants offend the sensibilities of some consumers with their artificial and often irritating products. Now available in natural-food stores are deodorants that dry with an astringent (like witch hazel) or absorbent powders (like cornstarch, cornflour, clay, and silk powder). Their chemical ingredients are emollients, emulsifiers, humectants, soapy substances (sodium stearate), and citric acid preservatives. Herbal teas, extracts, and oils are used as fragrance. A few natural deodorants contain alcohol and zinc salts, which are known to be irritating, but all must be lauded for not containing aluminum as an ingredient.

Lotions

Lotions, like moisturizers, are emollients—that is, they have a softening and soothing effect on surface tissues of the body. Natural emollient products contain softening oils, emulsifiers, thickeners, and herbal ingredients. Many contain vitamins, fragrances, and preservatives.

It is a popular misconception that oil in and of itself makes skin soft. Skin needs water. Oil shields the skin from outside factors that can dry it. Oil also nourishes the skin with vitamins A and E. Unrefined vegetable oils feed the skin with good-quality polyunsaturates. Some oils used in natural cosmetics are primarily included for nourishment, such as wheat germ oil and avocado oil.

Certain oils, such as olive, peanut, almond, and cocoa butter, are nondrying. They are best used on delicate, dry skin. Others, like sesame, safflower, sunflower, apricot kernel, and corn, are semidrying, thus suitable for people with normal to oily skin. Soy oil is the most drying and is acceptable for use on oily skin only.

Makeup

Natural base powders consist of silk powder and inorganic earth colors. Zinc stearate is a stearic acid salt used for its adhesive properties in a powder base.

One powder blush on the market is as simple as silk powder with natural plant and mineral colors.

By looking at the label on a tube of lipstick one might assume that not much can be done to simplify lipstick manufacture. The primary hardening ingredients are castor oil, candelilla, oleyl alcohol, beeswax, and ozokerite. Added to these are several emollient oils, vitamins, a wetting agent, a solvent, and an antioxidant. Most lipstick on the market contains coal-tar derivatives.

Liquid foundation includes chemical and vegetable oil emollients, wetting agents, humectants, thickeners, emulsifiers, talc, vitamins, inorganic colors, and preservatives.

Rouges on the market likewise contain agents such as candelilla wax, beeswax, carnauba wax, and ozokerite to give solid body to the cosmetic. Like lipstick, they also have vegetable oils and fat-soluble vitamins. Beyond this, some brands only have mineral colors and antioxidants, while others have coal-tar colors and preservatives.

Masks

After the initial facial cleansing, masks provide deeper cleaning, tightening of pores, and conditioning in the form of lubrication and hydration. These frequently consist of the same grains, nuts, and clays used in scrubs. They are mixed with water to form a paste that is applied to a clean face and left on for ten to twenty minutes.

Herbs used in scrubs and masks can be stimulating like lavender; cooling like elder flowers; soothing and demulcent like aloe vera, ginseng, and comfrey root; or healing for skin problems like goldenseal, ivy, and eucalyptus.

Fruit and vegetable ingredients in masks are cooling, stimulating to the skin, toning to haggard flesh, and refining to the pores. Dry skin responds well to avocados, apples, watermelon, and honeydew melon. Normal skin is helped by citrus fruits, carrots, zucchini, and bananas. Berries (especially strawberries), lemons, and tomatoes absorb excess oil and are good for oily complexions.

Moisturizers

The finishing touch to facial care is a moisturizer. A moisturizer is like a lotion, but it more effectively keeps facial skin soft and supple. A few ingredients actually draw moisture from the air and hold it to the skin. These include lanolin, honey, and glycerin. They are popular additives to facial moisturizers and body lotions.

Rinses

A good homemade rinse need include only a herbal infusion and astringent rinse. An astringent rinse softens the hair, making it more manageable, and neutralizes the alkalinity of soap. Appropriate astringents are lemon juice, apple cider vinegar, and seawater. Herbs used in rinses vary according to hair color and condition.

Scrubs

A scrub in its simplest form contains a gritty, grainy substance used to lift out dirt and oil. Oatmeal, cornmeal, rye flour, wheat germ, rice bran, and clay are frequently used. Oats are the fattiest grain and are preferred for dry skin. Cornmeal, rye flour, and bran are better for normal or oily skin. Almond and apricot kernel meals are added for their soothing properties. Some scrubs include vitamins, chemical emollients, emulsifiers, cleansers, and preservatives.

Shampoos

The simplest effective natural shampoo would include a neutral soap such as olive oil castile, gentle herbal extracts, and possibly a protein additive. If homemade, the simplest protein to use would be an egg.

The soap should remove surface dirt without stripping the hair of its natural oils. Detergent shampoos overcleanse, which dries the hair. It then becomes unmanageable and excessively oily in response to its dry condition.

No natural soaps duplicate the slightly acidic pH of hair and skin without adding extra ingredients. Yet healthy scalp and hair can easily return to its proper pH, especially if assisted with a slightly acidic astringent rinse.

Herbal extracts and essential oils add supportive emollient conditioning, highlights, or coloring and fragrance. Naturally derived essential oils are extremely expensive; thus when an essential oil is a cosmetic ingredient it is probably synthetic.

Some emollient herbs are comfrey root, peppermint, aloe vera, marigold, calendula, and orange flowers. Conditioning herbs used in shampoos and rinses are camomile, lemongrass and nettles. Herbs used to increase highlights or color are camomile, clove, and henna.

Natural shampoos are scented with clove, orange peel, lavender, and azulene (camomile).

Soaps

Soap is made when sodium hydroxide is added to fatty acids. Fatty acids may be of animal or vegetable origin. The only fatty acid that is definitely of vegetable origin is lauric acid, and it is derived from coconut oil. Myristic, palmitic, and oleic acid may be of either vegetable or animal origin. Stearic acid comes primarily from animal fat.

Quality soaps are available in great variety. Olive oil castile soap is always a good choice. Detergents are harsh to the skin and not recommended.

Toothpastes

Not to leave a pearly smile ignored, cosmetic companies are marketing more natural toothpastes. The ingredients in these dentifrices are not significantly different from those in standard commercial brands, but there are fewer ingredients. They accomplish the same results: cleansing tooth surfaces, stimulating gums, and freshening breath.

Natural toothpastes contain simple dentifrices like calcium carbonate (chalk), clay, dicalcium phosphate, baking powder, or sea salt. Humectants like glycerin and sorbitol help prevent the paste from drying out; sodium lauryl sulfate makes the product sudsy; carrageenan or guar gum thickens it. Myrrh extract is often added as an astringent, chlorophyll as a freshener, and various flavors like anise, mint, and cinnamon are for taste. Vitamins C, E, and A in their various forms serve as antioxidants.

Peelu toothpaste is a "natural tooth whitener" that comes from the peelu tree. Some stores also carry peelu chewsticks, which may be used in place of both toothbrush and toothpaste. Since biblical times people in the Mideast and Asia have scrubbed their teeth with this fibrous, bristlelike stick. The mechanical brushing action removes debris, and the stick's juice contains natural germ-killing and whitening chemicals. One stick affords about one month's use.

COSMETIC INGREDIENTS

Name	Description	Function	Products*	Toxicity
Agar-agar	Mineral-rich seaweed	Thickener	M	None known
Algin	Derivative of alginic acid; the sodium carbonate extract of seaweed	Thickener, stabilizer	SC	None known
Allantoin	Naturally derived from comfrey; synthetically from uric acid	Used to promote growth of healthy tissue; has cell regenerative properties	B, C, D, L, LP, M, SC, SP	None known
Almond meal	Pulverized, blanched almonds	Mild skin bleach; soothing, scrubbing action	MK, SC	None known, but causes allergies in some
Almond oil	From bitter or sweet almonds; refined to remove toxic prussic acid	Emollient	L, M, S	—

*Key: B, blush; C, conditioner; CL, cleanser; D, deodorant; F, foundation; FP, face powder; L, lotion; LP, lipstick; M, moisturizer; MK, mask; R, rinse; RG, rouge; S, soap; SC, scrub; SP, shampoo; T, toothpaste.

Name	Description	Function	Products*	Toxicity
Aloe vera	Mucilaginous, desert plant	Soothing for burns; softening to skin	C, CL, M, MK, S, SC, SP	None known when used externally
Amphoteric 2	Either a coconut derivative, or completely synthesized	Surface active agent; adjusts acid-alkaline balance	C, SP	—
Annatto	Derived from a red, waxy substance found on seeds of Central American plant	Dye	B, L, R, SP	None known
Apple cider vinegar	Acetic acid produced by apple fermentation	Removes soap after shampooing; solvent for cosmetic oils and resins	C, SP	None known
Apricot kernel	Powdered apricot pits	Soothing, scrubbing action	SC	Can be toxic if ingested in large amounts
Apricot kernel oil	Oil expressed from apricot pits	Emollient	L, M, MK, S, SC	None known
Ascorbic acid	Vitamin C; naturally occurs in citrus and other fruits; synthetically derived from glucose	Antioxidant, preservative	C, D, L, MK, SP	None known
Avocado oil	Oil expressed from avocados	Nutritive emollient	C, L, M	None known
Azulene	Blue liquid derived from distilled essential oil of camomile flowers	Fragrance, color	D, MK	None known
Balsam	Fragrant, brown viscous liquid obtained from Peruvian balsam trees	Disinfectant for skin disease; promotes healthy epithelial growth; leaves hair feeling soft and shiny after shampoo	C, SP	None known, but can cause dermatitis and stuffy nose
Barley waters	Liquid from cooking barley	Demulcent	C, L, SC, SP	None known
Bee pollen	Contains complete protein, Vitamins A, C, D, E, K, and B complex; rich in minerals; natural antibiotic	Nutritive additive for promoting healthy scalp	SP	—

Name	Description	Function	Products*	Toxicity
Beet juice	Juice expressed from beet root	Reddish coloring agent	C, SP	None known
Bentonite	White clay found in Midwest and Canada	Absorbs oil; thickener, emulsifier	L, MK	—
Benzalkonium chloride	Ammonium detergent; synthetic derivative of ammonium chloride	Detergent, germicide, preservative	C	Irritating to eyes
Biotin	B-complex vitamin	Texturizer; prevents hair loss	C, SP	—
Birch	Bark of birch tree	Astringent; used for skin and scalp disorders	SP	—
Bismuth oxychloride	Gray-white powder, "synthetic pearl"	Imparts a frost or shine in cosmetics	RG	May cause allergic reaction on skin
Blackberry	Leaves of blackberry bush	Astringent	L, MK, SC	—
Bois de rose	Essential oil	Fragrance	L, SP	—
Burdock	Root	Restores skin tone and smoothness		—
Calcium carbonate	Chalk; tasteless, odorless powder occurring in limestone	Absorbent, dentifrice, abrasive	SC, T	—
Camomile	Daisylike yellow or white flowers	Healing to mucous membranes; brightens light hair	C, L, MK, SC, SP	—
Camphor oil	Aromatic oil; originally derived from camphor trees; now synthetic	Renders a cool feeling to skin; preservative	CL	May cause rashes
Candelilla wax	Obtained from candelilla plant	Gives body	LP, RG	None known
Caramel	Scorched sugar or glucose with added alkali or trace mineral	Coloring; soothing agent	R	—
Carbopol	Slightly acidic white powder	Reacts with fat particles creating stable emulsions	L, M	None known

*Key: B, blush; C, conditioner; CL, cleanser; D, deodorant; F, foundation; FP, face powder; L, lotion; LP, lipstick; M, moisturizer; MK, mask; R, rinse; RG, rouge; S, soap; SC, scrub; SP, shampoo; T, toothpaste.

Name	Description	Function	Products*	Toxicity
Carmine	Derivative of a Central American insect	Crimson pigment	B, R, RG, SP	May cause allergic reactions
Carnanuba wax	Derived from leaves of Brazilian wax palm tree	Lends body and texture	RG, LP	Rarely causes allergic reactions
Carrageenan	Derived from Irish moss	Stabilizer, emulsifier, stiffener; soothes skin	MK, TP	None known
Casein	Milk protein	Thickens hair and makes more manageable	C, SP	None known
Castile soap	Hard soap made from olive oil and sodium hydroxide	Cleansing	C, SP, S	None known
Castor oil	Obtained from castor bean	Soothing to skin	C, LP	Can cause pelvic congestion if ingested in large amounts
Cetearyl alcohol	Mixture of cetyl and stearyl alcohols	Emulsifier	C	None known
Cetereth 5	Oily distilled liquid from cetyl alcohol and stearyl alcohol	Emollient, emulsifier, antifoam agent, lubricant	C, SC	None known
Ceteth 2	Compound of fatty alcohols mixed with ethylene oxide	Starting material for detergents, oily liquids, or waxy solids	L	
Chalk	(See calcium carbonate)			
Chlorophyll	Green coloring matter of plants	Deodorant	D, C, SP, T	—
Choline	B-complex vitamin; basic constituent of lecithin	Good for hair problems	C, SP	—
Citric acid	Vitamin C; a constituent of citrus fruits	Preservative, sequestering agent, pH balancer	C, L, SP T	None known
Clove oil	Essential oil from cloves	Fragrance, hair color	C, SP	—
Cocamide DEA	Coconut oil derivative	Lathering, cleansing	C, D, SP	May be irritating to skin
Cocamide-propyl betaine	Coconut oil derivative	Lathering, cleansing	L, SC, SP	—
Coconut oil	White, semisolid fat expressed from coconut flesh	Lathering, cleansing, lubricating	C, L, S, SC, SP	—

Name	Description	Function	Products*	Toxicity
Cocoa butter	Solid fats expressed from cocoa plant seeds	Lubricant	L, S	May cause allergic reactions
Collagen	Connective tissue protein	Strengthening, nourishing to hair	C, M, SP	None known
Comfrey	Roots and leaves of comfrey	Emollient, demulcent, astringent	C, L, SP	—
Cornmeal	Ground from yellow or white corn	Scrubbing agent	MK, SC	None known
Cornstarch	Highly refined corn by-product	Thickener, absorbent	D	May cause allergic reaction
Cucumber	Pulp	Cooling, soothing	MK	—
Cysteine	Amino acid	Strengthening and nourishing to hair	C, SP	—
DEA lauryl sulfate	Synthetic derivative of ammonium chloride	Preservative	SP	Can be irritating to mucous membranes
Dicalcium phosphate	White odorless powder	Dentrifice	T	—
EDTA	Ethylenediamine tetracetic acid	Sequestering agent	L, S, SP	On FDA list of additives to be studied for toxicity
Elastin	Polypetide amino acid	Maintains elasticity	M, SP	—
Elder	Flowers from elder trees	Cools, softens skin, mild astringent	CL, SP	—
Ergocalciferal	Vitamin D	Healing to skin	C, L, SC, SP, T	—
Eucalyptus	Aromatic oil and leaves of eucalyptus tree	Antiseptic, aromatic; for scalp conditions	CL, MK	—
Evening primrose oil	Oil of the evening primrose plant	Healing to skin	C, SP	—
F, D, & C	Coal-tar colors	Coloring in makeup	LP, RG	May be toxic
Folic acid	B-complex vitamin	For scalp conditions	C, SP	—
Geranium oil	Oil from geranium plant	Fragrance	C, SP	—
Ginseng	Root	Healing to skin	M, SP	—
Glutaral	An amino acid found in immature sugar beets	Preservative	SP	—
Glycerin	Residue from soap making	Solvent, humectant, emollient	C, D, L, M, S, SC, SP, T	In concentrated solutions irritating to mucous membranes

Key: B, blush; C, conditioner; CL, cleanser; D, deodorant; F, foundation; FP, face powder; L, lotion; LP, lipstick; M, moisturizer; MK, mask; R, rinse; RG, rouge; S, soap; SC, scrub; SP, shampoo; T, toothpaste.

Name	Description	Function	Products*	Toxicity
Glycerin stearate	(See glycerin)		CL, C, M	—
Goldenseal	Powdered medicinal root	Healing to skin	MK, SC	—
Guar bean gum	Nutritive seed tissues of guar plants cultivated in India	Thickener (thickens five to eight times as much as starch)	C, T	—
Gum arabic	Gum from acacia trees	Emulsifer, binder, stabilizer, gelling agent	MK	May cause allergic reaction
Gum benzoin	Balsamic resin from benzoin tree	Preservative	L	None known
Henna	Green powder made from leaves of North African henna shrub	Coloring, highlighting	C, SP	—
Hematite	Earth color	Reddish coloring in makeup	B	—
Honey	Sweet viscous material	Emollient, hydrator	C, MK	—
Hydroxyethyl-cellulose	Prepared from wood pulp	Binder, emulsifying agent	RG	
Imidazolidinyl urea	Partially made from urine	Antiseptic; bactericide	C, CL, L, SC	
Inositol	B-complex vitamin	Vital for hair growth	C, SP	
Iris	Flower	Controls water absorption	CL	—
Irish moss	Seaweed	Healing to skin	CL, M	—
Iron oxides	Inorganic mineral colors	Coloring in makeup	B, LP, RG	—
Isopropyl myristate	Mixture of myristate and fatty acids	Finishing agent	L, SP	None known
Ivy	Leaves of a creeping ivy vine	For problem skin	M, MK	—
Jojoba	Oil from desert jojoba plant	Cleaning, conditioning, emollient	C, L, M, SP	None known
Kaolin	Clay	Absorbs oil, emollient	MK, SC	—
Keratin	Hair protein	Strengthening, nourishing to hair	C, SP	—
Krameria extract	Synthetic flavoring derived from root shrubs	Flavoring	T	—
Lanolin	Wool oil	Emollient, absorbs water, emulsifier	C, CL, L, M, S, SC, SP	
Lecithin	Obtained from eggs and soybeans	Emollient, antioxidant, emulsifier	C, L, M, S, SP	None known
Magnesium aluminum silicate	Hard, porous, granular substance	Coloring agent	M, MK	None known

Name	Description	Function	Products*	Toxicity
Magnesium citrate	Citric acid salt	Finishing agent; leaves shine after drying	C, SP	None known
Manganese violet	Inorganic mineral	Coloring	B	Toxic when inhaled
Methyl paraben	Small colorless petroleum-derived crystals	Preservative	C, CL, L, M, MK, SC, SP	Allergic skin reactions
Mica	Crystallized mineral	Coloring	B	None known
Mineral oil	Petroleum-derived oil	Lubricant, binder	SC	None known
Mint	Leaves of mint plant	Emollient, healing to skin	CL, SM	—
Myrrh	Aromatic bitter gum resin from East Africa and Mideast	Astringent, aromatic	T	—
Nettles	Leaves of nettle	Healing to scalp, stimulates hair growth	C, SP	—
Niacin	B-complex vitamin	Healing to scalp	C, SP	None known
Oats	Meal from the grain	Drying, scrubbing	D, MK, SC	—
Octyl palmitate	A salt of palmitic acid	Used in makeup	FP	None known
Olive oil	Oil from ripe olives	Emollient	C, L, M, S, SP	—
Orange peel	Dried skin of oranges	Scent; healing to skin	C	—
Orris root	Fragrant root of the orris plant	Scent; healing to scalp; fixative	SP	—
Ozokerite	Waxlike mineral	Solidifier	LS	None known
PABA	B-complex vitamin	Sunscreen	C, L, M, SP	—
Panthenol	Vitamin B_5	Thickens hair, good for tissues	C, CL, L, M, SP	—
Papain	Protein-digesting enzyme from papaya	Digestive enzyme; dissolves dead material	MK, T	—
Pectin	Found in roots, stems, and fruits of plants	Emulsifier, thickener	SP	None known
PEG 8 distearate	Derived from oleic acid	Carrier or base	C, L	None known
PEG 100 stearate	Derived from stearic acid	Emulsifier	C, L, SC	—
Polysorbate 20	Oily liquid from lauric acid	Emulsifier, stabilizer of essential oils in water	L, SP	May cause allergic reactions

*Key: B, blush; C, conditioner; CL, cleanser; D, deodorant; F, foundation; FP, face powder; L, lotion; LP, lipstick; M, moisturizer; MK, mask; R, rinse; RG, rouge; S, soap; SC, scrub; SP, shampoo; T, toothpaste.

Name	Description	Function	Products*	Toxicity
Potassium chlorate	Potassium salt	Astringent		
Potassium sorbate	Potassium salt	Mold and yeast inhibiter	L, SC	May cause mild skin irritation
Propolis	Bee product	Nutritive substance	T	—
Propylene glycol	Clear, colorless, viscous liquid	Humectant, solvent	C, CL, D, SC, SP	—
Propyl gallate	White odorless powder	Preservative	LS	None known
Propylparaben	Ester of hydro-benzoic acid	Preservative	C, CL, L, M, MK, SC, SP	May cause contact dermatitis
Pyridoxine	Vitamin B_6	Hair and scalp conditioner	C	—
Quaternium 31	Synthetic derivative of ammonium chloride	Surfactant, preservative	C	Can be toxic
Quaternium 57	Grapefruit extract	Preservative	L, SC	—
Quillaja	Bark of South American tree	Sudsing agent	SP	—
Retinyl palmitate	Vitamin A	Healing to skin	C, CL, L, MK, SC, SP, T	—
Rose	Petals, water	Scent, astringent	M, SC	—
Rosemary oil	Herbal essential oil	Scalp conditioner	C, SP	—
Royal jelly	Bee product	Rejuvenator	L	—
Safflower	Oil from seed of a thistlelike plant	Emollient	C, L, M	—
Sage	Herb	Conditioner, skin stimulant	C, SP	—
Sesame oil	Oil extracted from sesame seeds	Emollient	L, M	—
Silk powder	White solid obtained from silkworm secretions	Coloring	FP	Causes severe skin reactions
Sodium alginate	Sodium salt from acid extracted from seaweed	Thickener, stabilizer, emulsifier		
Sodium lauryl sulfate	Coconut oil derivative	Wetting agent, cleanser, emulsifier	SC, SP, T	None known
Sodium stearate	Fatty acid	Deodorant	D	—
Sodium sulfate	Occurs naturally as mirabilite and thenardite	Soap; cleansing	S	
Sorbitol	Found in fruit and seaweed	Humectant, sequestering agent	T	—
Stearalkonium chloride	Synthetic derivative of ammonium chloride	Surfactant, preservative	C	May be toxic

Name	Description	Function	Products*	Toxicity
Steareth 2	Polyethylene ether of fatty alcohol	Surfactant	C	None known
Stearic acid	Naturally occurring in many animal and vegetable fats and oils	Major ingredient in soaps and lubricants	CL, L, M, MK, SP	Can cause allergic reactions
Stearyl alcohol	Mixture of solid alcohols; originally from whale oil	Emulsifier, lubricant, antifoam agent	C, D, L	None known
Sweet basil	Essential oil of the herb	Fragrance, stimulates hair growth	C, D, SP	—
Talc	A soft mineral, magnesium silicate	Coloring, gives slippery feel to powders and lotions	L, FP, MK, SC	Irritant if inhaled
Titanium dioxide	Natural powder of a crystal	Pigment	MK	None known
Tocopherol	Vitamin E	Antioxidant, healing to skin	C, CL, D, L, M, MK, SC, SP	—
Ultramarine blue	Mineral	Coloring in makeup	F	—
Wild cherry	Bark of the tree	Rinse for ease in combing	C, SP	—
Witch hazel	Made from leaves and twigs of a plant	Astringent, skin freshener	CL, D	—
Xanthan gum	Made from a microorganism	Thickener	D, L, M	—
Yarrow	Yarrow leaves and twigs	Stimulates hair growth	C, SP	—
Ylang-ylang	Oil of an Oriental flower	Scent	L, SP	May cause allergic reaction
Yucca	Root of a desert plant	Sudsing agent	SP	—
Zinc oxide	White ointment	Imparts opacity to makeup; healing to skin	FP	Generally harmless
Zinc stearate	Mixture of zinc salts of stearic acid	Adhesive property in makeup	FP	None known

*Key: B, blush; C, conditioner; CL, cleanser; D, deodorant; F, foundation; FP, face powder; L, lotion; LP, lipstick; M, moisturizer; MK, mask; R, rinse; RG, rouge; S, soap; SC, scrub; SP, shampoo; T, toothpaste.

Appendix 2
Recommended Reading List
(cookbooks, food books, natural healing books, and periodicals)

COOKBOOKS

The Art of Dieting without Dieting, Kathy Hoshijo. Glendale, Calif.: Self-Sufficiency Association, 1986.

Asian Pasta, Linda Burum. Berkeley, Calif.: Aris Books, 1985.

Aveline Kushi's Macrobiotic Cooking, Aveline Kushi. New York: Warner Books, 1985.

Basic Macrobiotic Cooking, Julia Ferré. Oroville, Calif.: George Ohsawa Macrobiotic Foundation, 1987.

The Book of Miso, William Shurtleff and Akiko Aoyagi. Kanagawa-Ken, Japan: Autumn Press, 1976.

The Book of Tempeh, William Shurtleff and Akiko Aoyagi. New York: Harper & Row, 1979.

The Book of Tofu, William Shurtleff and Akiko Aoyagi. Brookline, Mass.: Autumn Press, 1975.

The Book of Whole Meals, Annemarie Colbin. Brookline, Mass.: Autumn Press, 1979.

Cooking with Care and Purpose, Michel Abehsera. Brooklyn, N.Y.: Swan House, 1978.

Cooking with Japanese Foods, Jan and John Belleme. Brookline, Mass.: East West Health Books, 1986.

Cooking with Sea Vegetables, Sharon Ann Rhoads with Patricia Zunic. Brookline, Mass.: Autumn Press, 1978.

Deaf Smith Country Cookbook, Marjorie Winn Ford, Susan Hillyard, and Mary Faulk Koock. New York: Collier Books, 1973.

The Dō of Cooking, Cornelia Aihara. Oroville, Calif.: George Ohsawa Macrobiotic Foundation, 1982.

English Bread and Yeast Cookery, Elizabeth David. New York: Viking Press, 1977.

Laurel's Kitchen, Laurel Robertson et al. Petaluma, Calif.: Nilgiri Press, 1976.

Moosewood Cookbook, Molly Katzen. Berkeley, Calif.: Ten Speed Press, 1977.

Natural Foods Cookbook, Mary Estella. Tokyo: Japan Publications, 1985.

The Natural Healing Cookbook: Over Four Hundred Ways to Get Better and Stay Healthy, Mark Bricklin and Charon Claessens. Emmaus, Pa.: Rodale Press, 1981.

The New American Vegetable Cookbook, Georgeanne Brennan, Isaac Cronin, and Charlotte Glenn. Berkeley, Calif.: Aris Books, 1985.

The New York Times Natural Foods Cookbook, Jean Hewitt. New York: Avon Books, 1971.

Putting Food By (2d ed.), Ruth Hertzberg, Beatrice Vaughan, and Janet Greene. New York: Bantam Books, 1976.

Tassajara Breadbook, Edward Espe Brown. Boulder, Colo.: Shambhala Publications, 1970.

Tassajara Cookbook, Edward Espe Brown. Boulder, Colo.: Shambhala Publications, 1973.

FOOD BOOKS

Book of Whole Grains, Marlene Anne Bumgarner. New York: St. Martin's Press, 1976.

The Complete Book of Natural Foods, Fred Rohé. Boulder, Colo.: Shambhala Publications, 1983.

The Complete Food Handbook, Roger P. Doyle and James L. Redding. New York: Grove Press, 1976.

Consumer Beware! Beatrice Trum Hunter. New York: Touchstone Books, 1971.

Diet for a Small Planet, Frances Moore Lappé. New York: Ballantine Books, 1971.

Eater's Digest: The Consumer's Factbook of Food Additives, Michael F. Jacobson. Garden City, N.Y.: Doubleday/Anchor Books, 1976.

Food: An Authoritative and Visual History and Dictionary of the Foods of the World, Waverley Root. New York: Simon & Schuster, 1980.

Food Facts, A Compendium on Whole Foods, Evelyn Roehl. Seattle, Wash.: Food Learning Center, 1986.

Oxford Book of Food Plants. London: Oxford University Press.

Produce, Bruce Beck. New York: Friendly Press, 1984.

Stalking the Healthful Herbs, Euell Gibbons. New York: David McKay, 1966.

Uncommon Fruits and Vegetables: A Commonsense Guide, Elizabeth Schneider. New York: Harper & Row, 1986.

Vegetables from the Sea, Arasaki, Seibin, and Teruko. Tokyo: Japan Publications, 1983.

Whole Foods: Nutrition and Cuisine, Karen MacNeil. New York: Vintage Books, 1981.

World Hunger: 10 Myths, Frances Moore Lappé and Joseph Collins. San Francisco: Institute for Food and Development Policy, 1979.

NATURAL HEALTH BOOKS

Acid and Alkaline, (rev. ed.), Herman Aihara. Oroville, Calif.: George Ohsawa Macrobiotic Foundation, 1982.

The Book of Macrobiotics, Michio Kushi. Tokyo: Japan Publications, 1977.

The Five Phases of Food: How to Begin. John W. Garvy, N.D., D.Ac. Brookline, Mass.: Wellbeing Books, 1983.

Food and Healing, Annemarie Colbin. New York: Ballantine Books, 1986.

Food for Thought, Saul and Jo Anne Miller. Englewood Cliffs, N.J.: Prentice-Hall, Inc., 1979.

Healing Ourselves, Naboru Muramoto. New York: Avon Books, 1973.

Living Well Naturally, Anthony J. Sattilaro, M.D., with Tom Monte. Boston, Mass.: Houghton Mifflin, 1984.

Macrobiotic Home Remedies, Michio Kushi. Tokyo: Japan Publications, 1985.

Natural Healing Through Macrobiotics, Michio Kushi. Tokyo: Japan Publications, 1984.

Sugar Blues, William Dufty. New York: Warner Books, 1976.

Tom Brown's Guide to Wild Edible and Medicinal Plants, Tom Brown, Jr. New York: Berkeley Books, 1985.

The Way of Herbs, Michael Tierra, C.A., N.D. New York: Washington Square Press, 1983.

PERIODICALS

American Health, 80 Fifth Avenue, New York, NY 10010.

Bestways, Box 2028, Carson City, NV 89702.

East West: A Journal of Natural Health and Living, PO Box 1200, Brookline, MA 02147.

Harrowsmith, The Creamery, Charlotte, VT 05445.

Herbalgram, P.O. Box 12006, Austin, TX 78711.

Macromuse, 4905 Del Ray Ave., Bethesda, MD 20814.

Medical Self Care, P.O. Box 717, Inverness, CA 94937.

New Age, 342 Western Avenue, Brighton, MA 02135.

Nontoxic & Natural News, Box 475, Inverness, CA 94937.

Nutrition Action, Center for Science in the Public Interest, 1755 S St. NW, Washington, DC 20009.

Vegetarian Times, P.O. Box 570, Oak Park, IL 60303.

Whole Life, Journal for Personal and Planetary Health, Suite 600, 89 Fifth Avenue, New York, NY 10003.

208

Appendix 3
Natural Foods by Mail

Arrowhead Mills
Box 866
Herford, TX 79045
Full selection of health-food staples and a natural home food-storage program. Minimum order is 300 pounds.

Baldwin Hill Bakery
Baldwin Hill Road
Phillipston, MA 01331
(617) 249–4691
Natural sourdough European country bread containing organic stone-milled grain and baked on a brick hearth over a hardwood fire.

Garden Spot
Rt 1, Box 729A
New Holland, PA 17557
(800) 445-5100
Organic grains, nuts, beans, and herbs.

GEM Cultures
30301 Sherwood Road
Ft. Bragg, CA 95437
(707) 964–2922
Good cultures for tempeh, miso, shoyu, sourdough, kefir, and more.

Jaffe Brothers
P.O. Box 636
Valley Center, CA 92082
(619) 749-1133
Dried fruits, grains, beans, and candy.

Mendocino Sea Vegetable Company
P.O. Box 372
Navarro, CA 95463
Sea vegetables.

Mountain Ark Trading Company
120 S. East Street
Fayetteville, AR 72701
(800) 643–8909
A comprehensive catalog of macrobiotic food and kitchenware.

Oak Feed Store
3030 Grand Avenue
Coconut Grove
Miami, FL 33133
(305) 448–7595
Natural foods, specialty foods, and books.

Sanctuary Farms
RD #1 Butler Road
New London, OH 44851
(419) 929–8177
Specializing in certified organic grains and beans.

South River Miso
South River Farm
Conway, MA 01341
(413) 369–4057
Traditional farmhouse-style miso, naturally aged and fermented.

Walnut Acres
Penns Creek, PA 17862
Full selection of freshly made natural products.

Notes

A

1. *Health Foods Business,* "Lactobacillus, Acidophilus and Bulgaricus," pp. 62–64.
2. Sharon Ann Rhoads, *Cooking with Sea Vegetables,* p. 102.
3. Kathy Hoshijo, *The Art of Dieting without Dieting,* p. 525.
4. *Natural Foods Network Newsletter,* "Aloe Vera."
5. E. J. Kahn, Jr., "The Staffs of Life," p. 80.
6. Anasazi information supplied by Colorado State University Department of Food Science and Human Nutrition.
7. Gary Paul Nabhan, "Viable Seeds from Prehistoric Caches? Archaeobotanical Remains in Southwestern Folklore," pp. 143–46.
8. Waverley Root, *Food,* p. 12.
9. *Vegetarian Times,* "Apples at Core of Chemical Controversy," pp. 8–9.
10. Edward J. Ryder, Neal E. De Vos, and Mohammad A. Bari, "The Globe Artichoke (Cynara scolymus L.)," p. 646.
11. Florence Graves, "How Safe Is Your Diet Soft Drink?" pp. 25–29.
12. Department of Health and Human Services, "Quarterly Report on Adverse Reactions Associated with Aspartame Ingestion," p. 1.

B

1. Elizabeth David, *English Bread and Yeast Cookery,* p. 296.
2. Annemarie Colbin, *Food and Healing,* pp. 169–70.
3. Daniel McSweeney, "Bee Pollen," pp. 44–49.
4. Keith Henderson, "Drugs in Meat: Views on Congressional Findings," p. 25.
5. Cornelia Aihara, *The Dō of Cooking,* p. 117.
6. Naboru Muramoto, *Healing Ourselves,* pp. 14–19.
7. Bolita information supplied by Colorado State University Department of Food Science and Human Nutrition.
8. Diane B. Stoy, "The Buffalo-Cholesterol Connection."
9. Fred Rohé, *The Complete Book of Natural Foods,* p. 79.
10. Roger J. Williams, *Nutrition Against Disease,* pp. 83, 296.

C

1. Gail A. Levey, "King Cabbage and His Nobel Kin," pp. 87–96.
2. Phyllis Hanes, "Where is Cabbage Heading?" pp. 25–26.
3. Bruce Beck, *Produce,* p. 39.
4. Hanes, "Homely but Tasty Catfish," p. 25.
5. Roger J. Williams, *Nutrition Against Disease,* p. 295.
6. *Vegetarian Times,* "Imitation Cheese Raises Suspicions in Natural Foods World," p. 6.

7. Elizabeth Schneider, *Uncommon Fruits and Vegetables: A Common Sense Guide,* p. 116.
8. Bob Flaws and Honora Wolfe, *Prince Wen Hui's Cook: Chinese Dietary Therapy,* p. 21.
9. Beatrice Trum Hunter, *Consumer Beware!* p. 153.
10. *Health Foods Business,* Supplement Guide, p. 67.
11. Ellen Miller, "Chocolates to Tempt Your Valentine," pp. 1–2.
12. Michael Jacobson, "Caffeine's Role in Birth Defects," pp. 8–9.
13. Ronald E. Kotzsch, "From the Grounds Up," p. 55.
14. Kirk Johnson, "Chemical Coffee," p. 14.
15. Richard I. Ford, "The Color of Survival," pp. 17–29.
16. Thom Leonard, "Finding America's Staple Grain," pp. 42–47.
17. Food Protein Research and Development Center, *Cottonseed Cookery,* pp. 4–5.
18. Waverley Root, *Food,* pp. 99–100.
19. Evelyn Roehl, *Food Facts,* p. 152.

D

1. *California Natural Products Newsletter,* "From Dahlia Flowers to Dacopa."
2. *American Herb Association Quarterly Newsletter,* "Herbal Roots."
3. Jan and John Belleme, "Daikon—Japanese Radish Takes Root in America," p. 12.
4. Belleme, *Cooking with Japanese Foods,* p. 115.
5. Annemarie Colbin, *Food and Healing,* p. 154.
6. Northedge Natural Foods, *A California Food Products Notebook,* p. 31.
7. Roger P. Doyle and James L. Redding, *The Complete Food Handbook,* p. 55.
8. Ruth Hertzberg, Beatrice Vaughan, and Janet Greene, *Putting Food By,* p. 380.
9. Ford Heritage, *Composition and Facts about Foods,* p. 36.

E

1. Steven Foster, "Echinacea and the Immune System," pp. 8–14.
2. Michio Kushi, *Natural Healing Through Macrobiotics,* pp. 32–33.
3. Beatrice Trum Hunter, *Consumer Beware!* pp. 166–67.
4. Fred Rohé, *The Complete Book of Natural Foods,* p. 67.
5. Saul Miller, *Food for Thought,* p. 104.

F

1. Jan and John Belleme, *Cooking with Japanese Foods,* p. 2.
2. Ibid.

3. Thom Leonard, "Fermentation," p. 69.
4. William Helferich and D. Westhoff, *All About Yogurt.*
5. *Oxford Book of Food Plants,* p. 94.
6. Northedge Natural Foods, *A California Food Products Notebook,* pp. 25–26.
7. Paul Gingerich, Interview in *Natural Horizons.*
8. Georgeanne Brennan, Isaac Cronin, and Charlotte Glenn, *The New American Vegetable Cookbook,* p. 305.

G

1. Michael Tierra, *The Way of Herbs,* pp. 92–93.
2. Edna Zeavin, "Ginger: The Healing Spice," p. 38.
3. Ellen Lesser, "Taking Root," pp. 52–53.
4. Arthur Rashap and Beverly Braly, "Is Ginseng Safe?" p. 16.
5. Ibid.
6. Karen MacNeil, *Whole Foods: Nutrition and Cuisine,* p. 217.

H

1. John Heinerman, "What You Should Know Before Buying Herbs," p. 54.
2. Steven Foster and Jennifer Bennet, "The Herbal Ricochet," pp. 30–39.
3. Paul Bergner, "Elasticity Can Stretch Your Profits in Herb Sales."
4. *East West Journal,* Shopper's Guide to Natural Foods, pp. 72–72.
5. Roger W. Miller, "Honey: Making Sure It's Pure," p. 12.

I

1. Clare Barret Obis, "Ice Cream: The Chilling Truth," pp. 49–52.

J

1. Jan and John Belleme, *Cooking with Japanese Foods,* pp. 130–31.
2. Ibid., p. 93.
3. Betty Kamen, "Getting Fresh," p. 16.

K

1. Seibin and Teruko Arasaki, *Vegetables from the Sea,* pp. 53–58.
2. Ibid.
3. Leonard Jacobs, "Menage," pp. 16–18.
4. William Shurtleff and Akiko Aoyagi, *The Book of Kudzu,* pp. 53–55.

L

1. Harold McGee, *On Food and Cooking,* p. 263.
2. Mitoku Co., Ltd., "Japanese Food Guide," #5.

M

1. Laura Ingalls Wilder, *Little House in the Big Woods,* p. 151.
2. Fred Rohé, *The Complete Book of Natural Foods,* pp. 74–75.
3. Roger P. Doyle and James L. Redding, *The Complete Food Handbook,* pp. 140–41.
4. Rohé, p. 75.
5. William Shurtleff and Akiko Aoyagi, *The Book of Miso,* pp. 22–28.
6. Peggy Rossoff, "Is Dried Miso Good for You?" p. 11.
7. Shurtleff and Aoyagi, pp. 26–27.
8. Elizabeth Schneider, *Uncommon Fruits and Vegetables,* p. 307.

N

1. Norman Franklin Childers, *Childers' Diet to Stop Arthritis: The Nightshades and Ill Health.*
2. John Bardach, *Harvest of the Sea,* p. 206.

O

1. Herbert Kaufmann, "Skin Care in the Present Day," p. 18.
2. Phil Levy, *Vegetable Oil: The Unsaturated Facts.*
3. Barry Browstein, "Natural Wisdom in the Marketplace," p. 13.
4. Jeffrey Bland, "Calcium Pushers," p. 73.
5. John McDougall, "Healthy by Choice," p. 53.

P

1. *Oxford Book of Food Plants,* p. 20.
2. Corby Kummer, "Pasta," p. 41.
3. Linda Burum, *Asian Pasta.*
4. Bob Flaws and Honora Wolfe, *Prince Wen Hui's Cook: Chinese Dietary Therapy,* p. 28.
5. William Carlos Williams, *Collected Earlier Poems.*
6. Betty Kamen, "Hi-Q Protein: Quality, Not Quantity," p. 26.
7. Francis Moore Lappé, *Diet for a Small Planet.*
8. Ibid., p. 26.

Q

1. David F. Cusak, "Quinoa: Grain of the Incas," pp. 21–30.
2. Rebecca Theurer Wood, "Quinoa: Tale of a Food Survivor," pp. 63–64.

R

1. Northedge Natural Foods, *A California Food Products Notebook,* p. 18.
2. Richard Leviton, "A Shopper's Guide to Sweeteners," pp. 35–41.
3. Cheryl Mitchell, telephone interview, November 1986.
4. Bob Flaws and Honora Wolfe, *Prince Wen Hui's Cook: Chinese Dietary Therapy,* p. 30.
5. Aveline Kushi, cooking demonstration, June 1983.
6. Waverley Root, *Food,* p. 545.

S

1. Wayne L. Pines and Nancy Glick, "The Saccharin Ban."
2. Michael Jacobson, "Shaking Out the Truth About Salt."
3. United States Senate, *Dietary Goals for the United States.*
4. Phil Levy, *Salt: Walking the Briny Line.*
5. Ibid.
6. Lino Stanchich, *The Story of Balanced Minerals: Sea Salt.*
7. Judith Cooper Madlener, *The Sea Vegetable Book,* pp. 24–27.
8. Seibin and Teruko Arasaki, *Vegetables from the Sea,* pp. 52–58.
9. Thom Leonard, "Testing Sea Vegetables," pp. 16–22.
10. Leonard, p. 20.
11. Sharon Ann Rhoads and Patricia Zunic, *Cooking with Sea Vegetables,* p. 26.
12. Fred Rohé, *The Complete Book of Natural Foods,* p. 236.
13. Leonard and Barbara Jacobs, "Flour Power!" pp. 37–38.
14. Cornelia Aihara, *The Dō of Cooking,* p. 22.
15. Kisaku Mori, *Mushrooms as Health Foods,* pp. 41–76.
16. William Shurtleff and Akiko Aoyagi, *The Book of Tofu,* p. 200.
17. Ibid., p. 202.
18. Mariclare Barrett, "Sweet Things Are Made of These," p. 38.
19. Steve Meyerowitz, "Sprout Man, Raw Foodist," p. 24.
20. Marcy Barbour, "Squash: Colors of Health."
21. Mariclare Barrett, "Sweet Things Are Made of These," p. 38.
22. Levy, *Sugar and How It Gets That Way.*
23. William Dufty, *Sugar Blues.*

T

1. Mary Estella, *Natural Foods Cookbook,* p. 59.
2. Karen MacNeil, *Whole Foods: Nutrition and Cuisine,* p. 293.

3. New Age Foods Study Center, "Move Over Big Mac, Here Comes Tempeh."
4. Euell Gibbons, *Stalking the Healthful Herbs.*
5. Beatrice Trum Hunter, *Consumer Beware!* p. 284.
6. Julee Rosso and Sheila Lukins, *The Silver Palate Good Times Cookbook,* p. 252.
7. George P. Hammond and Agapito Rey, *The Rediscovery of New Mexico.*
8. Gail A. Levey, "An In-Depth Look at Texturized Vegetable Protein," pp. 56–59.

U

1. Steve Earl, "Salt Plums: Japan's Alka-Seltzer," pp. 70–71.

V

1. David Wollner, "How to Select Produce," p. 52.
2. American Cancer Society, "Taking Control."
3. Jan and John Belleme, *Cooking with Japanese Foods,* p. 25.

W

1. Sara Shannon, *Diet for the Atomic Age,* pp. 152–54.
2. Waverley Root, *Food,* p. 559.
3. Jan and John Belleme, *Cooking with Japanese Foods,* p. 190.
4. Kirk Johnson, "Plastic Water," p. 12.
5. Wheat Flour Institute, *From Wheat to Flour,* p. 14.
6. Annemarie Colbin, *Food and Healing,* p. 291.

Y

1. John McDougall, "Healthy by Choice," p. 52.

Bibliography

ABC News. "Is There Danger in Our Food?" 20/20 transcript, June 20, 1985.

Abehsera, Michel. *Cooking with Care and Purpose.* Brooklyn, N.Y.: Swan House, 1978.

Aihara, Cornelia. *The Dō of Cooking.* Oroville, Calif.: George Ohsawa Macrobiotic Foundation, 1982.

American Cancer Society. "Taking Control." 1985.

American Herb Association Quarterly Newsletter. "Herbal Roots." vol. 1, no. 4 (1986).

Angier, Natalie, and Geoffrey Leavenworth. "The Electronic Guinea Pig." *Discover* (September 1983).

Arasaki, Seibin and Teruko. *Vegetables from the Sea.* Tokyo: Japan Publications, Inc., 1983.

Bailey, Adrian. *Cook's Ingredients.* New York: William Morrow, 1980.

Barbour, Marcy, R.D. "Squash: Colors of Health." *American Health* (October 1986).

Bardach, John. *Harvest of the Sea.* New York: Harper & Row, 1968.

Barrett, Mariclare. "The Cook's Glossary of Soyfoods." *Vegetarian Times* (November 1986).

———. "Sweet Things Are Made of These." *Vegetarian Times* (October 1985).

Beck, Bruce. *Produce.* New York: Friendly Press, 1984.

Belleme, Jan and John. *Cooking with Japanese Foods.* Brookline, Mass.: East West Health Books, 1986.

———. "Daikon—Japanese Radish Takes Root in America." *Macromuse* (Autumn 1986).

Bergner, Paul. "Elasticity Can Stretch Your Profits in Herb Sales." *The Herb Magazine* (September/October 1986).

Bland, Jeffrey. "Calcium Pushers." *East West* (January 1987).

Brennan, Georgeanne, Isaac Cronin, and Charlotte Glenn. *The New American Vegetable Cookbook.* Berkeley, Calif.: Aris Books, 1985.

Brown, Tom, Jr. *Tom Brown's Guide to Wild Edible and Medicinal Plants.* New York: Berkeley Books, 1985.

Browstein, Barry, Ph.D. "Natural Wisdom in the Marketplace." *Macromuse* (Winter 1986).

Bumgarner, Marlene Anne. *Book of Whole Grains.* New York: St. Martin's Press, 1976.

Burns, Ken. "In Search of Wild Ginseng." *East West* (October 1984).

Burum, Linda. *Asian Pasta.* Berkeley, Calif.: Aris Books, 1985.

California Natural Products Newsletter. "From Dahlia Flowers to Dacopa." (February 1986.)

Cheraskin, E., M.D., D.M.D., W. M. Ringsdorf, Jr., D.M.D., and J. W. Clark, D.D.S. *Diet and Disease.* New Canaan, Conn.: Keats, 1968.

Childers, Norman Franklin, Ph.D. *Childers' Diet to Stop Arthritis: The Nightshades and Ill Health.* Somerville, N.J.: Horticulture Publications, 1981.

Cleland, Nona. "Vitamins: To Megadose or Not to Megadose?" *New Age* (October 1985).

Colbin, Annemarie. *Food and Healing.* New York: Ballantine Books, 1986.

Colorado State University Department of Food Science and Human Nutrition. "Nutritional Values for Anasazi and Bolita Beans." 1984.

Consumer Affairs Committee. *Yellow Pages.* American Meat Institute, 1982.

Cornucopia Project. *Empty Breadbasket?* Emmaus, Pa.: Rodale Press, 1981.

Cusack, David F. "Quinoa: Grain of the Incas." *The Ecologist* vol. 14, no. 1 (1984).

Daems, Willem F., Ph.D. "Plant and Man." *Weleda News* 2 (1980).

David, Elizabeth. *English Bread and Yeast Cookery.* New York: Viking Press, 1977.

Department of Health and Human Services. "Quarterly Report on Adverse Reactions Associated with Aspartame Ingestion." Washington, D.C., April 1, 1987.

Dharmananda, Subhuti, Ph.D. "Ma-huang: The 'Energy Herb.'" *Bestways* (September 1984).

Doyle, Roger P., and James L. Redding. *The Complete Food Handbook.* New York: Grove Press, 1976.

Dried Fruit Association. "The Dried Fruit Story." Santa Clara, Calif., 1973.

Dufty, William. *Sugar Blues.* New York: Warner Books, 1976.

Earl, Steve. "Salt Plums: Japan's Alka-Seltzer." *East West* (January 1979).

Eden Foods. "Ume Plum Concentrate." Clinton, Mich., 1984.

Elias, Thomas S. *Trees of North America.* New York: Van Nostrand Reinhold, 1980.

Estella, Mary. *Natural Foods Cookbook.* Tokyo: Japan Publications, 1985.

FDA Consumer. "Saccharin: Where Do We Go From Here?" (April 1978.)

Fillip, Janice. "Salt, with a Grain Of." *Whole Foods* (April 1980).

Fitzgibbon, Theodora. *The Food of the Western World.* New York: Quadrangle/New York Times Book Co., 1976.

Flaws, Bob, and Honora Wolfe. *Prince Wen Hui's Cook: Chinese Dietary Therapy.* Boulder, Colo.: Blue Poppy Press, 1983.

Food Protein Research and Development Center. *Cottonseed Cookery.* Texas A & M University, College Station, Tex., 1985.

Ford, Richard I. "The Color of Survival." *Museum of Anthropology Magazine,* Ann Arbor: University of Michigan, 1981.

Foster, Steven. "Echinacea and the Immune System." *The Herb Magazine* (September/October 1986).

———. "Herb Quality: A Tempest in Your Teacup?" *Whole Life Times* (July/August 1985).

Foster, Steven, and Jennifer Bennett. "The Herbal Ricochet." *Harrowsmith* 54 (April/May 1984).

Freuchen, Peter. *Book of the Eskimos.* New York: Bramhall House, 1961.

Frieda's Finest Produce Specialties, Inc. "Speciality Recipe Brochures." Los Angeles, Calif.

Friedlander, Barbara. *The Vegetable, Fruit and Nut Book.* New York: Grosset & Dunlap, 1974.

Fryer, Lee, and Annette Dickinson. *A Dictionary of Food Supplements.* New York: Mason/Charter, 1975.

Gibbons, Euell. *Stalking the Healthful Herbs.* New York: David McKay, 1966.

Gingerich, Paul. Interview, *Natural Horizons* (April 1986).

Goldbeck, David and Nikki. "Fried Foods." *Vegetarian Times* (April 1986).

———. *The Supermarket Handbook.* New York: Signet, 1976.

Graves, Florence. "How Safe Is Your Diet Soft Drink?" *Common Cause Magazine* (July/August 1984).

Hammond, George P., and Agapito Rey. *The Rediscovery of New Mexico.* Albuquerque: University of New Mexico Press, 1966.

Hanes, Phyllis. "Homely But Tasty Catfish." *Christian Science Monitor* (April 16, 1986).

———. "Where Is Cabbage Heading?" *Christian Science Monitor* (October 22, 1986).

Harrington, H. D. *Edible Native Plants of the Rocky Mountains.* Albuquerque: University of New Mexico Press, 1967.

Hausman, Patricia. "Unscrambling the Egg 'Controversy.'" *Nutrition Action* (December 1978).

Hayhow, Sally. "Peanut Butter's Brothers: Almond, Cashew and Sesame Butters." *Vegetarian Times* (January 1987).

Health Foods Business. "Research Roundup: Lactobacillus, Acidophilus and Bulgaricus" (July 1986).

———. "Specialty Supplement Guide" (June 1986).

Hearne, Shelley A. *Harvest of Unknowns: Pesticide Contamination in Imported Foods.* New York: Natural Resources Defense Council, 1984.

Heinerman, John. "What You Should Know Before Buying Herbs." *Vegetarian Times* (August 1984).

Helferich, William, and D. Westhoff. *All About Yogurt.* New York: Prentice-Hall, 1980.

Henderson, Keith. "Drugs in Meat: Views on Congressional Findings." *Christian Science Monitor* (January 29, 1986).

Heritage, Ford. *Composition and Facts about Foods.* Mokelumne Hill, Calif.: Health Research, 1971.

Hertzberg, Ruth, Beatrice Vaughan, and Janet Greene. *Putting Food By,* 2d ed. New York: Bantam Books, 1976.

Hibbolt, H. W., ed. *Handbook of Cosmetic Science.* Oxford, England: Pergamon Press, 1963.

Hoshijo, Kathy. *The Art of Dieting without Dieting.* Glendale, Calif.: Self-Sufficiency Association, 1986.

Houston, D. F., and G. O. Kohler. "Nutritional Properties of Rice." *National Academy of Sciences,* Washington, D.C., 1970.

Humane Society of the United States. *Close-up Report, LD50: A Cruel Waste of Animals.* Washington, D.C., March 1983.

Hunter, Beatrice Trum. *Consumer Beware!* New York: Touchstone Books, 1971.

Jacobs, Leonard and Barbara. "Flour Power!" *East West* (October 1985).

Jacobson, Michael F. *Eater's Digest: The Consumer's Factbook of Food Additives.* Garden City, N.Y.: Doubleday, 1976.

Jacobson, Michael, Bonnie Liebman, and Greg Moyer. "Salt, Salt Everywhere." *Nutrition Action* (November 1983).

———. "Shaking Out the Truth About Salt. *Nutrition Action* (March 1978).

———. "Caffeine's Role in Birth Defects." *Nutrition Action* (October 1978).

Jarrell, Nancy. "Animal Welfare Discussed by Livestock Group." *Rocky Mountain Union Farmer* (November 1986).

Johnson, Kirk. "Chemical Coffee." *East West* (August 1986).

———. "Plastic Water." *East West* (December 1986).

Jonassen, Gaylord D. "What You Should Know About Sesame Seed!" International Protein Industries, Inc., Smithtown, NY., 1976.

Kahn, E. J., Jr. "The Staffs of Life." *The New Yorker* (March 11, 1985).

Kamen, Dr. Betty. "Getting Fresh." *Health Food Business* (April 1986).

———. "Hi-Q Protein: Quality, Not Quantity." Health Food Business (March 1986).

Kaufmann, Herbert, M.D. "Skin Care in the Present Day." *Weleda News* 2 (1980).

Kilham, Christopher. *The Complete Shopper's Guide to Natural Foods.* Brookline, Mass.: Autumn Press, 1980.

Kotzsch, Ronald E. "From the Grounds Up." *East West* (July 1983).

Kummer, Corby. "Pasta." *Atlantic Monthly* (July 1986).

Kushi, Aveline Tomoko. *How to Cook with Miso.* Tokyo: Japan Publications, 1978.

Kushi, Michio. *The Book of Macrobiotics.* Tokyo: Japan Publications, 1977.

———. *Natural Healing Through Macrobiotics.* Tokyo: Japan Publications, 1978.

Langer, Stephen E., M.D., and James F. Sheer. "Not a Cosmetic But a Nutrient Powerhouse—Evening Primrose Oil, Storehouse of Essential Prostaglandins." *Health News and Review* (November/December 1986).

Lappé, Frances Moore. *Diet for a Small Planet.* New York: Ballantine Books, 1975.

———. "Beyond Diet For a Small Planet." *East West* (February 1982).

Lappé, Frances Moore, and Joseph Collins. *World Hunger: 10 Myths.* San Francisco: Institute for Food and Development Policy, 1979.

Leonard, Thom. "Fermentation." *East West* (December 1984).

———. "Finding America's Staple Grain." *East West* (July 1980).

———. "Testing Sea Vegetables." *East West* (September 1983).

Leonard, Thom, and Leonard Jacobs. "Choosing the Best Sea Salt." *East West* (November 1983).

Lesser, Ellen. "Taking Root." *New Age Journal* (February 1986).

Leveille, Gilbert A., Mary Ellen Zabik, and Karen J. Morgan. *Nutrients in Foods.* Cambridge, Mass.: The Nutrition Guild, 1983.

Levey, Gail A., M.S., R.D. "An In-Depth Look at Texturized Vegetable Protein." *Vegetarian Times* (January/February 1980).

———. "King Cabbage and His Noble Kin." *American Health* (January/February 1987).

Leviton, Richard. "A Shopper's Guide to Sweeteners." *East West* (May 1986).

Levy, Phil. *Salt: Walking the Briny Line.* Salem, Mass.: Talking Food, 1976.

———. *Vegetable Oil: The Unsaturated Facts.* Salem, Mass.: Talking Food, 1977.

———. *Sugar and How It Gets That Way.* Salem, Mass.: Talking Food, 1978.

Levy, Phil, and Christiane Levy. *Remedial Sweeteners.* Salem, Mass.: Talking Food, 1976.

Lewis Laboratories International, Ltd. "Aren't We Lucky There is Lecithin." Westport, Conn., 1985.

MacNeil, Karen. *Whole Foods: Nutrition and Cuisine.* New York: Vintage Books, 1981.

Madlener, Judith Cooper. *The Sea Vegetable Book.* New York: Clarkson N. Potter, 1977.

Mayall, Mark. "Beating the Sugar Blues." *East West* (September 1983).

McDougall, John, M.D. "Healthy by Choice." *Vegetarian Times* (October 1986).

McDougall, John, M.D., and Mary McDougall. "The Latest Thinking on Protein." *Vegetarian Times* (March 1986).

McGee, Harold. *On Food and Cooking.* New York: Charles Scribner's Sons, 1984.

McPartland, Christine, and Patsy Vigderman. "Vitamin ABC." *New Age Journal* (July 1984).

McSweeney, Daniel. "Bee Pollen: A Honey of a Product." *Whole Foods* (September 1984).

Meyerowitz, Steve. "Sprout Man, Raw Foodist." *Vegetarian Times* (July/August 1979).

Miller, Ellen. "Chocolates to Tempt Your Valentine." *Natural Horizons* (February 1986).

Miller, Roger W. "Honey: Making Sure It's Pure." *FDA Consumer* (September 1979).

Miller, Saul, with Jo Anne Miller. *Food for Thought.* Englewood Cliffs, N.J.: Prentice-Hall, 1979.

Mitoku Co., Ltd. "Japanese Food Guide #3, Umeboshi." Tokyo, 1981.

———. "Japanese Food Guide #5, Teas and Beverages." Tokyo, 1982.

Mori, Kisaku. *Mushrooms as Health Foods (Shiitake Kinkoko).* Tokyo: Japan Publications, 1974.

Mott, Lawrie, with Martha Broad. *Pesticides in Food: What the Public Needs to Know.* San Francisco: Natural Resources Defense Council, 1984.

Mullarkey, Barbara. "Continuing Reports of Side-effects Add to Aspartame Controversy." *Wednesday Journal* (February 19, 1986).

Muramoto, Naboru. *Healing Ourselves.* New York: Swan House Books, 1973.

Nabhan, Gary Paul. "Viable Seeds From Prehistoric Caches? Archaeobotanical Remains in Southwestern Folklore." *The Kiva* vol. 43, no. 2 (1977).

National Buckwheat Institute. "A History of Buckwheat." Penn Yan, N.Y., 1986.

National Dairy Council. "Milk." Rosemont, Il., 1983.

National Peach Council. "What's Unique About a Peach." Martinsburg, W. Va., 1985.

Natural Foods Merchandiser. "The Calcium Craze: Soaring Supplement Sales" (October 1986).

———. "Green Foods Category Grows in Popularity" (December 1986).

———. "State of Affairs: Legislative Review" (June 1986).

Natural Foods Network Newsletter. vol. 1, no. 2. "Aloe Vera." (August 1985).

New Age Foods Study Center. "Move Over Big Mac, Here Comes Tempeh." Lafayette, Calif., 1983.

Northedge Natural Foods, Inc. *A California Food Products Notebook.* Shelburne, Mass.: Northedge Natural Foods Cooperative, 1983.

Nutrition Search, Inc. *Nutrition Almanac.* New York: McGraw-Hill, 1975.

Obis, Clare Barret. "Ice Cream: The Chilling Truth." *Vegetarian Times* (July/August 1979).

Orr, Robert T. and Margaret C. *Wildflowers of Western America.* New York: Alfred A. Knopf, 1974.

Oxford Book of Food Plants. London, England: Oxford University Press, 1982.

Peterson, Vicki. *The Natural Food Catalog.* New York: Arco Publishing Co., 1978.

Pines, Wayne L., and Nancy Glick. "The Saccharin Ban." U.S. Department of Health, Education, and Welfare (HEW Publication No. [FDA] 77-2079).

Pomeranz, Yeshajahu, and George S. Robbins. "Amino Acid Composition of Buckwheat." *Agricultural and Food Chemistry* vol. 20, no. 2 (March/April 1972).

Popcorn Institute. "Popcorn Industry Fact Sheet." Chicago: Popcorn Institute (September 1978).

Rashap, Arthur, and Beverly Braly. "Is Ginseng Safe?" *The Herb Magazine* (September/October, 1986).

Reed, Patsy Bostick. *Nutrition: An Applied Science.* St. Paul, Minn.: West Publishing Co., 1980.

Rhoads, Sharon Ann, with Patricia Zunic. *Cooking with Sea Vegetables.* Brookline, Mass.: Autumn Press, 1978.

Rice Council for Market Development. *U.S. Rice Handbook.* Houston, Tex., 1985.

Robinson, Corinne H. *Fundamentals of Normal Nutrition,* 3d ed. New York: Macmillan, 1978.

Roehl, Evelyn. *Food Facts: A Compendium on Whole Foods.* Seattle, Wash.: Food Learning Center, 1986.

Rohé, Fred. *The Complete Book of Natural Foods.* Boulder, Colo.: Shambhala Publications, 1983.

Rombauer, Irma S., and Marion Rombauer Becker. *The Joy of Cooking,* New York: Bobbs-Merrill Co., 1964.

Root, Waverley. *Food: An Authoritative and Visual History and Dictionary of the Foods of the World.* New York: Simon & Schuster, 1980.

Rosso, Julee, and Sheila Lukins. *The Silver Palate Good Times Cookbook.* New York: Workman Publishing, 1985.

Rossoff, Peggy. "Is Dried Miso Good for You?" *Macromuse* (Winter 1986).

Ryder, Edward J., Neal E. De Vos, and Mohammad A. Bari. "The Globe Artichoke (Cynara scolymus L.)." *Hortscience* vol. 18 no. 5 (October 1983).

Schneider, Elizabeth. *Uncommon Fruits and Vegetables: A Common Sense Guide.* New York: Harper & Row, 1986.

Seamens, Dan, and David Wollner. *Shopper's Guide to Natural Foods.* Brookline, Mass.: East West, 1985.

Shannon, Sara. *Diet for the Atomic Age.* Wayne, N.J.: Avery, 1987.

Shurtleff, William, and Akiko Aoyagi. *The Book of Kudzu: A Culinary and Healing Guide.* Brookline, Mass.: Autumn Press, 1977.

———. *The Book of Miso.* Kanagawa-Ken, Japan: Autumn Press, 1976.

———. *The Book of Tofu: Food for Mankind.* Brookline, Mass.: Autumn Press, 1975.

Simon, Andre L., and Robin Howe. *Dictionary of Gastronomy.* New York: Overlook Press, 1978.

Stanchich, Lino. *The Story of Balanced Minerals: Sea Salt.* Escondido, Calif.: Great Life Products, 1982.

Stepro, Keith. "Amino Acids: The Building Blocks of Life." *Let's Live* (July 1986).

Stoy, Diane B. "The Buffalo-Cholesterol Connection." Fort Pierre, S. Dak.: Traditional Buffalo Association, 1986.

Switzer, Larry. *Spirulina: The Whole Food Revolution.* New York: Bantam Books, 1982.

Talub, Lynn. "Friendly Fats: Evening Primrose Oil and GLA." *Let's Live* (July 1986).

Thomson, Bill, "A Shopper's Guide to Fruit." *East West* (June 1985).

Tierra, Michael, C.A., N.D. *The Way of Herbs.* New York: Washington Square Press, 1983.

Tsuji, Shizuo. *Japanese Cooking: A Simple Art.* New York: Kodansha International, 1980.

United States Department of Agriculture. *Composition of Foods: Spices and Herbs.* Washington, D.C.: Agricultural Research Service, Agriculture Handbook No. 8–2, revised January 1977.

———. *Handbook of the Nutritional Contents of Foods.* New York: Dover Publications, 1975.

United States Senate, Select Committee on Nutrition and Human Needs. *Dietary Goals for the United States.* Washington, D.C., February 1977.

Universal Foods Corporation, Fermentation Division. *Nutritional Information: Nutrex Nutritional Yeasts.* Milwaukee, Wisc., 1983.

Valentine, William, and Frances Moore Lappé. *What Can We Do?* San Francisco: Institute for Food and Development Policy, 1980.

Vegetarian Times. "Apples at Core of Chemical Controversy." (December 1986).

———. "Imitation Cheese Raises Suspicions in Natural Foods World." (October 1986).

Walters, Enoch P. "What About Bottled Water?" *FDA Consumer* (May 1974).

Walton, Izaak. *The Compleat Angler.* New York: Everyman Press, 1975.

Washington Asparagus Growers. "Asparagus." Sunnyside, Wash., 1986.

Wheat Flour Institute. *From Wheat to Flour.* Washington, D.C., 1976.

Whittenberg, Margaret. *Experiencing Quality.* Austin, Tex.: Whole Foods, 1984.

Whole Foods. "Supreme Court Gives Nod to Nutrasweet." (June 1986).

Whole Foods Natural Foods Guide. Berkeley, Calif.: And/Or Press, 1979.

Wilder, Laura Ingalls. *Little House in the Big Woods.* New York: Harper & Row, 1971.

Williams, Dr. Roger J. *Nutrition Against Disease.* New York: Bantam Books, 1981.

Williams, William Carlos. *Collected Earlier Poems.* London: New Directions, 1938.

Winter, Ruth. *A Consumer's Dictionary of Cosmetic Ingredients.* New York: Crown Publishers, 1976.

Wollner, David. "How to Select Produce." *East West* (June 1982).

Wood, Rebecca. Quinoa cookbook. (In Press)

Zeavin, Edna. "Ginger: The Healing Spice." *Bestways* (March 1985).